Humanistic Concerns
in Punjabi Literature

DAKSHINAYAN
INDIAN THOUGHT

Humanistic Concerns
in Punjabi Literature

Edited by
Atamjit
Harbhajan Singh Bhatia

Translated by
Vivek Sachdeva
Pushpinder Syal
Swaraj Raj
Madhvi Kataria

Series Editor
G.N. Devy

All rights reserved. No part of this book may be modified, reproduced or utilised in any form, or by any means, electronic or mechanical, including photocopying, recording or by any information storage and retrieval system, in any form of binding or cover other than in which it is published, without permission in writing from the publisher.

The **Dakshinayan Indian Thought** series has received funding from the Rajiv Gandhi Foundation, New Delhi.

HUMANISTIC CONCERNS IN PUNJABI LITERATURE

ORIENT BLACKSWAN PRIVATE LIMITED

Registered Office
3-6-752 Himayatnagar, Hyderabad 500 029, Telangana, India
e-mail: centraloffice@orientblackswan.com

Other Offices
Bengaluru, Chennai, Guwahati, Hyderabad,
Kolkata, Mumbai, New Delhi, Noida, Patna

© Orient Blackswan Private Limited 2025
First published 2025

ISBN 978-93-5442-794-7

Typeset in Minion Pro 11/13.5 *by*
Shine Graphics, Delhi 110 094

Printed at
Yash Printographics, Greater Noida 201 310

Published by
Orient Blackswan Private Limited
3-6-752, Himayatnagar, Hyderabad 500 029, Telangana, India
e-mail: info@orientblackswan.com

Contents

Publisher's Acknowledgements   xi

1. Introduction   1
2. Folklore   25
3. Medieval Poetry   46
       Sheikh Farid   *Salok*   46
       Shah Hussain   *Without Good Deeds*   48
         What Makes You So Proud   49
       Sultan Bahu   *Everyone Wishes for a Stronger Imaan*   50
         Let Eyes Sprout   50
         Attaining Knowledge They Inflate Their Ego   50
         Neither Hindus, nor Muslims   51
       Bulleh Shah   *I Know Not Who I Am*   51
         One Point Holds the Whole Truth   53
         The Spring of Love   54
       Wajeed   *Who Should Tell Him*   56
       Bhagat Namdev   *Namdev Has Seen Vithal*   57
         Forget Me Not   58
       Dhanna Bhagat   *Gopala, I Worship You*   59
       Bhagat Pipa   *One Who Seeks Him, Finds Him*   60
       Bhagat Kabir   *Gardener*   61
         The True Brahmin   62
         Of One Light   62
         True Valour   63
       Bhagat Beni   *The True Seeker*   64
       Bhagat Ravidas   *Begumpura, the Ideal Town*   66
       Guru Nanak   *Has Your Heart Not Melted Yet?*   67
         When Stained with Blood   68
         Grabbing What Rightfully Belongs to Others   68

Greed, the King	68
The Dance of Devotion	69
The Simmal Tree	70
Fake Religiosity	70
Man and Woman	71
Guru Arjan Dev *The Door to Salvation*	72
Guru Gobind Singh *To God, My Friend*	73
From 'Chandi Di Vaar'	73
Bhai Gurdas *Four Varnas and Four Sects*	74
If A Dog Sits on a Throne	75
Man in Kalyug	75
Waris Shah *On Friends' Request*	76
As People Think of Brothers	77
A Dialogue Between Mullah and Ranjha	77
Heer's Reply to Her Mother	78
Heer's Wailing	78
Hashim Shah *I Will Go and Return Not*	79
Shah Mohammad *The Battle Scene*	80
4. Modern Poetry	82
Bhai Veer Singh *Time*	82
Dhani Ram Chatrik *Radha's Message*	83
Prof. Puran Singh *Farmers*	86
Heera Singh 'Dard' *Dream of a New World*	87
Babu Rajab Ali *The Pain of the Punjabi Language*	88
Diwan Singh 'Kalepani' *Dusk Has Fallen*	89
Firoz Deen Sharaf *I Love My Language*	91
Prof. Mohan Singh *Mother*	92
Breeze Like Life	92
Nand Lal Nurpuri *Jutti Kasuri (The Shoes of Kasur)*	93
The Guest with the Kaintha	**94**
Ustaad Daaman *The Other Side*	95
Cried We Both	96
Ishwar Chitarkar *The Flight of Imagination*	97
Sharif Kunjahi *Brother, Are You from Kunjah?*	99
Bawa Balwant *The World and the Truth*	101

Contents

Pritam Singh Safir *The Cranes of* Katak	103
Amrita Pritam *I Call Upon Waris Shah*	107
Bread Giver	108
Harbhajan Singh *I Fear*	110
A Man Without a Head	110
Ahmed Rahi *You, Who Have Homes*	113
Jaswant Singh Neki *Ordeal*	114
Tara Singh *Don't Light Candles*	116
The Bull Beneath the Earth	117
Gurcharan Rampuri *Words*	118
Mannu Bhai *Those Wonderful Times*	119
Rauf Sheikh *Ghazal*	120
Sohan Singh Meesha *A Loud Cry*	121
Jagtar *Shackles on Every Foot*	124
Droplets	124
Harbhajan Hundal *Poesy and People*	125
Shiv Kumar Batalvi *My Father Did Me Wrong*	127
Trees	129
Ravinder Ravi *The Void in Relations*	130
Navtej Bharti *A Poem in Three Parts*	131
Mohanjit *Walking is a Must*	133
Sant Ram Udaasi *To August, the Fifteenth*	134
A Call to the Farmers	135
Ajaib Singh Hundal *Dupattas with Lace*	136
Ajmer Rode *A Notice to the Man*	138
Gurumel *Mind*	139
Satinder Singh Noor *In My Country*	140
Dr. S. Tarsem *Ghazal*	141
Harbhajan Halwarvi *Bridges*	142
Ravinder Bhathal *I Do Not Write Poetry*	143
Fakhar Zamaan *A Sparrow in the Drawing Room*	146
Brittle Relations	146
Lal Singh Dil *Prostitutes*	147
A Poem	148
Ahmed Salim *Wagha*	148

Surjit Patar *Quivering Water*	149
A Song	150
Beeba Balwant *Incessant Battle*	151
Sain Akhtar Lahori *Dear God, Come Down to the Earth*	152
Iqbal Ramoowalia *G. B. Road*	153
Parminderjeet *The Bird of Ego*	155
Sulakhan Sarhadi *Ghazal*	156
Dev *How Shall I Return Home*	157
Amitoj *Evening*	158
Shaista Habib *A Backward Area*	160
Jagtar Dhaa *Walls*	161
Baba Najmi *Ghazal*	162
Ghazal	162
Devinder Kaur *Relationships*	163
Amar Jyoti *How Does It Bother Me*	164
Paash *Refusal*	165
The Most Dangerous	167
Surinder Dhanjal *The Crazy Poet*	169
Dr Ravinder *Sad Mother*	170
Manjit Indra *The Song of a Shattered Embrace*	172
Darshan Bulandwi *Lamp Burning in the Sun*	173
Ambrish *A Military Tank and a Butterfly*	175
Sukhwinder Kamboj *Rootless Green Trees*	176
Gurbhajan Singh Gill *A Song*	177
Vanita *When Language Overwhelms Me*	179
Darshan Buttar from *The Grand Trembling*	179
Hardial Sagar *Ghazal*	181
Jaswant Deed *Roof*	182
Nirupama Dutt *Apology*	184
Sant Sandhu *War*	185
Lakhwinder Johal *Words*	188
Paul Kaur *Immunity*	190
Jaswinder *Ghazal*	191
Varinder Parihar *Heart*	192
Vijay Vivek *Ghazal*	193

Surjit Jajj *Ghazal*		194
Swaranjit Savi *Mother*		195
Sukhpal *I And Nanak*		196
Gurmeet Kallarmajri *Change*		197
Parminder Sodhi *Earthquake and God*		198
Barjinder Chauhan *Ghazal*		199
Gurtej Koharwala *Ghazal*		200
Satish Gulati *Ghazal*		201
Manmohan *Disagreement*		202
Sukhwinder Amrit *Mothers and Daughters*		203
Amarjeet Kaunke *On Speaking the Truth*		205
Jaswant Zafar *Man*		206
Neeru Aseem *A Girl*		207
Tariq Gujjar *A Poem for Undivided Punjab*		209
Swami Antar Nirav *Lewd Laughter*		209
Neetu Arora *Roti and Life*		210
Sabir Ali Sabir *O God, Without Your Will*		212
Speech and Silence		212
5. Fiction		213
Nanak Singh *An Overflow of Affection*		213
Gurmukh Singh Musafir *The Revolutionary's Daughter*		220
Sant Singh Sekhon *The Ploughman*		228
Jaswant Singh Kanwal *Honesty*		235
Sujaan Singh *Kulfi*		238
Kartar Singh Duggal *Neeli*		244
Santokh Singh Dheer *A Shared Wall*		250
Kulwant Singh Virk *The Earth Stands On the Horns of a Bull*		261
Ram Saroop Ankhi *The Cycle Race*		267
Manmohan Bawa *Neelma*		271
Gurdial Singh *Common Ground*		284
Ajeet Kaur *Gulbano*		290
Raghubir Dhand *On The Other Side*		295
Gulzar Singh Sandhu *Disgraced*		301
Dalip Kaur Tiwana *The Confession*		308
Gurbachan Singh Bhullar *The Toy Car*		315

Afzal Ahsan Randhawa	*The Generous Elder*	323
Mohan Bhandari	*The Wooden Pestle*	330
Jasbir Bhullar	*The Snow Demon*	337
Kirpal Kazak	*Roots*	345
Baldev Singh Moga	*The Business of Life*	353
Waryam Singh Sandhu	*Each One Must Have Their Share*	357
Khalid Hussain	*Eye Witness*	367
Mitter Sen Meet	*The Investigation*	372

6. Drama — 383

I. C. Nanda	*The Bride*	383
Harcharan Singh	*Unfulfilled Desire*	389
Balwant Gargi	*The Night of the Tempest*	400
Harsaran Singh	*A Helpless Mother*	416
Gursharan Singh	*The Old Man Speaks*	432
Charan Das Sidhu	*Alexander's Victory*	448
Ajmer Singh Aulakh	*Satyr*	457
Atamjit	*Come Back from the War*	471
Swaraj Bir	*Fragrance*	481
Pali Bhupinder Singh	*The Thirsty Crow*	491
Kewal Dhaliwal	*Bonhomie in the Jungle*	498

7. Prose — 505

Teja Singh	*The Love of Home*	505
Gurbax Singh Preetlarhi	*A War-free World*	511
Bhagat Singh	*Communal Riots and Their Remedy*	518
Harinder Singh Roop	*Of Sycophants*	522
Balraj Sahni	*My Pakistan Travelogue*	527
Pritam Singh	*The Importance of History*	535
Giani Gurdit Singh	*Be Blessed, O Father!*	543
Gurbachan	*This is not Punjab*	547
Narinder Singh Kapoor	*A Flight in The Sky*	559
Harpal Singh Pannu	*Mansur*	565
Balbir Madhopuri	*The Humanist Slap*	575

Glossary — 581

Publisher's Acknowledgements

Navi Duniya Da Supna by Hira Singh Dard, translated from the original Punjabi by Vivek Sachdeva 'Dream of a New World'. Used with permission from the publisher Unistar Books

Dard Punjabi Boli Da by Babu Rajab Ali, translated from the original Punjabi by Vivek Sachdeva 'The Pain of Punjabi Language'. Used with permission from the publisher Chetna Parkashan

Maa by Prof. Mohan Singh, translated from the original Punjabi by Vivek Sachdeva 'Mother'. Used with permission from the author's grandson

Hawa Da Jivan by Prof. Mohan Singh, translated from the original Punjabi by Vivek Sachdeva 'Breeze Like Life'. Used with permission from the author's grandson

Jutti Kasuri Pairi Na by Nand Lal Nurpuri, translated from the original Punjabi by Vivek Sachdeva 'Jutti Kasuri'. Used with permission from the author's grandson Mr Inderjit Nurpuri

Kainthe Wala by Nand Lal Nurpuri, translated from the original Punjabi by Vivek Sachdeva 'The Guest with the Kaintha'. Used with permission from the author's grandson Mr Inderjit Nurpuri

Jorha Os Passe by Ustaad Daaman, translated from the original Punjabi by Vivek Sachdeva 'The Other Side'. Used with permission from the publisher Unistar Books

Roe Assin Vee Haan by Ustaad Daaman, translated from the original Punjabi by Vivek Sachdeva 'Cried We Both'. Used with permission from the publisher Unistar Books

Pankheru (Poem) by Ishwar Chitarkar, translated from the original Punjabi by Vivek Sachdeva 'The Flight of Imagination'. Used with permission from the publisher Navyug Publication

Veer tun Kunjah da en (poem) by Sharif Kunjahi, translated from the original Punjabi by Vivek Sachdeva 'Brother, are you from Kunjah?' Used with permission from the author's grandson Mr Kursheed Yusuf

Duniya by Bawa Balwant, translated from the original Punjabi by Vivek Sachdeva 'The World and the Truth'. Used with permission from the publisher Lokgeet Parkashan

Katak Koonjan (poem) by Pritam Singh Safeer, translated from the original Punjabi by Vivek Sachdeva 'The Cranes of Kattak'. Used with permission from the publisher Navyug Publication

Aakhaan Wars Shah Nu by Amrita Pritam, translated from the original Punjabi by Vivek Sachdeva 'I Call Upon Waris Shah'. Used with permission from the publisher Shilalekh Publisher

Ann Daata by Amrita Pritam, translated from the original Punjabi by Vivek Sachdeva 'Bread Giver'. Used with permission from the publisher Shilalekh Publisher

Apramanik by Harbhajan Singh, translated from the original Punjabi by Vivek Sachdeva 'Unsubstantiated'. Used with permission from the publisher Navyug Publication

Tere Huzoor Meri Hazri Dee Dastan by Harbhajan Singh, translated from the original Punjabi by Vivek Sachdeva 'The Tale of My Presence in Your Noble Presence'. Used with permission from the publisher Navyug Publication

Desan Walyo from Zulmon Kook Gangi by Ahmed Rahi, translated from the original Punjabi by Vivek Sachdeva 'You, Who Have Homes'. Used with permission from the publisher

Parkh (poem) by Dr. Jaswant Singh Neki, translated from the original Punjabi by Vivek Sachdeva 'Ordeal'. Used with permission from the publisher Navyug Publication

Mombattian by Tara Singh, translated from the original Punjabi by Vivek Sachdeva 'Don't Light Candles'. Used with permission from the publisher Navyug Publication

Dharti Hethla Baulad by Tara Singh, translated from the original Punjabi by Vivek Sachdeva 'The Bull Beneath The Earth'. Used with permission from the publisher Navyug Publication

Shabd (poem) by Gurcharan Rampuri, translated from the original Punjabi by Vivek Sachdeva 'Words'. Used with permission from the author

Publisher's Acknowledgements

Oh Khoob Diharhe San, from Academy's literary magazine Shabd Boond's issue of Oct–Dec 2004 by Manoo Bhai, translated from the original Punjabi by Vivek Sachdeva 'Those Wonderful Times'. Used with permission from the publisher Haryana Punjabi Sahitya Academy

Cheek Bulbule by Sohan Singh Meesha, translated from the original Punjabi by Vivek Sachdeva 'A Loud Cry'. Used with permission from the publisher Unistar Books

Har Pair Te Saliban by Jagtar, translated from the original Punjabi by Vivek Sachdeva 'Shackles on Every Foot'. Used with permission from the publisher Unistar Books

Jal Kan by Jagtar, translated from the original Punjabi by Vivek Sachdeva 'Droplets'. Used with permission from the author

Kavita Te Lok by Harbhajan Hundal, translated from the original Punjabi by Vivek Sachdeva 'Poesy and People'. Used with permission from the author

Dharmi Babal Paap Kamaya by Shiv Kumar Batalvi, translated from the original Punjabi by Vivek Sachdeva 'My Father Did ME Wrong'. Used with permission from the author's son Meherban Batalvi

Rukh by Shiv Kumar Batalvi, translated from the original Punjabi by Vivek Sachdeva 'Tree'. Used with permission from the author's son Meherban Batalvi

Rishtiaan Dee Shunyata by Ravinder Ravi, translated from the original Punjabi by Vivek Sachdeva 'The Void in Relations'. Used with permission from the author

Ahalya, Sarupnaka, Yashodra by Navtej Bharti, translated from the original Punjabi by Vivek Sachdeva 'A Poem In Three Parts'. Used with permission from the author

Turna He Banada Hai by Mohanjit, translated from the original Punjabi by Vivek Sachdeva 'Walking is a Must'. Used with permission from the author

15 August De Naa by Sant Ram Udasi, translated from the original Punjabi by Vivek Sachdeva 'To August, the Fifteenth'. Used with permission from the publisher Unistar Books

Haarhian Dev Haani by Sant Ram Udasi, translated from the original Punjabi by Vivek Sachdeva 'The Friends of Summer Crops'. Used with permission from the publisher Unistar Books

Gotte Waliaan Chunnian by Ajaib Singh Hundal, translated from the original Punjabi by Vivek Sachdeva 'Dupattas With Lace'. Used with permission from the author

Bande Nu Notice by Ajmer Rode, translated from the original Punjabi by Vivek Sachdeva 'A Notice to the Man'. Used with permission from the author

Zehen by Gurumen Sidhu, translated from the original Punjabi by Vivek Sachdeva 'Mind'. Used with permission from the author

Mere Desh Vich by Sutinder Singh Noor, translated from the original Punjabi by Vivek Sachdeva 'In My Country'. Used with permission from the publisher Navyug Publication

Allah Mian Thalle aa from Academy's literary magazine Shabd Boond's issue of Oct–Dec 2004 by Sain Akhtar Lahori, translated from the original Punjabi by Vivek Sachdeva 'Dear God, Come Down on Earth'. Used with permission from the publisher Haryana Punjabi Sahitya Academy.

Ghazal by Dr. S. Tarsem, translated from the original Punjabi by Vivek Sachdeva 'Na Roshandan'. Used with permission from the author

Pulan to Paar by Harbhajan Halwarvi, translated from the original Punjabi by Vivek Sachdeva 'Bridges'. Used with permission from the author's wife Dr. Pritpalkaur Halwarvi

Mein Kadon Kavita Likha Haan By Ravinder Bhathal, translated from the original Punjabi by Vivek Sachdeva 'I Do Not Write Poetry'. Used with permission from the author

Drawing Room Vich Chirhi by Fakhar Zaman, translated from the original Punjabi by Vivek Sachdeva 'A Sparrow in the Drawing Room'. Used with permission from the author.

Kach De Rishte by Fakhar Zaman, translated from the original Punjabi by Vivek Sachdeva 'Brittle Relations'. Used with permission from the author.

Vesva Trimtan by Lal Singh Dil, translated from the original Punjabi by Vivek Sachdeva 'Prostitutes'. Used with permission from the publisher Chetna Parkashan

Publisher's Acknowledgements

Wagha by Ahmed Salim, translated from the original Punjabi by Vivek Sachdeva 'Wagha'. Used with permission from the author

Ikk Larzda Neer See by Surjit Patar, translated from the original Punjabi by Vivek Sachdeva 'Quivering Water'. Used with permission from the author

Nirantar Yudh by Beeba Balwant, translated from the original Punjabi by Vivek Sachdeva 'Incessant Battle'. Used with permission from the author

G B Road by Iqbal Ramoowalia, translated from the original Punjabi by Vivek Sachdeva 'G. B. Road'. Used with permission from the author's wife

Haankar De Parinde by Parminderjit, translated from the original Punjabi by Vivek Sachdeva 'Bird of Ego'. Used with permission from the publisher Unistar Books

Hun Mein Ghar Kiven Partaanga by Dev, translated from the original Punjabi by Vivek Sachdeva 'How Shall I Return Home'. Used with permission from the publisher Navyug Publication

Sandhya (poem) by Amitoj, translated from the original Punjabi by Vivek Sachdeva 'Evening'. Used with permission from the publisher Chetna Parkashan

Kandhaan (poem) by Jagtar Dhaa, translated from the original Punjabi by Vivek Sachdeva 'Walls'. Used with permission from the publisher Chetna Parkashan

Ghazal by Baba Najmi, translated from the original Punjabi by Vivek Sachdeva 'Ghazal'. Used with permission from the author

Ghazal by Baba Najmi, translated from the original Punjabi by Vivek Sachdeva 'Ghazal'. Used with permission from the author

Rishte by Devinder Kaur, translated from the original Punjabi by Vivek Sachdeva 'Relationship'. Used with permission from the author

Saanu Kee (poem) by Amitoj, translated from the original Punjabi by Vivek Sachdeva 'How Does It Bother Me'. Used with permission from the publisher Chetna Parkashan

Inkaar by Paash, translated from the original Punjabi by Vivek Sachdeva 'Refusal'. Used with permission from the publisher Unistar Books

Khatarnak by Paash, translated from the original Punjabi by Vivek Sachdeva 'The Most Dangerous'. Used with permission from the publisher Unistar Books

Jhalla Kavi by Surinder Dhanjal, translated from the original Punjabi by Vivek Sachdeva 'The Crazy Poet'. Used with permission from the author

Maa Udaas Hai by Dr. Ravinder, translated from the original Punjabi by Vivek Sachdeva 'Sad Mother'. Used with permission from the publisher Unistar Books

Bhajjiaan Bahin da Geet by Manjit Indra, translated from the original Punjabi by Vivek Sachdeva 'The Song of a Shattered Embrace'. Used with permission from the author

A Backward Area by Shyasta Habib, translated from the original Punjabi by Vivek Sachdeva 'A Backward Area'. Used with permission from the author's husband Fakhar Zaman

Dhup Ch Jagda Deeva by Darshan Bulandvi, translated from the original Punjabi by Vivek Sachdeva 'Lamp Burning in the Sun'. Used with permission from the publisher Unistar Books

Jarhheen (Poem) by Sukhwinder Kamboj, translated from the original Punjabi by Vivek Sachdeva 'Rootless Green Trees'. Used with permission from the publisher Chetna Parkashan

Tank Te Titlee (Poem) by Ambrish, translated from the original Punjabi by Vivek Sachdeva 'A Military Tank and a Butterfly'. Used with permission from the publisher Chetna Parkashan

Geet by Gurbhajan Gill, translated from the original Punjabi by Vivek Sachdeva 'A Song'. Used with permission from the author

Jadon Bhasha Hon Lagge Mere Te Haavi by Vanita, translated from the original Punjabi by Vivek Sachdeva 'When Language Starts Dominating Me'. Used with permission from the author

Maha Kambni Vichon by Darshan Buttar, translated from the original Punjabi by Vivek Sachdeva 'From the Grand Trembling'. Used with permission from the author

Chatti by Jaswant Deed, translated from the original Punjabi by Vivek Sachdeva 'Roof'. Used with permission from the author

Publisher's Acknowledgements

Ujli Nazar Pal Bhar by Hardial Sagar, translated from the original Punjabi by Vivek Sachdeva 'Ghazal'. Used with permission from the publisher Chetna Parkashan

Muafi by Nirupama Dutt, translated from the original Punjabi by Vivek Sachdeva 'Apology'. Used with permission from the author

Jang by Sant Sandhu, translated from the original Punjabi by Vivek Sachdeva 'War'. Used with permission from the author

Shabd by Lakhwinder, translated from the original Punjabi by Vivek Sachdeva 'Words'. Used with permission from the author

Unmukti by Paul Kaur, translated from the original Punjabi by Vivek Sachdeva 'Immunity'. Used with permission from the author

Dil by Varinder Parihar, translated from the original Punjabi by Vivek Sachdeva 'Dil'. Used with permission from the author

Ghazal by Jaswinder, translated from the original Punjabi by Vivek Sachdeva 'Ghazal'. Used with permission from the author

Ghazal by Vijay Vivek, translated from the original Punjabi by Vivek Sachdeva 'Ghazal'. Used with permission from the author

Ghazal by Surjit Jajj, translated from the original Punjabi by Vivek Sachdeva 'Ghazal'. Used with permission from the author

Maa by Swanjit Savi, translated from the original Punjabi by Vivek Sachdeva 'Mother'. Used with permission from the author

Mein Te Nanak by Sukhpal, translated from the original Punjabi by Vivek Sachdeva 'I and Nanak'. Used with permission from the publisher Unistar Books

Daawa by Gurmeet Kallarmajri, translated from the original Punjabi by Vivek Sachdeva 'Change'. Used with permission from the author's son

Bhuchal te Rabb (Poem) by Parminder Sodhi, translated from the original Punjabi by Vivek Sachdeva 'Earthquake and God'. Used with permission from the publisher Chetna Parkashan

Ghazal by Barjinder Chauhan, translated from the original Punjabi by Vivek Sachdeva 'Ghazal'. Used with permission from the author

Kraange Zikar Us Da by, translated from the original Punjabi by Vivek Sachdeva 'Ghazal'. Used with permission from the author

Ghazal by Satish Gulati, translated from the original Punjabi by Vivek Sachdeva 'Ghazal'. Used with permission from the author

Asahmati by Manmohan Singh, translated from the original Punjabi by Vivek Sachdeva 'Disagreement'. Used with permission from the author

Maavan Te Dhiaan by Sukhwinder Amrit, translated from the original Punjabi by Vivek Sachdeva 'Mothers and Daughters'. Used with permission from the author

Jadon Mein by Amarjeet Kaunke, translated from the original Punjabi by Vivek Sachdeva 'On Speaking Truth'. Used with permission from the author

Banda by Jaswant Zafar, translated from the original Punjabi by Vivek Sachdeva 'Man'. Used with permission from the author

Kurhi by Neera Aseem, translated from the original Punjabi by Vivek Sachdeva 'A Girl'. Used with permission from the author

Poore Punjab Layi Adhhi Nazam by Tariq Gujjar, translated from the original Punjabi by Vivek Sachdeva 'A Poem for Undivided Punjab'. Used with permission from the author

Ashlil Hassa by Swami Antar Neerav, translated from the original Punjabi by Vivek Sachdeva 'Lewd Laughter'. Used with permission from the author

Roti Te Zindagi by Neetu Arora, translated from the original Punjabi by Vivek Sachdeva 'Roti and Life'. Used with permission from the author

Rabba Tere Hukam Bina by Sabir Ali Sabir, translated from the original Punjabi by Vivek Sachdeva 'O God, Without Your Will'. Used with permission from the author

Jibhan Vech Ke by Sabir Ali Sabir, translated from the original Punjabi by Vivek Sachdeva 'Speech and Silence'. Used with permission from the author

Bhua by Nanak Singh, translated from the original Punjabi by Pushpinder Syal 'An Overflow of Affection'. Used with permission from the author

Baghi Dee Dhee by Gurmukh Singh Musafir, translated from the original Punjabi by Pushpinder Syal 'The Revolutionary's Daughter'. Used with permission from the author's daughter

Publisher's Acknowledgements

Hal Wah by Sant Singh Sekhon, translated from the original Punjabi by Pushpinder Syal 'The Ploughman'. Used with permission from the author's son

Imandari by Jaswant Singh Kanwal, translated from the original Punjabi by Pushpinder Syal 'Honesty'. Used with permission from the publisher Unistar Books

Kulfi by Sujan Singh, translated from the original Punjabi by Pushpinder Syal 'Kulfi'. Used with permission from the author's son

Neeli by Kartar Singh Duggal, translated from the original Punjabi by Pushpinder Syal 'Neeli'. Used with permission from the publisher Navyug Publication

Saanjhi Kandh by Santokh Singh Dheer, translated from the original Punjabi by Pushpinder Syal 'A Shared Wall'. Used with permission from the author's son

Dharti Hethla Bauld by Kulwant Singh Virk, translated from the original Punjabi by Pushpinder Syal 'The Earth Stands on the Horns of the Bull'. Used with permission from the author's son

Cycle Daur by Ram Sarup Anakha, translated from the original Punjabi by Pushpinder Syal 'The Cycle Race'. Used with permission from the author's father

Neelma by Manmohan Bawa, translated from the original Punjabi by Pushpinder Syal 'Neelam'. Used with permission from the author

Saanjh by Gurdial Singh, translated from the original Punjabi by Pushpinder Syal 'Common Ground'. Used with permission from the publisher Unistar Books

Gulbano by Ajit Kaur, translated from the original Punjabi by Pushpinder Syal 'Gulbano'. Used with permission from the author.

Us Par by Raghubir Dhand, translated from the original Punjabi by Pushpinder Syal 'On the Other Side'. Used with permission from the publisher Unistar Books

Kulachhne by Gulzar Singh Sandhu, translated from the original Punjabi by Pushpinder Syal 'Disgraced'. Used with permission from the author

Oh Sochdi by Dalip Kaur Tiwana, translated from the original Punjabi by Pushpinder Syal 'The Confession'. Used with permission from the author

Car Khidona by Gurbachan Singh Bullar, translated from the original Punjabi by Pushpinder Syal 'The Toy Car'. Used with permission from the author

Vadda Aadmi by Afzal Ahsan Randhawa, translated from the original Punjabi by Pushpinder Syal 'The Generous Elder'. Used with permission from the publisher Unistar Books

Ghotna by Mohan Bhandari, translated from the original Punjabi by Pushpinder Syal 'The Wooden Pestle'. Used with permission from the author

Barf Da Danav by Jasbir Bhullar, translated from the original Punjabi by Pushpinder Syal 'The Snow Demon'. Used with permission from the author

Jarhan by Kirpal Kazak, translated from the original Punjabi by Pushpinder Syal 'Roota'. Used with permission from the author

Novel 'Lal Batti Da Akhri Kaand' by Baldev Singh, translated from the original Punjabi by Pushpinder Syal 'The Business of Life'. Used with permission from the author

Apna Apna Hissa by Waryam Singh Sandhu, translated from the original Punjabi by Pushpinder Syal 'Each One Must Have their Share'. Used with permission from the author

Jeodeean Akhaan Dee Dastan by Khalid Hussain, translated from the original Punjabi by Pushpinder Syal 'Eye Witness'. Used with permission from the author

Tafteesh by Mittar Sen Meet, translated from the original Punjabi by Pushpinder Syal 'The Investigation'. Used with permission from the author

Suhag Kujh Ansh by I C Nanda, translated from the original Punjabi by Swaraj Raj 'The Bride'. Used with permission from the Publisher Punjab University, Patiala

Man Deean Man Vich by Harcharan SIngh, translated from the original Punjabi by Swaraj Raj 'Unfulfilled Desire'. Used with permission from the author's son

Pattan Dee Berhi by Balwant Gargi, translated from the original Punjabi by Swaraj Raj 'The Night of the Tempest'. Used with permission from the publisher Navyug Publication

Publisher's Acknowledgements

Ikk Vichari Ma by Harsaran Singh, translated from the original Punjabi by Swaraj Raj 'The Helpless Mother'. Used with permission from the author's son Navchetan Singh

Baba Bolda Hai by Gursharan Singh, translated from the original Punjabi by Tajinder Kaur 'The old Man Speaks'. Used with permission from the author

Sikandar Dee Jitt 'Kujh Ansh' by Charan Das Sidhu, translated from the original Punjabi by Swaraj Raj 'Alexander's Victory (An Excerpt)'. Used with permission from the author's son and daughter

Dhaanda (play) by Ajmer Aulakh and Manjeet Aulakh, translated from the original Punjabi by Swaraj Raj 'Satyr'. Used with permission from the publisher Chetna Parkashan

Murh As Lama Ton 'Kujh Ansh' by Atamjit, translated from the original Punjabi by Snehalata Jaiswal 'Excerpt from Come Back from the War'. Used with permission from the author

Khushbo by Swaraj Bir Singh, translated from the original Punjabi by Swaraj Raj 'The Fragrance'. Used with permission from the author

Pyasa Kaa 'Kujh Ansh' by Pali Bhupinder Singh, translated from the original Punjabi by Swaraj Raj 'Excerpts from The Thirsty Crow'. Used with permission from the author

Janglam Manglam by Kewal Dhaliwal, translated from the original Punjabi by Swaraj Raj 'Bonhomie in the Jungle'. Used with permission from the author

Jang Mukt Duniya by Gurbaksh Singh Preetlarhi, translated from the original Punjabi by Madhvi Kataria 'A War Free World'. Used with permission from the author's daughter Ms Uma Singh

Excerpts from Mera Pakistani Safarnama by Balraj Sahni, translated from the original Punjabi by Madhvi Kataria 'My Pakistan Travelogue'. Used with permission from the publisher Navyug Publication

Itihasmukhta Di Lorh by Prof. Pritam Singh, translated from the original Punjabi by Madhvi Kataria 'The Importance of History'. Used with permission from the author's son

Babul Tera Punn Hove by Gyani Gurdit Singh, translated from the original Punjabi by Madhvi Kataria 'Be Blessed! O Father!'. Used with permission from the author's son

Eh Punjab Nahin by Gurbachan, translated from the original Punjabi by Madhvi Kataria 'This is Not Punjab'. Used with permission from the publisher Unistar Books

Ambar Vich Udaan by Narinder Singh Kapoor, translated from the original Punjabi by Madhvi Kataria 'A Flight in the Sky'. Used with permission from the author

Mansur by Harpal Singh Pannu, translated from the original Punjabi by Madhvi Kataria 'Mansur'. Used with permission from the author

'The Humanist Slap' from *Changiya Rukh Against the Night* by Balbir Madhopuri and translated by Tripti Jain, reproduced with permission of © Oxford University Press 2010.

1
Introduction

Literature is a creation by human beings for fellow human beings in a human society. Without human concerns, the very idea of literature is inconceivable. Literature may have regional hues, tones or melodies, yet it transcends the boundaries of region, caste, colour, race and gender. The visible superficies of literature highlights its unique and distinctive characteristics, but its undercurrents are always related to fundamental human concerns. Thus, literature strings together the whole world in a single thread. Its most distinctive feature is to embody human emotions, feelings, experiences and incidents, ideas and thoughts using appropriate tropes and narrative structures in a way that gives human emotions and experiences a concrete shape, in the form of a text. Literature is a verbal art, but every piece of writing cannot be called literature; it is rooted in society, but every writing presenting different facets of society is not literature; it is meant to be read and enjoyed, yet everything that readers enjoy does not deserve to be called literature. There has to be something in a work that makes it 'literary', something pertaining to aesthetics, that elevates a piece of writing to the level of literature. Taking ideas from reality, using imagination and creativity, a writer transforms real-life incidents into a work of art, and gives them an aesthetic form. It is a construct in which the experiences, creativity and perspective of an artist entwine or blend with one another. In the aesthetic design of literature, nothing is ugly, indecorous, dreadful or horrible; rather, in literature human concerns are fused with beauty and sublimity. Literature is a thing of beauty. The unique aesthetic design of literature is not the result of divine inspiration; rather, it is the result of amalgamation of human experiences, creative labour and constant practice. Literature, as human creation, also lays down the foundation for understanding and transforming human society.

Nearly 2500 years ago, Socrates, the son of Sophroniscus, a sculptor, asked his father questions on the soul, art and the creative process. While looking into art, he discovered the shores of sublimity, aesthetic design and the purpose of human welfare through art. Although, at this nascent stage of discovery, he associated creation of art and its purposiveness with divine inspiration yet he did not turn his back on the welfare of humanity as one of the purposes of art. His student Plato did not agree with the social and human purpose of literature. He argued that the influence of poetry was corrupting and capable of igniting baser passions in the human mind. His epistemology made him conclude that poetry was thrice removed from reality. Plato's disciple Aristotle, taking a formalist stance, rejected his teacher's deterministic epistemology and proposed the view that it is the form of a literary work that determines its ontology. Owing to the capacity of a literary work to lead the audiences to catharsis, aesthetic pleasure and moral instruction, Aristotle attached greater importance to literature (drama). In fact, he ranked literature higher than history. Aristotle believed that literature may lack empirical truth, but it abounds in poetic truth. In the long history of ideas about art and its relation to life, there have been movements like 'art for art's sake' which dwelt on the cult of beauty in art, but such ideas have been negated time and again as such aestheticism tended to divorce literature from society and human concerns. Thus, while appreciating the value of aesthetic dimensions of art, the role of imagination, the importance of craftsmanship and the function of tropes in art and literature, art has been celebrated for its fundamental concerns involving human existence and values.

The question is, if literature is a verbal art, does every construct of words deserve to be called literature? Can any writing, confined within the narrow limits of race, caste, colour, religion and gender and operating within such parochial frames, be called literature with human concerns? Contrariwise, is writing that entertains us or expresses free human spirit a work of literature expressing humanistic concerns? Nevertheless, art, with its heightened language of passion, is an expression of the intent to live and understand human life. It would not be wrong to suggest that mostly and in general, it is the human heart that leads the human self. Other disciplines of knowledge grow under the ambit of mind, rationality and intellect, but in art truth peeps out through the veil of emotion and imagination. In the case of art and literature, it is the faculty of imagination that makes it possible for the truths dwelling in the world within and without to emerge. Discovery of truth through aesthetics is unique to art in general and literature in particular. A composite amalgam of truth, aesthetic pleasure, historical truth of the times in which art is created and the universal truth of human values can only be found in literature/art. Literature that connects human beings with each other, keeps them away from malice, teaches humankind the beauty of love and trust, widens an individual's mental horizons and frees the human mind from parochialism and insular thought, teaches love for all humanity and raises the voice of protest with full artistic beauty; this is humanistic literature. Humanity is its sole identity.

A sincere attempt has been made in this book to introduce readers to the best of Punjabi literature dealing with the saga of human values and concerns: desire, achievement, failure, love, rebellion, complaint, dilemma and struggle. It is with this touchstone that the present anthology was tested, selections made and representative texts included. As we are aware that the vast gamut of Punjabi literature cannot be reproduced in a single anthology, each work included in this collection represents a particular shade of Punjabi literature.

I

Any literary work written in the Punjabi language would be known as Punjabi literature. There are different opinions about the origin of Punjabi literature. Principal Teja Singh's assertion that the Vedas were written in Punjabi is more of an emotional proclamation than a factual statement. However, Mohan Singh Diwana opines that the earlier form of Punjabi literature is found in the writings of Nath Jogis. According to him, the period of Gorakhnath Jogi is circa 940–1040 CE. Thus, it can be said that the Punjabi language is more than a thousand years old. Punjabi language never looked up to the ruling class or elites. It has always been people's language. It has flourished and developed because of its extensive use by the masses and also because it was the medium of expression of Punjabi literary writers. Scholars place Punjabi in the family of Indo-European languages and its roots are traced to Sanskrit. It was during this developmental stage of Punjabi language that the Rig Veda was composed in Punjab. That is why the influence of Sanskrit on Punjabi cannot be denied. With the arrival of Islam, it was natural for Punjabi to be influenced by Persian and Arabic. Words from Sanskrit, Arabic, Persian and later English (because of colonial intervention) found their way into Punjabi.

Its form is deeply coloured by Punjabi culture, conventions and literary tradition. While studying Punjabi literature of any particular period, glimpses of the history and culture of those times can be seen. Dr Diwana not only discovered traces of Punjabi language in the writings of Nath Jogis, he also found hues of Punjabi language in the writings of Chand Bardai, Amir Khusrau and Masood. With his keen eye, he discovered folk songs and *vaars*[1] of those times as well. He declared Baba Farid (1173–1266 CE) to be the first known poet of the Punjabi language. Undoubtedly, Baba Farid by expressing his thoughts and experiences in a dialect of Punjabi did yeoman's service for the Punjabi language. People accepted Baba Farid's poetry without any religious or communal discrimination. Guru Arjan Dev preserved the poetry of Baba Farid in Guru Granth Sahib[2] (1604 CE), the holy book of the Sikhs. During medieval times, Punjabi language flourished in five streams of Punjabi literature such as Sufi poetry, *Gurbani, Qissa Kaav, Veer Kaav* and prose. The people of Punjab used two scripts – Gurmukhi and Shahmukhi – to express themselves in Punjabi. Due to political reasons, the users of these scripts have distanced from each other. Unfortunately, the grandeur of Punjabi literature and its variety cannot be fully appreciated and enjoyed

---

[1] It refers to poems telling stories. There are two kinds of vaars available in Punjabi literature. One telling stories of heroic deeds and the other, telling stories of spiritual growth of an individual.

[2] Adi Granth was the title of its first rendition.

without familiarity with these two scripts or considering literatures written in both scripts.

In the present times, Punjabi is one of the major languages of India, but is not confined only to India. A member of the Indo-Aryan family, this language is spoken by over 130 million people all over the world. Punjabi is the tenth most spoken language of the world. It is spoken in Indian (East or *charhda*) Punjab and Pakistani (West or *lehnda*) Punjab alike. Punjabi is an essential part of the day-to-day interaction and culture in both the Punjabs. Although in Pakistan, because of the state policies, Punjabi is not given the honour of the state language, nor is it much respected, yet most people in Pakistan speak Punjabi. A sizable population from both India and Pakistan is settled in different parts of the world such as America, Canada, Britain, Australia and New Zealand. The history of these migrating people is more than a century old. From this point of view, Punjabi has virtually become an international language. At airports and market places in various cities of Canada, many signboards are in Punjabi. The Punjabi population in Canada has the legal right to government services in Punjabi. In 2015, after English and French, Punjabi was declared as the third national language in Canada.

Besides *charhda* or East (Indian) Punjab and *lehnda* or West (Pakistani) Punjab, many Punjabi authors live in other parts of the world. Similarly, works of Punjabi authors settled in England, America, Canada, Switzerland, Japan, etc. have also been included. It is interesting that Punjabis born and brought up in foreign lands have yet to contribute to this literature in some significant manner. However, it is heartening to note that the next diaspora generation too has shown interest in Punjabi language. Since the emergence of diasporic literature, the tension between literary expression and readers is evident as the new generation is not fully aware of the subtlety and complexity of the experience that Punjabi literature expresses to. However, they are not completely ignorant of their roots either. In fact, Punjabi literature serves as a bridge between the experience of the people of earlier generations of their culture and that of their own in a foreign land. The touchstone for any work of art is that it should be close or similar to the reality it is rooted in, even if it is not an identical representation of reality. Undoubtedly, the diasporic writers find themselves in a kind of crisis that asserts itself especially in a diasporic situation where reading Punjabi in Gurmukhi and Shahmukhi scripts also poses a big challenge. Another challenge is that migrated Punjabi writers are confined to the native themes; they are generally not equipped to address the reality of the land they have opted to live in. For literature to thrive, there has to be, not only a wide readership, but also a community of literary critics and thinkers to evaluate and comment upon the worth of the literature in terms of its relevance to the scenario where it originates from; wether it is Punjab on both sides of the border or the foreign land of their choice. It is imperative to recognize and appreciate its regional and local elements. Some people believe that the enthusiasm of the third-generation diaspora with their native language might have fallen considerably. But this is not the case. The new generation does exhibit interest in its language primarily through Punjabi music and films and secondarily through Punjabi literature. There are courses being offered in Punjabi language and literature in universities abroad. Despite their limitations, newspapers, cultural programmes, and radio and TV contribute to the promotion of Punjabi language and literature. Interviews with and talks by Punjabi writers and local productions of many films and plays in Punjabi point towards this fact. All this indicates that the Punjabi language is growing and flourishing.

II

The present anthology has a selection from folklore, poetry, narrative, drama and prose, representing different streams of Punjabi literature. Like the folklore of any culture, there are expressions of basic human emotions such as love, jealousy, anger, pride and sacrifice in Punjabi folklore as well. On the one hand, if determinism and surrendering to the will of God are values which are integral to the Punjabi psyche; on the other hand, protest and rebellion are also equally a part of it. Critics and thinkers too have responded to Punjabi folklore in an interesting manner: either by completely rejecting it or placing it at the zenith of appreciation. Undoubtedly, popular

Punjabi sensibility weaves history, culture, dreams, pain, sorrow and tragedy into the folklore of Punjab. This inclusiveness of folklore is one important reason that writers from all over the world have urged for the preservation of folklore. Maxim Gorky accepted and celebrated the importance of folklore over literature. He believed that to understand our present we need to understand our past and asserts that 'most profound, striking and artistically perfect types of heroes have been created by folk-lore, the oral art of the working people' ('On Literature').

There cannot be any disagreement on the importance of preserving folklore of any culture. It is important not only because folklore helps us understand the cultural moorings, values and tradition present therein; without understanding folklore neither can good literature be created, nor can what have been created be understood. From Vanjara Bedi to Nahar Singh, many intellectuals have made successful efforts to preserve Punjabi folklore, the success of which can be seen in new writings of Punjabi literature. In doing this, they have also brought out new dimensions of criticism. It is firmly believed that modern and medieval Punjabi literature is rooted in Punjabi folklore, which should be understood putting aside our emotional investment in these.

III

The second part of the anthology presents samples of medieval Punjabi poetry. The medieval period (1150 AD to 1850 AD) is known for Sufi poetry, *Gurmat Kaav, Qissa Kaav, Veer Kaav*[3] and traditional prose. Most of the medieval Punjabi literature is rooted in Punjabi folklore.

---

[3] *Gurmat Kaav* refers to the poetry written by poets included in the Guru Granth Sahib and also the poetry rooted in Sikh philosophy, but are not a part of the Granth Sahib. *Qissa Kaav* refers to long narrative poems of epic proportion written in Punjabi. *Veer Kaav* refers to ballads or narrative poems telling stories of bravery and valour. The term ballad should not be confused with Ballad as a literary form in English literature which has a particular form. *Veer Kaav* is the poetic rendition of episodes from wars, battles or conflicts in which heroism of an individual is celebrated and glorified.

Thus, medieval Punjabi literature can be seen as a continuation and persistence of the folklore of Punjab. While creating their works, the medieval Punjabi poets did not simply adopt the folklore of Punjab, they also transformed it according to the sociocultural context in which they lived. That is why the medieval Punjabi literature is valued for dealing with fundamental issues, for its unique form and novelty of expression, and its socio-historical relevance.

During this period, the folklore was not mechanically reproduced, it was trans-created. In the warp and woof of its fabric reside the ideas of the time such as God, fate, the worthlessness of worldly pursuits, the artificial nature of social system or its structure and its inalterability. These issues are a part of the medieval consciousness, and can be seen operating in the backdrop of *Qissa Kaav* and *Veer Kaav*. Belief in the divine, romance, struggle and protest are its integral elements. Medieval Punjabi literature, despite being rooted in a particular cultural and historical context, never turned its back on fundamental human values. While being a part of the continuum of folklore, medieval literature is a complete and independent unit in itself. Its different strands or genres also stand as forms of literature on their own, and complement one another. These strands (the poetry of Naths, Siddhs and Sufis, and *Gurbani*) can be seen extending or transforming meanings of each other, and sometimes, exhibit strong points of convergence and confluence with each other, for example in Sufi poetry and *Gurbani*. Folklore, deeply rooted in these writings, plays an important role in arousing and circulating the popular sentiment prevailing among people.

Besides *Gurmat Kaav*, *Qissa Kaav*, *Veer Kaav* and traditional prose, Sufi poetry is an important component of medieval poetry. The sources of Sufi poetry are rooted in the Islamic mystic traditions. Sufi poetry held at its centre three principles of Islam—God is one, the Quran Sharif is a holy book and Prophet Mohammed is the last prophet. *Namaz, shahada, roza, zakat* and *hajj* are rituals which some Sufi poets have rejected, while others have accepted them. Love for God and suffering the pangs of separation are two fundamental emotions in Sufi poetry. The imagery, symbols, love legends and metaphors from Punjabi culture embedded in Sufi poetry signify its deep-rooted connection with the Punjab. The fundamental values of human concerns and notes of rebellion embedded in Punjabi poetry constitute the centre of Sufi poetry. Both values operate within the frame of religious thought. For example, Baba Farid, following the prevalent Indian religious thought, preached abstaining from materialism, and also reflected on death. He also underlined the value of peace, endurance, patience, humility, service and self-restraint in his poetry. As Attar Singh points out 'Baba Farid has given the Punjabi literary tradition its humanist complexion and ideals'; his poetry is important 'not because of its religious nature, but because it is firmly rooted in the truth of life and is flowing with the stream of life.' Najam Hussain Syed, a scholar from the West Punjab, echoes this: 'The basis of Farid's poetry is his lived experiences which are also the experiences of a common man.' Sheikh Farid and Shah Hussain were defiant, and they denounced dogmas and rituals:

> O Farid, the prayer-mat is hanging on your shoulder,
> You are wearing the *Sufa* robes,
> You utter words sweet like jaggery
> But in your heart, you carry stinging malice.

Shah Hussain says,

> You are pure from without, from within you are filled with filth,
> Why should anyone call you a Sheikh?

Bulleh Shah, who also rejected religious dogmatism and ritualism vehemently, stands close to Farid. Bulleh Shah is bolder in challenging the hegemonic religious and political structures. He says:

> In the inn stay invaders, in the temples dwell the thieves
> In the mosques reside the crooked ones, lovers are chaste for they are recluse.

Despite Sufi poetry being rooted in Islamic thought and culture, Punjabi Sufi poetry has its distinct identity. Attar Singh says that this tradition was conceived in the womb of the land of Punjab. Besides Baba Farid, other poets such as Shah Hussain, Sultan Bahu and Bulleh Shah have also contributed significantly to make Sufi poetry a part of the popular consciousness of Punjab. It has the simplicity and innocence of the people of Punjab. Attar Singh concludes that during this period, 'Punjabi poetry was Islamicized and Islam was Punjabiized.' That is why in Punjabi Sufi poetry conventional Sufi metaphors of wine, cup and flasks are not found; nor is there formalistic stylization of Persian poetry. Punjabi Sufi poetry is miles away from communalism, discrimination and violence; and in this poetic tradition dwell values like tolerance, liberal thinking and love for humanity. When seen from this perspective, the Punjabi Sufi poetry holds a value even in our present times.

In the *Gurmat Kaav* too, one God and an invisible divine power has been mentioned repeatedly. *Gurmat Kaav* is also an example of poetry rich in human values and social issues. This poetic tradition denounced religious dogmas, rituals, social inequalities, and excesses and atrocities of the ruling class. Guru Nanak has called the king a lion and his officials the dogs. He did not shy away from calling ignorant masses 'blind'. The voice that *Gurmat Kaav* raised against social injustice and inequality had a great impact on the minds of the people. The foundation of the *Gurmat Kaav* was laid down by Guru Nanak, who presented before the people a new cultural model. On the one hand, Guru Nanak condemned the invading Muslims; on the other, he embraced the ordinary people, irrespective of their caste or creed: 'no one is Hindu, no one is Muslim'. Jagbir Singh in his book, *Gurmat Kaav da Itihaas* (*The History of Gurmat Kaav*) says that the ideology of *Gurmat Kaav* is that of the deprived, the common and the subservient. The ideology, which empowers the ordinary, helps them raise their voice against all kinds of oppression and exploitation. It criticises religious orthodoxy in the feudal setup of the Mughal period and economic exploitation of people. It debunks Brahminical ritualism and hegemonic social structure based on Manu's ideas, which in a systemic manner facilitates the oppression of the poor and the lower castes.

> I am lowly, my caste is lowly, I am lowlier than the lowest
> Nanak says—In you I have found the company of the higher
> Wherever you shower your grace, the lowly is embraced by the higher.
>
> (Guru Nanak)

The message of equality, raising voice against tyranny, fearlessness and to stand for the weak, embedded in *Gurbani,* is relevant even today.

Qissa Kaav of Punjabi literature are stories of love and romance. The love legends of Heer–Ranjha, Sohni–Mehiwal, Mirza–Sahiban, Sassi–Punnu etc. belong as much to Punjab as to other regions outside Punjab. It would be inappropriate to reduce these tales to class conflict or to call these legends as stories of poets' indifference to social issues. These love legends highlight the value and importance of human life in the mortal world. They give voice to universal human values, culture, syncretic cultural practices and linguistic beauty. *Qissa Kaav* presents a glimpse of human values in which love, valour and devotion are simultaneously present. In this poetic tradition, there is neither contemplation on the other world, nor is there its dominance. Using the backdrop of these stories, the poets have presented their socio-cultural context, a wide range of human emotions and deeper understanding of cultural values, as well as the feudal social structure and their worldview. By making the theme of love, a prohibited subject, the central idea in these *qissas,* the poets made an attempt to transform the ideal of love into reality. The mode of story-telling and the way in which sociological and cultural aspects are highlighted shows that the *qissa,* as a genre, has the potential of challenging the values of the ruling class and express protest. Many of these poems were written by Muslim poets, which highlight the Islamic cultural backdrop. The Sufi and *qissa* poets of Punjab had a bigger role to play in leaving a lasting influence of Islam in Punjab than the invaders and rulers. The people of Punjab struggled against Muslim invaders, but embraced poetry entrenched predominantly in Islamic culture. These literary works laid down the foundation of syncretic culture in Punjab, which was later preserved in the Guru Granth Sahib. The cultural consciousness of Punjab accepted female protagonists of these narratives as daughters of Punjab, who belonged to different socio-cultural backgrounds. These female characters challenge hypocritical social values and provide a counter-viewpoint to the dominant discourse.

The category of *Veer Kaav* includes *vaars* and *jangnamas*. Description of war is central to this genre of Punjabi poetry. However, the central theme of the medieval *vaar* is valour. These are the accounts of exploits of brave men and women. When the people of Punjab fought against Nadir Shah's invasions, Najabat, the poet, describes the scene in *Nadir Shah di Vaar*. Vaars that belong to the era before Guru Nanak, had the complexion of spiritual *vaars*. *Chandi di Vaar*, by Guru Gobind Singh, exhibits the confluence between valour and spirituality. Invoking the goddess Chandi, Guru Gobind Singh in this work provides alternative models of womanhood to Punjabi women. The second form under this category is called *jangnama*, which is rooted in the battle of Karbala in which the grandchildren of Prophet Mohammad lost their lives. This feature of *jangnama* becomes the basis of tales of valour associated with battles fought by the Sikhs. The best example of this category of poetry is found in Shah Mohammad's *Jang Hind-Punjab*. Telling the story of the times after the death of Ranjit Singh, Shah Mohammad in this work portrays Sikh chiefs as traitors and forces of the Raj in a heroic mode. Using his understanding of the times and poetic talents, Shah Mohammad transforms it into a historical narrative. He highlights the lasting bond of love between Hindus and Muslims, the valour of Punjabis, the abuse by feudal lords, and the prevalent anti-British sentiment. The glorious body of his work shows the poet's deep understanding of history, his unstinted empathy with Sikh/Khalsa Raj, his secularism and an exceptional talent of poetic expression; small wonder that this *jangnama* is a classic of Punjabi literature.

The religious literature of Punjab, especially *Gurmat Kaav*, does not propagate the idea of renouncing the world; rather it encourages humans to encounter and resolve the challenges of life. This can be attributed to the fact that most of Sikh Gurus were either workmen or warriors. One major contribution of Sikhism to Punjab is that it brought society and religion close to each other. From the people's point of view, it was a unique and exceptional initiative, which brought society and religion together. The compilation of Guru

Granth Sahib was an exemplary and extraordinary task. It is a rare holy book which includes poetry not only by the Sikh gurus, but also by various sadhus, saints, Bhakti and Sufi poets. Kabir, Namdev, Ravidas, Baba Farid and *bhatt* poets have also been included in the book. After the compilation of the Granth Sahib, the idea of establishing it as Guru took birth. While compiling the Granth, Guru Arjan Dev totally ignored the caste, religion or regional affiliation of the poet and selected texts on the basis of the merit of the poetry. Besides the poetry of six Sikh Gurus, works of four Sikh followers, poetry of fifteen *bhakts* and eleven *bhatts* have been included in the Granth. This book provided society with values like patience and creativity, and also gave people a fresh perspective. This compilation enlightens the human mind and inspires humanity to live life with a broader perspective and an open mind.

IV

The third, fourth, fifth and sixth sections of this book comprise select samples of modern Punjabi poetry, narrative (novel and short story), drama and prose. Although some scholars believe that modern Punjabi literature began in 1850 CE, whereas modernity entered Punjabi literature somewhere close to the twentieth century. The modern outlook resulted in scathing criticism of the past, while establishing a dialogue with tradition. There is an appreciation for rationality, logic, scientific outlook and justice. Scientific outlook replaced belief in divine power, God, determinism and fate. Romance with realism gave a new perspective to the understanding of human life. Along with the British also came the new educational system, which changed the lifestyle and worldview of the people of Punjab. The new reality resulted in new experiences, which required a new idiom of expression. The old forms were replaced by the new. It was because of the new outlook that human behavior and human concerns came to be at the centre of the new literature. Although Punjabi has a long history of prose writing, discussion of contemporary issues entered these writings comparatively recently. Genres like autobiography emerged in the middle of the twentieth century. Autobiographies by women emerged two decades later.

The twentieth century presented before us various shades of modernity. Drama, novel, short-story, history and criticism had a powerful beginning. In the twentieth century, human needs and political circumstances became more complex than before. British rule offered new challenges to Punjab. The injustice of colonialism, wars and emigration made people compare their circumstances (of slavery and mistreatment) with that of the West. The western education system gave the people of Punjab an opportunity to read English literature. People, who earlier believed in fate, destiny and God, now began to trust rationality and empirical reality. The changing environment introduced modernity to Punjabi literature. Bhai Veer Singh, the pioneer of modern Punjabi poetry, changed the idiom of Punjabi poetry. Taking it away from the traditional narrative poetry, he invested modern thought in Punjabi poetry. He introduced Punjabis to 'western' forms of literature such as short poems, novel, drama and epic. Poets like Puran Singh, Dhani Ram Chatrik, Diwan Singh Kalepani, Bawa Balwant, Mohan Singh, Amrita Pritam further enriched Punjabi poetry and transformed its form, nature, and concerns completely. If somebody wants to have a glimpse of the reality of life, harsh contemporary circumstances, shades of Punjabi culture and identity, simplicity of Punjabi culture, and pure language in use, one should read poets like Dhani Ram Chatrik.

Reinventing itself and breaking new grounds is an integral part of Punjabi poetry. But the shift to modernity was a difficult process because the British colonialism and other ruling powers, directly or indirectly, strengthened those regressive structures that the Guru Granth Sahib had earlier challenged and broken. Punjabi poetry enjoys an ambivalent relationship with the British Raj. On the one hand, the British rule gave Punjab new ideas; on the other, it also committed atrocities on the people. The British empire executed its policies to strengthen itself but the seeds of new ideas sown by the British rule gave people a new outlook, facilitating the agenda of western modernity in India. Those who had emigrated to foreign countries, where they experienced and lived individual freedom, became critical of British rule in India, and wanted to free their own country. This gave birth to anti-British sentiment in the form of Ghadar movement and Babbar Akali movement, which made open declarations to root out foreign rule.

The tradition of stage-poetry in Punjab was at its peak during the first half of the twentieth century. It performed an important role in social reforms and political movements, led by stage-poets such as Mohammad Ramzan Hamdam, Firoz Din Sharf, Kartar Singh Balaggan and Ustad Daman. Besides, progressive poetry in the 1940s was an important influence against western imperialism. It created class consciousness among people for changing the existing social structure. These poets expressed their concerns on issues like freedom, peace, struggle, class structures, revolution, imperial loot and dignity of labour. This poetry gave a new consciousness and idiom to Punjabi poetry.

After the war with China, the dream of nation building was shattered. The notes of hope in Punjabi poetry were replaced with despondency. This shift gave birth to experimental poetry. A new generation of poets such as Ravinder Ravi, Jasbir Singh Ahluwalia and Ajaib Kamal joined the movement of experimental poetry in Punjabi. These poets believed that industrialisation would lead to urbanisation and their reality would change. This poetry became a space for expressing intellectual thought rather than discussing prohibited relationships, sexual fantasies and expressing extreme emotions; individual morality instead of social morality and idealism; and contemporaneity instead of historicity. Directly or indirectly, it became a counter-discourse to progressive poetry. Since this kind of poetry did not reflect the culture and lived reality of Punjab, not many readers identified with experimental poetry.

Modern Punjabi poetry after this phase distanced itself from romance, idealism and experimental strains. It created a niche for itself by engaging with social issues, which is called *suhajwadi kavita*.[4]

---

[4] *Suhaj* means aesthetics. This school of poetry was rooted in high formalistic consciousness among its practitioners.

This poetry was written keeping in mind human dilemmas and social issues. This school of poetry is seemingly free from all 'isms'. Harbhajan Singh laid emphasis on the aesthetics of poetry, Jaswant Singh Neki emphasised complexities, Tara Singh expressed broken relationships through irony and sarcasm, and Sohan Singh Misha lent voice to suppressed human emotions, particularly the intimacies of the man–woman relationship. Shiv Kumar Batalvi enunciated from the depths of Punjabi culture and his voice reached every nook and corner of Punjab, across all sections of society. Personal pain and agony left a great impact on everyone. Simultaneously, by presenting the pain of women through Loona, he touched the core of Punjabi society. Besides, another form of poetry took birth in Punjab which is known as Naxalite poetry or *vidrohi kavita* (poetry of protest), or *jujhaaru kavita* (poetry of militant struggle) or *itihasmukh chetna wali kavita* (poetry with historical consciousness). Jagtar, Paash, Sant Sandhu, Sant Ram Udasi, Lal Singh Dil, Amarjit Chandan and Harbhajan Halwarvi belong to this movement. Committed to the idea of revolution, this school of poetry deals with poverty, and the lives of the poor: their pain, struggle, dreams and oppression. Simultaneously, it unmasks exploitative structures, violence of the state and inhuman deeds of the powerful and the haves. Paash declared his poetic creed and purpose by announcing:

> Do not expect of me that I,
> Despite being the son of the soil,
> Will talk about your
> Despicable pleasures and deplorable tastes

Simultaneously, other poets such as Mohanjit, Surjit Patar and Parminderjit also contributed to Punjabi poetry. During the phase of militancy in Punjab, Punjabi poets opposed political suppression of people and also articulated and protected human values through their poetry.

* * *

The fourth part of the book offers a selection of narrative prose (short stories and excerpts from novels). The position of Punjabi novel is peculiar. It can be seen as a continuation of the tradition of long narrative love poems written during the medieval period, or as a new genre flourishing under the influence of western literature. The British prepared the first dictionary of Punjabi and also established the first printing press in Punjab. The missionaries had two novels translated into Punjabi: *Masihi Musafir di Yatra* (1859), a Punjabi translation of Bunyan's *The Pilgrim's Progress* and the second one is *Jyotirudya* (1879). Since the purpose of these translations was to pave the path for Christianity in Punjab, the texts were naturally critical of Hinduism and Islam, but it is interesting to note that the literary idiom of *Gurbani* and Sikhism was used in these translations. The birth of Singh Sabha Movement in Punjab was a reaction to protect the Sikh community from conversion to Christianity under the influence of these books. Other religious groups too began protecting the interests of their respective communities, dividing people along communal lines.

To counter Punjabi translations of novels by Christian missionaries, Bhai Veer Singh, Bhai Mohan Singh Vaid and Charan Singh Shaheed wrote novels from the Sikh point of view. The Christian missionaries and the British worked towards presenting an exalted view of Western culture and religion by showing Punjab, and its language, culture and religions in a poor light. It would further their likely intent of kindling a sense of inferiority among the Punjabi people. It was natural on the part of these writers to react and respond. Their writings achieved the purpose without maligning the syncretic culture of Punjab flowing in the five rivers of the land. Later novelists changed the form, nature and idiom of the Punjabi novel. Nanak Singh, who is considered to be the father of the Punjabi novel, renounced the communal worldview and wrote novels with a secular vision. His novels dealt with realistic issues and he tried to find their solution from a progressive-idealist position. Surinder Singh Narula was a champion of naturalist realism in Punjabi literature. He is known for a humanist portrayal, through realistic representation. Sant Singh Sekhon is a progressive realist novelist. By rendering tensions between economic compulsions and love for the (home)land in *Baba Asman*, he exhibits his rational and critical understanding of the human situation. The fourth important novelist of this generation is Jaswant Singh Kanwal, who started his literary career as a progressive idealist but his worldview later changed. At the beginning of his career, he earned fame by using folklore, *qissas* and *veer sahit* in his writings. Themes like love, progressive thought, rebellion and freedom gradually acquired centrality in his writings. He explored the rural psyche, and also the psyche of the ruling class in his writings. In the 1980s, progressive and revolutionary concerns were replaced by concerns of identity and nation. When he accused the working class people, coming from other parts of India to Punjab, of 'polluting' Punjabi culture, his progressive outlook was questioned. However, it cannot be denied that in his writings he has always focused on Punjab, its economy and pride.

Due to constraints of space, we could not include complete novels in this project. However, some excerpts from different novels have been included as representative samples. Short stories of some novelists such as Nanak Singh, Jaswant Singh Kanwal, Dalip Kaur Tiwana and Mitter Sain Meet, have been included along with a story by Gurdial Singh, a Jnanpith Awardee humanist writer. Owing to the paucity of space, Amrita Pritam could not be included as a narrative writer in this selection, the reason being no writer has been included under more than one category. This list includes writers such as Sant Singh Sekhon, Balwant Gargi, Fakhar Zaman, Gurmukh Singh Musafir, etc. Sekhon is not included in the drama category; Gargi does not figure in the prose section. Similarly, Fakhar Zaman is not included in the prose section and Musafir has not been included in the poetry section.

There are four major milestones in the journey of the Punjabi short story. Short stories from Pakistan can be discussed as a separate category and those written by diaspora writers can also be discussed independently. There is also the category of the Dalit short story and the category of women's short stories written from the feminist point of view. When seen collectively, the trajectory of the Punjabi short story moves from idealism to realism. There is a vast body of Punjabi short story writers and their writings, but we do not have a frame large enough to include everyone. We offer our apologies to all diaspora writers, writers of the third generation and the new generation of writers for not being able to include them. We could include only Afzal Ahsan Randhawa from Pakistan. Perhaps the grand picture of Punjabi short story can be shared with readers through another project.

* * *

Any discussion of modern Punjabi literature is incomplete without reference to Punjabi drama. Punjabi drama began with translations of Sanskrit and English drama into Punjabi. Bhai Veer Singh and Bawa Budh Singh are the pioneers of Punjabi drama. Bhai Veer Singh wrote plays on Sikh identity. Bawa Budh Singh wrote plays on women's emancipation. While, the drama of Bhai Veer Singh was somewhat sectarian and focused on the question of Sikh identity, Bawa Budh Singh's plays were secular in nature. I. C. Nanda is the real pioneer in this regard. He not only blended the seriousness of Bhai Veer Singh with the secularism of Bawa Budh Singh but also acted in and directed his own plays dealing with rich human concerns. Norah Richards, the Irish actress who was earlier associated with the productions of Abbey Theatre and who came to Lahore, was I. C. Nanda's primary inspiration.

Owing to Norah Richards' unparalleled influence on Punjabi drama, for the next three to four decades, her ideas continued to inspire Punjabi drama. Bawa Budh Singh gradually embraced fundamental human concerns. Nanda, Gargi, Harcharan Singh and Sekhon contemplated themes of women's emancipation and human concerns in their plays. The second-generation playwrights like Surjit Singh Sethi, Kapur Singh Ghuman, Harsaran Singh and G. S. Jasuja paved the way for the next generation of playwrights who were entrenched in social and human problems on the one hand and were enthusiastic theatre doers on the other. They took dramatic writing to the next level. Given the pace at which Punjabi drama is growing, we hope that very soon it will be included among important drama traditions of India. Satish Kumar Verma says that 'Punjabi drama is at its best now because one, it connects itself with postcolonialism, globalisation, postmodernism, feminist consciousness and Dalit consciousness; two, it has achieved its distinct form; three, while searching for new theatrical devices it adopts and adapts electronic media into theatre; and four, it is looking for new grounds in different cities of India, Pakistan and overseas.'

* * *

In the last section of the book, there are samples of Punjabi prose. The British commissioned Punjabi writers to write textbooks. Shardha Ram Phillauri is the most popular name in this category: his best known works are *Punjabi Baat-Cheet* and *Sikhan De Raaj Di Vithya*. In order to protect Punjab from the influence of Christianity, many prose writers, like the novelists, wrote accounts of Sikh history and Sikhism, obviously to glorify them. Karam Singh Historian and Bawa Prem Singh Hoti have made a major contribution in this direction. Among the prose writers, Giani Gian Singh, Professor Gurmukh Singh, Giani Ditt Singh, Bhai Kahan Singh Nabha and Bhai Veer Singh are also well known.

At the beginning of the twentieth century, implementation of the new education policy, availability of western knowledge, presence of science books in school and college libraries, Punjabi writers gaining access to modern education, their exposure to the outer world and the rise of different sociopolitical movements in Punjab are among the important factors which inspired Punjabi writers to reflect, think and write. Major prose writers of the twentieth century had before them the agenda of enlightening the Punjabi reader. This task began with a purpose to motivate the modern person to live life better, purposefully, happily and with sensitivity. Principal Teja Singh chose the subject of love, new ideas, new times, simplicity and highlighted human values in a very simple manner. Gurbax Singh Preetlari brought prose out of mystery and romance, and placed it very close to the ordinary man. Instead of the other world, he discussed the mortal world; instead of God, he talked about the human; instead of fate, he wrote about human potential. He reached out to common people. Ideas like *sahaj preet* (spontaneous love) and *pyar kabza nahin pehchan hai* (love is not possession, but identification) gave people a fresh perspective. Harinder Singh Roop spread the message of Sikhism and welfare of humanity through his writings. Through works like *Chunjha Pahunche*, he convinced his readers that complex issues like uncommon reality and the truth of contemporary times can be dealt with through common themes. Narinder Singh Kapoor is doing the same task in the present times. Undoubtedly, this prose gave hope and inspired the Punjabi people to adopt a rationalist view of life. This consciousness contributed to making Punjabi readers more humane, thoughtful and sensitive human beings.

There are many forms of modern Punjabi prose: essays, articles, travelogues, autobiography, biography, character sketches, memoirs and short essays. This book includes essays, excerpts from autobiographies and a travelogue.

In the twentieth century, criticism, theory, literary history and literary studies too grew at a fast pace. But all this is linked to the study of literature and literary criticism. In this book, we have confined our task to literature in which a creative writer, according to his/her linguistic prowess and capability, reflects on life and searches for truth. Taking his discovery to the realm of imagination, he/she brings it back to the real world. Created with the writer's full creative might and humanist perspective, it transcends all boundaries of time and space, and attains universality.

***

In the present times, market forces, commerce and trade dictate the overall tenor of life, and human values have been pushed to the margins. Life is fast-paced, anxiety-ridden and full of absurd pursuits. The human dimensions in modernity are under serious threat as the spaces for aesthetic pursuits that demand leisure and contemplation have shrunk. Political forces in the market-driven economy are not interested in human values; their prime concern is to grab power and reproduce such enabling conditions that allow them to remain in power. The easiest way to acquire power and maintain it is by distancing people from each other through divisive identity politics. Division of any kind in human society, making a mockery of life-affirming human values, will surely lead to chaos. And this is what we see happening around us. As a civil society, we need to understand that sacrificing human values for worldly pleasures, power and parochial gain is most unfortunate. Our humanity is our most cherished possession; without it we are robots or machines, incapable of love, compassion and sympathy. Art and literature have a great role to play here, the role of making us compassionate and sympathetic to all life forms; in other words, art and literature have it in them to humanise us by liberating our minds from hedonistic pursuits and egomania. We hope the present volume of humanistic texts will make a humble contribution in this regard.

***

We are thankful to Dr. Ganesh Devy, who gave us this honourable and marathon task to serve Punjabi literature. We are thankful to Vivek Sachdeva (Professor of English, GGSIP University, New Delhi), Pushpinder Syal (former Head and Professor of English and Cultural Studies, Panjab University, Chandigarh), Swaraj Raj (former Head and Professor of English, Shri Guru Granth Sahib World University, Fatehgarh Sahib, Punjab) and Madhvi Kataria (IAS) for translating different sections of the book. We also take this opportunity to extend our special gratitude to Rana Nayar (former Head and Professor, Department of English and Cultural Studies, Panjab University, Chandigarh), Sneh Jaswal (Professor of Psychology, Chaudhary Charan Singh University, Meerut), Jaishree Kapur (Asst. Professor, University of Delhi), Tripti Jain, Tejinder Kaur, Amandeep Kaur Sra, Kanika Bhalla, Ravinder Bhathal (President, Punjabi Sahit Academy), S. K. Verma (former Head and Professor of Punjabi, Punjabi University, Patiala), Chaman Lal (former Professor, Jawaharlal Nehru University, New Delhi), Gagandeep Sharma, Neetu Arora, Queeny Pradhan, Madan Gopal Singh, Yadwinder Singh (Department of Punjabi, University of Delhi), Gurbhajan Gill, Rawail Singh, Harish Jain, Renuka Singh, Satish Gulati, and Sugra Sadaf and Tariq Gujjar from Pakistan for their valuable contribution and help in the present project.

We also take this opportunity to thank our friends who helped us during the entire project in varied ways. Owing to the paucity of space, it is not possible for us to name and thank each of them. They are like the invisible angels who helped us at every critical moment. We are deeply indebted to all of them for their unstinted cooperation, support and help. We also apologise for not being able to include a few important writers because of the copyright limitations.

We hope that, despite shortcomings, the readers will appreciate our sincere efforts. We are aware that, as compared to the vast body of Punjabi literature, this book only offers a glimpse of Punjabi literature written over almost ten centuries. Despite that we are still hopeful that this volume will introduce readers, especially those who cannot read Punjabi, to the vast and rich tradition of Punjabi literature. It will help our readers get an idea of human concerns and values expressed in Punjabi literature. From the vast ocean of Punjabi literature, this book is only a drop.

We are sure readers will enjoy reading this book.

Atamjit
Playwright and Director

Harbhajan Singh Bhatia
Former Head and Dean, Languages
Guru Nanak Dev University
Amritsar

(Translated from Punjabi by Vivek Sachdeva)

2

FOLKLORE

Tappe

Redness pricks my eyes, though
But it hurts my lover more.

You get a fever, I groan
You and I are one.

The pain of parting I cannot forget
All other pains of life I can.

Not a widow, I'll be a *suhagan* again,
If the war of Basra ends today.

O *firangi*, strike off his name from the list,
He is the only son my mother-in-law has.

Making pretence that the smoke of hurts,
The wife of a soldier hides her tears.

You may take one hundred holy dips
The filth of your heart is not washed away.

Having sown *keekar*,
It's foolish to expect the dates of Bijaur.

One who promised to remain thick like milk forever,
Turned out to be thinner than water later.

Above there only your deeds will carry you through
No one will ask you which caste you belong to.

Fair complexion will get you no reward,
People will love you only for your virtues.

Beauty, youth and parents
If gone, are gone for good.

I'll work equally hard with you in the field,
First you buy me some anklets for my sickle.

Songs of the Maiden

I

A Flock of Sparrows

(A Dialogue Between the Daughter and the Father)

Daughter:

We are like a flock of sparrows,
    We will fly away one day, my *babul*.
We will take a long flight,
    Don't know where we may end up, my *babul*.
Through the doors of your mansion
    My *doli* refuses to move, my *babul*.

Father:

If my mansion stops you
    I shall knock down a wall for you,
Find your way to your new home, my daughter.

Daughter:

We are like a flock of sparrows,
    We will fly away one day, my *babul*.
My *doli* refuses to budge,
    In your orchards it is stuck, my *babul*.

Father:

If it is this *tahli* that blocks your way
    I shall cut it down for you
Find your way to your new home, my daughter.

Daughter:

We are like a flock of sparrows,
    One day we'll fly away, my *babul*.
Tell me, in your mansion now
    Who will play with dolls?

Father:

My grand-daughters will play
    In due course of time
Find your way to your new home, my daughter.

Daughter:

We are like a flock of sparrows
    We will fly away one day, my *babul*.
In your mansion now
    Who will spin the yarn?

Father:

My grand-daughters shall spin the yarn
    When they grow up like you
Find your way to your new home, my daughter.

Daughter:

We are like a flock of sparrows
    We will fly away one day, my *babul*.
We will take a long flight
    Don't know where we may end up, my *babul*.

A Wedding Song

Wake up, O sleeping *babul*
    It is time to part with your daughter,
It's time to do fatherly duty
    It's time to earn some honour;
Pigeons in your mansion coo
    The koel in your garden chant the name of Rama.

Wake up, O sleeping brother
    It is time to part with your sister,
It's time to do brotherly duty
    It is time to earn some honour;
Pigeons in your mansion coo
    The koel in your garden chant the name of Rama.

Wake up, O sleeping *chacha ji*
    It is time to part with your niece,
It's time to do your duty
    It's time to earn some honour;
Pigeons in your mansion coo
    The koel in your garden chant the name of Rama.

Wake up, O sleeping *mama ji*
    It is time to part with your niece,
It's time to do your duty
    It is time to earn some honour;
Pigeons in your mansion coo
    The koel in your garden chant the name of Rama.

Standing by the Sandal Tree

My dear sister, why were you hiding?
    Why were you standing behind the tree?
I was standing there with my brother.
    Find me a match, brother.
What match do you desire, my sister?
    Among stars, he should be the moon
Among moons, he should be like Krishna;
    Find me a Krishna, my brother.

My dear daughter, why were you hiding?
    Why were you standing behind the tree?
I was standing with my father.
    Find me a match, father.

What match do you desire, my daughter?
    Among stars, he should be the moon
Among moons, he should be like Krishna;
    Find me a Krishna, my father.

My dear niece, why were you hiding?
    Why were you standing behind the tree?
I was standing with my *mama ji*.
    Find me a match, *mama ji*.
What match you desire, my dear niece.
    Among stars, he should be the moon
Among moons, he should be like Krishna;
    Find me a Krishna, my father.
Traditional

A Vanjara Selling Bangles

A *vanjara* has come –
    A *vanjara* is there in the street
Buy new bangles for yourself
    Give yourself a treat.

I asked my mother-in-law
    I asked my husband's sister,
I asked them to buy me bangles,
    But no one bought me any.

My husband came home after the day's fun
    My *jethani* poisoned his mind
Getting angry, he picked up a stick
    And smashed all of my bangles.

What should I do with your money?
    Ask your sister-in-law to cook for you.
I've eaten enough food cooked by her,
    Now I wish to eat what you'll cook, says my husband.

A Suitable Match

My father found me an old man,
    He sold me for a handful of coins;
My friends, the old man slips
    When he gets onto the wedding-bed,
How can I help him?
    Should I give him a walking stick?
This way only the false sound of the *been* can be made
But you cannot create the joyous melody of the *algoza*.

My father found me a child
    And gave him some pieces of sugarcane;
My friends, the child throws a tantrum
    When he gets onto the wedding-bed,
How can I help him?
    Should I sing him a lullaby?
This way only the false sound of the *been* can be made
But you cannot create the joyous melody of the *algoza*.

My father found me a suitable match,
    He came riding a fine mare;
My friends, he plays the game of love
    When he gets onto the wedding-bed, my friends
Lord Rama has blessed us both
    Lord Rama has created a perfect match.
Now we'll make the soulful music of the *been*
Now we'll create the joyous melody of the *algoza*.

A Wife's Wish

That scoundrel always gambles
    And has all sorts of fun;
He never forsakes meat and wine,
    Just look at what he sports.

He has taken away my clothes and jewels
    Oh, I cry aloud;

If I utter a word, he hits me hard
    I endure a lot of pain.

He is good at back-stabbing
    For which I scold him oft;
If, by chance, he comes home
    I plead before him hard
Forsake your vices
    Think of your suffering wife.

Married Woman's Pain – 1

Seething with rage, he came back home
    And opened the door,
I had kneaded the dough,
    Lentils I had boiled though.
Sitting among other ladies
    I had sewn my *saree* too.
While going out in the morning,
    By chance he had touched a stick
With the same stick in the evening,
    He hit me hard,
All the pearls of my necklace
    Lay scattered in the sand.

Married Woman's Pain – 2

I bought those ear-rings for myself,
    Which my husband gave to his *bhabho*.
Look at my simpleton man
    He serves his *bhabhi* more.
Like a slave, he does her chores
    He throws the cow-dung; he fetches her water;
My *jethani* is no less than a dictator
    I will never fetch her water.
A ripe juicy lemon I need
    We will pluck it from the garden.

Married Woman's Pain – 3

I was born in beautiful Doaba
    I got married into this wilderness.
My love has gone to the war,
    I am like a crane parted from the flock.
Tears roll down from my eyes like a stream,
    No news of his return I ever receive
Come back, my love!
    I have given you my heart and soul.

All sides are lit up
    Wherever you sit, my lovely lady.
But your father has shown no regard
    To your youth, beauty and passion;
He has sent you far away
    By arranging your match in a far-off land,
Nothing was in your control, nothing was in mine
    Your father got you married to a soldier.

Married Woman's Pain – 4

In the middle of the night you leave, O young man
    And come back at the break of the dawn;
Dogs bark at you when cross the street
    Thinking you may be caught, my heart sinks;
People will come carrying sticks
    By now your affair is an open secret;
Everybody knows about
    Your furtive visits to a *telan*.

A Warning

There are many villages,
Among many villages,
    There is one called Dina,

Every day there is a fight
    Every day a piece of land is sold.

The youth migrating to cities,
    Opium has consumed everything,
Their fathers are rendered useless
    Nobody is willing to work.
The evil is at its worst
    With bodies their spirits are rotten too.

O man, if you do not plough the land
    You cannot survive now,
Come out of the world of addiction,
    And go back to your fields.

Remembering Parents

Flying crow, flying crow
    Flying crow, you go flying.
Go flying and stop once
    Stop at my parent's house.

Tell my mother nothing
    Tell her nothing about me,
She'll cry over my plight
    Holding my dolls tight.
O crow, I'll be indebted to you.

Tell my sister nothing
    Tell her nothing about me,
Finding the empty yard
    She will cry hard.
O crow, I'll be indebted to you.

Tell my sister-in-law nothing
    Tell her nothing about me,
She would laugh and cackle
    When she visits her parents.
O crow, I'll be indebted to you.

Tell my father nothing
    Tell him nothing about me,

Leaving all his affairs
    He would cry bitterly.
O crow, I'll be indebted to you.

Go and tell my dear brother
    Tell him everything about me,
He will come rushing to save me
    Trotting on his Arab horse.
O crow, I'll be indebted to you.

The Clay-Baby

A baby of clay I make for myself
Give him a dress to wear,
Wrapping him with a shawl
I keep him warm;
O my baby, cry you not
For your father has gone to
Faraway lands.

My clay-baby speaks not
My clay-baby moves not
When I call my baby
He responds not.
When I gave my baby a bath
He dissolved in water.
Oh, what a loss to me!
Ah! my baby is gone.

A Wedding Song

O *malin*, it's time for ceremonial green leaves,
O Sister, it's time for ceremonial green leaves,
It's time for joy; it's time to revel;
Let's celebrate the day
Hanging auspicious green leaves on the door
The day he was born, that day was auspicious.

When he was born, he was covered with a cloth
Elderly women also held him once
Giving him a bath, he was wrapped with a silk-drape
Each sister carried him once in her lap.

What reward did the midwives get?
What reward did the old women get?
What rewards did his sisters get?
Five rupees were given
To midwives and old women each,
To sisters were given
Three pieces of silk cloth each.

Asking people, *malin* reaches the street
Which house is blessed with joys?
The house with a large tent
And green tent-walls
That is the house blessed with joys.
Come, *malin*, sit at the door
Tell me the price of the *sehra*.

Chamba is for one lakh, *marua* is for two only
The price of the *sehra* is three lakhs
Go ahead, *malin*, you may tie the *sehra*
Tie it on the groom's head.

O *malin*, it's time for the ceremonial green leaves,
O Sister, it's time for the ceremonial green leaves,
It's time for joy; it's time to revel;
Let's celebrate the day
Hanging auspicious green leaves on the door,
The day he was born, that day was auspicious.

Another Colour of Life

My father-in-law has fallen sick
My mother-in-law cries like a crane.
She fondly serves her ailing husband,

She presses his aching limbs.
To show her love for him,
She joins two cots for themselves in *chobara*.
Boiling dried dates in milk
She offers him daily.

To buy his wife a double layered *jutti*
My father-in-law often goes to Patiala.
Seeing their love for each other
My husband blushes shyly.

The Song of Saavan

It is the month of *saavan*
    It is the month of showers.
It is the month to refresh our hearts
    It is the month of downpour.

While swinging in the garden
    Mariam has got drenched
And along with her, Ram Piyari is dripping wet
    And the *kurti* of Haro,
Which she brought in her dowry,
    is soaked to the weave.
    And so is the *phulkari* worth ninety rupees.
Harnami's *sutthan*, decorated with lace,
    Is drenched in rain.
Small thin braids of Janto,
    To count they were forty in total,
Are also sopping wet.

They all ran towards the village
    When it began to pour,
The rain caught them all
    Running in a flurry.
While swinging Sassi fell down
    And also Noori from Nabha,

Shamo lost her anklets
> That Rakhi found for her,
And even Lajjo, the proud one,
> Is also soaking wet.
Listen, the clouds of *saavan*,
> Even Heer of Syal stands drenched today.

The Vaar *of Bhagat Singh*

When the granary lay empty,
> And the pitchers were dry;
Without milk, the churning-stick began to sob
> Hitting the pitcher harder.
Then woke up the lion of Punjab
> Taking his comrades along,
He stood up against oppression,
> Injustice and wrong.
He pledged to uproot poverty
> from the land forever,
Hearing his loud roar,
> The British trembled with fear.
Only his death, thought the sinful jury
> Could save the British from his fury
When he was about to be hanged
> Even his noose shrank
When he died people cried so hard
> The sweet water of Sutlej turned saline.

All his mother's wishes
> In the heart were smothered;
No one tied a *gaana*, nor did he get married;
No one decked his hands with *henna*,
> His mother regrets;
Nor could his mother perform
Any rituals of his wedding.

When the moon of Punjab set,
> All the stars drowned with him,

While kissing the brim of the noose
    A smile shone on *his lips.*
The dream of his country
    In his eyes flashed,
Buried long in his heart,
    His emotions then surged.

Swang: I Shall Not Speak

First Woman: You have come home at midnight, I shall never speak to you.

All Women: You have come home at midnight, I shall never speak to you.

Husband: Where are the children? Where are the elders? Where are you lying?

First Woman: I'll never speak to you.

All Women: You have come home at midnight,
Will never speak to you.

First Woman: Your children are lying here,
Your elders are lying there,
I'm lying on the ground.

All Women: You have come home at midnight,
Will never speak to you.

Husband: Where is the food?
  Where is *roti* and *daal*?

All Women: You have come home at midnight,
Will never speak to you.

Wife: Your *roti* is in the niche
And your *daal* is on the *chulah*
I'll never speak to you.

All Women: You have come home at midnight,
Will never speak to you.

Husband:	Where are the children?
	Where are the elders?
	Where are you?
	I'll never speak to you.
All Women:	You have come home at midnight,
	Will never speak to you.
Wife:	Children and elders are lying on the bed.
	I am lying on the floor.
	I'll never speak to you.
All Women:	You have come home at midnight,
	Will never speak to you.

A Fight Between Love Rivals

One:

You have all the utensils, I am left with nothing but a ladle
Still you fight; still you argue with me, my rival.
Go and fight that scoundrel, go and pull his beard
Who married you and brought you home in a red palanquin
That palanquin cries and waits for your *bhabho*.

All:

Delhi is yours, mine is Agra, we face each other
Today two love rivals fight each other.
Today two love rivals fight each other.
Now you fight me, I am no less than you.
Now you fight me, I am no less than you.

If I Speak Now...

When utensils were distributed, I was given only this bowl
You, the people of the village, take note of this.
If I speak now, you'll say I howl.
I become a bad woman.

When cattle were distributed, I was given only this calf
You, the people of the village, take note of this.

If I speak now, you'll say I roar.
I become a bad woman.

When in-laws were distributed, I was given this nasty mother-in-law
You, the people of the village, take note of this.
If I speak now, you'll say I bawl.
I become a bad woman.

When families were distributed, I was given this horrible sister-in-law
You, the people of the village, may take note of this.
If I speak now, you'll say I scream.
I become a bad woman.

My Heart Winces

First: O my son's father
All: Aye!
First: I am dying of pain
All: Aye!
First: Are you good only for an 'Aye'?
All: Aye!
First: Let your Aye be cursed!
All: Aye!
First: Please call a doctor.
All: Aye!
First: Let your Aye be cursed
All: Aye!
First: I am dying of pain
All: Aye!
First: Get me some lemons
All: Aye!
First: Get me something sweet
All: Aye!
      My dear, get me a lemon please.
      My heart winces with pain
      My heart winces with pain.

Sadhu

First Woman:	O good people
	I am a sadhu
	I am a celibate
	I liked a girl once
	Since then I have taken a vow
	Since then I am an ascetic.
	My dear people,
	I am a sadhu
	I am a celibate.
Second Woman:	Baba ji, Ah! Please examine my daughter-in-law. Something ails her.
	(*Baba ji whispers something into her ears and then they elope*)
All:	Sadhu has run away with his *belle* follower
	Our mother now screams loudly.
	Sadhu has run away with his female follower
	Our mother now screams loudly.

A Monkey and the Moon

Once upon a time, a monkey, walking aimlessly, reached a well. When it peered into the well, it saw the shadow of Moon there. The monkey thought—'It is terrible that Moon has fallen into the well. We should do something to save Moon.'

It ran to the jungle and, gathering other monkeys, said to them, Brothers, a terrible thing has happened. Moon has fallen into the well. We should haul it up, lest our nights should be dark.'

Hearing this, all the other monkeys also peered into the well. They could see Moon in the well. The monkey said, 'I'll hold the wall of the well and go down. The next monkey should hold my tail.

Holding the tail of the next monkey, let's make a chain of monkeys. By doing so, we will pull Moon out of the well.'

All the monkeys acted accordingly. They worked the whole night to pull Moon out of the well. By dawn, Moon had set and its shadow was no longer seen in the well.

They were all proud of themselves thinking that they had saved Moon.

One Coin of the Poor

One day, a group of dacoits attacked a village. The dacoits said to the villagers that if they were given gold, silver and gems equal to the weight of their leader, they would not harm anybody. If not, they would create havoc in the village. The rich men of the village thought that it would be better to give them money. If they survived, they could earn more.

So, on one side of the scales sat the leader of the dacoits and on the other side they piled up items of gold and silver. But the scales remained tilted towards the leader's side. The rich men brought out every precious thing from their homes to save their lives, but all in vain. Finally, they went to the *Pir*, who lived near the pond, and asked him for a solution. The *Pir* said, 'These dacoits are devils, who have come to gather your ill-gotten money. They can be defeated only by hard-earned money. You should put hard-earned money on the scales. The scales will shift.'

When the rich men were returning from the *Pir*, they crossed the poor men's shacks in the village. The family of a blacksmith was at work. One was blowing into the furnace, another was beating the iron and a third was working to cast the iron. Sweat was dripping from their bodies. The rich men stood at the shack of the blacksmith and said, 'Please give us a coin. We will return you many folds.'

The blacksmith said, 'But I have only one coin.'

The rich man said, 'Give me this coin. I'll give you more money tomorrow.'

The blacksmith said, 'No, please return my coin tomorrow. I don't want your wealth.'

When the rich men put that one coin on the scales, it shifted. The poor hard-working men said, 'The entire wealth of the rich people is equal to one hard-earned coin.'

A Little Sparrow

Once a hunter, who was very fond of sparrows, was playing with a colourful sparrow at the crossing. A mahout riding an elephant passed the crossing. On seeing the hunter, the mahout said, 'You foolish man, move aside lest my elephant should crush you and your sparrow. Just look at him, he has just a little sparrow and there is no end to his elation.' The hunter got angry and said brashly, 'Don't you take pride in your oversized elephant. You can have a wrestling match between my sparrow and your elephant. You may change my name, if your elephant does not run away from the arena.' On being challenged, the mahout got down from his elephant and said to the hunter, 'Bravo! You may call me anytime. I accept your challenge.'

'In a month,' the hunter said emphatically, 'At the same place.'

'Okay, then.' Saying this, the mahout left the place.

After the mahout left, the hunter began to think, 'There cannot be a match between a sparrow and an elephant. I was foolish to challenge him. What'll happen now?' He thought about the competition for a couple of days. Finally, he had an idea. He asked a painter to paint a picture of the elephant on the wall, which looked like a real elephant. Then he made two ears of elephant with paper, which were more real than the real ears. He placed some grain in the ears of the elephant.

The next day, the hunter kept the bird hungry for the entire day. When the sparrow was famished, he led the sparrow to the paper ears of the elephant, that had grain inside. The sparrow ate its fill and came out. He repeated this for some days. Consequently, whenever the sparrow was hungry, it would look into the ears of the elephant for grain. Gradually, the sparrow got used to eating grain from the ears, so much so that even if there was grain lying around, it would ignore it and look for grain inside the elephant's 'ears'. Now the hunter was satisfied.

Finally, the day the sparrow would wrestle the elephant arrived. People of the village gathered at the crossing to watch the match. The hunter had kept the sparrow in a cage and given it nothing to eat for a few hours. When the elephant approached the birdcage, the sparrow struggled to come out of it. As soon as the cage was opened, the sparrow flew straight into the ears of the elephant to look for grain. In doing so, the sparrow hurt the elephant, pecking inside its ear. The elephant cried with pain and left the arena. The people of the village were happy to see the show and they congratulated the hunter for his clever thinking.

A Piece of Just Bread

Once in the court of a King came a Holy Man. They talked over various matters for a long time. When it was time to eat, the King offered varied kinds of eatables to the Holy Man. The Holy Man asked the King, 'Honourable King, I always break just bread. Is this food just?'

The puzzled King looked at the Holy Man. With utmost humility, he asked the Holy Man, 'What is just bread? What do you mean by this? Kindly explain.'

The Holy Man said, 'In your town, behind your palace, lives an old woman. Her name is Mai Daultan. Go and ask her for a piece of just bread. You will then understand what I mean.'

The King, disguised as a sadhu, reached the old woman's house, 'Mother! I am hungry. Give me something to eat. God will bless you.' When the old woman was about to give him alms, he said to the old woman, 'Mother! I need a piece of just bread.'

The old woman said, 'I have only this food with me today. Half of it is just and the other half is unjust.'

The confused King asked, 'How come the other half is unjust?'

The old woman told the King, 'I was spinning my wheel yesterday sitting at the door. I had finished only the half of my work when it began to get dark. I was about to get up from my spinning wheel when the king's men, who were waiting for an officer, gathered here. They were carrying torches. With the light from their torches, I finished the rest of my work. After selling the thread, I bought flour for myself and cooked this food. That's why, one half of it is just and the other half of it is unjust.'

Hearing the old woman's story, the King touched her feet. Running back, he came to the Holy Man and said, 'Most revered Holy Man, all my food is unjust.'

3

Medieval Poetry

Sheikh Farid

Sheikh Farid-ud-Din Masood Ganjshakar (Sheikh Farid) (1173–1266 CE) was born in Khotwal, near Multan (now in Pakistan). It is believed that he would talk so sweetly that people called him Shakarganj. After leaving Delhi, he spent some time at Hansi (now in Haryana, India) and later settled down at Pakpattan (now in Pakistan), where he died. He is also known as Baba Farid in Punjab. Farid is the first Muslim poet who wrote poetry in a dialect of Punjab. He belongs to the Chishti Sufi order and is among the earliest Sufi poets in India. Hazrat Nizam-ud-Din, the famous Sufi Fakir and Master, is one of his disciples. Sheikh Farid's writings are important in the history of Punjabi literature because, including Guru Nanak, three Sikh Gurus have written on his poetry. Besides Baba Farid's two *shabad* and 112 *salok*, writings on Farid by Sikh gurus are also included in the Guru Granth Sahib. According to Attar Singh, Baba Farid's poetry brought about 'Islamisation of Punjab and Punjabisation of Islam'. Imagery rooted in Punjabi culture can be found in all his works. Along with love for God, he reflects on the importance of moral integrity.

Salok

O Farida! If your mind is sharp as a razor's edge
Then why not be discerning, why pile up deeds so black?
Only if you were to peep into the heart divine
Your own faults, and not of others, shall shine.

O Farida! I, too, have seen the eyes that transport the world
To dizzying heights, and mesmerize; the eyes

They darken the lids, smudging the kohl when it's applied,
Now birds have found a resting perch in these very eyes.

O Farida! If this world is what you're still lusting for
That all your professions of love for *Sahib* are false
Like the claims of a poor man, who claims to be calm
When the roof of his thatched hut has sprung a leak.

O Farida! Walking on your spindly legs and thighs
You have scaled the mountains, low and high
In your old age, you've become an empty, earthen bowl
Everyone uses for ablutions, before hastening for *namaz*.

O Farida! Some sow the seeds of a thorny *keekar*
And yet want to reap grapes, so sweet and rich
Some go through life, spinning yarn of coarse wool
And yet want to drape their body in colourful silk.

O Farida! You condemned me to wait outside a stranger's door
O *Sain*! If this be my fate, I'd rather not accept the offer
If you refuse to listen, and don't write my destiny anew
Then refusing to keep this body, I just offer it unto you.

Canopies sprawling over their heads, they walked merrily
To the beat and rhythm of the kettle drums, trumpeting along
Bards sang their praise while they lived; but now when they are dead
They lie quietly in their graves, like orphans, forlorn and sad.

O Farida! With a prayer mat on my shoulder, and a loose,
Woolen garment around my neck, I walk with a swagger,
A dagger in my heart, and honey dripping off my tongue
You see the halo, but I, only the darkness invading my heart.

O Farida! Where are your parents, who brought you into this world
Some time earlier, they did walk this earth, but is it so, anymore?
Leaving you alone, they have departed to another world, and yet,
You don't accept that one day, it could happen to you, just as well.

O Farida! To all those who do an evil turn unto you
Return only the good; do nothing less, nothing more

Purge your mind of anger, and your body shall be pure
Otherwise, it's not easy to proclaim, 'O, I love this life so.'

O Farida! I thought I alone was the sufferer, little did I know
That all those who visit this world, are condemned to suffer too,
Clambering up the roof-top, when I screened my eyes to view,
Each house, I saw, caught in flames of desire, burning down slowly.

Translated by Rana Nayar

Shah Hussain

Shah Hussain (1539–1599 CE) was a Sufi poet of the Qadri Sufi order. He was a weaver by profession. Three hundred years after Baba Farid, Shah Hussain gave a new lease of life to Punjabi Sufi poetry. He made Sufi poetry the centre of Punjabi thought and reflection in his times. His poetry is marked by the spirit of freedom, which attempted to liberate Sufi poetry from the confines of religious thought. He was unmindful of worldly affairs and customs. Shah Hussain's poetry is replete with references to the culture and folk heroes of Punjab. It is believed that he was in love with Madho Lal, a Hindu man, because of which he is also known as Madho Lal Hussain.

Without Good Deeds

What did you do
    While living in this world?
What will you get, when you die
    And go to the other world?

Neither did you wash the cotton
Nor did the carding happen
    No spinning did you do either.

Nor did you spin the wheel
Nor did you reel up the thread
    You did not tighten the thread either.

Nor did you gin the cotton
Nor did you basket the rolls
　　You have not woven the cloth either.

Shah Hussain says, you stand with no dowry
Without good deeds, sweet talk is of no use
You could not please your Lord either.

What Makes You So Proud

What makes you so proud,
　　That you walk with a swagger? /pause/

Eating delicious food, wearing beautiful clothes,
　　Is no profitable venture;
　　You finally become the fodder of Yama.
Three yards and a half long shall be your grave
　　So why capture lands, while you are alive?
Shah Hussain, the Fakir of *Sain*, says,
　　Do not take pride in your worldly possessions
　　Finally, with dust shall we all mingle.

SULTAN BAHU

Sultan Bahu (1630–1691 CE) belonged to the Qadri Sufi order, which was established by Sheikh Abdul Qadri Jilani. Sultan Bahu was born in Avaan, in Jhhang district. He has written most of his poetry in *siharfi*,[1] a form of Sufi poetry. The unique feature of his poetry is that it ends with 'Hu', which encapsulates the meaning of God. His poetry brims with pain and singing it is an intense experience. Sultan Bahu shied

---

[1] *Siharfi* (Golden Alphabet) is a form of Sufi poetry in which every line of a poem or stanza begins with the succeeding letter of the Arabic alphabet. The first two poems in this collection begin with *alif* and the last two poems begin with *noon*.

away from the religious thought in his poetry; rather, he was critical of Islamic customs and rituals.

Everyone Wishes for a Stronger Imaan

Everyone wishes for a stronger *imaan*[2]
    Seldom someone yearns for love, *Hu!*
Evading love, people value *imaan* more
    Their dignity is dearer to them, *Hu!*
The stage to which love takes a seeker
    Of it *imaan* knows nothing, *Hu!*
Preserve your love, says Bahu
    For *imaan* will let you down, *Hu!*

Let Eyes Sprout

Let eyes sprout from every pore of my body
    Forever may I gaze upon my *murshid*, *Hu!*
In every pore, let there be a million eyes
    I'll close one and open another, *Hu!*
The longer I gaze, the more my yearning increases
    How can I quench my thirst, *Hu?*
One glimpse of my *murshid*, says Bahu
    Is more than a million pilgrimages, *Hu!*

Attaining Knowledge They Inflate Their Ego

Attaining knowledge people inflate their ego
    They win accolades from *Hafiz*, *Hu!*
Tucking books under their arms
    Poor fellows wander in the streets, *Hu!*
Finding patrons among the well-off, to them
    They read scripture to make money, *Hu!*

---

[2] *Imaan* refers to religious faith, integrity and dignity. A person who follows rituals and discipline of religion, and has a strong religion-based sense of righteousness will have a stronger *imaan*. Sultan Bahu in his philosophical view prefers *ishq* or love for the divine over observing religious discipline.

Selling the name of God, they lose their souls
> They fail in this world, also in the other, *Hu!*

Neither Hindus, nor Muslims

They are neither Hindus, nor are they Muslims
> Lovers don't bow in any mosque, *Hu!*

They see God everywhere
> Lovers don't perform any ritual, *Hu!*

They know all yet they feign ignorance
> Lovers hide who they are, *Hu!*

I sacrifice my life for them, says Bahu
> Who have won the game of love, *Hu!*

Bulleh Shah

Bulleh Shah (1680–1758 CE) was born at Pandoke, Tehsil Kasoor in Lahore district. Belonging to the Qadri Sufi order, he was a Sufi poet who had also imbibed the philosophical tradition of the subcontinent. His poetry is replete with human emotions. According to Prof. Puran Singh, the flow of emotions is so strong in his poetry that all humanity is swayed by it. He rejected the principles of Sharia, and in his relationship with God, but for his spiritual Master, Shah Inayat Qadri, he did not accept anybody else as an intermediate. He pointed out the wretched state of Islam and held the preachers of Islam, including Maulvis, responsible for its condition. His poetry, written in the form of *Kafi*, has always been popular among common people, yet it plumbs the depths of Sufi thought and state of consciousness.

I Know Not Who I Am

Bullah says,
> I know not who I am.

I am not a believer praying in the mosque
> Nor in the rituals of infidels I am

I am not the pure among the impure
    I am not Moses, nor Pharaoh I am
Bullah says,
    I know not who I am.

I am not present in the holy books
    Nor in hemp or liquor I am
I am not found among drunkards either
    I am not sleeping, nor awake I am
Bullah says,
    I know not who I am.

I am neither happy, nor sad I am
    Neither pure, nor impure I am.
I am not of water, nor of dust
    I am not fire, nor wind I am
Bullah says,
    I know not who I am.

I am not from Arabia, nor from Lahore I am
    Nor from the city Nagaur of Hind I am
I am not a Hindu, nor a Turk from Peshawar
    Nor from the city of Nadaun I am
Bullah says,
    I know not, who I am.

I know not the mystery of religion
    Nor am I born to Eve and Adam
I do not want to have an identity
    I am neither settled, nor a wanderer I am
Bullah says,
    I know not who I am.

I am the beginning, I am the end
    Any other thing I acknowledge not
Who is standing there, Bulleh Shah?
    No one is wiser than I am

Bullah says,
> I know not who I am.

One Point Holds the Whole Truth

Let go your cleverness and grasp this point simple,
> Forget the infidel's lessons that always swindle;

Forget the torture, ignore fears of death and hell,
> From your heart all doubts dispel;

In a pure heart dwells the truth
> One point holds the whole truth.

Why bow and rub your head on the ground in vain?
> Prostrating at the mosque, what do you gain?

Reading *kalma* you make people laugh,
> Not a word you ever understand;

Can anyone ever hide the truth?
> One point holds the whole truth.

Some go to the *Hajj* and are called Haji,
> Coming back they wear robes blue;

Going to the Haj is no more than a trade
> No one appreciates what they do there;

For no one can hide the truth,
> One point holds the whole truth.

Some people go to jungles in vain,
> They live there on a little grain;

The fools get tired keeping themselves unfed,
> Finally, they come back home half-dead;

In ascetic rituals they waste their youth,
> One point holds the whole truth.

He is no less than God, you follow your *murshid* benign
> You'd forget everything in the ecstasy divine;

Purge yourself of desire and worries thine,
> Cleansed of all impurities, let your heart shine;

Bullah says, he cannot help uttering the truth,
  One point holds the whole truth.

The Spring of Love

When I learnt the lesson of love
  I dreaded entering the mosque;
I entered a temple of *thakur*
  Where echoes tumultuous sounds;
The spring of love is ever fresh
  The spring of love is ever divine.

When I deciphered the mystery of love
  In all its forms died this ego of mine;
From within to without, I became chaste
  Wherever I looked, I saw my beloved divine;
The spring of love is ever fresh
  The spring of love is ever divine.

Heer and Ranjha are one in love,
  Mistaken, she looks for him in the woods;
Though Ranjha is playing next to her.
  I've lost the sense of mine and thine;
The spring of love is ever fresh
  The spring of love is ever divine.

Reading the Book, you get tired
  Bowing, you've worn off your head;
Neither in mosques, nor in temples God dwells
  He can only be seen in the Light Divine;
The spring of love is ever fresh
  The spring of love is ever divine.

Burn your prayer mats, smash your begging bowls
  Throw away the rosary and the stick;
Lovers call out at the top of their voice
  Forsake the code of *halaal*, on whatever you may dine;

The spring of love is ever fresh
> The spring of love is ever divine.

Going to the mosque you've wasted your life
> With filth you are filled deep inside;
You've never prayed, nor observed any restrain,
> Now it is meaningless—this crying of thine;
The spring of love is ever fresh
> The spring of love is ever divine.

In love I forgot all rituals of worship
> Why quibble over any matter now?
Bullah says, observing silence is now better
> Love is soaring high, there's no way to confine.
The spring of love is ever fresh
> The spring of love is ever divine.

Miscellaneous Verses

I) *Mullah* and the torchbearer, in similarities both are stark
They spread light in the world, but live in the dark.

II) A rooster is better than a *mullah* that wakes up the sleeping world
A broken pot, that gives water to thirsty dogs, is better than an idol.

III) If I tell a lie, I stay safe a bit,
If I speak the truth, the world may throw a fit;
I weigh both the options, I utter with much caution,
What comes to my lips, I stop not.

IV) *Hajis* always go to Mecca, I go to Takht Hazara,[3]
My Mecca is where my love resides;
You may search all holy books,
I am mad in love.

---

[3] Takhat Hazara is a town in Pakistan, the birth place of Ranjha, the protagonist of the famous love legend of Heer-Ranjha.

V) Bullah says, in the inn stay invaders, in temples dwell the thieves,
In the mosques the crooked ones, lovers live the life of a recluse.

Wajeed

Wajeed (1525–85 CE) was a Sufi poet. His unique contribution was introducing sarcasm in Sufi poetry. He would sometimes complain to God, which is rarely seen in Sufi poetry. Wajeed questioned God about inequalities prevailing in the social, economic and domestic spheres. He is known for his quatrains in Punjabi.

Who Should Tell Him

If He makes fools ride horses and elephants,
And wise men drag their feet in torn shoes;
If He makes the wise men labour and serve the foolish master,
Wajeed says, who should tell Him, don't do it this way, but the other.

If He gives grass to the cow and rich food to dogs,
If He, snatching from the enlightened ones, gives it to the ignorant lot;
There is no dearth, all ponds are brimful with water,
Wajeed says, who should tell Him, don't do it this way, but the other.

If thieves bring home their plunder
And eat sumptuously with milk and butter;
If those who have faith in You, rather starve,
Wajeed says, who should tell Him, don't do it this way, but the other.

If some have built palaces and live in big mansions,
While others carry girders and stones on their heads;
If some ride horses, while others like beggars wander,
Wajeed says, who should tell Him, don't do it this way, but the other.

Bhagat Namdev

Bhagat Namdev (1270–1350 CE) was born in Narsi in Maharashtra. Later, his family shifted to Pandharpur. He was a Dalit and was a great champion of equality among human beings. He suggested that instead of attaining salvation after life, one should aim at attaining it during one's lifetime. He is among those who have supported progressive new consciousness in religion in India. He is believed to have spent the last years of his life at Ghuman, a village near Qadian in Punjab. Guru Arjun Dev included his poetry in the Guru Granth Sahib.

Namdev Has Seen Vithal

Namdev has seen Vithal today.
    I'll tell you what I know
You may listen to me
    O, the ignorant lot! /pause/

O Pandit, your Gayatri grazed away
    The crop in Lodha's field,
Since the farmer broke her leg with a stick
    She walks with a limp.

O Pandit, I saw your Mahadev ride a white bull
    At the house of Modi, the merchant,
A feast was prepared for Mahadev,
    He partook the food and later, killed his son.

O Pandit, I have seen it
  What Ram Chandra also did,
He fought against Ravana
  And later forsook his own wife.

Hindus are blind
  Muslims are one-eyed
Only the Enlightened one
  Is wiser than the both.

Hindus worship in temples
  Muslims in the mosque
Namdev serves the Lord, who dwells
  Neither in temples, nor in mosques.

Forget Me Not

O God, forget me not!
  I implore you,
  Forget me not.
Forget me not, dear Rama.
  Forget me not. /pause/

Their high caste is nothing but an illusion,
  They are ignorant of this truth;
In their ignorance and false pride
  They spit their anger on me.

Calling me *shudra*, they hit me oft
  O God! I feel so pained and aggrieved;
Salvation holds no meaning
  If it's given after one's death.
O Pandit, you do not understand
  When you call me lowly
It lowers you too;
  Why would you call me so?

O God! You are benevolent,
    Infinite, mighty and compassionate
You have turned the temple's face to Namdev
    And its back towards pandits.

Dhanna Bhagat

Not much is known about Dhanna Bhagat's life. According to Macauliffe, Dhanna Bhagat was born in 1415 CE. He belonged to the Jat caste. In his poetry, he reflects more on the material world than the spiritual world, and defined religion and spirituality in simple terms. He found his spiritual path in leading a life of high moral integrity. Though he was not a prolific poet, his poetry is close to the common man in Punjab. Guru Arjun Dev included his poetry in the Guru Granth Sahib.

Gopala, I Worship You

Gopala, I worship you
    I perform your *aarta*[4]
Whosoever worships you
    You solve his problems.

Give me some lentil, ghee and flour to eat
May peace eternally dwell on me,
    I pray to You!

---

[4] *Aarti* is a Hindu ritual of worship. Devotees chant and light a lamp while performing *aarti*. Since Dhanna Jat was a peasant, he wrote an *aarta*, which literally means a bigger *aarti*; it could also be interpreted as an unsophisticated *aarti* without brahminical rituals.

Water, shoes and grains of seven kinds
Give me a cow and a buffalo,
    I pray to You!

A fine Turkish horse and a good wife
    These things only
Your humble servant Dhanna
    Begs of you.

Bhagat Pipa

Bhagat Pipa or Sant Pipaji was a Bhakti poet. It is believed that he lived during the fourteenth and fifteenth centuries. He was born in the present-day Jhalawar district of Rajasthan. Initially, he was under the influence of Shaivism and Shakti worship. Later, he became a disciple of Ravidas.

One Who Seeks Him, Finds Him

In this body dwells the God
    This mortal frame is His abode,
In this body lie the incense, lamps
    And also leaves for the offering;
This body is the holy place
    Where I make my pilgrimage.

I've searched in all realms though
    In this body I found nine treasures too.
Nothing ever comes, nothing ever goes
    It is His mercy, I forever seek.
He, who pervades the universe, dwells in this body too.
    Seek Him in your body, you shall find Him there.
Pipa says, God is the supreme Truth
    With the grace of a True Guru, you can find Him.

Bhagat Kabir

Bhagat Kabir is one of the major medieval poets in India. Scholars believe that he was born in Varanasi in 1398 CE. There are varied views regarding his personal life. Some believe that he was born to a Brahmin woman, whereas the followers of *Kabir Panth* believe that he was an incarnation of the divine light. Most scholars agree that he was raised in the house of a poor Muslim weaver. Later, he became a disciple of Swami Ramanand. According to Kabir, one does not become a brahmin because one is born in a brahmin family. He believed that one who reflects on *brahm* is the true brahmin. Kabir was a prolific poet. From his voluminous writings, 541 *shalok* have been included in the Guru Granth Sahib.

Gardener

You pluck leaves for your prayers, O gardener
    Knowing not that every leaf pulsates with life.
The idol, for which you pluck the leaves,
    Is dead and stiff.
You miss the point, O gardener
    Your Guru is the living God. /pause/

Brahma lives in the leaves, Vishnu in the branches
    And Shankar dwells in the flowers,
Severing these three gods from there
    Which God do you serve, my dear?

A sculptor to carve an idol
    Places it under his feet;
If the God of stone were true,
    It'd devour the sculptor—an apt treatment to mete.

Rice, beans and sweets are
>   Enjoyable delicacies all,
After offering to the idol once
>   It's the Pandit who enjoys them all.

The gardener is mistaken, and so is the world
>   But not I, says Kabir,
I am under God's protection
>   Hallowed by His incessant blessings.

The True Brahmin

No child is born with a caste
>   It is from one *brahm* all creation is made;
What makes you a brahmin
>   Would you mind telling me, Pandit?
Taking false pride, exulting in your caste
>   You lay waste your life. /pause/

That to a brahmin woman you are born
>   Doesn't make you a brahmin.
Everybody is born the same way
>   Were you born in a different fashion?
How come I am a *shudra*?
>   What makes you a twice-born?
If blood runs in my body
>   No milk runs in your body either.
Kabir says, the true brahmin is the one
>   Who meditates on *brahm* and knows Him.

Of One Light

First God created the Light
>   From one Light, He created the world;
If from His Light all are born
>   Then all are good, no one is bad.

Do not let doubt overcome you
    The creation and the Creator are one.
The Creator dwells in His creation
    He lives through His creation;

Using the same clay,
    The Creator has fashioned different figures;
Nothing is wrong with the potter
    Nothing is wrong with the clay.

One God dwells in us all
    By His actions everything happens,
One who surrenders before His will
    And knows Him, serves Him the best.

True Valour

The war-drum echoes,
    Hitting the target, the arrow inflicts a wound.
The battlefield calls for the brave
    It's time to fight till the end.
True valour lies in
    Defending the defenseless,
He is a true warrior
    Who fights for the weak;
Even hacked limb by limb,
    He never retreats.
You cannot divine easily
    The mystery of God,
My Guru asked me to describe
    The sweetness of jaggery,
Kabir says, all his doubts have vanished
    After seeing the true God.

Bhagat Beni

Not much is known about when and where Bhagat Beni was born. It is believed that he was a contemporary of Guru Nanak; three of his writings were included in the Guru Granth Sahib. He fiercely criticised ritualism in religion. Bhagat Beni believed that all rituals are shallow and hold no value unless humans look into the depths of their consciousness.

The True Seeker

You rub sandal paste on your body
    And place basil leaves on the forehead
But deep in your heart
    You carry malice.

You pretend to be a seeker,
    But inside you are a thug
You pose like a crane to cheat,
    In deceiving others, you deceive yourself too.

You pretend to be a *vaishnav*
    But you are a fake worshipper
For hours you may pray;
    For hours you may meditate,
But there is evil in your mind
    There is malice in your heart
In this essential conflict
    Your life goes waste. /pause/

You keep your body clean
    And you wear fresh clothes,
You perform all rituals
    Drink only milk and nothing else.

But in your heart you hide a dagger
    You indulge in evil; you covet wealth
You are easily tempted
    To collect heaps of money.

You worship an idol of Ganesha
    All night you remain awake
But your heart is not one with Him
    You only pretend to meditate.
You pretend to dance in ecstasy
    But your mind is filled with filth.
You are lewd; you are low
    And your dance is wicked too.
You sit on the skin of the deer
    You may tell a rosary of *tulsi* seeds,
You place a glowing mark of sandal paste on your forehead,
    But your heart is full of deceit;
You are lustful; you are low
    You do not chant the name of God.

Without realising the truth of one's soul
    All rituals are absurd;
Beni says, learning from the Guru
    Meditating like a *Gurmukh*,[5]
Is the only way
    You may find Him.
Without the blessings of a Guru,
    No one can know Him.

From Sri Guru Granth Sahib

---

[5] *Gurmukh* means one who listens to his Guru and acts according to his Guru's instructions. It is the opposite of *Manmukh*, one who follows his own mind.

Bhagat Ravidas

Bhagat Ravidas (circa 1450–1520 CE) was probably born in a village near Varanasi, although scholars differ in their opinions about these facts. Like Kabir, Ravidas was also a disciple of Swami Ramananda. Meera Bai accepted Ravidas as her spiritual guide. He was a Dalit and believed in the *nirguna* concept of god. He was not ashamed of his caste; rather his sense of pride in his caste was instrumental in challenging the hegemony of the brahmins. His poetry has been included in the Guru Granth Sahib. In his famous poem 'Begumpura', he conceives an ideal state for the oppressed and downtrodden.

Begumpura, the Ideal Town

God's place is in your heart
    The town is called Begumpura.
Free of misery—no worry ever touches the town,
    Free of taxes—there is no reason to fret and frown.
There is no room for fear, folly or fall,
    My real home I have found,
Which in peace and joy abound.

That is my God's eternal kingdom
    He rules there forever.
No one is low, no one is high
    His city stays populous forever.
Its dwellers are wealthy; they live content
    Freely they walk; freely His mansion they enter.
Ravidas, the liberated shoemaker, says
    Whosoever lives there is his companion.

Guru Nanak

Guru Nanak (1469–1639 CE) was born at Rai Bhoye Ki Talwandi, now known as Nankana Sahib, in Pakistan. He is the first Sikh Guru and the founder of Sikhism. Guru Nanak spread the message of equality. He vociferously spoke against orthodoxy, ritualism and superstitions. He laid emphasis on hard work and sharing food. One of the unique features of Guru Nanak's poetry is that he presented the affairs of the material world from the point of view of the spiritual world. His poetry is alive with images of day-to-day life, making him a poet of human concerns and values.

Has Your Heart Not Melted Yet?

Having conquered Khorasana, Babar terrified Hindustan.
    Deflecting blame from Himself, God has sent the Mughals;
Like the messengers of Death, they ruthlessly murder people.
    Seeing slaughter all around, people tremble with fear and fret;
O God, has your heart not melted yet?

It is the duty of the Creator
    To take care of all,
If the strong strikes an equal
    No one complains at all. /pause/
But if the mighty kills the helpless
    O God, You should intervene at once.
Dogs have defiled this glorious land,
    This jewel-like beautiful country is ruined,
To our utter dismay, no one pays attention.
    You unite people; You separate them,
Your ways are mysterious to men,
    Your glory is beyond human comprehension.

Thinking highly of oneself
   One may revel in one's false glory,
But in the eyes of God such a man
   Is nothing but a worm—no matter of celebration.
Nanak says, one who transcends one's ego
   May win God's blessings and His benediction.

When Stained with Blood

When stained with blood, the cloak is filthy and impure,
   Drinking blood then, how can your soul remain pure?
Nanak says, chant God's name with a pure heart,
   All other deeds are false, like a deceptive craft.

Grabbing What Rightfully Belongs to Others

Grabbing what rightfully belongs to others
   For a Muslim is like eating Pig, for a Hindu, cow.
Our Guru, the spiritual Master, blesses us
   If we do not feed on the dead.
Just by exalted talk, no one enters heaven,
   Salvation comes only if by Truth you are driven.
By adding spices to foul food,
   You cannot make it palatable.
Nanak says, the untrue begets the untrue
   The wrong begets the wrong.

Greed, the King

Greed, the King; Sin, the Minister; Falsehood, their Treasurer; and
   Lust, the Advisor;
They are summoned, together they sit and conspire.
   People are blind; they lack wisdom,
Offering bribe they wish to smother the fire of greed,
   Oh, they are so dumb!

The Enlightened and the Wise, decking up with jewels fine
   Play instruments, sing and dance.

They sing aloud epics of battles
    And tales of valour.
In the present times, fools claim to be scholars
    They are so phony,
For their only intent is,
    Through illicit means, to amass money.

Even by nursing the desire to achieve salvation,
    The righteous lose righteousness,
    The upright lose uprightness.
People renounce their homes and live a life of celibacy,
    But they know not the true path of love and its ecstasy.
Fools think they are always right;
    Their ignorance, they never suspect.

Nanak says, if one's honour is weighed on a scale,
    Only then can one measure one's worth, without fail.

The Dance of Devotion

Disciples play the music and the Guru dances,
    They move their feet, they shake their heads in a trance.
The dust rises and then settles on them,
    Beholding the sight, people laugh
They go home shaking their heads.

To make a living, they play music
    To earn money, they dance.
They sing of gopis, they sing of Krishna,
    They sing of Sita, they sing of Rama.

Only the Name of God is true
    He is fearless, He is formless,
It's He who has created the universe;
    They are fortunate who can serve Him.

Those whose hearts are brimful
    With love and devotion,

Their minds are calm
>   Like a night bedewed.

Contemplating on my Guru's teachings,
>   I now know the Truth;
With His grace and benevolence
>   He has lead my boat ashore.

The Simmal Tree

The *Simmal* tree grows like an arrow,
>   It looks tall, straight and thick.
Birds perch on it buoyantly
>   Hoping to get some fruits to eat,
But finding what the tree has to offer
>   They fly away disappointedly.
Its fruits are tasteless, and flowers repulsive,
>   Its leaves are of no use to anyone.
Nanak says, the real essence of goodness and virtue
>   Lies in humility and sweetness of being.

Everyone wants others to be modest,
>   Everyone wants others to be humble;
But no one is willing to let one's pride go,
>   That's where they all stumble.
It is a truth well-known all around
>   In a scale, the heavier side goes down.
The sinner bows twice, but like a hunter
>   He bends only to kill the deer.
What shall you gain even if you bow to hurt,
>   While in your heart you carry loads of dirt.

Fake Religiosity

Pilgrims may take holy dips,
>   But they commit heinous sins;
They carry filth in their hearts,

They are like wicked thieves.

Taking a bath, it's only from their bodies
    They can remove the dirt;
But their souls gather another layer
    Of the filth of pride instead.

Using the gourd, rubbing it hard
    They clean only their skin,
But inside, to the core they are
    Filled with venom and sin.

A true sadhu is better, even if
    He performs no ablution,
However many baths a liar may take
    He always treads on the wrong path.

Man and Woman

To a woman, the man is born
    In a woman's body, he is conceived.
To a woman, he is engaged
    To a woman, he is married.

A man loves a woman
    Through her, future generations are found.
When a man's wife dies, he seeks another woman
    To a woman, the man is so deeply bound.

So why curse the woman?
    To whom even kings are born
A woman is born to another woman
    Without a woman, life comes to an end.

Nanak says, only the True God lives without a woman,
    One who praises Him is fortunate, he's bless'd with the divine beauty;
In the court of the True God
    Their faces shall be radiant, they will shine with divinity.

Guru Arjan Dev

Guru Arjan Dev (1563–1606 CE) was born at Goindwal, district Amritsar and is the fifth Guru of the Sikhs. He was a man of many talents. He invited Mian Meer, a Sufi saint, to lay the foundation of Harmandir Sahib (the Golden Temple) Amritsar in 1589. The Harmandir Sahib was given four doors in four directions suggesting that it welcomes people from all directions and four varnas. He compiled the Holy Book of Sikhs, the Guru Granth Sahib. The book is placed inside the shrine. The task of the compilation of the book ended in 1604. Besides the poetry of the Sikh gurus, the Guru Granth Sahib contains poetry written by Bhakti poets, Sufi poets and other saints.

The Door to Salvation

Spreading your *dhoti* like a mat you sit on it,
    Like a donkey you shovel food into your stomach's pit.
But for good deeds, you may find no redemption,
    Your devotion opens the door to salvation.
Wearing a *tilak*, taking holy dips you perform the ritual,
    To nurture a viper in your heart, you are habitual.
Skillfully you perform the melodious incantation,
    But to deceive your followers, you have no hesitation.
Nanak says, whosoever He blesses, shall find
    Goodness of heart and shall contemplate God.

Guru Gobind Singh

Guru Gobind Singh (1666–1708 CE), the tenth Guru of the Sikhs, was born in Patna, Bihar. Instead of appointing a successor, he declared the Guru Granth Sahib to be the Guru of all Sikhs. His poetry is included in the *Dasam Granth*, although its authorship is contested by various scholars. They opine that most of his writings were composed by court poets. He arranged for the translation of several Sanskrit scriptures into Punjabi. Guru Gobind Singh wrote in Persian, Sanskrit and Braj. He wrote 'Chandi di Vaar' (that describes the victory of good over evil), a poem in *veer rasa*, and two *shabad* in Punjabi.

To God, My Friend

Please tell my dearest Friend
    The plight His disciples suffer.
But for Him, the quilt offers no warmth;
    The household, like a snake bites.
The cup pierces like a dagger;
    Like thorns, pricks the pitcher.
Living without my beloved Friend
    I mourn earnestly;
Without Him enjoying pleasures
    Is like burning in a furnace.

From 'Chandi Di Vaar'

The war trumpet blew, two sides showed their might,
    Both the armies came forward, and began the fight.
From the scabbard, Durga, the Invincible, pulled out her sword,
    And with a blow Chandi slayed all the demons she abhorred.
The skull and body of demons were all cut in two,
    Running through the saddle and then the horse too.
The sword struck the Earth in a single blow,
    It sliced through to the horns[6] of the Bull below.
Then it hit the tortoise standing below the Bull,
    Beheading her enemies, She killed them all.
In the battlefield, she cut demons' heads,
    Like a carpenter saws wood into shreds.

---

[6] The reference is to the mythological bull on whose horns it is believed that the Earth rests.

With the soil of the field, blood and marrow mixed,
  The story of Her sword be told for eons to come.
Such is the might of the sword that killed Mahishasur.

Bhai Gurdas

Bhai Gurdas (1553–1637 CE) was born in village Gillwali, near Amritsar. He was well-versed in Persian, Punjabi and Braj. He wrote 49 spiritual *vaars* in Punjabi. The first *vaar* deals with the life of Guru Nanak Dev. He studied Hindu scriptures and Hindu religion at Varanasi. Besides writings *vaars* in Punjabi, he wrote in Sanskrit and Braj. Though the writings of Bhai Gurdas have not been included in the Guru Granth Sahib yet they are placed under the category of *Gurmat Kaav*. The first manuscript of the Granth Sahib (or Adi Granth as it was known earlier) was handwritten by Bhai Gurdas.

Four Varnas and Four Sects

Hindus have four varnas, Muslims have four sects
  Full of bigotry, they are always eager to fight.
The Ganga and Benaras are sacred to the Hindu,
  So is the Kaba of Mecca to the Muslim.
Hindus wear the sacred thread and a *tilak* on the forehead
  Muslims choose circumcision, instead.
Hindus worship Rama and Muslims worship Allah,
  But both have missed out on the True name of God.
Forgetting God's message, the knowledge
  Given in the Vedas and the Quran.
Greed torments them both,
  They both fight and kill each other.
From the cycle of life and death,
  Neither will find liberation.

If A Dog Sits on a Throne

Even though a dog sits on a throne
    It will still lick the stone of the flour mill.
You may feed a snake with milk
    It will spit venom still.

Even though under water for ages
    A stone will never soften.
Forsaking the fragrance of sandal
    A donkey rolls in the mud often.

Like them, a backbiter too
    Would backbite incessantly,
By not changing the habit
    One destroys oneself spiritually.

Man in Kalyug

O God! In *Kalyug* men have fallen so low,
    Like dogs they crave to eat the dead.
The kings sin rampantly,
    The fence destroys the crop it's supposed to protect.

Bereft of knowledge, the ignorant
    Do not utter a truthful word,
The Guru now dances
    To the tune of his disciples, instead.

Students sit at home and
    Teachers go to teach them.
Qazis are crooked and corrupt
    Accepting bribes, they make false judgments.

People love each other for their riches
    Without knowing, how ill-begotten the money is.
Now sin is spread all around,
    Now sin all-pervading is.

Waris Shah

Waris Shah (1722–1798 CE) was born at Jandiala Sher Khan, Shekhupura. His work *Qissa Heer Ranjha* (also referred to as *Heer*) is a masterpiece in the Punjabi language. The work is replete with historical, social, political and cultural information about Punjab and Punjabi. The character of Heer portrays the honesty, bravery, truthfulness and the rebellious nature of the Punjabi people. Before Waris Shah, Damodar and Muqbal had also written the legend of Heer, but Waris Shah immortalised Heer and Heer immortalised Waris Shah. A few excerpts from *Heer* are included here.

Excerpts from Heer

On Friends' Request

My friends came to me and said,
    'Tell us the story of Heer once more,
Using your poetic fecundity,
    Tell the tale of love once again.
Writing couplets, showing your talent,
    Let Ranjha and Heer in your verse meet
Sharing the tale in the company of friends,
    Let's enjoy the tale of love once again.'

Acting upon my friends' words, I am ordained;
    A beautiful tale of love I have told,
Rhyming words and correcting lines,
    A new flower of poetry thus bloomed
After planning long in his mind,
    Farhad carved stairs out of a mountain,
Extracting ideas a thing beautiful was made,
    Like *attar* from roses is obtained.

As People Think of Brothers

Without brothers there can be no gatherings,
    Without brothers there is no spring ever,
Your arms crumble when your brother dies,
    But for brothers there is no true kin either
Brothers are the buttress—a truth you should know.
    As long as they live no defeat touches you;
But for them there are no companions,
    For brothers break you, your brothers make you.

If the father loves one dearly, other brothers get envious;
    Fearing father's wrath, they say nothing, yet
They make taunts subtle, and speak stinging words;
    Like snakes from their mouths they do venom spit.
If they could, they would throw one out of the house;
    They'll make yet new remarks undeserved,
Waris Shah says, self-interest is dear to all;
    There is no other bond like your body, which stays with you.

A Dialogue Between Mullah and Ranjha

It may smell sweet like *halva*,
    But in fact it is terrible like news of death.
It seems in one breath you bless people,
    And they are cursed in the next.

Sitting here like the blind, the leper and the cripple,
    You do nothing but wrong.
Sitting in the village assembly,
    You defend the culprit with authority.
Waris Shah says, whosoever crosses the village street,
    You talk to everyone haughtily.

Mullah says, 'Arrogant *Jat*,
    Stay here tonight, you may depart in the morning,
You may go as soon as the night ends
    Covering your head, you may leave the mosque.

Fight not uselessly with God,
> Do not invite calamities on you.'
Waris Shah says, to these blessed places of God
> *Mullahs* cause misery and pain undeserved.

Heer's Reply to Her Mother

Those who kill their daughter,
> Carry the burden of the heinous sin,
Hurting daughters is like hewing them to pieces.
> On Judgment Day
You will be cursed to eat,
The flesh of your daughters you kill today.
I have always been obedient to you, my parents,
> My *dupatta* always covered my head; I obeyed you.
Heer is committed and loyal to Ranjha
> Please don't talk about him the way you do.

Heer's Wailing

Heer wails and says, 'O *Jogi*, you lie to me
> When a friend is displeased, no one placates;
I have not found a single soul yet,
> Who can unite lovers whom fate separates.
I shall make shoes of my skin for the one,
> Who can once relieve my pain;
Those who have been separated for long,
> Tell me, does God ever unite them again?
Have the dead and the parted ever met?
> People weave pleasant lies to soothe;
A crow has snatched a crane from the hawk,
> Let's see if it is quiet or it cries aloud.
The field of a *jat* is set ablaze,
> Let's see if he comes to put the fire out.'

Hashim Shah

Hashim Shah (1752–17821 CE) was born at Jagdev Kalan, tehsil Ajnala, district Amritsar. He wrote the Qissas of Shirin–Farhad, Heer–Ranjha and Sohni–Mehiwal, but the *qissa* of Sassi–Punnu is his masterpiece. He excels in expressing pain in his poetry. He stands apart from his predecessors and successors as he has portrayed the suffering of Sassi as a woman. He is also known as the poet of pain. The following extract is from Sassi–Punnu.

I Will Go and Return Not

With readiness to sacrifice my life, I will go and return not,
    As long as I breathe, hope I lose not, death I fear not.
I shall go and meet Punnu, if God hears the cries of Sassi,
    Hashim says, in the vast desert, there is no other martyr of love like Sassi.

The blazing sun is up in the sky, scorching heat is all around,
    Hot winds blow, dead birds lie on the ground.
The ever-expansive burning desert spreads like a river of fire,
Hashim says, though unconsciousness, she still calls for Punnu;
Once she has taken a step forward, Sassi refuses to retreat.

Her feet are soft, they are painted with henna,
    Burning, blistering and sizzling sand parches her feet like grains.
The sun hides behind a cloud as if frightened by its own heat,
    Hashim wonders at Sassi's resolve. So determined! She refuses to retreat.

She falls and gets up again; tired, she sits down to catch her breath,
    Like the irresistible urge of a drunkard, she strides further,
She looks for Punnu's camel's footprints. She finds none, her search is in vain;
Hashim says, her love is so great, the whole world will tell her tale.

Shah Mohammad

Shah Mohammad (1780–1839 CE) was born at Wadala Veeram in Amritsar district. He was a prolific poet. *Jangnama* is his masterpiece and tells the story of the first Anglo-Sikh War after the death of Maharaja Ranjit Singh. He was well-versed in history: one of his close relatives was an employee in the army of Maharaja Ranjit Singh. Of the 105 verses in *Jangnama*, 53 verses describe the context of the war and the war itself. Shah Mohammad's work exemplifies the syncretic culture of Punjab as Hindus and Muslims used to live in mutual harmony. His vivid descriptions of war are characteristic of his work and are unique in Punjabi literature. *Jangnama* shows the spirit of Punjabi nationalism against the British. The excerpt included here is from *Jangnama*.

The Battle Scene

This world fascinates everyone
    But it deceives all like a fraudster,
Parents, youth and fun are transient
    Nor does your childhood stay forever.

Wealth, horses and camels—all shall perish
    No kingdom of any king is perpetual.
Shah Muhammad says, your beauty is fleeting too
    Your hair won't stay black forever.

Those who have killed my brother
    I'll pull their hair out,
All invaders will go back
    When, like a lioness, I'll roar aloud.

Many women shall become widows today
    Their nose-rings shall be removed.

Shah Mohammad says, there'll be loud wailing all around
   If Punjabi women are widowed today.

When with fear they were stricken
   The young infantry began to talk,
From whence these white men attacked us,
   Let's sneak out in the cover of the dark.

We were happy ploughing our fields
   We are the sons of affluent farmers,
Shah Mohammad says, we are the people of lands and wells
   We can toil and harness the plough.

The battle between the Hind and Punjab has begun
   Both sides have brought their armies to the front.
I wish our lords were here to see for themselves
   The way swords of the Khalsas swung today.

Men were falling as bullets were fired,
   Along with the palanquins, elephants also fell.
Shah Muhammad says, caused by the treason of a couple of chiefs
   The valiant Sikh army lost the battle, otherwise won.

Platoons came marching in rows along with the artillery
   They were crushed badly. The Sikhs fought with peerless
   bravery.
Mewa Singh and Madhey Khan displayed valour unrivaled
   Three attacks of *firangis* they thwarted heroically.

Sham Singh from Attari, the General of the Sikh Army,
   Broke the bones of the enemy—their weapons lay scattered.
Shah Muhammad says, the Sikhs crushed *firangis* in the battle
   Like juice from lemons, their blood was squeezed out.

4

Modern Poetry

Bhai Veer Singh

Bhai Veer Singh (1872–1957) was born in Amritsar. He is the pioneer of modern Punjabi poetry. Besides poetry, he also wrote prose, fiction and drama. He was awarded the Sahitya Akademi award for his book of poetry *Mere Saiyan Jio* in 1955. Panjab University bestowed upon him the Doctor of Oriental Learning award in 1949. He was awarded the Padma Bhushan in 1956. His poetry emphasises moral integrity, and also reflects his philosophical and mystical experiences. He preferred to stay close to nature. Bhai Veer Singh acts as the bridge between traditional and modern Punjabi poetry.

Time

I implored hard, but
    Time heeded not,
Whenever I tried to hold it
    Time slipped out of my hands,
I raised many walls
    But time broke them all,
Taking quick paces it flew away
    Jumping from one roof to another,
O human! Don't waste your time
    Make the most of it, for time flies fast
It knows not how to stop
    Once gone, it never comes back again.

Dhani Ram Chatrik

Dhani Ram Chatrik (1876–1954) was born in Passian Wala in district Sialkot (now in Pakistan). His vast oeuvre includes tales from mythology to the everyday life of Punjab, and the use of rich idiomatic language, poetic devices and diction. His poetry reflects his wide-ranging imagination as well as understanding of his cultural roots. Marked with the spontaneity of folk songs and simultaneously, it also encompasses modernity in its ambit. An avid supporter of Punjabi language and culture, he was proud of his Punjabi identity. The spirit of the culture of Punjab was so deeply imbued in his consciousness that Radha in his famous poem, 'Radha's Message', comes across as a Punjabi woman. This poem transcends all boundaries of time and space.

Radha's Message

(1)

Tell me something about Krishna
    Why do you set my heart ablaze, Udho?
After long, my wounds were about to heal
    Krishna has given me fresh wounds again.
I struggled to smother my feelings,
    You have rekindled my pain that lay in slumber.
Your words of wisdom cure me not,
    For my wounds need some other cure.
Tell Krishna to do away with his pretense,
    If he intends not to come again;
If he cannot douse the fire that burns me
    Why does he add fuel to it?

(2)

Tell him to come and see me once
    I wail like a crane,

Praying to see him once
>   I spend sleepless nights.
My heart, filled with sorrow, lies at his altar
>   I wither away rapidly among the tormenting sorrows.
I eternally grieve my loss
>   Repenting for having sent my bounties away.
Tell Krishna, he has settled down in Mathura
>   Here Gokul is bleak without him.
He has forgotten the way back home
Curse the moment when he left!

(3)

Your sweet tongue can beguile me no more, Udho
>   For I have tested how deep Krishna's love is,
Keep these words of wisdom aside for Kubjan
>   Who in no time has beguiled him.
Udho, loving Krishna is a hopeless affair
>   I have lost everything I had once,
My sorrows have consumed me; my pain has drunk me
>   My gold like precious body rots
Beseeching him is a worthless affair
>   I know him to the core now,
May god bless him! May he prosper wherever he is!
>   No one can snatch him away from my heart.

(4)

Tell the fickle lover that he has insulted my true love
>   For he has not kept his word.
Like a black moth he has acted lately,
>   He settles on the flower where he finds one.
He sends me words of wisdom to make me content,
>   He is swayed by the charms of the *malin*.
Herding cattle here, he's gone to the palace
>   From thence he talks profound to me.

Instead of being here with me
   He sits on the throne of Kansa;[1]
I wouldn't have torn away his curtains and tassels,
   Had he shown me his palace once.

(5)

Tell him, my love for him is constant
   The boat of my heart shall ever sail.
As long as sun and moon are in the sky,
   We shall be one, like skin and nail.
Whenever people sit together,
   They'll sing the tale of our love;
No one will remember Kubjan
   Radha's name will stay joined with Krishna's.
Krishna may have three hundred and sixty wives
   And his fame may increase manifold,
Till eternity even in temples, says Chatrik,
   Radha shall stay forever with Krishna.

Prof. Puran Singh

Puran Singh (1881–1931) was born in Salhad, Abbottabad (now in Pakistan). A scientist and a man of liberal views, he rejected shackles of any sort. Consequently, he changed many jobs and practised different religions in his life. The titles of the most of his books begin with the word 'Khulley' (Punjabi for *pen*) such as *Khulley Maidan, Khulley Ghund, Khulley Lekh* (prose) and *Khulley Asmani Rang*. He wrote in free verse and was greatly influenced by Walt Whitman. He derided the use of meter in poetry, calling it 'a golden shoe'. He represents the free spirit and syncretism of Punjabi culture and lifestyle.

---

[1] In Hindu mythology, Kansa is a tyrant, who ruled from Mathura. He is Lord Krishna's mother's brother. Lord Krishna killed him.

Farmers

Listen!
I have thrown away my books,
And the knowledge therein.
I have lost my heart to ploughs
I am devoted to the fields now.
These farms are my books
Rustic farmers my fellow friends
They offer a bowlful of lassi
And *bajra* roti.
They also offer a handful of butter
And plenty of milk for all to drink.
They give rice, wheat and corn
And other coarse grains like millet too.
Cool water from the well they give to all;
They give us joys to drink and delights to live on
They are like God's own hands.
To God's will they surrender;
They are happy as God keeps them.
They plough the fields, they sow the seed
They toil hard day and night.
They eat less and wear coarse cloth
Hoping for rains they look up at the sky
They keep the granary of the world full
Even kings look up to them for their share of bread.

Heera Singh 'Dard'

Heera Singh 'Dard' (1887–1965) was born in village Ghagrot, Rawalpindi (now in Pakistan). He was a journalist and freedom fighter. While being actively associated with various political and social organisations, he devoted time to writing consistently. Initially, he would read his poetry in Sikh Educational Conferences. Later, he worked with the Congress party. The British government confiscated his house and sent him to jail for his political views. He was one of the founders of the Central Punjabi Writers' Association. Under the influence of Marxism, he was critical of Bhai Veer Singh. Besides writing poetry, he also wrote stories, prose, criticism and biographies.

Dream of a New World

In this world laden with
Fear, danger and wailing
Where we toil day and night for others,
This world is like hell
To Hindus and Muslims alike;
Where we, the owners of the land, work like slaves
At the waking hour, we wake not;
At the sleeping hour, we sleep not.

Come, let's create a new world—
A new free world!
Let's knock down the walls
And wipe away all boundaries that divide us.
Let's crush everything that separates us.
The garden of life belongs to us all,
Let's spread its sweet fragrance
Let's have a world where all are one
A world where there is no Pandit; and there is no Mullah.

BABU RAJAB ALI

Babu Rajab Ali (1894–1979) was born in the village Sahoke, Firozpur district (now Moga district). Babu Rajab Ali was a *kavishar* in the Malwa region of Punjab and wrote many patriotic poems. He also wrote on Hindu mythology, Sikh history and semitic themes, including poems on Prophet Muhammad and Jesus Christ. During the partition of 1947, he moved to Pakistan. Most of his works were published posthumously.

The Pain of the Punjabi Language

Sweeter than candy is the language of my dear Punjab,
    It flows down sweetly like the *attar* of roses.
Other languages hurt me, from my eyes tears have sprung,
    For you feel not the pain of your mother-tongue.

The accursed one, which dwells in the country of Pathans
    Coming here, Pashto bathed in the land of shastras and vedas;
As compared to your wife, a servant girl is given a higher rung
    You feel not the pain of your mother-tongue.

Then came Persian, another sister of Pashto;
    It hurts my soul, my heart wails bitterly
I, the guileless, the innocent, am thrown, flung far
    Oh! You feel not the pain of your mother-tongue.

Again, I suffered the loss, when Urdu came up here
    This new rival of mine occupied all the court-rooms,
Weak and hapless as I was; with poison I was deep stung
    And you feel not the pain of your mother-tongue.

From Britain thence came another, dancing with no shame,
    Fair complexion, calamitous eyes, tough-tongued;
It took people some time to realize, what a brutal song English had sung
O, compassionate ones! You feel not the pain of your mother-tongue.

Then came Hindi, yet another love-rival
    I am always silent, she barks incessantly;
An old toothless woman, her bell has been rung
    And you feel not the pain of your mother-tongue.

Dear Punjabis, be watchful! No one spares the weak
    Dead for a long time, others have looted even its remnants,
Having swallowed eight–nine provinces, her thirst is still young
    For you feel not the pain of your mother-tongue.

Why can't our modern men grasp a simple truth?
    Men always look handsome in their traditional gear,
Babu remembers his friends from school—we studied together at
    Moga.
    Why don't you feel the pain of your mother-tongue?

Diwan Singh 'Kalepani'

Diwan Singh 'Kalepani' (1897–1944) was born in village Galhotian, tehsil Daska, Sialkot (now in Pakistan). He fought against the British rule, but he was killed by the Japanese fascist forces in 1944. He was an army doctor by profession and was stationed in the Andaman islands (commonly referred to as Kalapani in Punjabi), which gave him the name Kalepani. Like Prof. Puran Singh, he too wrote poetry in free verse. He was a progressive poet with a modern sensibility and a critic of regressive thought and ritualism. His use of sarcasm in poetry is masterly.

Dusk Has Fallen

The sun has set
It's getting dark,
As the light fades
And the darkness deepens
Those who have homes, are headed homeward,
I have not reached my destination yet
Nor have I found any place to rest.
The evening deepens

I am only half way through my journey.
On the banks of a deep river
Suddenly my path is blocked
The untameable! The unfathomable! It flows vigorously.
The evening is spread out
And the light fades,
When the sun could do me no good
What good would this fading light do?

There is no bridge, no boat, no boatman either
On this bank I stand alone,
I cannot wade through the water
I cannot swim either.
There is no one to take me across
I am told
My destination is the other side;
I don't have the address
I am not certain where it is
The path has suddenly come to an end
On the bank of this fathomless river.
Is there anyone with a boat?
Is there anyone who can take me across?
A dark evening is spread out.

I can see a scary night approaching fast
Clouds are gathering in the sky
Calamity is 'loosed upon the world'
There is no moon, no sun, no stars,
I am scared;
My life is like a tiny earthen lamp
Which is about to die;
I can see the world on the other side,
As if it were calling me.

I am but a young helpless woman
I stand here alone
I do not know how to swim

If it were a shallow river
I would have crossed it
But the river is flooded
The tide is high
Is there a kind soul nearby?
Is there someone who will show me mercy
And take me across?

Firoz Deen Sharaf

Firoz Deen Sharaf (1898–1955) was born in Lahore, but his paternal grandparents belonged to Tola in district Amritsar. He learnt poetry from Ustad Hamdam and was one of the leading stage-poets of Punjab. He wrote in Urdu and Punjabi. He had good command over the theory of *pingal* and *aarooz*. After Waris Shah, Sharaf was one of the few poets who used idiomatic language and wrote poetry in chaste Punjabi. His themes were patriotism, communal harmony between Hindus and Muslims and social reform. As he had a melodious voice, he was also known as the 'Nightingale of Punjab.

I Love My Language

I never hesitate to say that
    My love for my mother-tongue would never cease to be;
I am a pearl in the nose-ring of a married woman
    Of a Punjabi lass's bangles, I am a piece.

My mother-tongue should get the honour it deserves
    Like a lover this dream in my heart I keep;
From Waris Shah to Bulleh Shah—a spectrum vast
I have coloured my life with these colours deep.

While living here in Lahore, why should I speak the lingo of U.P.?
    To me this wisdom is with ignorance entwined;

Sharaf, I am a Punjabi and I serve Punjabi
The wellbeing of my mother-tongue, I always keep in mind.

Prof. Mohan Singh

Prof. Mohan Singh (1905–1978) was born in Hoti, near Mardaan in Peshawar (now in Pakistan). He was a romantic poet who also wrote on social issues. Love with its various facets was the most popular subject of his poetry. Even his progressive poetry has a touch of Romanticism. He was well-versed in Persian. He was awarded the Sahitya Akademi award for his book *Wadda Vela* in 1959. He has narrated the story of Guru Nanak in his long poem 'Nanakain'. He translated *Light of Asia* into Punjabi as 'Asia Da Chanan'.

Mother

I cannot see a tree
With shade more dense than
That of a Mother's.
Borrowing from her a little shade
Even God has His heavens made.
All plants in this world die
When their roots go dry,
But, Mother is a plant that perishes
When its flowers shrivel and wither.

Breeze Like Life

Grant us a breeze like life!
    Let us be eternally in quest;
Every moment we should pine for our beloved,
    Let the flame of love always burn in our breasts.

We may walk through forests or deserts,
    Or we may climb the mountains high;

Ceaselessly we may remain in search,
    We may rest not when a stop is nigh.

Finding a bed of flowers on the way,
    We may halt not, and stop not to rest;
Even if we cross a sea of beautiful sights,
    We digress not from the path of our quest.

We may plug our ears
    When a haunting melody distracts us;
If ever our cloak is caught in thorns,
    We shake it vigorously and move on thus.

Grant us a breeze like life!
    Let us be eternally in quest;
Every moment we should pine for our beloved,
    Let the flame of love always burn in our breasts.

Nand Lal Nurpuri

Nand Lal (1906-1966) was born in Nurpur, Lyallpur (now known as Faisalabad, in Pakistan). He joined the police service at a young age. He received a medal for displaying exemplary bravery. Seeing the atrocities committed by the police, he resigned from his job. He is one of the most famous songwriters of Punjab. His songs portray the culture of Punjab. Almost all of his contemporary singers sang his songs. He also wrote the songs of a famous Punjabi film, *Mangati*. His life was full of economic hardships and deprivation. He lived in extreme poverty; it eventually drove him to suicide.

Jutti Kasuri *(The Shoes of Kasur)*

Jutti Kasuri won't fit me well
    Oh God, ahead lies a long walk;
Paths that I know not so well
    Such paths now I'll have to walk.

It's a long journey to my in-laws'
    And worse, to my dismay;
My man did not hire a cart
    He made me walk all the way.

When on the way for *muklawa*
    He is walking along the road;
My veil covers my face, I can say nothing,
    For shyness is the newly wedded woman's code.

My calves are soft and feet delicate
    I cannot take a step more,
My youth and beauty, and this heat of the noon!
    For me he has no pity to pour.

Blisters appear on my feet
    And my face wilts and wanes;
My dear man walks ahead of me
    To look back, he takes no pains.

Jutti Kasuri won't fit me well
    Oh God, ahead lies a long walk
Paths that I know not well
    Such paths now I'll have to walk.

The Guest with the Kaintha[2]

The guest with the *kaintha* has come
    O mother, your chores are not done yet.
He will not visit us soon again
    O mother, your chores are not done yet.

When he walks, his gold-laced *jutti* sparkles
    Crimson light flares in my eyes;
Give me the keys to the trunk, Mother
    I will spread out the silken cover for him;

---

[2] *Kaintha* is a kind of necklace men and women wear in Punjab.

The guest with *kaintha* has come
    O mother, your chores are not done yet.

He feels shy when my bangles tinkle
    I tried persuading him, but he won't come in;
He looks up once, then lowers his eyes
    He hesitates and smiles shyly;
The guest with *kaintha* has come
    O mother, your chores are not done yet.

I wish I could make him sit close to me
    And let my eyes feast on him;
Noorpuri says, If he leaves in anger
    I'll beseech desperately;
The guest with *kaintha* has come
    O mother, your chores are not done yet.

Ustaad Daaman

Ustaad Daaman (1911–1984) was born in Lahore. He spent his entire life in Lahore as he deeply loved the city. Daaman was famous in his lifetime. His poetry, written in chaste Punjabi, would express the pain of ordinary people, which won him many hearts. In his poetry, he criticized the regime in Pakistan. Faiz Ahmed Faiz, the famous Urdu poet, opined that Daaman was gifted to match the talent of Bulleh Shah and Waris Shah. Daaman was a champion of the oneness of humanity. A critic of the Partition, he believed that the creation of Pakistan was only to serve the vested interests of a handful of leaders.

The Other Side

A strange partition of Pakistan has taken place,
One part is here; one part is there.

What cure could these ignorant people offer?
The ointment is here; the boil is there.

How can we reach our destination ever?
The horse is here; the cart is there.

What honour can you find in the marriage of convenience?
One pair is here; one pair is there.

Cried We Both

You may or may not say it aloud, but you know it deep in your heart;
You've suffered a great loss, and we have suffered too.

This freedom has ruined us both alike,
You were wrecked by it; and it has wrecked us too.

There is some hope that we may find life soon,
But for now you are dead; and we are dead too.

The life was thrust into the jaws of death,
You were carried there; and we were carried too.

Those who were awake looted us to their fill,
You've been sleeping; we've been sleeping too.

The redness in the eyes tells the whole tale
That you cried bitterly; and we've cried too.

Ishwar Chitarkar

Ishwar Chitarkar (1912–1968) was born at Paddi, Hoshiarpur district. During his early days, he used to teach fine arts at a school. After shifting to England, he became a full-time artist. He experimented with writing sonnets in Punjabi. Love and separation constitute the dominant themes in his poetry. According to Narinjan Tasneem, he was a melancholic or sad poet, but not pessimist. He knew the craft of *ghazal* very well. The painter within him gave his poetic imagination well-defined images.

The Flight of Imagination

The wings are ablaze
The bird is soaring high,
Seeing the bird's flight
Hunters are getting ready.
Along with the bird also flies
The dagger pierced into its heart.
Wings flapping slowly,
Along with the gust of the wind,
Tiny flowers are blooming in the sky.
The blood of courage,
Dripping from the heart,
Guides mankind for ages to come.
Perhaps, it needs something else
To douse the fire burning in its heart.
Who can quench
The fire that love ignites?
Once again, the bird is flying
Towards the nest of lightning.
The wings are ablaze
And the bird is soaring high.

Many cages has it broken,
Spent many days and nights;
To fulfil its cherished dreams
It has spent many sleepless nights.
For moments, days and months,
Unmindful of seasons,
It has spread its songs.
Unless Time wills
Saplings of these songs will not grow.
Is there any one

Who can dare pick
These burning ambers?
Borrowing colours from the dawn
It shall embrace
A dying star.

The wings are ablaze
Singed feathers are falling down
Stars, that these wings kiss,
Are burning too.
Only a brave one can bear
The heat of love.
Every dawn is the harbinger
Of the death of old stars.
Numerous unsung songs
Burn in its heart,
These unsung songs
Are its life-stream now—
Who sees the obvious?
Who deciphers the subtle?
But pain keeps everyone in their place—
As much as one can endure
As much as one can survive.

Why has the entire expanse of creation
Become too small for the bird?
The wings are ablaze
The bird is soaring high.

Sharif Kunjahi

Sharif Kunjahi (1914–2007) was born at Kunjah in district Gujarat, Pakistan. He was one of the leading Punjabi poets of Pakistan. He was a poet, painter, lexicographer, translator, scholar, critic and teacher. He was one of the founding teachers at the Department of Punjabi, the University of Punjab, Lahore. He had studied Urdu and Persian. He lends voice to the pain of the ordinary people and expresses the idea of universal love in his poetry. He has also articulated the trauma of partition and the concerns of peasants in his poetry. He discusses religion without being communal. He is said to be the representative poet of Pakistani Punjabi poetry.

Brother, Are You from Kunjah?

Brother, are you from Kunjah?
Is your name Sharif?
I thought as much.
What a fortunate day it is!
With the grace of God,
I've met my brother today.
Son, look at him
This man is your uncle.
I am sure you couldn't recognize me.
We used to play together when we were children
Do you remember?
My name is Niamat.
I am the granddaughter of Mehar Noor Deen.
You know,
Your friends and relatives
Kith and kin hold a meaning
As long as you meet them
The wells remain alive as long as you haul water from them.
Sometimes, I used to stay there for as long as a year.
I hardly get a chance to have a glimpse of those places now.
Tell me
Is my aunt still cross with me?
Tell me, my brother.
What was my fault in the whole affair?
Can there be any place more dear to me than my maternal grandparents'?

But, daughters are not supposed to retort
We are not supposed to answer back to our elders.
The sense of shame seals our lips.
We never cross the line.
They gave birth to us
They let us breathe in this world – that's an obligation
That's the best thing that can happen in a girl's life
We daughters are grateful to our parents for that.
They never wish their daughters ill, I know.
But we all stumble in times of dearth.
Wisdom betrayed my father
Winds of sorrow had begun to blow
The mountain of grief broke on me
Even my maternal grandparents, uncles and aunts
Began to avoid me
When they met me
Instead of blooming with happiness
They steered clear of me and shrank into themselves.
I was young and those were testing times
I was like a half-baked brick and the fire in the furnace had gone
    out.
Nobody could think straight.
Times were such
Everybody was deserting us.
My husband's father persuaded my father
On his deathbed, my father gave him his word.
It's okay if my man is older than me by many years.
My brother, you are an intelligent man
You understand everything
The daughter, who doesn't value what her parents did for her,
Is not a good daughter.
I reconciled with my fate
I accepted the man who once had pleasures with his first wife;
I accepted the bowl of milk
From which the other woman had already drunk

To make my share of curd.
God has kindly rewarded my endurance
He has blessed me with this beautiful son.
Okay, I'll get down here.
Why don't you also get down here today?
Stay for a night at your forsaken sister's place.
It's okay.
The world is a celebration for those who live to enjoy it.
Remember me to everyone at home
Pay my regards to everyone there.

Bawa Balwant

Bawa Balwant (1915–1972) was born in Neshta, Amritsar. He was one of the greatest poets of the twentieth century. His progressive poetry had many hues. He thoroughly imbibed the Indian philosophical tradition and was also greatly inspired by Marx and Trotsky. His poems would directly address his reader and raise rebellious questions. He would find revolution even in nature. Along with the idea of revolution, he gave equal importance to the aesthetics of poetry. Though not very popular, he is an important Punjabi poet.

The World and the Truth

Having lived through all sorrows and joys in this world
They left this world calling it a dream.
One, who called the world an illusion,
That wise man—
Ate the grain he got from this world
And lived on this very earth.
He drank its water
And found friends in this very world.

One wise man said, 'This world is no more than a figure of smoke.'
Another said, ' This world is nothing, but an illusion.'

You live here on this earth for a hundred years
Eat its fruit, drink its honey
And then dare say,
'This world is a mirage; it stays not forever.
Life is shortlived;
The world is ephemeral.'
After having enjoyed all joys of this world, someone said,
'This world is like a fleeting shadow.'
Having raised many memorials on this earth,
He said, 'This world is nothing but *maya*.'
'This world is not true; Truth dwells somewhere else.'
Another wise man said, 'The world is transitory.'

(2)

Since ages, many have said that the world is transient
Those who said so are also dead;
But this world continues.
Those who said, 'This world is perishable.'
Missed the point terribly.

It may have its own serpentine, meandering course, I agree;
But it goes on forever.
It never dies,
It only changes.
The change is the dawn of life
The world is not a dark abyss of death.
One who says, 'There is nothing in this world.'
He may be a Messiah or some Avatar
A sage or an artist,
Knowingly or unknowingly,
He sits in the company of the rulers;
For this idea makes
The root of slavery and poverty in the world.

(3)

This world is the truth; this world is the reality.
Man's wishes, his dreams and his hard work
Have made this world yet more beautiful.
The sun is the truth, the water is the truth,
Matter is the truth, its movement is the truth.
Billowing fields are a fact; the yield is a verity
This factory of facts is a great reality.
Matter and its movement are eternal
Intellect, soul and mankind are its manifestations.
This world is not an illusion, nor a dream;
This world is a reality; this world is the truth.

Pritam Singh Safir

Pritam Singh Safir (1916–1999) was born in Mulkpur, district Rawalpindi. He was a lawyer by profession and later became a magistrate in the Delhi High Court. He is a romantic poet from the school of Amrita Pritam and Mohan Singh. His mysticism makes him different from the rest. The first phase of his poetic career is marked by social issues; the second phase is dominated by the question of the self. Earlier he focused on the outside world; but later on the world within. He won the Sahitya Akademi award in 1983 for his book *Anik Bisthar*.

The Cranes of Katak

Lakhs of *Katak*[3] months have come and gone
    Lakhs of cranes have died.
Equal number of religions and nations
    Have been born in this world.

---

[3] *Katak* or Kartik in Hindi coincides with October and November of the Gregorian calendar

Lakhs of nights have spread on earth
    And lost in the vast arena of time;
Equal number of Adams have passed on
    Embracing Eves tight,
Unmindful of their deaths.

Lakhs of lakes, brimful with water, have dried;
    Lakhs of mountains fractured and chasms have opened.
Equal numbers of *Pirs* and Messiahs have died
    The world is stuck mid-stream.

I do not believe in these stars or in the *nav khand*[4];
    Nor do I believe in their power over us.
Lakhs of gods have been destroyed
    Who knows them?

There have been many Vishnus, Brahmas and Shivas
    As many as blades of grass are there
Why should any Parvati
    Cry for any Shiva today?

Below these brackish seas innumerable Ravanas rule,
    For many of these *avatars* enjoyed lustful pleasures
They caused their own downfall
    They lost their bodies, their souls;
    Losing everything, they sit there.

Armies of gods and demons
    Fairy-like princesses,
Lakhs of armies from all directions
    Have drowned in the river of time.

---

[4] Sikhism believes in nine divisions of the cosmos. In this scheme of thoughts, *Sach Khand* is the highest, which is the abode of formless God and *Narak* or Hell is the lowest. In ancient Hindu thought, the cosmos was also divided into nine divisions. However, in Hinduism there is also a concept of seven Heavens and seven Hells. Guru Nanak has used this expression in his famous verse Japuji and it means all the realms, universes, and all creation.

Every age has waged wars
    Destroying old civilizations;
New lives keep coming to the world
    Old ones continue to die.

Time and again, with the coming of *Katak* every year
    New cranes are born
Thinking, reflecting and pain-ridden
    They fly down from the sky.

In the human heart, filled with illusions,
    Brightly they come and sit;
And say, 'Lakhs of prisoners have died
    Shackles are not broken yet
Sheets of iron are still forged into bayonets.'

Love for god and love for country – such grand talk!
    Despite the tides of tears and cries of suffering people,
Since times immemorial,
    Nothing could knock down the palaces of bloodsuckers.

Supplicating and imploring, humanity is dying;
    Ruined in embarrassments, taking their defeat as Providence
Not even a single step the suffering people take
    Towards the goal of revolution.

Change is seen as a perilous task,
    Initiative and enterprise as horrendous scheming;
Who can save the world
    Where people have such opinions?

Nobody can stop those who are ready to sacrifice their lives,
    After fighting battles fierce, crushing all obstacles
This world will become a heaven;
    Why shouldn't this miracle happen?

Gold and silver do not ever die
    Capitals of continents are destroyed and rebuilt;

With no other goal but gold, silver and power
    In seas and on mountains the blood of millions is spilt.

May the hope of a better world live!
    May the pleasant winds blow!
May everyone share the warmth of labour!
    May we all share the shades of joy!

Don't cut short the lives of suffering and pain;
    If you wish to kill, kill for a cause;
Gather all that you need at one place
    To raise a palace of pleasure on the burning land.

Where prisons are demolished and shackles are broken
    I dream of a world where there is no injustice;
A world where every man is free –
    Every man is a king, and every woman a queen.

New cranes in the month of *Katak*
    Inflame new passions,
Flying down into human hearts
    They wake up the sleeping pain in us.

I wish, from their calling
    A new world were born;
Where everybody is happy
    And hapless remains none.

Amrita Pritam

Amrita Pritam (1919–2005) was born in Gujranwala (now in Pakistan). She represents the romantic–progressive tradition of poetry. Her poetic career can be divided into three phases. In her early days, she wrote religious and idealist poetry under the influence of her father. In the second phase, when she was part of the progressive movement, she expressed personal emotions and also responded to social issues. Her poetry written on the Partition is exceptionally famous. She gave voice to the woman's concerns and expressed the innermost feelings of a woman in her poetry. In the third phase of her career, she wrote experimental poetry. She won the Sahitya Akademi award for her collection *Sunehrhe* in 1956. She has also written prose and fiction. She was the editor of the literary journal *Nagmani* for nearly three decades.

I Call Upon Waris Shah

I call upon Waris Shah to speak up from his grave
And urge him to turn over love-saga's next page.

Once cried a daughter of Punjab, you wrote a long wailing verse
Millions of them cry today, and call upon your name.

O, the compassionate one. Rise. Look once at your Punjab
Corpses lay spread in fields and blood runs in the Chenab.

Some wicked hands have poisoned the sweet water of five rivers
Irrigated with the same, every field of Punjab shivers.

Every corner of this land now is spitting venom high
The fields have turned red, calamity touches the sky.

A poisonous wind began to blow, every forest did it shake
Every flute it changed into a terrible deadly snake.

With its first bite, all charmers lost their charm
Another bite made them serpents, it did a grave harm.

Stung by its bite, everyone grew a sting
Its venom spread into Punjab's every limb.

The songs of Punjab have died, from spindles the thread is snapped
Sundering girls from *trinjan*, their spinning-wheels are cracked.

Along with the beds, the rowers let our boats sink
The boughs of *peepal* cracked along with the swing.

The storm has broken Ranjha's melodious flute,
The songs of lovers have sadly turned mute.

With the downpour of blood, the land of Punjab is drenched;
Damsels cry at shrines, with pain they are wrenched.

All men are Qaidon[5] now, who love and beauty smother
From whence can we find now, Waris Shah another.

I call upon Waris Shah to speak up from his grave
And urge him to turn over love-saga's next page.

Bread Giver

My bread giver!
Like debt your salt sits heavy on my tongue
Your name is on my father's lips
And in my mortal frame runs his blood.
How can I dare speak?
Before I utter a word, your grain speaks up.
I had only a few words to say
But we, the worms of the grain,
Are crushed under its weight,
With me
My words are crushed too.

My bread giver!
My toiling and working parents bore me
I too am destined to toil,
My body can do all jobs of the flesh
That was a job,
This is also a job.

My bread giver!
I am a doll of flesh,

---

[5] Qaidon is Heer's maternal uncle, who arranged Heer's marriage in the family of Kheras against her wishes.

You may play with it
And make it play—as it pleases you.
A cup of blood, you may drink it or offer it,
I stand in front of you,
I am but an object to play with
You may use me any way you wish.
I grew... I was ground... I was kneaded like dough and rolled out like roti
Put me on a burning *tawa* if it gratifies you.
I am no more than a morsel,
Consume me any way you wish;
And you...
You are no more than lava;
Burn me, melt me to your heart's content
Wrap your lava around me.
I stand at your feet,
Embrace me.
You may kiss me, you may lick me,
And do whatever you wish to do
With whatever is left of me.

My bread giver!
A 'No' on my lips?
How is it possible?

Love?
That's not your cup of tea.

Harbhajan Singh

Harbhajan Singh (1920–2002) was born in Lumding, Assam. A literary critic, thinker and poet, his creative world was vast. A modern poet of the post-progressive movement, he used sarcasm effectively and highlighted the pettiness of human nature in his poetry. He expressed the complexities of human emotions with ease. Besides the Soviet Land Nehru Award, he also won the Sahitya Akademi award for his book *Na Dhuppe, Na Chhaven* in 1970. He also received the Kabir Samman (1987), the Saraswati Samman (1994) and a fellowship from Sahitya Akademi.

I Fear

Every night, in the street, the stars and I sleep together,
Companions of each other's dull smoldering bodies
We are too shy to appear in each other's dreams
When every morning the newspaper-vendor wakes me up
I know that the sun has visited my home
All the stars have been swept away,
Next is my turn, I am quite sure.

When the broom strokes the back of the street
I know life will soon pick up its speed
I wake up lest I should shatter into pieces
And am scattered all around like smithereens;
Or should get stuck in someone's sharp forked gaze,
A small piece of naked and half-ripe flesh, which nobody will eat
Nor would anybody save me from impalement.

My door opens like a yawn
I throw myself into the house from the street
The stuffy house becomes my covering
I am always stark naked in the open
My wife sweeps the floor
And throws the garbage out in the street,
I fear
Lest my wife should see me.

A Man Without a Head

I was there
When the naked sword in your hand,

Writhed in pain;
When the swelling, smoldering fair
Shrunk into silence like a dead dried pond,
Barren land like silence stretched to the horizon,
So barren was it
That even a single breath could not grow there.

I was there
When you uttered your amber-like words:
'Offer me a head; if someone has one.'
I was there
Sitting like a man without a head on his shoulders.
Something within me stood up instinctively
Like a sudden wave
And then quietened like a still river.
I was not more than a thin line
But for my physical existence, I was nothing.
I was there like a stump
Which, but for four feet from the ground,
Was wholly cut down and felled.
A sense of disgust and shame overwhelmed me
There was no shade over my head, not even my own.

I was there
When your sharp gaze
Pierced through my empty self
Something like the sun you had set in my inner being
My inner self was restless in its light.
I asked myself—
Is it my head on my shoulders
Or a sham—
Which I can show, but cannot use?
Am I really myself or somebody else?
Am I a man sitting in the presence of my Guru

Or a woman,
Who left her home to go somewhere
Carrying an additional organ on her body?
But in broad daylight, in front of everybody
That organ shattered,
Her unadorned truth revealed unto all
My own existence became a burden to me
And the burden of the silence of the fair
Mocked me.

I was there again
When the miracle happened.
That incredible man was sitting next to me
Who readily gave away his head;
With extreme humility, he placed his head at your feet.

Seeing the magic
The inert sword in your hand
Also shook for a moment.
Those, who have the courage to make sacrifices,
Do not need a sword.

The courageous man placed his head
At your feet with such ease and grace
The way dawn places the young sun
At the feet of the sky.

I was startled!
My soul shook a little
To emerge from the interstices of my being,
The spellbound fair
Shook a little before it was stunned;
The silence mumbled for a while
And fell asleep again.

Ahmed Rahi

Ahmed Rahi (1923–2002) was born in Amritsar. He was a professional writer who wrote more than four dozen films. He wrote songs for several Punjabi and Urdu films. It is believed that he penned around 1900 songs in his life. He was an active member of the Progressive Writers' Club in Pakistan, and was closely associated with Faiz Ahmed Faiz. His writings have the spontaneity and simplicity of folk songs. He lamented the pain of partition in his anthology titled *Trinjan*. He died in Lahore.

You, Who Have Homes

O friends, you live in your home,
I have come home like a visitor.

> You are fortunate to live in your homes
> I have come home like a guest.

Buried in this land
My mother is like a haunting call of time.

> My tears have turned to water
> My hopes have crumpled.

Like a lonely tree on the bank of a river
I bear the heat and sway.

> I search my mother's grave
> And look for my kin's remains.

You are in your homes
I am homeless ... I am a foreigner.

> You hugged me, smiling
> I cried and consoled myself.

Dim stars once again sparkled in the sky
Hopes, that I had forgotten, came to fruition.

    May my city live forever! May its people live forever!
    I, the foreigner, shower my blessings on you.

'You may see,
    My hands are empty,
I take nothing along
    When I go from here...'[6]

Jaswant Singh Neki

Jaswant Singh Neki (1925–2015) was born in Mureed in Jhelum district (now Pakistan). He was a renowned psychologist. A multi-faceted personality, he wrote robust and assertive poetry on psychological issues and mystic intellectual poetry; sometimes, he comes across as a religious poet following the tradition of Bhai Veer Singh. He juxtaposes religion with science. Instead of showing dominance of one over the other, he is keen to learn from all sources. His real strength is his inquisitive mind. He also wrote prose. He won the Sahitya Akademi award for his anthology of poetry titled *Karuna di Chhoh Ton Magron* in 1979.

Ordeal

Here are my words, you may test them if you wish;
Throw them on a stone and check their clinking sound
If they are genuine or not—
Test them in the market, my dear friend!

Look at my deep intent;
Sift it in your winnowing eyes,

---

[6] The last two lines allude to *Heer* by Waris Shah.

Whatever chaff is in my gaze
Blow it away in the wind, my dear friend!

Here are my actions, rub them hard,
Throw some water on them,
If you find even a grain of dust
Wash it away beating hard on a stone, my dear friend!

Here are my emotions. Give them
The wick of the pain of separation,
If they burn, throw their ash
In the fields, my dear friend!

From dust, test my body made of dust
From winds, the breath
From dew drops, you may test my tears
Throw this existence in the pyre, my dear friend!

Let there be only one ordeal
Let the whole world tremble with fear
Let the four elements challenge me
My faith fears nothing, my dear friend!

I ask for my test
Whilst the world escapes and seeks shelter;
Is there any god
Who undergoes an ordeal, my dear friend?

TARA SINGH

Tara Singh (1929–1993) was born in Hookran, Hoshiarpur. Many of his major works were written in a humorous strain. He occupies an important position in the history of Punjabi literature. In his times, on the one hand, there was the tradition of Mohan Singh and Amrita

Pritam, and on the other, of experimental poetry of Jasbir Singh Ahluwalia and Ravinder Ravi. Tara Singh placed himself in the middle of these two traditions.

Don't Light Candles

Why do you light candles on the parapet?
Let hot winds cross these lanes first.

Blotches of embarrassment mark the doors, let them be
There are signs of blemished politics, let them be
Generations to come shall blame us for our deeds of today
There are some burnt-out-lamps in the houses, let them be
Where would you go? All sides are stained with blood
Why do you light candles on the parapet?

Spare the place besmeared with pure blood
Let there be some names engraved on the walls
Let there be some fields echoing with innocent cries
Let there be some villages that fell to conspiracies
Do not look for blooming flowers, it is autumn still
Do not light candles on the parapet.

Let dried blood come off the swords first
Let anger shake off phoney thoughts
Houses that have marks of blood on them
Let those marks vanish from the walls first
All fragrances sweet are smothered by the dark times' fret
Do not light candles on the parapet yet.

Where words and debates have lost their might
Both the sword and the scabbard've turned absurd
Such winds have blown, I've seen with my own eyes
Friends, who loved you once, are no longer with you
Listen to me, those winds haven't stopped yet,
Do not light candles on the parapet
Let hot winds cross these lanes first.

The Bull Beneath the Earth[7]

You haven't heard it yet
But the whole world knows,
The bull beneath the earth
Is missing.

That's why the earth shakes,
The government speaks only on radio,
Gigantic lies resound in the parliament;
People seek refuge in gurudwaras
And search for solace in scriptures,
The ruler moves amidst high security
From his duty he is constantly slipping;
The bull beneath the earth
Is missing.

That's why offices do not function, they only open
That's why officers are always late;
That's why bribes are common,
That's why workers starve
And their condition worsens;
The container craves for flour,
And instead of feeding people
Flour eats human flesh
What incongruity!
The bull beneath the earth
Is missing.

That's why people eat chicken and drink whisky
Instead of arguments, shoes are hurled in parliament,
In foreign countries, 'Hey Ram' works

---

[7] It refers to a mythic bull. It is believed that the bull bears the burden of the earth on its back and horns. The idea of a mythic bull is similarly present in Islamic mythology. Kujata is the name of a mythic bull in Islamic mythology that carries the angel on its back who shoulders the earth.

In India, it is somebody's reference,
Criminals are more influential
It is wealth, whisky and flesh
Everybody is worshipping;
The bull beneath the earth
Is missing.

People say that politicians have duped us
The custodians of faith have betrayed us
Traders, poets and singers have failed us
Scholars, artists and heroes have depleted it
The wise or the stupid have harmed it
Everybody is accused of stealing;
The bull beneath the earth
Is missing.

Gurcharan Rampuri

Gurharan Rampuri (1929-2018) was born in Rampur in Ludhiana district. Later, he moved to Canada. A progressive poet, he had been writing poetry since 1944. He has been translated into English by American English scholar Amritjit Singh under the title *The Circle of Illusion*. Rampuri's work has also been included in an anthology of Punjabi poetry published in Russian.

Words

Kindly return words their old meanings
Words have been plundered;
Some 'gentlemen' have ransacked their homes.

These poor, harmless and wounded words—
Loud cries of 'scholars' and lewd lies of politicians
Have made them numb forever.

Taking off a poor man's clothes,
They are rather given
Fascinating, frightening masks to wear.

In this village, simple honourable words
Are rendered homeless,
They have even lost their identity.

Somebody should return their clothes
A self-respecting man does not wear discards,
Even if it belongs to a king.

Mannu Bhai

Mannu Bhai or Munir Ahmed Qureshi (1933–2018) was born in Wazirabad, Pakistan. He is a poet, translator and playwright. He wrote many TV serials for Pakistan TV. Under the influence of Javed Shaheen, he became a Marxist. He was greatly influenced by the ideas of Trotsky. He also admired South African revolutionary thinker, Ted Grant. He was unhappy with poverty in Pakistan as well as some political leaders of the country, whom he was openly critical of.

Those Wonderful Times

Those were wonderful times!
If we were hungry
We would simply demand;
If we got it
We would eat it;
If didn't,
We would cry;
Crying, we would fall asleep.

These are strange times now!
We do feel hungry,

But we cannot demand;
If we get it
We cannot eat it;
If we don't get it
We cannot cry;
If we don't cry, we can't sleep.

Rauf Sheikh

Rauf Sheikh (b. 1934) expresses his views on society, the role of money, the pace of modern life through his poetry. Through striking images he conveys the conflict between money and love. 'Where coins are minted, love cannot grow' exemplifies the conflict he expresses in his poetry.

Ghazal

Which emotion should I hide? What should I articulate?
How can I be a foe to them whom I've loved the most?

Every new face looks more innocent than the former
Who should I doubt now, and who should I trust?

We equally share the heritage which belongs to us all
Why raise a wall over a trifle that matters least?

I wish on this earth, burning with atrocities and lies,
I should spread love all over the world and let its pain placate.

My soul trembled initially while crossing the threshold of morality
Now nothing shakes within me whichever line I may thwart.

Corruption has become the order of the day
A crane is called a flock; sometimes the flock, the crane.

They cannot tolerate each other while living in the same house
The more I think about it, the more confused I get.

Intelligent people do not commit the same mistake twice
How can I, in public, my foolishness accept?

Rauf says, waking up those in slumber is not a difficult task
How can I wake up those who are already alert?

Sohan Singh Meesha

Sohan Singh Meesha (1934–1985) was born in Bhet, Kapurthala State (Punjab). He is an important modern poet. While defining his poetic cult, he distanced himself from both of the important literary movements prevailing his time – the progressive movement and the romantic movement. He is sometimes called an anti-romantic poet. As a poet, he dedicated his life to writing about the common man. His work occasionally exhibits sarcasm and dramatic elements. His book *Kach De Vastar* was given the Sahitya Akademi award in 1977.

A Loud Cry

Do you remember the story of Nandu—the bachelor
Who was granted permission
By the village council
To deliver one or two loud cries
In the wee hours every morning?
When he made this humble request—
'I have no rivals in this village
Every woman of the village is like my sister or mother
Only when I am drunk
My heart swells up,
A strange uneasiness overpowers me;

I can't smother it, however hard I may try
A cry comes out unwittingly.'

Even if
I don't find liquor in the cruel city too often
I live here silently
Holding a cry tight inside me,
Quietly, I carry a storm inside me.
So many times
Listening to a speech during elections,
When the crowd was singing the national anthem,
Or in the silence of a condolence meeting
I wanted to cry out aloud,
But I smothered the cry surging inside me.

During weekly meetings
In the office
When a cryptic argument
Was presented in a dramatic fashion
I choked the cry rising inside
Tightening my neck-tie a little more.

Every new month
On payday
Strangulating simple wishes
Swallowing my pain, enduring it silently
I almost drank my own blood
When I asked my son to wait for another month
For a new pair of shoes,
Every time I postponed the cry rising in me.
When in the next cabin
A gossip session was in progress
Thinking of hardships and bitterness
While opening a soda bottle,
I felt as if I were tearing apart.

This way and that
I chewed on my cry
With the betel leaf and a pinch of tobacco,
I put my cry to sleep with tranquilisers,
And sometimes, I pacified it with the aroma of bodies.

But now
I can no longer hold it back.
It resists my endurance
And overpowers my senses,
It pricks me from inside
And doesn't let me sleep at night.
Now I wish,
Tomorrow,
While standing at the Gandhi Chowk,
Near the judicial court
I should give vent to my anger
Bottled up for a long time.
I should send out a loud cry
Taking the stick from the smiling Gandhi's statue
I should bring it down hard on my head.

Drenched with my own blood
I should fall at the feet of the statue
And say Rama once or twice
Before I die.

Jagtar

Jagtar (1935–2010) was born in Rajgumal, Jallandhar district. Besides poetry, he also wrote literary criticism and research papers. He was also an editor and a translator. He began his poetic career as a progressive poet. He wrote experimental poetry and in the later phase of his career, he was sympathetic to the Naxalite movement. However, the poetry written in the last phase of his life is relatively mild. He did not indulge in sloganeering through art. His poetry is marked with seriousness and deep thought. He was awarded the Sahitya Akademi for his work *Jugnu, Diva Te Dariya* in 1995.

Shackles on Every Foot

There are shackles on every foot, there is darkness at every step
You should marvel at our courage, yet we stop not.

How long can the clay remain silent
How long will my blood boil not?

I am an inscription on stone, not a script on the sand
The more they erased me, the deeper I went; I vanished not.

On the pages of history, on the wings of time
Your name is written with fingers in blood-ink dipped.

Your memory cuts through the thick jungle of pain
Like glow-worms it lights up a dark cave.

Droplets

The season of autumn.
Naked branches of trees.
Rain has just stopped.
Tiny little droplets
Dangle on naked branches.
The gravitational pull;
And branches stretching themselves.
Strong piercing wind is
Shaking the tree,
At every step
As they come closer to each other
The death of a droplet is certain.

Existence of other droplets
Has become an unbearable burden—
Every droplet is wary of the other.

What times are these!
We, like chameleon,
Pretend to show what we are not;
Skittish of the other's existence
Crucified on the cross of time
We are like droplets.

Harbhajan Hundal

Harbhajan Hundal (1934–2023) was born in Lyallpur (now known as Faisalabad in Pakistan). He was a prolific writer. Besides poetry, he wrote an autobiography and many sketches. He was the editor of *Chirag*, a quarterly literary magazine. A staunch Marxist, and a bold progressive poet, he used poetry to inspire people to stand against capitalism. A fierce critic of communalism and narrow nationalism, he believed in establishing a dialogue with people. He felt that modern poetry is disconnected from the common people. He wrote about political issues in simple language. He translated Hikmet, Pablo Neruda, Brecht and Lorca into Punjabi.

Poesy and People

Poesy!
No one shall visit you—
Neither a worker
Nor a shopkeeper
Nor the one who parches grain
Nor a loyal servant.

You will have to reach out
To listen to their grief

To tell them your sorrows
And to share common heaves of sighs.

They don't have time
To sit by your side;
They don't have time
To show their hunger-stricken shrunk bellies
Lifting up their *kurta*;
They don't have time
To solve complications
To know mysteries.

You will have to go
To them
To their menial wards
To their heaths and furnaces
To their courtyards
To the meeting points of their Panchayat
And their shops.

If you don't wish to go to them
Let it be so
You can sit comfortably in your glass palaces
On cushioned seats
Switching on your room-coolers.

People will manage to live without you
Singing folk songs
Playing popular music on cassettes
Enjoying vulgar songs on TV
Crying and wailing.

If you wish to bloom like a rose
If you wish to dance like a butterfly
If you wish to sing like a koel
If you wish to drop the way a mango drops from a tree
If you wish to be filled with juice like sugarcane

If you wish to swing freely like a flag
Then you will have to go
To your audience
To your connoisseurs.

If you go, you shall live;
If not,
May god help you!

Shiv Kumar Batalvi

Shiv Kumar Batalvi (1937–1973) is one of the most popular and well-known Punjabi poets. He was born in Lohtian, Sialkot (Pakistan). As a poet, he was independent of all literary movements and different from his contemporaries. His rustic vocabulary and fresh images made him stand out. The pain of separation constitutes the central emotion in his poetry. He was exceedingly critical of traditional customs and values in the society. He commented on the condition of women in a patriarchal society in an inimitable style in his poetry. He attacked the values of his time in his verse-play, *Loona*, which won him the Sahitya Akademi in 1967. The excerpt below is from his work *Loona*.

My Father Did Me Wrong

My father did me wrong
He committed a sin
He tied my lot with Salwan, a withered flower,
Who had conjugal pleasures with Ichhran;
I am of Puran's age, though
I am made his mother now.
I am not much older to him
He is only a kiss away.
How can I be his mother?
He is not born to me.

Friends, I am rather
Like Salwan's daughter.

When a man espouses a girl
Of his daughter's age
People find no shame in it,
If Loona loves Puran,
Why does the world
Call her a fallen woman?

Let people call Loona a fallen woman
If she trifles, if she flirts;
But, if her parents do not find her a fit match
A match that matches her age
What is wrong
If she finds herself a fitting match?
People may call Loona a fallen woman
If she is married to someone she loves,
Yet she philanders.
Her soul is not blemished,
She is as pure as *kanjak*
Only Loona knows this.

Friends, give me not words of wisdom
How can I tell you what wrings my heart?
How can Loona be discreet
If she is not granted
A matching passion?

Desire lasts until you are cremated
Its fire leads you to the light
It lasts till it burns itself
Youth knows no other relation,
But of desire and passion.

Friends, this luminous body of mine
When it sleeps on the smoldering bed

I smell foul to myself,
The pain of such a moment
No one else can know.

The ecstasy of the conjugal moment is greater than heaven's bliss;
Besmeared with a fragrance sweet
Bathed in a pond of wine
That moment of pleasure extreme
Only a rare one enjoys in one's lifetime.

But when that moment reaches me
A Loona within this Loona dies,
The bed of Salwan
Pricks me like thorns,
Nor do I enjoy that moment with him.

When that moment smolders in my body
Snakes crawl in my head
Friends, I feel
My womb rips apart,
I sift my dreams
From the dust of my body.

Trees

Some trees are like sons to me
Some trees are like mothers
Some trees are like daughters and
Some are like daughters-in-law;
Some trees are like brothers to me
Some are like my grandfather
With leaves rare on the boughs
Some are like grandmother's embrace
Offering *choori* to the crows.

Some trees are like friends to me
Some trees I wish to hug and kiss

One is like my dear beloved
Sweet, yet pain-giving;
Some trees I wish to play with
Lifting them on my shoulders,
Some trees I wish to kiss and die
Some trees will always swing together
Even when tough winds blow.

All trees have the verdure tongue
I wish to pen down what they say
If ever I am born again
I wish to be born a tree
If you wish me to sing you a song ever
I wish to sing through trees
Trees to me are like my mother
May their shade live forever!

Ravinder Ravi

Ravinder Ravi (b. 1937) was born in Sialkot, now in Pakistan. He taught in schools in India, Kenya and Canada. Besides writing poetry, he has also written many plays, stories and travelogues, some of which are included in academic curricula. He expresses his experiences in a unique way and through original imagery. He also addresses global issues in his poetry. The authenticity of his experience, its fearless expression, simplicity and poetic expanse make him a fascinating writer.

The Void in Relations

We are awake in the nightclubs
And asleep at homes,
Our time does not follow the sun
Our time follows us.

As we close our eyes
The night falls,
Dreams enter
The colourful world of dreams.

High on drugs
We are lost in the world of fantasy
We are so full of ourselves
That we are lost in our own clutter.
Spreading, shrinking, rising
In the void of meaningless relationships
We are nothing, but only ourselves—
Empty and hollow!

We don't belong to the world
Even while being present in the world.

Navtej Bharti

Navtej Bharti (b. 1938) was born in Rodey, Faridkot district. He moved to Canada in 1966. Along with his brother, Ajmer Rode, he wrote a full-length poetic work *Leela*, which is deemed an important text of Punjabi literature. Navtej Bharti is among those diaspora poets who, instead of longing for the homeland, consider the entire world as their home. Prof. Prem Prakash has beautifully described his poetry as: 'There is no bitterness or anger in Bharti's poetry, rather his poetry is subtle, philosophical and is marked with the freshness of aesthetics.' Navtej Bharti writes in English as well.

A Poem in Three Parts

As soon as a man realizes that
The woman has begun to see
He blindfolds her;
As soon as a woman begins to see

Also begins her curse
But she can still see
There are eyes on her entire body
When man is dazzled by her beauty
And lost in her body
She is still awake
Woman is consciousness
Awakened in her entire body.

Ahilya

A woman can still manage to laugh.
Even now?
He wondered;
But woman
Is beyond all boundaries of man's world
When she laughs
She does not merely open her mouth
She opens her world too.

Shoorpnakha

Woman is beyond
Both—the world and the renunciation
She is eternally in the state of *samadhi*
She doesn't have to undergo
Arduous meditation for self-realisation
She is eternally awake
For, like earth, she also creates.

Yashodha

Mohanjit

Mohanjit (1938–2024) was born in Adliwala, Amritsar district. He was a poet, critic, translator and editor. He showed lifelong commitment to progressive and experimental poetry. The simplicity of his language, spontaneity of expression, prosody, imagery, and depth of subjects made him stand out among other poets. According to Satinder Noor, every word in his work expands like a sign and has multiple layers of signification.

Walking is a Must

Come! Sit down!
Please wait for a couple of moments
For I am in conversation with the breeze,
With the morning, with the evening and the night spread quietly
And with everything that we can see
Yet beyond our reach.

I wonder
What is the relation between a flower and its fragrance?
The mind and time?
Love is everywhere alike
Why does the pain of friendship sting?

Does it mean I should stand still
Like a mountain
Like an eternal waiting;
Or should I
Flow like a river
Like the breath of time?

How can you know
Where the beginning is
And where is the end?
How can you know the Fundamental—
Its beginning and its end?

If you are concerned with the path,
Then it is imperative to walk—
Walking is a must.

Sant Ram Udaasi

Sant Ram Udaasi (1939–1986) was born in Raisar, Sangrur. He is a famous poet of the Naxalite movement in Punjab. He addresses his reader directly in colloquial language. Under the influence of communist ideology, he raises his voice aloud against profiteers, capitalism, feudalism and industrialists. To strengthen his message, he incorporates Sikh history in his poetry. He also views women as fighters, and includes them in the struggle of the working class. Owing to the rich musicality of his poetry, his poems have often been sung publicly.

To August, the Fifteenth

We have broken the shackles of slavery
We have endured the endless pain
Tell the people who rule now
Pawn not our country once again.

Imperial traders wait to strike
Friendship, based on money, always fails
Tell the dark night not to fight against the light
And not to cause stress or strain;
Tell the people who rule now
Pawn not our country once again.

The more you trust, the deeper you are stabbed.
The more we sought out a cure, the sicker we returned
No one should offer us such a cure again;
Tell the people who rule now
Pawn not our country once again.

The machine that belches fire pretends to follow Buddha,
It murders our rights, soiling the hands with blood
Tell it not to enter our blood or brain;

Ask the people who rule now
Pawn not our country once again.

The workers have woken up now, and also the farmers
All deceit should end, that's the demand of the hour
No one should curtail our rights again;
Tell the people who rule now
Pawn not our country once again.

Raising the voice high, workers speak aloud
We'll claim our share of freedom, it is avowed
No one should place any obstacles yet again;
Tell the people who rule now
Pawn not our country once again.

A Call to the Farmers

The friends of the summer crop
The friends of the winter crop
Sharpen your sickles,
Pick up your hammers
Break the breasts of stones
For today, it is embers that we need.

Why on the golden skirt of wheat
Are spread
Shreds of the smut of disease.
Sturdy stalks and sharp spikes
Shall pierce the chest of
What sickens the wheat.
A new age of awareness is ushered in
Protect your grain, guard your yield
Do not trust the idlers
Who do nothing,
But suck our blood and amass gains.
A sea of peasants and workers surges
Give them their due and let them go.
We cannot bear their agony

Their soaring cries and stinging sighs.
Do not beg of these rishis – the rich and the haves
You cannot borrow laughter.
Pick up your hammers
Break the breasts of stones
For today, it is embers that we need.

If we begin to lose our grain
Who will then hold the world?
If we ask a dead moon for moonlight
Who will call us wise?
Come! Let's show the new sun
How the assault on our share of the sunlight was made.
Pick up your hammers;
Break the breasts of stones
For today, it is embers that we need.

Ajaib Singh Hundal

Ajaib Hundal (b. 1939) was born and grew up in Verka; later, he moved to Amritsar. His journey from the village to the city is of becoming and unbecoming, which he expresses skillfully in his poetry. He has written on the theme of a daughter who is absent in her presence and is present in her absence. As a lawyer, he would daily come across stories of suffering and become a witness of their being in a state of eternal limbo, like *Trishanku*. That's why he doesn't spend his evenings listening to *ghazals* sung by Jagjit Singh but heeding to cries rising from a lace dupatta.

Dupattas *with Lace*

She wanted to remove the *mangalsutra*[8]
She was wearing around her neck.

---

[8] In Hindu culture, a necklace that only married women wear.

I said to her
Every *mangalsutra* is like that
It feels strange in the beginning.

She said:
'But this *mangalsutra* feels strange even after ten years.'

Pointing at her dress, I said again:
'Those who wish to remove their *mangalsutra*
Do not wear *dupattas* with gold or silver lace.'

She said:
'It is outrageous
To bear a *mangalsutra* around the neck
To wear *dupattas* with gold or silver lace.
I have been counting for years
Legs of the chairs in the court room
I have been seeing
Mangalsutra and lace *dupattas*
Tied to benches.

I do not spend my evenings
Listening to ghazals sung by Jagjit Singh,
My evenings are spent
Heeding cries rising from a lace-edged *dupatta,*
My day does not begin
With the newspaper vendor's call
Rather it begins with the knocking of a *mangalsutra.*
I always think
While going to the court and
Coming back home
What kind of chairs are lying in the courts?
Benches do not have four legs
What sort of benches are these?

Mangalsutra tied to them
Are dying for the necks of their choice,

And *dupattas* tied to them
Are dying for the heads of their choice.'

Ajmer Rode

Ajmer Rode (b. 1940) was born in Rodey, Faridkot. Along with his brother, Navtej Bharti, he has produced the famous work, *Leela*. Besides poetry, he has written drama and prose, and is also a translator. He is considered to be the founder of Punjabi theatre in Canada. He writes simple poetry addressing issues of humanity. Gifted with a wide intellectual horizon, he doesn't perceive human beings in narrow frames. His poems include ideas from science and philosophy making his poetry stand out.

A Notice to the Man

The Machine has sent
A notice to the Man
Would you run me, or
Should I run you?

The Man
Has bought some time
From the Machine
To think over the issue.

Gurumel

Gurumel Sidhu (1940–2022) was born in Paasla, Jallandhar. He was a scientist and a professor of Genetics and Biotechnology at California State University. Writing as a humanist, his poetry combines emotions with rationality. While residing in America, his mind dwelt on Punjab. The following lines convey his concern about increasing pollution in Punjab: 'It has dripped drop by drop, the dirty water of towns and villages/The clean water of five rivers of Punjab, has turned red ochre.'

Mind

For a minute
Look deep within yourself
If at the door of your mind,
Any frightened, scared wish
Sits timidly
And crawls,
Or an innocent word
Is losing its meaning,
Or an aborted desire
Is crying itself to death.

Sometimes, a lot
Intended, unintended
Burns inside;
Or a man dies every moment
Lying on the thorny bed of time.

Mind is really a horrible thing.

SATINDER SINGH NOOR

Satinder Singh Noor (1940–2011) was born in Kotkapura in Faridkot district. He was an established critic of Punjabi literature. His first book of poetry came out in 1970. He took twenty-five years to bring out his second book. He has written extensively on love and poetics. His poetry has tranquility and is rich in aesthetics. His work on criticism titled *Kavita di Bhoomika* was awarded the Sahitya Akademi prize in 2011.

In My Country

In my country
Every prostitute has a name
Salma, Rukhsana, Hussaina, Alam Ara
Or any other Muslim name.
She looks at you
As if offering apologies for the mistakes of the past,
She is now inviting men to ravish her.

I, in the city of Dushyant,
Listening to *ghazals* and *dadra*,[9]
Too became acquainted with Hussaina.
I said unwittingly
If there is a good singer, it has to be a Muslim girl.
Listening to me,
Hussaina said instantaneously,
'No, no...
I was brought here from Punjab
My name is Jamuna
This is Rukmani and that one is Meera.'

When I heard of Alam Ara
In the city of Kalidasa
And reached his magnificent palace
Decked with sandalwood,
While seeing me off
She whispered to me,
'Come again...
My real name is Urvashi,
That beautiful girl is Shakuntala,
And she...'
While climbing down the stairs
I said,
'I know. Her name must be Kamla.

---

[9] *Dadra* is a form of light classical singing in Hindustani music.

My name is Siddharth
I am in a hurry.
Yashoda and Rahul are waiting for me
At home.'

Dr. S. Tarsem

Dr. S. Tarsem (1942–2019) was born in Tapa, Sangrur. He began losing his eyesight in his childhood, and by the age of thirty, had lost his vision completely. He fought against all odds, including poverty. He wrote almost two dozen books. His oeuvre includes short stories, an autobiography and poetry. The *ghazal* has been his primary form of self-expression. A Marxist since his early days, the issues of peace, communal harmony, love, unity, social justice and class conflict are closer to his heart. In 2000, he was given the Millennium award by the All India Confederation of the Blind.

Ghazal

Not ventilators, nor windows, nor doors he makes
Now it's only chairs, every carpenter of my city makes.

One makes beds and the other makes biers
But there is one person who only flutes makes.

Neither is there any Sun, nor any rain, why then
Everyman for himself an umbrella makes?

We're bothered so much about future, even when a child plays
Sometimes he makes a house; sometimes a boat he makes.

Look how a painter uses his eyes these days
Sometimes a desert, sometimes an ocean or lightning he makes.

Imagine what he would undergo when
A bier of someone dear to him he makes.

Tell the gardener to go, we can water our garden,
If the fragrance of flowers his puppets he makes

When in the evening Tarsem sees flowers in bloom
A butterfly fluttering in his heart, gladly he makes.

Harbhajan Halwarvi

Harbhajan Halwarvi (1943–2000) was born in Halwara in Ludhiana district. He has written travelogues and prose. He was the editor of *Punjabi Tribune*. During the phase of Naxalism in Punjab, he had to remain underground. He was an ardent supporter of the ideology of protest and struggle, but his poetry was never loud. Despite his circumstances, he did not relinquish his commitment to Marxism and optimism. He never lost hope in human relationships, and believed in building new bridges and transcending borders through poetry.

Bridges

Rivers are the blood streams
Of the sturdy body of the earth,
In their waters are the cells of life
Flowed and lost on the sands of time,
But the signs of generations
The signs of civilisations
Earth, Life and Rivers
Can never be separated.

Whichever river it may be
Ganga, Brahmputra, Kaveri
Satluj, Ravi or Chenab
There is no difference
The water is one
Yet they flow independently,

Separately
Like men,
Who despite having red blood in common,
Are unique.

Flourishing on the banks of a river
Water that joins everybody,
Separates them too;
There are humans on this side of the bank
There are humans on the other side too.
The gap between two banks of the river
Like magnetic waves
Creates a pull;
Unknown people living on this side
Crave for the other
Using their arms, or boats
Or sometimes bridges;
Bridges connect two banks of a river.

Ravinder Bhathal

Ravinder Bhathal (b. 1943) was born in Mahila, Sangrur. Deeply imbued with Punjabi culture, his free poetry expresses the sentiment of the common man in a simple diction. In the age of globalization, his poetry calls for old Punjabi values. His poetry laments the loss of innocence of the rural people of Punjab crushed under the weight of modernity. Bhattal weaves the pain of modernity with the folklore of Punjab, which he presents mixing it with the melody of the Malwa dialect of Punjabi.

I Do Not Write Poetry

I do not write poetry
I only give meaning

To the innocent lisping
Meaningless sounds
Made by a child,
I translate into words
A child's smile,
His cries from behind the door
And his moans.

I only give
Cloak of words to dreams
Beaming in the eyes of a lover,
Desire and cravings on the lips,
Emotions throbbing in the heart,
I do not write poetry.

I only
Become a witness to
Vanishing water,
A drying bough,
A tale of scattering vows,
An unsaid prayer,
An unacknowledged copy
Of what I feel and see,
I do not write poetry.

I only
Try to weave into my lines
The worker's dream for a better future,
An innocent girl's fondness for picking words,
Writhing motherhood in dry breasts,
Someone tired of truthfulness,
Sobs of a humble innocent man,
I do not write poetry.

Poetry to me
Is not the merry jingling of anklets,

It is like the blood
Drying drop by drop in the human heart,
It is like an untimely cry
Rising from a painful heart,
It is like a long wait
Of a loyal wedded wife turned into stone,
I do not write poetry.

It is like a
Feeble whimper of pain
Rising from a dry throat,
It is like the heat of the soul
Emanating from fingertips,
It is like a long wait
For good times stuck in the breath,
I do not write poetry.

I only
Make an attempt
To give a form to
The fundamental human emotion of pain,
Tears falling from the eyes,
I try to draw
The heat of human suffering on a paper,
Blaming a few culprits
I try to abate human pain,
I do not write poetry.

Fakhar Zamaan

Fakhar Zamaan (b. 1943) was born in Gujrat district in Pakistan. He has written fiction, drama and poetry. A trilingual poet, he writes in English, Urdu and Punjabi, but Punjabi is his favoured language. He started a movement in support of Punjabi in Pakistan and has vociferously criticized the imposition of restrictions on the people of Pakistan. For this reason, his magazines, *The Wise, Baazgasht* and *Vangar* were banned. His novel *Bandiwan* was published by UNESCO. Many of his novels have been translated into various languages of the world. He was the Minister of Culture in the government of Benazir Bhutto. He was given the award of Sitara-e-Imtiaz in 1994 and Hilal-e-Imtiaz in 2008. He held the office of the Chairperson, Pakistan Academy of Letters. He has also been honoured by the Government of India.

A Sparrow in the Drawing Room

Close all exits
Shut all doors, windows and ventilators
Do not let it sit for a moment
It will get tired and automatically fall.

Brittle Relations

Everything has broken down
Bangles, Dreams and Glass!

Once broken, they cannot be fixed
Bangles, Dreams and Glass!

Lal Singh Dil

Like Sant Ram Udaasi and Paash, Lal Singh Dil (1943–2007) is also a poet of protest. He was born in a Dalit family at Ghungrali, a village in Ludhiana district. He worked as a daily wager, a watchman, farm labourer and a cook to earn his livelihood. He also ran a tea stall. During the Naxalite movement, he emerged as a major poet from Punjab. His strong assertion of his caste identity in his struggle makes him a unique poet. As recorded in one of his letters, he embraced

Islam in 1973. Unlike Paash, he never used explicit political language in his poetry.

Prostitutes

Friends
You may think poorly of me
As much as you want,
But these prostitutes
Are my sisters, mothers and daughters
And yours too;
They are the mothers, daughters and sisters
Of Hindustan that worships cows,
They are the mothers, daughters and sisters
Of Bharat that worships non-violence and Buddha,
They are the sisters, mothers and daughters
Of great priests and worshippers.

If not,
Then they are
The mothers, daughters and sisters
Of some impending revolution.

We, the Great Wrestlers,
We tie up our loincloths in the morning
To fight hunger and poverty.
Endless permutations and combinations is our exercise.
Our moves are intriguing—
Instead of speaking up, we become silent
Instead of drinking water, we die of thirst
Instead of taking food, we take vows to fight until eternity
Placing our knees on the neck of the opponent
We can defeat any big name in the world of wrestling,
But we live the life of a donkey slogging in the field;
Yet we, the Great Wrestlers,
Tie up our loincloths in the morning.

A Poem

It always remained a dream
That we would place the prisoner's cap
On the heads of the so-called honourable men,
We will make them yield and crawl
They will stand accountable to us.

On the other hand,
The marching feet of anti-revolution
Stood fast on our chests,
Perhaps
Only humiliation
Was written in our destiny.

Ahmed Salim

Ahmed Salim (1945–2023) was born in Gondal, Bahaudin (now in Pakistan). He cherished progressive ideas and supported friendship between India and Pakistan. He is said to be the poet of united Punjab. Only he could have written the poem 'Sada Jiye Bangladesh' while staying in Pakistan. For his political views, he was sent to jail.

Wagha

There are flowers between us
    A wall is a wall even if it is of flowers,
There are letters between us that we exchange
    Which awaken the pain of separation in us,
There are tears between us that blur our vision
    We cannot see each other's face,
There is pain that spreads
    Like a desert between us,

Though there is also love between us
    Wagha makes us two from one.
So, my dear mean friend!
    I wish to hate you
    Hug you
    And cry...

Surjit Patar

Surjit Patar (1945–2024), an important contemporary poet, was born in Pattar Kalan, Jallandhar district in 1945. He wrote *ghazal, nazm* and *geet*. His themes are love, the crisis of Punjab and duplicity in human nature. As a poet, he sang gently about unrequited love among the middle-class. His poetic sensibility established a new complexion of Punjabi poetry and language. According to Rajinder Pal Brar, 'His uniqueness lies in being a gentle lover. He is not a rebel lover, but a love-stricken poet.' He was given the Sahitya Akademi award for his work *Hanerey* in 1993.

Quivering Water

Once there was some quivering water
It died and turned to stone.

The second one, fearing this accident
Turned to stone.

The third was going to tell the tale
When another stone frowned at it;
And it also turned to stone.

Only a poet was left
Pulsating with sensitivity and quivering
He thought, 'So many stones!'

Counting the stones
He also turned to stone.

A Song

Earlier Waris Shah was divided
    Now it is Shiv Kumar's turn,
Since people have forgotten the old wounds
    New boils shall erupt now.

Without Sheikh Farid, even honey
    Is unsavory to me,
Without Kabir, even the vast horizon
    Looks lesser and tiny.

All that burns like a flame is mine
    I love all flames, light in all forms,
He to whom the sky was like a prayer-platter
    The Sun and the Moon were like the lighted lamps.
Stars were like pearls to him
    Day and night winds a circumambulate.[10]
Who has ruined that poem of the great poet
    By drawing a line?

Those who have turned their backs on their mother tongue
    And have gone afar
Shall live their entire lives
    Without its comforting shade.

Forsaking the deceptive warmth of the foreign tongue
    I am sure
One day they will return.

---

[10] This refers to the 'Aarti' composed by Guru Nanak

Beeba Balwant

Beeba Balwant (b. 1945) was born in Rurka, Ludhiana district, but he has been living in Gurdaspur for a long time. A painter, creative photographer and a theatre actor, he is primarily known as a poet. Images and painting occupy an important position in his poetry. Beeba's poetry expresses the pain and agony of humankind. His poetry is unique for its complexity, aesthetics, melody and freshness.

Incessant Battle

Khap Panchayat
Is not limited
To one area
It is present
In every house.

Khap Panchayat
Persuades
Frightens
Threatens
If you do not listen to it;
It can even kill you.

Khap Panchayat –
First mother
Then mother+father+rotten values
+all distant and close relations –
Warns you.

The battle has been going on
For a long time,
The battle will go on
For a long time to come.

Neither Heer Ranjha would die,
Nor would Qaidon.

Sain Akhtar Lahori

Sain Akhtar Lahori (n.d.) is a famous poet of West Punjab. Though he lives in Lahore, glimpses of the rural life of Punjab can be seen in his poetry. He is a disciple of Ustaad Daaman. His poetry is a blend of sarcasm and humour, which he has exploited to its fullest potential to raise issues of society, politics and religion.

Dear God, Come Down to the Earth

O God, come down on earth for once
Come down and look around,
Either give us the food we need
Or end this life, pain and misery abound.

If you too have daughters to marry off
Or have to offer dowry—
   that every maternal uncle gives to his niece,
Or you have to placate your angry sister
You would forget all pleasures with glory crowned;
O God, come down on earth for once
Come down and look around.

If you too have daughters, and
You have to bear the stinging comments of her in-laws
You would never sit with your relations—
   less of relations, more of rivals
If dust has eaten away your robes
And with insults you are wounded;
O God, come down on earth for once
Come down and look around.

If your granary too were empty
If you were to wear rags
If the fools were taken as wise in your world
You would lose your composure and calm;
O God, come down on earth for once
Come down and look around.

If your roofs were leaking
If your nights were spent drenched, sitting up
Watching the water drip
You too would lose your sense of time
In your house, grass would grow all around;
O God, come down on earth for once
Come down and look around.

Iqbal Ramoowalia

Iqbal Ramoowalia (1946–2017) was born in Ramoowal in Moga district. His father, Karnail Singh Paaras, was a famous *kavishar*. He inherited the tradition of writing and singing from his father. He sings about the pitiable condition of humans in industrialised cities. During the initial years of his poetic career, he was under the influence of Naxalism, which is evident from: 'Taking sickles in hands we cut ourselves in the heat/ And in the machines we sift ourselves,/That is also us, what comes to the market to be sold.' He wrote poetry, verse plays and fiction.

G. B. Road

Delhi is a strange city, my friends.
Billboards are safer
Than human lives.
You can have high-priced hotel rooms
And wear them on your sleeves.

In brothels on G.B. Road
Colourful fishes
Trapped in bright coloured bottles
Are for sale;
Lather like soft bodies,
Like tinkling marbles in the pocket,
Look tempting;
Delhi is a strange city, my friends.

Every man and woman is
More than a body here
The pen, the voice
And the musical instruments
Everything is for sale –
The law, the vote and the political party.
G. B. Road is not the only an ill-reputed part of the city,
The vile can also be found
In the police station, and its registers,
Vice is present in the drawers of the office-tables,
And in the spectacle of cross-examinations,
In the bags of the M.L.A.s,
In the chairs of the Lok Sabha.

Delhi is really a strange city, my friend!

Parminderjeet

Parminderjeet (1946–2015) was born in Jaura, Tarn Taran (now a district near Amritsar). Satinder Singh Noor, a famous critic, identified two recurrent images in his poetry: letters and journey. Parminderjeet sees humans as victims of their failures, fighting the battle of life alone. To negotiate with the loneliness, they need to connect with people, for which they need letters and journeys. Parminderjeet's poetry is poignant and profound.

The Bird of Ego

How high would you let your ego fly?
How long would you feed it?

Tired and worn out
One day the bird would eventually peck
Its own threshold
And spill the birdseed.

It cannot be domesticated
It is a bird of prey;
Violent and ferocious
It nips the hands that launch it;
Do not feed it with your blood.
Do not dote too much on it.

It is loyal
As long as its beak is moist with blood,
Beware!
It is carnivorous.
Do not give the bird the shelter of your mind.

It is friends only to
High soaring burning ambitions and desires.
It stings the body that feeds it.
It stings the mind that nourishes it.
Do not feed the bird of ego with your blood.

Sulakhan Sarhadi

Sulakhan Sarhadi (b. 1946) was born in Kuhar in Gurdaspur district. He was a teacher by profession. He has written both *geet* and *ghazal*. He mastered the craft of ghazal. His ghazals resonate with human concerns and with Sufi thought.

Ghazal

The design of the palace of justice amazes me
In its every corner, there are loopholes many.

Words grow in the womb of silence
In thoughts lies sensitivity, sensitivity the music be.

The old wounds are the signs of the past,
The freshly erupted pain is my new identity.

You have shackled the wings of my spirit with etiquettes
Now my vale of fragrances is just a barren valley.

It is commendable to stand firm becoming a bridge
But to flow smoothly like water is high simplicity.

It stays in the pocket and teases Socrates
These days the cup of poison performs buffoonery.

They tell me that it is a day, I've accepted it
But if Night tells me to accept it, that's sheer impotency.

This is the translation of my pain and its commentary too
Poetry is my life; pain is the breath of my poetry.

For victory is too close, let me lose from here
My manhood lies in losing after ensuring victory.

When the wings of butterflies looked like love letters
O that flower like age of mine! Where are thee?

DEV

Dev (b. 1947) was born in Jagraon, near Ludhiana. He resides in Switzerland. Dev is not only an accomplished poet but also a talented painter. He feels that Switzerland inspires him to paint and India inspires him to write. His poetry is rich in visual imagery. He recurrently uses the image of the bird in his poetry. The metaphor of bird represents his restless and inquisitive self, ever exploring new worlds. He often talks about the human dilemma in the context of modernity. He was given the Sahitya Akademi award for his work *Shabadant* in 2001.

How Shall I Return Home

To save the dying flame of the lamp
    The Guru lighted the *jot*.
Letting little dreams and innocent laughters
      Bury alive in the wall,
Punjab, what has happened to that beautiful history?
People are turning against their own soil
Becoming
    Shrieks
        Swords
           Walls

Did you know that
For my Guru
Humanity was his religion?
Punjab, why are you bent upon
Killing and butchering your own people?
The roots of violence are not outside,
Not even across the border;
They are always present somewhere within us.
Punjab, how come you have begun hating yourself?
Running through your veins,
Am I a Sikh stream
    Or a Hindu stream?

So many times, to beat you down,
To crush you and to slaughter you
Cantering horses came from outside,

But this time
You take pleasure in slaughtering yourself.
Punjab, how shall now I return home
Like carefree birds and children?

Amitoj

Amitoj (1947-2005) was born in Muridke, Gurdaspur. He was a multifaceted personality. He was a teacher, director, scriptwriter, songwriter and poet. To him, poetry was not a source of entertainment, but to express fundamental aspects of human reality. He has presented the conflict between the human self and society through his poetry. His book, *Khali Tarkash*, presents the dynamics of human helplessness and hope.

Evening

The sun sets differently in my village.

Not the way it sets in your city
Where it falls abruptly on the road from a balcony
And dies instantly;
In my village
It sets differently.

Even if the sun knows that
It will come again tomorrow
Like an obstinate child
It throws a tantrum,
It feels the pangs of separation very intensely;
Sometimes like a golden wasp
It plays with hemp flowers;
Sometimes, like a wild cat

It plays in the shoulder-high sugarcane field;
Sometimes, like a kite with its string cut
It is caught in the graveyard *keekar* tree;
Sometimes, like a widow's earthen lamp
It burns on a shrine.
I told you
It throws a tantrum
When it sets.

First it hops like a playful pigeon
Behind the dome of a mosque,
Like free spirited cattle
It takes a dip in the pond,
It sees off every child playing on the hillock
To his home,
Chants evening prayers
Prostrates in front of them
Prays to *pirs* and *fakirs*,
I told you
It feels strongly the pangs of separation.

Not like in your cities
Where it falls abruptly on the road from a balcony
And dies instantly;
In my village
The sun sets differently.

Shaista Habib

Shaista Habib (1948–2004) was born in Lahore. Her poetry explores the condition of women in society. One can see that the condition of women, and of female poets in particular, is the same across the subcontinent. In

Punjab, the state of all women is similar; she does not see any hope of better circumstances for women. Shaista compares women to sparrows as neither of them have ever laughed to their heart's content. Renouncing the conventional form, she embraced the modern form of poetry. Her *nazms* explore the changes taking place in society.

A Backward Area

I am in heavy debt
The debts of the world;
To keep up my existence
Seeking grants from powerful countries
Sometimes, I bent towards the West
Sometimes, the East.
I broke my limbs
My being has always remained stifled
With the chains of slavery
I have spent my childhood serving others
My youth was crushed under the burden of loans;
In the prime of my youth, when the winds of spring should have caressed me,
I was burning under the scorching sun
Craving for the shade of happiness.
The youth of the poor and the moonlit nights of winters
Are invisible entities.
I fought my war against
Poverty, ignorance, slavery and fanaticism;
But I was alone.
No one so much as sat beside me
My sentiments were crushed under heavy boots
My dreams had no value for them
Clouds over my head dispelled
Without giving me a rain
And cruel winds
Blew away my *chunni*.
My identity was taken away from me.

My voice was choked,
My life was circumscribed.
Throughout my life
In this entire world
Like a backward area
I kept craving for
The wind and the clouds
And other small moments of happiness.

Jagtar Dhaa

Jagtar Dhaa (b. 1948) was born in Sirgundi, Jallandhar. The renowned poet had a tough childhood which he describes as 'wanderlust'. Although in his work titled *Guache Ghar di Talaash*, he is nostalgic and relives his past memories. Currently, he lives in Britain. Generally, he does not write on diasporic themes like longing for homeland, generation gap, racism and cultural differences.

Walls

One can jump over the walls,
One can even break down the walls,
One can be buried alive in the walls,
One can break one's head
Banging it against the walls,
But one cannot enter into a dialogue
With the walls.
You have to knock them down.

But in order to knock down the walls
First you have to enter into a dialogue
With yourself.

Baba Najmi

Baba Najmi (b. 1948) was born in Lahore. He is a popular poet in Pakistan. A poet of human relationships, he writes about hope and believes in the extraordinary potential of human beings. He is an ardent advocate of friendship across both sides of the border. He is an enthusiast of Punjabi language and culture. According to him, Waris Shah and Sultan Bahu are greatly respectable and exceedingly sophisticated poets, whose poetic sensibility can match any other great poet in the world.

Ghazal

They are cowards, who sit idle and complain about their fate
Those who have guts, tear apart stones and emerge great.

Only their names shall be written on the facade of destinations
Who map their journey at home, before the first step they take.

They would not have crucified Mansoor the way they did
Had a wise man told them the sense his words made.

If we all make it a habit to fulfil our duties first
No one in front of others shall his begging bowl shake.

Baba Najmi, no one has covered the head in your city
The appeal for *burqas* and *chadars* why should here I make?

Ghazal

Rotten elements exist on both sides of the border
Thugs and ruffians exist on both sides of the border.

Please tell me who should I praise, *Maulvi ji?*
Easy money is ill-begotten on both sides of the border.

Those who grab everything threatening with their horns
Such bulls sadly exist on both sides of the border.

Nobody does the hoeing, they only pretend to do so
Fake hoes do exist on both sides of the border.

Why can't we all pick together from our lands
Thorns which are spread on both sides of the border?

Those who raise the voice of truth in this world
Are tortured and humiliated on both sides of the border.

Devinder Kaur

Devinder Kaur (b. 1948) was born in Kanjhali, Kapurthala. Although she is a prolific writer of prose and criticism, she is also recognised as a poet. She portrays bitter and harsh experiences from a woman's point of view. She also examines the complexities of man–woman relationships in her poetry.

Relationships

Some relationships are like
Houses with open windows,
There are colourful pictures on the walls,
Beautiful carpets are spread on the floors,
And there are many other things
To make these houses beautiful homes.
Homes
Where walls and floors
Have almost disappeared.

Some relationships are like those houses
Which have walls and windows

Made of concrete,
Cement is tightly
Packed into their foundations;
But things that
Make them beautiful,
Things that make them homes
Are missing.

Amar Jyoti

Amar Jyoti (b. 1949) was born in Amritsar. She was the editor of children's magazine, *Pankhariyan*. A woman's and diasporic consciousness are simultaneously present in her poetry. She is also critical of consumerism and globalisation, and uses sarcasm effectively in her poetry. She currently lives in Amsterdam.

How Does It Bother Me

Multinationals,
You are most welcome.
You may open your branches here
And become the god of India's destiny
...*bharat bhagya vidhata!*
Open your branches
Sell your products
And take the profit back home.
The citizens of modern age
Modern daughters and sons
Modern parents,
Children of global civilisation,
Forsaking *rajma*
You may accept
Noodles and hamburger
Pizza and lasagne

Chilli corn and tortilla,
Get used to drinking
Draught beer that now quenches your thirst,
Get used to bibbing wine
Wine, whisky and brandy.
In the new age
Let people be dazzled by money
Make them follow you
Delude them with advertisements
'You only live once.'
'Everybody is the master of one's life.'
'Beautify yourself – look good.'
'Live to make yourself happy.'
'Have fun.'
'Enjoy your life.'

Freedom?
May be you know the difference.

Paash

Paash or Avtar Singh Sandhu (1950-1988) was born in Talwandi Salem, Jallandhar. A major poet of the post-independence Punjab, he was highly critical of the Indian establishment and also of communalism. Paash was assassinated by Khalistani militants for his humanitarian views. He borrowed imagery from the rural landscape of Punjab and presented his experiences with artistry.

Refusal

Do not expect of me that I,
Despite being the son of the soil,
Will talk about your
Despicable pleasures and deplorable tastes

The flood of which wash away
The innocent lisping poems of our children
And the *kanjak*-like pure laughter of young girls.

Whenever I've uttered a word
I've spoken about the shortage of fertilisers
I'll talk about sugarcanes withered like
Shriveled breasts of a poor woman,
I'll talk about the harvest lying in the courtyard
And winter at the threshold.
Do not expect me to tell you the names of the flowers
That bloom in winter
And the names that boys give to young girls of the village.

I'll talk about
The thin mustache of the bank clerk
Or the tail of the *sarpanch*[11] that stretches all the way to the police station
Or the zoo that I carry in my chest
Or the museum which I carry in my heart
I'll speak rough and gruff.
To me, the heart is no more than a mass of tissue which looks like a *paan*
To me, beauty is like a *roti* made of flour kneaded with salt
To me, life is like country liquor, which we drink clandestinely.
Do not expect me to smell the wild flowers delicately like a rabbit,
I have taken every task head on
Like a pair of bulls harnessed to work in the fields.

I stand for the farmer's story
Before he becomes a sadhu in the heat of the summer
I am the vision of the old blind shoemaker's eyes
I am just a memory of the police constable's crippled right hand
I am just a smudge of a century on the body of time.

---

[11] Head of the village council

My imagination is like the charred flesh of a blacksmith,
Who is eternally annoyed with the unkind heavens
For a puff of wind,
In his hands the plough-nail
Becomes a sword and
Sometimes, ends up just being a pile of fodder.
I cannot become the bellow of a harmonium for your sake
I am a melody rising from the fingers of the domestic help
While washing the dishes.
I have many things to tell
Of beauty and imagination,
But for now I'll talk only about the night
Which looks like the black lips of a worker.

Do not expect of me that I,
Despite being the son of the soil,
Will talk about your
Despicable pleasures and deplorable tastes
The flood of which wash away
The innocent lisping poems of our children
And the *kanjak*-like pure laughter of young girls.

The Most Dangerous

Your labour getting plundered
Is not the most dangerous,
Nor is the torture of the police the most dangerous,
A wily handshake between Betrayal and Greed
Is not so treacherous.

It is surely unfortunate to get caught when you least expect it,
While you sit leisurely or are asleep;
No doubt, it is awful when fear and silence strike you
But it is still not the most dangerous.
No doubt, it is wrong to smother the voice of truth
In the noise of treachery and deceit,

It is unfortunate to read in the feeble light of a glow-worm.
All this is bad, but still
Not the most dangerous.

The most dangerous is
When death-like silence overpowers you,
To feel no pain, no anguish, and to swallow everything.
To follow the mechanical routine of
Home to work and work to home,
The most dangerous part is
The death of our dreams.
The most dangerous is that watch
Which, despite ticking on your wrist,
Stands still and tells you nothing.

The most dangerous is the eye, which
Sees all, yet remains icy cold like a dead body;
Which forgets to kiss people lovingly
And is blinded by the haze of material things
Accepting the ordinariness of the visible
It is lost in the vicious circle of absurd monotonous routines.

The most dangerous is the moon,
Which rises in the stunned yard
After every murder,
But does not hurt your eyes like red chillies would.

The most dangerous is the raunchy song
Which cuts through lamentations
To reach your ears,
At the door of the scared people
It coughs like a goon.

The most dangerous is the night
Which falls on living souls,
In which owls hoot and jackals howl
And cling fast to the thresholds and doors eternally shut.

The most dangerous is the direction
In which the sun of your soul sets forever,
And some splinters of its dead light
Pierce through the east of your body.

Your labour getting plundered
Is not dangerous,
Nor is the torture of the police the most dangerous;
Even a wily handshake between Betrayal and Greed
Is not so treacherous.

Surinder Dhanjal

Surinder Dhanjal (b. 1950) was born in Chakk Bhaika, Ludhiana district. He lives in Canada and he taught Computer Science at the University at Kamloops. Currently, he is Professor Emeritus at Thomson University. He was greatly influenced by Paash, his close associate. His initial poetry follows the sentiment of protest in the tradition of Naxalite literature. Later, he wrote many progressive poems from the Marxist perspective.

The Crazy Poet

The poet in slumber,
How can you write a poem matching the stature of Paash?
You do not have the eyes of Paash that see all.

The eyes in slumber,
How can you envision a poem matching the vision of Paash?
You do not have dreams that can match the dreams of Paash.

Dreams in slumber,
How can you fly like the poetry of Paash?
You do not have a life to match the intense life of Paash.

Life in slumber,
Why don't you have a poem that in stature matches Paash's?

Asking such questions
A foolish poet
Perhaps forgets that
If his life could match the life of Paash
Perhaps, Paash wouldn't have been Paash!
Perhaps, he wouldn't have been born!
Perhaps, he wouldn't have died!

Crazy poet!
Your life doesn't match the stature of Paash
O, the idiot poet!
Why doesn't your life match the stature of Paash?

Dr Ravinder

Dr Ravinder (b. 1950) was born in Batala in Gurdaspur district. He is a doctor of medicine by profession and also a serious poet. He dreams of a world free of suffering and tension, of a world rising above discrimination on the basis of caste, race, community and country. He seeks freedom from ego, hatred and conflict.

Sad Mother

Mother has been deeply saddened
By the loss of
Her life partner.

She has become paranoid
She thinks that
She is a burden on us;

Or, sometimes she would
Dress up and deck herself
She would take out her old clothes from the trunk—
    Which she brought along with herself when she got married—
She would try them again,
Every moment
She is ready for something.

She would show
Her daughters-in-law
And their daughters-in-law
The clothes she wishes to wear
During her last moments
She would ask them if they like the clothes
She would seek their opinion on the matter
But, she would not trust them completely.

Sometimes, she would ask her son
Not to spend too much money on her;
Or sometimes,
She would express her desire
To perform her final rites
With pomp and show.

Hiding in her heart
The strong desire to live,
She talks about death;
Time and again
She would talk about having become useless.

I don't know
What's wrong with her
Since she lost her life partner.

Manjit Indra

Manjit Indra (b. 1950) was born in Bajwara, Hoshiarpur. As a poet, she explores the complexities of human relationships in her poetry. She is critical of the institution of marriage as, in a patriarchal society, a woman is always expected to sacrifice her dreams.

The Song of a Shattered Embrace

There is no door, no window nor a parapet
    Where do we keep the burning lamp now?
There are roofs on my head and walls on my shoulders
    But where should I place these roofs and walls now?

Clasping trees in our hands
    We slept tight in the shade;
There is no tree, no shade, nor love
    My embrace is shattered when I wake up from a dream.

Neither father's home, nor mother's lullaby remains
    Leisure to spend time with friends is also forsaken;
There is no sound of footsteps, no anklets tinkle anywhere
    The bells from anklets are abruptly silenced.

Love is widowed, no bier is in sight,
    Reminiscent of good times
    Mango leaves still hang across the doorway;
Who can see how pain and sorrow
    Have saddened us?

There is no door, no window nor a parapet
    Where do we keep the burning lamp now?
There are roofs on my head and walls on my shoulders
    But where should I place these roofs and walls now?

Darshan Bulandwi

Darshan Bulandwi (b. 1951) was born at Mehmuwaal in Jallandhar district. His early life was full of struggle. When starting out as a poet, he kept company with Paash. Due to Paash's influence on his poetry, Darshan's poetry is idiomatic. His poetry reflects his progressive ideology that rejects all types of discrimination, divisions, borders and hatred. Currently, he lives in Britain. Nostalgia about the past and love for the homeland constitute the body of his poetic work. He portrays the pain of exploitation very sensitively.

Lamp Burning in the Sun

The East living in the West,
In front of the Sun of the West,
You are no more than a lamp
How long will you
Celebrate your feeble glow?
How long will you
Fight against the bright formidable rays of the Sun of the West?
Well, I too am born in the East
But beneath my sandy feet
Runs the river of the West
I also have to examine my boat
Time and again,
Who knows when
Stealthily
It may drown me in high tide,
And I may have no clue.
Yes, otherwise, seeing your steadfastness
I bow my head
To respect your unshakeable trust;
But you, while putting your signature

On the flowing waters of time,
Are so ignorant of every thing
You are not aware of how
Falling from your own interstices
How the Sun of the West
Has engulfed
Every photon of your existence.
All your plans
To light up your house
With the beam of your blood
Have been thwarted.
The dreams of giving flight to the birds
You carried in your womb,
From doors and windows
That you kept tightly shut
Its light has entered
And has planted climbers growing in your house
In its own flowerpots,
Disowning like a bastard son
Pasted you on the threshold of the house
And you never realised it.
You kept on searching
The last hummed word of the song
Which disappeared from your house.
The last hue of the dying colour,
Some last feature
Of your hazy face
You were just looking for all that
From the site of your defeat
Whereas every clipped wing of your flight
Has fallen to the ground.
In your own hands,
The iron of your every barrier
Has molten and spread
On its every road like charcoal.

In front of the Sun of the West
You, the East
Burning like a tiny lamp
How long will you celebrate your feeble glow
How long...?

Ambrish

Ambrish (b. 1952) was born in village Dhallian in Gurdaspur district. He is a doctor of medicine by profession. With great sensitivity, his poetry describes the pain of the common man.

A Military Tank and a Butterfly

A military tank,
The souvenir of the last war,
Is placed
At the crossroads in the centre of the city.

Around the black gun of the tank
Butterflies flutter,
On the turret of the tank
Small children are playing games,
Among the rust-ridden links of the chain
Grass with soft green stalks is growing,
Small yellow wildflowers
Are lifting their heads proudly,
And sparrows, carrying straws in their beaks,
Are looking for space in the cracks and crevices
For their nests.

In the end
There are always
Flowers, children and butterflies.

Sukhwinder Kamboj

Sukhwinder Kamboj (b. 1953) was born in Sultanpur Lodhi, Kapurthalla district. He worked as a principal of a college in Punjab, but later moved to the USA, where he runs his personal businesses He writes poetry of protest and diaspora, expressing his longing for the homeland.

Rootless Green Trees

We have work here
But no life.
Taking work away from our feet
We have loaded it on our backs,
We have made it the stress of our lives.
We have severed our ties with
Small roads leading to towns;
Forsaking the gatherings of friends
And people we love,
We have shaken hands with individualism.
The question is
Where are our roots?
What is our character?
Virtues like loyalty and commitment
Define our character.
How can we decide
Which is the immortal moment of our lives?
Where is the end of this road?
Sharp daggers of time broken into pieces

Pierce though our hearts.
When we change our work
The ways of being social and
The ways of friendships
Also change.
This tendency to move on—
Is it a virtue or a vice?
Is this a quality given to us by the flexible capital
Which you never tire of admiring?
This is not so simple;
Rather, this is an illusion of simplicity.
This is no life, but a parody of life,
We are perhaps those plastic trees
Placed in buildings
That always look green,
But are rootless.

Gurbhajan Singh Gill

Gurbhajan Singh Gill (b. 1953) was born at Basantkot in Gurdaspur district. He wrote poetry in several forms such as *geet* (song), *ghazal* and free verse, but he is best known for his songs. His family suffered extreme losses at the time of the Partition. During the period of militancy in Punjab, he favoured the humanistic ideas of love, the syncretic culture of Punjab and brotherhood.

A Song

Let's cover the distance from one home to another
Let's cover the distance from Lahore to Amritsar.

The lines were drawn, the land was divided
Mass murders transpired in the trains

Those who survived were forced to bear
Unbelievable agony; unimaginable pain.
Why doesn't this deep wound heal ever?
Let's cover the distance from one home to another
Let's cover the distance from Lahore to Amritsar.

May the lamps in their houses burn forever!
May the wick of the lamp is ever dipped in the oil!
The lamp of love, which dispels darkness,
May it burn, and burn forever
Let's cover the distance from one home to another
Let's cover the distance from Lahore to Amritsar.

The wedding procession is ready, the mare is decked
Sister, you may sing the wedding songs;
May the couple always sit together!
Those who long for peace,
May they live forever!
Let's cover the distance, from one home to another.

Oh! My friend, living across Wagha,
I hope you agree with me,
The Sun does not rest
As long as dark times inflicts the world;
Let's cover the distance from one home to another
Let's cover the distance from Lahore to Amritsar.

VANITA

Vanita (b. 1954) was born in Amritsar. She is a well-known poet and critic. She opines that poetry is not meant to be read; it is meant to be lived. To her, poetry is timeless. She was honoured with the national award by Sahitya Akademi for her collection *Kaal, Pehar, Gharhian* in 2010.

When Language Overwhelms Me

When language overwhelms me
I wish to forget
The language and its grammar,
I wish to talk in a language
In which trees and leaves
Birds and animals
Fruits and flowers
Stars in the sky
The Moon and the Ocean
The Earth and the Sun
Talk to each other.

Darshan Buttar

Darshan Buttar (b. 1954) was born in Thoohi in Patiala district. His poetry is passionate and intense, yet sensitive and subtle. His images are original and unique which provide a fresh perspective to life. He won the Sahitya Akademi award in 2012 for his collection of poems *Maha Kambani*.

from *The Grand Trembling*

I

While laying bricks to make a wall
Do not place all of your dreams along with the bricks
Keep some of them aside
Put them on the parapet
From where
It is easier for them
To fly.

II

When you shut your doors
Keep them slightly ajar
To let the light enter and leave;
Remove the curtain from your mind
Before you draw it in the room.

III

Trees
Never give their branches
Exclusively to leaves,
They always wait for
Birds, travelers and swings.

IV

There are some flights
Rebellious to the wings,
Some kites fly
Even without a wind,
Some poems are written
Even without words.

V

Some journeys are made
Not with the feet
But with the head,
Before you set your feet on your path
You must remove thorns from your mind.

VI

Never count
Snails and shells
Lying at the bottom of the lake;
Rather, let's gauge our thirst.

Hardial Sagar

Hardial Sagar (b. 1954) was born in Kapurthalla. The hardships of his childhood and the early loss of his mother made him a reflective and sensitive person. Sagar uses the form of the *ghazal* to explore themes such as love, humanity and integrity.

Ghazal

For once, with the long queue are my eyes entwined
The flock of swans, some herons have also joined.

That flourish in advertisements, not in hearts
Such relationships are destined to fail.

Wearing the *mizrab* is not enough to play the sitar
You pluck your heart before you play a tune.

I sat in the first row to receive the accolade
Though, I hid when difficult times arrived.

When the caravan of wounds met my body
It polished me further, more did I shine.

The sun will be divided into races, the wind into religions
If man had the power to execute his wily design.

Jaswant Deed

Jaswant Deed (b. 1954) was born at Shahkot, Jallandhar district. He lives in Canada. He retired from the Doordarshan, Jallandhar and has made documentaries on many writers. One of his documentary films won the National Award. His book *Kamandal* won the Sahitya Akademi Award in 2007. He is a subtle and profound poet, who uses images evocatively. He has control over his words; he has sarcasm; he has the nuanced touch of rich tradition and vividly depicts the double standards of people.

Roof[12]

Who is it?
Who gallops over me?

Perhaps, they are my forefathers
Buried in the roof.

Around my face
The halo of tensions and worries
The hooves of the horse beneath me
Belch embers
A strange face has taken away
All the words from my voice.

A sword moves restlessly in my being
I come out of my tent every day
And ask for my head;
With a severed head,
In the forest
I look for a place to sleep.

At the top of the mountain
I wander like a madman
In the misconstrued strength of my shattered concentration
My *baaz*[13] squabbles with me

---

[12] The poet invokes the history of Guru Gobind Singh and other figures from the Sikh history to comment on the predicament of the modern man.

[13] Goshawk or northern goshawk or *baaz* is always shown with Guru Gobind Singh in his pictorial representations. The bird is the symbol of his strength and tenacity.

We are both
Wounded
We cross rivers, hillocks and forts
Stuck in the hooves of the horse
We cry while writing
The instrument of abdication.

The ideals for which the father – the guru
Sacrificed his entire family
I write that dream again.
In the process of
Writing and re-writing,
My words are drowned in the Kali
My plume has gotten soiled
My royal robes are torn;
Sometimes, I ask Jito[14]
Sometimes, I call Tripta[15]
Gujri[16] is thinking—
Who is this who doesn't let her son sleep at night
I have kept the last arrow in my quiver
For myself

Scratching the halo of stress
Around my face
The arrow has lost its sharpness,
Waiting for the clarion of victory
My horse and my *baaz*
Look at me
I put on my uniform

Someone is galloping on my chest.

---

[14] Jito or Mata Jito or Mother Jito was Guru Gobind Singh's first wife. Guru Gobind Singh had three sons from her, Jujhar Singh, Zorawar Singh and Fateh Singh.
[15] Tripta or Mata Tripta is the mother of Guru Nanak Dev
[16] Gujri or Mata Gujri is the mother of Guru Gobind Singh

Nirupama Dutt

Nirupama Dutt (b. 1955) was born in Chandigarh. She is an English journalist, translator and a poet. She writes in Punjabi and translates her poetry into English. Her writings have been published in various Indian languages. She has written and spoken about issues of feminism, extremism and militancy.

Apology

Today
I offer my apologies
To all those women
From whom
I stole a moment or two
Of their bright light
And cheerfulness,
This small act of theft of mine
Caused them a lot of pain
And kept them awake for many nights.

What could we women do?
In order to escape the darkness of our lives
We run towards
Each other's sun,
Borrowing a ray of light
We fix them on the black *dupatta,*
We always
Leave the sun
Full, intact, unharmed.

Today
I forgive

All those women, who
Stole a moment or two
Of bright light and cheerfulness
From me.

Sant Sandhu

Sant Sandhu (b. 1945) was born in Talwandi Salem, Jallandhar district. He was closely associated with the tradition of Paash. His poetry shakes up the historical consciousness of the people. Sant Sandhu expresses the pain of the oppressed effortlessly. His poem on war, which has been included in this anthology, is one of the best anti-war poems in Punjabi.

War

Of friends' fall from high morals
War is an appeal of swords
War is a whim of governments
War is the intent of storms
War is a conspiracy of scoundrels
War is death of innocent souls
War is like the disease of pests
War is the sting of a scorpion
War is another name for black smoke.

It is like a loud wail
It is like losing a gem in the mud
It is like the burning hot summer month
It is like silver lace pulled from a *dupatta*
It is like a mad ox with blood on its head
It is quick, a stick hitting hard.

It means drying of wells once brimming with water
It means souls sinking into a long slumber
It means a song echoing in desolation.

It is like a neighbor with malevolence
It is like coveting someone else's money
It is like the withering of an innocent flower.

It is a widow in a demolished town
It is a trail in a forest
It is a place where Death frowns.

War is for you what fate has decreed
War is a field of grains badly burnt
War is sweet dreams' incineration.

It's like a swing with its rope snapped
It's like the dance of a demon on a fiery noon
It's like a snake spitting poison.

As if everyone has gone mad
As if life is stuck on a shoe-stretcher
As if there were a visible lump on the body.

It's like the snapping of young boughs
It's like listening to bad news
It's like the darkness of graves.

This is not a war of ideas plain
It's of love polluted and profaned
It's about a fallen character and its disdain

War is the downpour of blood
War is blood overflowing the kneading pan
War is a long dark night.

War is the gait of a lost traveler
War is a noose around the neck of humanity
War is the picture of devastation.

It is a path closed
It is a bag of books unread
It is a bloody crossing.

It is about the breathing souls expired
It is about dead doves somewhere
It is about burnt huts somewhere.

War is about shattered arms
War is about lost trails
War is a crime against humanity.

War is about destroyed orchards
War is like a chronic disease
Every war is our ill fortune.

It is about countries divided
It is about trees severed in two
It is a gift from the West to us.

The river-bank is full of thorns
It is sharp like a barber's razor
War is not a bed of roses.

It is about dried rivers
It is about desolations
It is about wailing mothers.

War is like backstabbing a friend
War is like sighs for a dead mother
War is like thorns of black *keekar*.

When a barren cloud thunders
When the war trumpet sounds
A demon dances in frenzy.

When bombs explode and the earth shakes
All eyes remain open
Leaving mothers in pain.

As if shade became hot
As if mothers' sons are lost
As if a river of blood flows.

War is a business of spoiled brothers
War is a business of lost travelers
Every war is a business of mad men.

There are no men or women
It is like a looted bazaar
No one wins or loses a war.

Brothers like Mirza die on both sides
Green forests turn to ashes on both sides
And tears roll down from both eyes.

Lakhwinder Johal

Lakhwinder Johal (b. 1956) was born in Jandiala, near Amritsar. He upholds progressive ideas. His writings reflect not only his progressive ideas but also give a sensitive portrayal of human psychology.

Words

Like wind words travel
Like buoyant water they leap
Like a cloud of dust they rise
Words are like tides
Hidden in a man's heart.

Words bow their heads
At the shrine of pain
They burn

In the flame of fire.

Words
See all
Blooming flowers
Gliding fragrance
Withering buds
And pierced
With their own thorns
They watch.

Words
When they fall on paper
Make the pages break down in tears.

Wailing crying pages
When they refuse
To accept
The touch of the pen
Then…
Words become sad.

Sad words
Travel
Hopping, jumping, flying
Words are like tides
Hidden in a man's heart.

Paul Kaur

Paul Kaur (b. 1956) was born in Kalo Majra, near Banur in Patiala district. Like her contemporary women poets, the female consciousness is evident in her poetry too. She raises women's questions through her prose as well. The argument in her poetry is rational and images are borrowed from mythology. She voices her concerns sensitively, challenges patriarchy boldly and daringly disturbs the existing order. Her rebellious female self says: 'I was born on this side of the threshold, But I lived on the other side of it.' She was given the Bhai Santokh Singh Puraskar in 2018.

Immunity

When I fell down
While I was learning to walk
My mother said to me,
'It's okay
You've just scattered flour for the ants.'

Throughout my life
I've walked and slipped,
When I outgrew the innocent belief
About scattering flour on the floor
I felt the real pain every time I fell
Every time I was hurt.
Sometimes, I would get a friend's shoulder to cry on
Or sometimes, their sympathy;
And sometimes, pity from relatives—if I can call them relatives—
But gradually
I became immune;
For every time I fell
Neither did I get hurt like before
Nor did I feel the pain.

But today if I slip or fall
And I feel that I am hurt somewhere
A voice comes from within
'It's okay
You've just scattered flour for the ants.'

Jaswinder

Jaswinder (b. 1956) was born in Kalalwala, Bathinda. He is a mature poet of the 'new ghazal' and is among the best contemporary *ghazal* poets in Punjabi. He has excellent control over its craft and expresses his humanist concerns through *ghazal*. A poet with left leanings, he exposes the capitalist system, which he says offers grain to the bird on the one hand, while preying on it on the other. Awarded by the Sahitya Akademi for his book Agarbatti in 2014, he currently lives in Canada.

Ghazal

I wonder, what sort of play is being staged
The role of a wound is by a knife played.

I was promised a melodious *taan*, and all I hear is noise
I came to enjoy music, and look. How music is slayed!

What war is this, where I fight on both the sides
Why do my hands always my life take?

With the script of fear on the pages of the forest – the Darvesh
Trees translate the fire. What a folly to make!

They are teaching the stones how to tear the water apart
They are teaching the glass how to get cracked.

Black bees are fed on the blood of buds
For butterflies, a dish of dead flowers is made.

Smoldering lava, acidic river and an island of fire
What sort of objects in my sleep populate?

Earthen lamp, you ponder, hidden from the sun
For what journey, is this light being arranged?

We drown daily in the deep river of our pain
We hear daily that a bridge over it is being made.

Varinder Parihar

Varinder Parihar (b. 1956) was born at Malsian, near Nakodar, Jallandhar. After finishing MA in English from Jallandhar, he went to England. Michael Hamburger, the famous poet and translator, motivated Varinder to write in his mother tongue. He opines that science and technology have done great harm to our environment. We have been divorced from nature and the world has been converted into a huge pile of plastic garbage. He converses with Nature in many of his poems. He believes that modern poets need to invent a new idiom to write poetry, and that images should be adapted to the modern context.

Heart

My heart is my heart
My heart is not a piece of land
Which will stay silent
When you trample it with your imperialist dreams.

From six in the morning to six in the evening
You will suck
Every drop of blood from my body
A morsel of food that you gave me yesterday
Becoming the blood
It will run through my body,
It will pass through my heart
It will listen to me
It will follow my heart.

My heart in my chest
Beats only for me

It may be a mass of flesh
As big as my fist
But it is not a helpless mute piece of land.

My heart is entirely mine
My heart is after all
My heart.

Vijay Vivek

Vijay Vivek (b. 1957) was born at Ratti Rori in Faridkot district. Vivek's poetry is spontaneous and profound. He does not cherish the idea of revolution, but works to make his readers aware of the flaws in society. He is critical of ideas that place humans against nature. He believes that matter is the basis of all truth.

Ghazal

We yearned for each other life long, but
    The distance between us we could not navigate;
I could not reach out to you
    You were not patient enough to wait.

A strange boat, like a dagger,
    Ran into the heart of the river;
Such tremendous pain! Even the sand beneath trembled,
    Such tremendous endurance! Even a cry I could not make.

I, the untalented painter of yours,
    Have filled the canvas with smudges;
I've lost my colours,
    Even your face I could not paint.

You were the dark cloud, I was the sandy bank
    Who could imagine the mishap impending?
I could not stifle my thirst,
    You could not hold the water, my mate.

Like tiny droplets is my existence
    Like straw my flesh is weak;
Like strewn pieces my thoughts are scattered
    Oh! To keep things gathered I have failed.

Surjit Jajj

Surjit Jajj (b. 1958) was born in Palakhan in Patiala district. He is associated with progressive ideas. Though he has a strong political consciousness, his poetry is not sloganeering. He experiments with new meters in *ghazal* and songs. He aptly expresses the condition of farmers worsened by globalisation.

Ghazal

Strange is the Qalandar and strange are his ways
He was murdering people and we called it devotion.

Pulling them out of water, we placed our boats on higher ground
How else could these boats find protection?

If they grow in jungles, winds would uproot them
Trees are safer in flowerpots. What a wise decision!

Uprooted from the fields, the bread-giver is now a beggar in the market
Such is the boon of global trade, so horrid is its vision.

In the mad race of trade we are all for sale
From the cradle to the grave, it's only trade and its commotion.

Every river that fell into the Sea was thirsty to the core
The Sea is asking the Land, 'Is this the rule of the man?'

What the Moon stole from the Sun and the Lake from the Moon
I need the same vision to read what you have written.

Why do you coerce the mirror by asking about your identity
Like you, the mirror knows when the image should change.

Whether you are a diamond or a stone, a gem or a piece of glass,
It depends on my viewpoint how you are perceived.

The graft of touch-me-not is planted next to a cactus
Surjit says—This is how they ensure their protection.

Swaranjit Savi

Swaranjit Savi (b. 1958) was born in village Gehlan of Sangrur district. He is a poet and a painter. During the first phase of his career, he wrote under the influence of Naxalism. Later, he concentrated on the physical relationship between men and women. In his books *Dehi Naad* and *Kameshwari*, he raised the debate around body-consciousness in Punjabi poetry. His poetry challenges orthodoxy.

Mother

Instead of killing a nation
Kill the mother of the nation first
Kill her rights of being a mother
Destroy her genitals completely;
Don't rape her
Leave her good for nothing.

If the mother of a nation dies today
By design the nation will die tomorrow.

This is how we—your children—
Think about you, Mother.

Sukhpal

Sukhpal (b. 1960) was born in Ludhiana. He studied at Punjab Agricultural University, Ludhiana, and taught there for ten years before moving to Canada. His poetry is emotionally intense but uses poetic logic to good effect, thus combining emotion and rationality.

I And Nanak

I hear ill words about him,
To save his honour
I raise arms,
But his honour does not need me.

I listen to everyone
Discussing his philosophy
Priests, scholars, followers, warriors;
It is only Nanak I do not listen to.

He was neither
A Muslim, nor a Hindu, nor a Sikh
It is only I
Who think it is important to be
A Muslim, a Hindu or a Sikh.

He took a dip in a river
He wandered like a *fakir*,
I, holding his book of verses tight;
Shut the door and sit down.

'I believe in one God', he said.
But I don't believe in the oneness of humanity;

One who wandered all around the world
Carrying love for humanity in his heart,
I have saddened him to the core.

I try to become Nanak's true follower
He waits for me to become another Nanak.

Gurmeet Kallarmajri

Gurmeet Kallarmajri was born in Kalar Majri, Patiala. He is a teacher, poet and critic. He writes poetry in free verse. A Marxist at heart and aware of caste discrimination in the society, he talks about the oppressed, the Dalit and the common man in his poetry.

Change

I have
Made my claims
Over the fresh and clean water of the pond
Where
Even the sound of my ancestor's footsteps
Was prohibited.

I have decided
To make that priest
Stand in the dock
Who denied me for ages
My share of
Benedictions
By keeping them with himself.

I have
Challenged the sky
To fill in my eyes

Its azure space
Which has always denied me wings
And my flight in the sky.

I have transcribed
That jungle into my songs
Where I had been fighting
The acidic dark,
And for the sake of
A handful of grain,
I was sold
Along with my freedom,
The bloody reality
Of my caste.

Parminder Sodhi

Parminder Sodhi (b. 1960) was born in Firozpur. Currently, he lives in Japan. He has translated the history of Japanese literature into Punjabi and has also written haikus. He has been influenced by Buddhism, Taoism and Osho. Love is the central theme in his poetry.

Earthquake and God

After an earthquake
Seeing the fallen lamp-posts
Knocked-down houses
Glass broken into smithereens
Opening chasms in the roads
And fire all around
A scared child
Asked me
'Who brings this earthquake?'

Inadvertently or perhaps unwittingly
I said, 'God—
He brings the earthquake.'

Immersed in
Fear, anger and innocence
The child said,
'God is mad!'

Barjinder Chauhan

Barjinder Chauhan (b. 1961) was born in Patiala district. He writes ghazals to expresses his innermost thoughts and emotions. He has mastered the craft of the *ghazal*. Gifted with a keen eye, he notices every small event around him. Depleting trust between human beings in the age of globalisation and insecurity that the modern world suffers from are some of the critical concerns in his poetry.

Ghazal

How long will you bear injustice
    Get up, look for a spark and ignite,
Hiding your head between your knees
    You cannot pass this wintry night.

As if after that incident
    My eyes have turned to stone,
Since then my eyes have not shed
    Even a tear over anybody's plight.

The heat has singed
    The trunk of this tree,
Go elsewhere to find shade
    Wrecked trees give nothing, that is their plight.

Don't get excited if
    Winds knock at your door,
Do not nurse false hopes
    Do not cling to your past so tight.

There are ruins of dreams
    Or the wreck of memories,
The quake has changed the scenario
    In no time, it has shown its might.

Barjinder, your one habit
    Will cost you dearly,
You never agree meekly
    And ask questions with all might.

Gurtej Koharwala

Gurtej Koharwala (b. 1961) was born in Koharwala, Faridkot. In many ways, Gurtej can be considered one of the outcomes of Naxalism in Punjab. He grew as a poet during the phase of terrorism in Punjab. He has written beautiful ghazals on the tragedy of Punjab, which gives us a sensitive humanistic perspective. Introspection and reflection are two important qualities that his poetry reflects.

Ghazal

I'll speak of my love and keep my heart restless
This evening, in my house, I welcome sadness.

I'm so lost that I can't even recall the names of colours
I once thought of giving a name to every fragrance.

It was we who threw flowerpots and vases on the road
How can we, for this accident, blame someone else?

Lest the essence of relationships should get diluted
Some relationships I would like to keep nameless, thus.

This is what happens when green trees are burnt
Smoke hurts our eyes, it also fills the air with sadness.

Satish Gulati

Satish Gulati (b. 1962) was born in Faridkot. Due to poor financial conditions, he could not study beyond matriculation. He was introduced to books by his father, who was also a novelist and translator. River and silence are two recurring metaphors in his poetry.

'The river does not talk, yet it can be noisy.
Its silence, on the contrary, can drown us.'

Ghazal

They race to fall into the sea, such are rivers;
They keep in mind the thirst of the land, such are rivers.

Quite innocently they spread out on burning lands
Oft I've seen them die like this, such are rivers.

Don't stop them from moving freely and playfully, for they too
Have dreams, hopes and a heart, such are rivers.

They bear many bridges of relationships in their hearts
Yet they act like bridges till the end, such are rivers.

Their world of silence intrigues us all
Who knows what they keep in their hearts? Such are rivers.

Mentors, leaders and judges, you may decide now;
Do they dupe or are they duped? Such are rivers.

Manmohan

Manmohan (b. 1963) was born in Amritsar. He is a poet, and also a researcher, translator and a novelist. He was awarded by the Sahitya Akademi for his first novel *Nirvaan* in 2013. He is not a romantic poet; rather, he is called a poet of human consciousness. His poetry, written in free verse, has a unique flavor. He is influenced by Marx, Buddha and Ambedkar.

Disagreement

Nanak of Rai Bhoye
Met Nanak of the Sikhs
At Nankana…

They discussed, debated and argued
On many contemporary issues.

While walking away Nanak said,
'Nanak Singh…
We have gone too far;
Swayed by our intellectual talk
I fear
We may not ever agree
On any point.'

Sukhwinder Amrit

Sukhwinder Amrit (b. 1963) was born in Ludhiana. She writes *ghazals*, and love poetry. She becomes the archetypal Heer who does not find it impossible to fight against the system. She trusts her womanhood and her love. Her poetry is celebratory. She is a poet of conjugal love.

Mothers and Daughters

Mothers of every era
Say one thing or another
To their daughters
That may help them
That may light their path

My mother told me:

Nice girls
Stay hidden
Keep smouldering throughout their lives
Walk with their heads bent down

Neither do they speak loudly
Nor do they laugh loudly
Girls do not share their sorrows
But cry on the pretext of smoke
And live happily behind the walls

Girls are an epitome of modesty and coyness
With their heads covered
And eyes downcast

Girls are like cows
Whichever post you tie them to
There they remain
These speechless creatures never say anything to anybody
....

No word of my mother
Ever helped me
Every sentence of hers

Raised before me like a wall
And I taught my daughter:

Don't make compromises with the walls
At every step

Don't mortgage your flights
With the cages
Ensure that your status is
So high
So enlightened

That every darkness is scared of your presence
Every wall trembles in your presence
Fetters break down in your presence

You live an honourable life
Die an honourable death
Don't make compromises with the walls at any cost
My daughter
Will also say one thing or another to her daughter
Perhaps more beautiful
Something that abounds with more love and freedom

Because
In every era
Mothers say one thing or another
To their daughters
That may help them
That may light their path

Perhaps it is the way
the eras change.

Translated by Amandeep Kaur Sra

Amarjeet Kaunke

Amarjit Kaunke (b. 1964) was born in Ludhiana city. While living in another city, he considers himself a diaspora because he cannot forget the streets of his native place. He feels he is in a state of exile in his homeland. He unravels layers of human relationships and presents its ironies. A scholar and a translator, he engages with the complex modern social reality in his writings but there is spontaneity and seriousness in his poetry.

On Speaking the Truth

When I called hunger, hunger
When I called poverty, poverty
When I called love, love
They didn't like it.

When I called a bird, bird
When I called the sky, sky
When I called a tree, tree
And a word, word
They didn't appreciate it.

But when I wrote
An unpoetic poem
Called the filth of slums a heaven on earth
When I called a woman only a vagina
Called a round *roti*, the moon
When I called black colour, the moonlight
And called a black crow, a guinea fowl
They all exclaimed
Wah! Wah!
What a great work of poetry!
Wah! Wah!

Jaswant Zafar

Jaswant Zafar (b. 1965), born in Sanghe Khalsa, Jallandhar, is an acclaimed Punjabi writer. He is an iconoclast in the true sense of the word. He uses sarcasm to its full potential. Using satire in his writings, he exposes and attacks double standards and hypocrisies in religion. Zafar carries forward the literary tradition of writing on Guru Nanak started by Harbhajan Singh. 'Only pictures of Nanak, painted by Sobha Singh, can hang/On the walls of our houses/For the weight of the true dangerous Nanak/No wall can bear.'

Man

I asked the River flowing towards the Sea
    'How do you manage to flow incessantly?'
The River asked me in turn
    'What is flowing?'

Walking along the River
I reached the Ocean
The Ocean was laughing looking at the Moon
I asked the Ocean
    'How come you are so deep?'
The Ocean asked me
    'What is being deep?'

Then I asked the Moon
    'How come you are so calm?'
The Moon was bewildered and said
    'What is being calm?'

At night in my dream
River, Ocean and Moon tell me—
    Be human

But, I cannot ask them back —
'What is being human?'

Neeru Aseem

Neeru Aseem (b. 1967) was born in Bathinda. She calls herself a cypher and sees her strength in her being a non-entity. As a woman, she has adopted a novel method of struggle. 'I have no address/I was once an artist/A mother, a wife, or an actor/These days I have ceased to be/My dear critic, what will you do now?/How will you catch from the air?' She has lost faith in social institutions and religion and hence, wants to 'become' poetry: so she may get dispersed into the air.

A Girl

They said to her
You are like a sparrow
You are like the breeze
Believing that
She was a sparrow and the breeze
She continued flying.

They said to her
You are weak and helpless,
She was puzzled
Yet she remained silent;
Innocently she believed it too
And began to wait for
The bright pathways.

They said to the girl
Wake up, you are Durga!
The girl stared at them,
At every step

She blew the war trumpet
She kept fighting;
She was exhausted fighting,
Exhausted,
She kept on dying in the battle.

Then the girl said
I am only a soul
I am nothing, but a simple soul,
I am
Life;
Nothing else.

Let there be no different systems for me
Let there be no other names for me
Let there be no sweet messages for me
I am what I am.

Since ages
I am a tradition
I am a long story.

I am a soul
I am life
Once again, the girl said
I am nothing else…

TARIQ GUJJAR

Tariq Gujjar (b. 1969) was born in Dujkot, Faislabad (Pakistan). His parents had migrated from India in 1947. He teaches Punjabi literature in a college in Pakistan and has published his collection of poetry *Ratt Rale Pani*. He is a supporter of the Punjabi Bachao Movement or Save Punjabi Movement in West Punjab.

A Poem for Undivided Punjab

While giving birth to me
Mother Earth split into two,
You may savour the bitterness on my lips
Then you will believe me;
The first food given to me
Was the nectar of five waters mixed with blood,
You cannot sing a complete song in its entirety
On broken instruments,
While crossing the river
The other half of my flute was left behind.

SWAMI ANTAR NIRAV

Born in 1971 Gurvinder Singh alias Swami Antar Nirav is a traveler and explorer. He was born in Poonch, the land adopted by Krishan Chander. In the last couple of years, his poetry, published in various journals, has received critical acclaim. His book *Kuchh Baki Hai* is rooted in the culture of Pothohari. His imagery is fresh and original. Currently, he lives in Jammu, and in his own words, is wedded to poetry.

Lewd Laughter

He plants hunger
Inside me

Nurturing, cultivating and cherishing it
I have become hunger myself
From the woman to the field
Everywhere
I see nothing, but hunger

He claims that
His every battle

Is a battle against my hunger

I find that
His last blow
Snatches my home from me
And also water from the well
In my backyard

While hungry
I am left thirsty
And homeless too

He doubts
My belonging to my country
And laughs
An obscene lewd laughter.

In response
I cry the same way.

Neetu Arora

Neetu Arora (b. 1978) was born at Bhullar in Muktsar district. She tries to understand society through her personal experiences. She believes Punjabi artists and poets have not been given the respect they deserve. 'When the poets of a language/Fail to grow/And end up being pygmies/Courage also remains dwarf/Reality and imagination/Even men and women/Fail to grow.'

Roti *and* Life

Many years ago
Quite naturally I had my first encounter
With the circularity of *roti*.

My mother taught me nothing
But I learnt it on my own
That a round *roti* has no edges,
It has no corners.

Then I understood
That life is also round
Like a *roti*
It has no edges, no corners.

How similar
Life and *roti* are!
The Kitchen and the World!
In the kitchen we have
Different utensils like
Cooker, pot, *karahi* and *tawa*;
In the world we have
Thoughts, ideas, debates, relations, values.
Everything is round.

We
While looking for edges and corners
Lose the thread;
We fail to grasp
The center of the issue.

A *roti* has no edges, no corners
But only a centre.

Sabir Ali Sabir

Sabir Ali Sabir (b. 1977) is a young promising poet and short story writer from West Punjab. He was born in Pandoki, Lahore. Sabir comes across as a Sufi of the modern times. He rejects the constructed ideas of god and institution of religion. He brutally exposes artificiality and hypocrisy. 'Be it Ganges or Mecca; both are simply unfair to us all. You are looking for god,/Is god fair to us all?' Besides writing poetry, he also writes short stories.

O God, Without Your Will

O god,
If not even a leaf moves without your will,
Does it mean
You are responsible
For the mighty and the weak?
Does it mean
You are responsible
For all wrongs being done to us?
Does it mean
You are responsible
For all the fights over temples, churches and mosques?
What pleasure do you find
In this bloodshed?
O god,
If not even a leaf trembles without your will.

Speech and Silence

We sold off our speech to earn silence
That's why silence is so hale and hearty
We are culprits
We betrayed our conscience;
Instead of imprisonment
We have endured the silence.

5

Fiction

Nanak Singh

Nanak Singh (1897–1971) was born Hans Raj in village Chak Hameed in Jhelum district (Pakistan). Though he authored many stories, plays and poems, it is as a novelist that he is best known. With him, the second and most significant era began in the history of the Punjabi novel. Nanak Singh took Punjabi literature out of its narrow concerns of religion and communality, and placed it in the realm of social reality. His work deals with issues such as widow remarriage, untouchability, unemployment, corruption, child marriage and prostitution. Many of his writings are concerned with the partition of India. It is not only as a social reformer that he is recognised, but as a writer who took literature away from the limited boundaries of religion and paved the way for progressive writing to take shape. Nanak Singh was awarded the Sahitya Akademi award in 1961 for his novel *Ek Miyaan Do Talwaran*.

An Overflow of Affection

There was no chance of getting any conveyance that day. Nothing could be arranged. I had no choice but to walk all the way, through fields and muddy paths, and on the road for some part, till at last I reached my Bhua's village. I felt a great sense of relief.

As soon as I arrived, I dashed up to my Bhua, greeted her with warmth, and touched her feet. She gestured her welcome and patted my back with affection, but I did not find the usual warmth emanating from her. This puzzled me, till I realised that she had not actually recognised me, owing to her poor eyesight.

When she asked, 'Where are you from, son?', I told her my name, and then she understood. She was beside herself with joy. She caught hold of me, hugging me tightly, kissing me all over my face, and at the same time, calling out in her excitement, 'O, Chandan Kaur, come here quick, look who's here, my Singh, by the grace of God! O, all you children, come, see, your Chacha is here.'

Her daughter-in-law came running. Bhua's grandchildren also rushed in and surrounded me. None of these little ones had seen me before but it was enough that their granny had called me their Chacha, for them to be excited.

Bhua's daughter-in-law was younger than me, and would not dare lift her veil, or speak to me. I was sitting on a low stool near Bhua, and she, sitting on the floor, was patting me on the back, stroking my head, touching my face; she couldn't have enough of me! While I—I could hardly say anything in response, except, 'Yes, Bhua, yes… *haan ji…haan ji…*', feeling like an overgrown schoolboy in the flood of her affection.

'O, my girl, go at once and get something to eat. Look at the poor boy, he must have been hungry all day on his journey, go…' sending the woman scuttling towards the kitchen. I was left protesting that there was no need, but to no avail.

The fact was that I was not in the least bit hungry. Rather, I was feeling stuffed after the wedding feast I had had earlier in the day and was determined to skip my evening meal. 'Oh, my God,' I groaned inwardly, and felt an actual fear when there appeared before me a large platter of food. Two large *parathas*, of the size of the big stone wheel of a wheat grinder, soaked in ghee to the extent that it dripped all round the platter, and seeped into a mound of sweet vermicelli covered with a sprinkling of powdered jaggery.

I stared in horror at the platter, and at my own belly. A saying cropped up in mind, 'Moses ran from death, and saw that death stood before him'.

I could not speak to Bharjai, it was not my place to do so. Nor was it any use trying to convince Bhua; it was futile to even think of it.

I did so, though. 'Bhua,' I said. 'I am not at all hungry. I ate a wedding feast, which was very heavy and I am feeling very full…' but

Bhua completely ignored what I was saying. She continued with her own talk, 'Now, this is hardly anything, son, just two small *rotis*... come on, eat it, my dear...'

'And, Bhua, how can I eat so much sweet vermicelli?' I tried to persuade her to let me off. 'Sure, you can eat it, you're my good son. What's it, only a little sweet, it's nothing, after all. What other delicacies do we have in a village? It's not like in towns, where you can get anything you fancy, you only have to ask and such things are made available. It is often said that cities and towns are for blessed angels, and only ghosts live in villages. So here we have only this simple food, son. Once we went to Amritsar when your Phhuphar was alive. It is the blessed city of the Gurus. And we were so lucky to have *darshan,* with the blessings of Guru Maharaj. Otherwise it is not easy to get away from the usual things going on at home. And even this was possible only when we had to go to Gangaji with Jethani's ashes. He said, 'Mother of Shankar, come with us, never mind about expenses, we can manage, so come along...' and so, it was a good chance for me, I could go. And now, I would like to go again, to bathe in the Ganga. Many times have I asked Shankar, my son, please, do take me there sometime, you have no problem in spending a little bit, but he doesn't listen...'

Bhua was rattling on with her stories, and I was thinking all the while, 'Is it now going to be the turn of her nephew's ashes to be consecrated in the Ganga?' But having no alternative, I thought that having put myself in this situation, I will have to bear it—and so I began to eat. I had barely had a few mouthfuls, when suddenly, before I could protest, Bharjai came up with a bowl of fresh ghee and poured it on the heap of vermicelli. It floated like a deadly sea all around the vermicelli, swilling around on the platter, as I stared at it, horrified.

How was I ever going to get relief from this self-inflicted torture? I sought a strategy. I could think of nothing, so I did somehow manage to stuff in one and a half of those *parathas,* but how should I deal with that sweet dish? It occurred to me that Bhua would hardly notice what I was doing, so I might be able to scoop a handful of vermicelli from the plate and throw it aside. But the other one, Bharjai, was also there, looking on intently from under her veil—how could anything escape her attention?

Slowly, I put a tiny morsel of vercimilli in my mouth and chewed it, waiting for it to finally go down my gullet. All of a sudden, Bharjai got up and went inside. Ah, at last, she had taken pity on me, I thought. I looked around surreptitiously, to see where I could throw the handful of food. I saw a clay oven near the wall. I could drop the food there, and then, later in the night, cover it over with the ashes of the tandoor—it would not be discovered.

Thus thinking, I scooped up as much as I could in my hand, and gathered courage. I had just lifted my hand away from the platter, when Bharjai appeared before me, and without even asking me, plonked another big *paratha* on to the plate!

I could do nothing. I put the handful of vermicelli back where it was, admitting defeat. There was no hope for me.

Finally I managed to eat half of whatever was there on that fatal platter, and was able to put the rest of it aside. But to be able to get up and move to my cot turned out to be a superhuman effort. My stomach felt like it was about to burst, while I could just about draw my breath with difficulty. I made it to the cot laid out for me in the courtyard and lay down. From the bottom of my heart, I regretted my visit—if I had to die, could I not have chosen to die in my own home?

After a while, I felt a little better. Still, I could not sleep. I tossed and turned restlessly on the cot, without finding a position in which I could be comfortable. There was no relief from the discomfort in my body, and I began to sweat profusely. There was a hand fan laid by my side, but in no circumstance could I have lifted it and fanned myself.

I became desperate after another half hour of flailing around on the cot like a fish, I felt I could not take it any more. I sat up and began to look around. Maybe if any of the children were around, I could ask them to get me a digestive that could help me. I saw with alarm that Bharjai was standing there, like an awful nemesis waiting to finish me once and for all.

She held a large bowl full of warm milk in her hands.

I refused—once, twice, three times. But Bharjai was immovable. She just stood there without speaking, holding out that infernal bowl of milk towards me.

When I could avoid it no longer, I took the bowl from her hand and placed it on the edge of the cot, and said, 'It's hot. I will drink it later, when its less warm.'

She could not allow her husband's respected elder brother to face any difficulty. She must have thought that he wanted to drink the milk at once, so she ran to the kitchen, got another vessel and began to cool the milk by transferring it from the bowl and back, till it was drinkable.

And the bowl was back in my hand again. I had hoped that she would retreat after this, but she had strict instructions from her mother-in-law that she was to return with the empty bowl, and so she did not move.

The bowl of milk might have been ambrosia for all it mattered; at that moment I would have preferred a dose of poison over it. I took a few sips, but some sips were not going to bring down the level of the milk in that big bowl.

I shed all appearance of politeness. I was not going to risk my life over this. I held the bowl towards her, and said, 'I've finished.' But she took a step back from me as though she thought it was untouchable. She did not take it back. I was out of my mind because of my extreme discomfort and irritation, and declared, 'All right, I will have it later.' And in my haste I tried to perch the bowl on the edge of the cot. Being so huge, it did not find a steady place there and crashed to the floor spilling the milk.

'Oh no!' I exclaimed, and hurriedly picked up the bowl from the floor, handing it to her, whereupon she immediately took it from me.

'What was that?' Bhua, hearing the noise, came hobbling with her cane and stood near me.

'Nothing. The milk spilled,' her daughter-in-law replied, nervous and abashed.

'O, all right, doesn't matter. There's no shortage of milk. Go bring some more,' said Bhua and sat down on the cot next to me. 'I wanted to sit and talk with you, son, open my heart to you on the ups and downs of life, but then I thought you might be so tired, I must allow you to rest, not disturb you.'

A moment later, her daughter-in-law came back and whispered into Bhua's ear, to which Bhua responded angrily. 'What did you say? You have used all the remaining milk for making curd? All of it? Oh God, I'm fed up of these people! Why did you have to make curd from all the milk? What will the boy have now? What will he think of us? He was hungry all day, then ate only a little bit. Is he to go to sleep hungry? Our boy does not come to visit us every day. Go quickly and get a bowl of milk from our neighbour's, go.'

I protested weakly. 'No, no, Bhua. There is no need. Please don't send her,' I pleaded.

'What, just listen to yourself!' Bhua spoke with affectionate reproach. 'Is this the way to talk? Since morning you have been roaming around hungry! Why, bless you, is this a stranger's house for you to be so formal? Do you know how much I prayed to have a child like you? You are the elder heir and survivor of all three families, so precious to us all. Only I can tell how many holy rituals we did to be blessed with you. Your father's side were three brothers. We arranged the marriage of the first one. But as fate decreed, his wife died even as the marriage ceremonies were being completed. He did not get married again and died a widower. The next one was Daulat Singh, your elder uncle, so handsome he was, as if an angel walked the earth and springs would burst forth from it's feet. But cruel death took him away.' Bhua's tears began to trickle down her cheeks as she narrated the story.

Bharjai had gone to the neighbour's. Bhua continued telling her stories, fascinating and heart-rending at the same time, but my mind was fixed on the reappearance of that bowl of milk, symbol of my own fate. Bhua continued, 'He was married for not even a year. The leaf decorations on the doorway had not even dried, when the hand of death snatched him away. His delicate little wife was left mourning. The youngest of the brothers was your father. Eight years passed after his marriage, but there was no issue. Son, we went everywhere—to every saint, baba and mendicant we could find.

We observed all the holy days, did all-night prayers to Hanuman, organised feasts for saints, made offerings to *fakirs* and to the holy Kambli Baba. O my son, we tried everything and travelled far and wide. We followed every suggestion that was made to us by anyone, but nothing came of all this. It was only when we went to the refuge of saint Pir Deene Shah, that our prayers were finally heard, and we were blessed with your birth. O, you are such a precious one for us, our dearest son!'

I was listening to her, but my attention was focussed on the doorway.

Bharjai returned, and I uttered a silent prayer of thanks. She held an empty bowl in her hand. In a most dejected and apologetic tone, she told her mother-in-law that there was no milk in the neighbour's house as the little calf had managed to get to the cow and suckled her dry.

Bhua could not contain her angry response. 'Now see, some blight has struck them all. There used to be so much milk that even the dogs had more than enough, and now suddenly they have no milk at all. Our boy will be ashamed to visit a house like ours where he couldn't even get a drop of milk to drink.'

She looked at me with a face full of tender compassion and said with deep concern, 'My son, I am so sorry, you will sleep hungry. I am myself not going to rest thinking about you, but what can I do?'

But I looked at the spilled milk on the floor, and felt a great sense of relief. I remembered what a poet had once said, 'Thank God, the spinning wheel had broken! I have been saved from the toil and suffering inflicted upon me!'

Gurmukh Singh Musafir

Giani Gurmukh Singh Musafir (1899–1976) was born in Adhwaal, Rawalpindi (Pakistan). He was Chief Minister of Punjab in 1966–1967 and a Member of Parliament. The stories and poems he wrote are highly respected in Punjabi literature, and are full of patriotic fervour and idealistic vision. During the freedom struggle, Musafir spent time in jail, and his writings contain descriptions of prison life from this perspective. The spirit of nationalist awakening pervades all his work. In 1978, he was awarded the Padma Vibhushan, and the Sahitya Akademi award for the short story collection *Urvar Paar*.

The Revolutionary's Daughter

1

On seeing the police appear, Kishan Singh spoke bravely, 'All right, the Khalsa is always ready and prepared', but the expression on his face belied his bold words.

'Look, if you hold up the police, and it gets late, you will have to spend the night in the detention room, not the jail. And you know the difference between them, don't you?' To this warning from the inspector, Kishan Singh retorted, 'It's all the same to me. It's not as if spending a night in detention is a new thing for me.'

'No, no, I don't mean that...' But Kishan Singh interrupted him. 'I will be ready in a moment. Let me say goodbye to my daughter'. Just then, someone came up to speak to the inspector, and he hurried off across the street to a factory-like building and entered it. One of the soldiers who was watching spoke up, 'Looks like Inspector Sahib has gone to make a telephone call to someone.'

Kishan Singh went into the room where the members of his family were waiting and his daughter Laj lay burning with fever. His sister Veeranwali seemed about to burst into tears. Kishan Singh understood the mood of each person, so he went to the other side of Laj's bed and sat on a stool near her. He caressed Laj's hair softly and said, 'My child, you are better now, I know. Your fever is down, and by tomorrow you may be completely out of it. If not for your fever, I would have already reached jail by now. All our comrades are already there.'

His beloved Laj replied to her father in a low voice. 'Father, this means I am not a good girl, to have stopped you from doing your duty!'

'No, my dear. How is it your fault? This fever is not something you can help. I wasn't ready at first to leave you in this state. The day the militants were caught in front of us, I made a speech for a few minutes, congratulating them. Since then, I have been occupied with your treatment. I did not have any time to spare to go out anywhere. Also, I think they will go after the leaders first, and then they will come after small fry like us. But what is it to us? They can come and pick us up even now. '

Kishan Singh had hardly uttered these words that Laj spoke up, 'Yes, they can do so.'

Kishan Singh feels a great sense of emotional release when talking to this darling daughter of his. As he talks, his heart grows lighter. Now he waits for his wife Sharan Kaur to come home, eyes glued to the entrance of the veranda. He is content that the inspector has not returned either.

Sitting close to both of them, Veeranwali has been unable to speak for fear that her emotions would get the better of her. Now she recovers herself sufficiently to say, 'Laj, if your father is taken away, who will get medicines for you? And won't you feel sad and upset about it?'

'Bhua ji, you are here with me, aren't you, and you will get me the medicines I need. Mother is here too. If I get sad, I can always go and stay with my Father in jail!' Veeranwali could not help but laugh out on hearing these words from Laj.

Laj said, 'No, Bhua ji, it's no laughing matter. It's not a bad thing to go to jail for one's country. I will definitely go this time.'

'Laj, you are not even twelve years old.' To this remark by her aunt, Laj replied, 'Father, do you hear what Bhua ji is saying? It seems she doesn't go to the gurudwara and listen to the sermons there. Father, will you tell Bhua ji what was the age of the young sons of the Guru, the Sahibzadas, when they sacrificed their lives for the faith? Were they not very young? And I can't even go to jail?' Now it was not just Veeranwali, but Kishan Singh whose eyes welled up with uncontrollable tears, but these were tears of happiness and gratitude.

Now Kishan Singh picked up the keys from their place at Laj's bedside. He went to the storeroom and changed his clothes there, then returned to her bedside. The answer to Laj's query, 'Father, why have you changed your clothes now, where are you going?' was quite obvious. He had so far been worried about how he would break the news of his arrest to his sick daughter. Now he brought out the books of daily prayers and the books of commentary on the scriptures from the cupboard in Laj's room, and placed them carefully in his little box. There was the sound of boots clattering in the veranda. Kishan Singh kissed the forehead of his daughter, still hot because of her fever, and murmered *My dear Laj*, softly, overcome with emotion. His frozen tears melted and poured down. The child Laj said, with great maturity and calm in her voice, 'Father, don't worry about me.' At this moment a young man slipped into the room, having dodged the police to find his way in. He whispered something into Kishan Singh's ear, and quickly slipped out. Again, Kishan Singh appeared to be disturbed. With a serious look, he gave brief instructions to Veeranwali about Laj's care, and got into the horse carriage accompanied by the police.

2

Though the guards at the town police station had been commanded to remain alert and ready as soon as the telephone call came, they waited for an hour before they were ordered to take action. So while the police dallied in their effort to cordon off the area round the Little Haveli near the bazaar, a *khadi*-clad woman ran out of a door that opened out to the street from the left side of the haveli. In one hand she held a national flag and in the other hand she was sporting a *kirpan, a* dagger that symbolised her religion. She was followed by a stream of women who rushed out, wearing similar homespun garments, shouting nationalist slogans. The policeman standing at the corner could only stare even as the large procession of women reached the centre of the bazaar. The sky reverberated with the shouts of 'Bharat Mata ki Jai!' Within a few minutes, a massive crowd gathered and the entrance to the *bazaar* was blocked. When the women shouted out the words to hail the national flag, the crowd followed suit and shouted in unison, 'Hail to the flag!'

One of the policemen, trying to snatch the flag, leapt forward while the woman holding it was advancing at full speed. The policeman's hand struck the *kirpan* in trying to stop her and in the altercation, the sheath of the dagger slid open. It scratched the policeman's hand, and blood spurted out. At this, the police reacted and began a *lathi* charge. People ran helter-skelter and the crowd began to disperse. The woman with the flag held on to it tightly with both her hands, and went up to the platform of a shop, where she sat down in protest mode, still holding the flag. The other women also sat down in the street beside her. As the crowd thinned out, the chief of the guards approached and spoke to the woman with flag, first with authority, and then with a milder, persuading manner, asking her to hand over the flag. But the determined woman declared, 'This flag will stay with me till I die'. Finally, the entire group was arrested and forced into horse carriages and taken away. The issue of the flag came up again at the entrance to the jail. The women were adamant that they would take the national flag into the jail and hoist it atop the jail barracks. While the argument was underway, the party bringing Kishan Singh to the jail also arrived. Kishan Singh was not surprised to see his wife Sharan Kaur holding the flag in the midst of a large group of women. He took it on himself to explain to the gathering, 'You have all done well to affirm your faith with the flag. You did not allow any disrespect to the flag even in the midst of everything. Now you have been arrested, so even if you do succeed in hoisting the flag on the barrack roof, the jail authorities will take it down at once after locking you inside the barracks. They will simply tear it down and this will not be a good thing'. Finally, it was decided that the flag would be borne with all honour to the office of the Congress and kept there. As she entered the jail, Sharan inquired about Laj, but before Kishan Singh could reply, the jail doors slammed shut and she did not hear the reply.

3

Though she was suffering both from intense fever and the deprivation caused by the absence of her parents, Laj was inspired by the fervour of the nationalist movement. Over the next few days, she felt better and left her bed. Bhua did not spare any effort in looking after her, and even took Laj to her own house so she could tend to her. Veerawali's husband Zamindaar Hushnaak Singh was in the army and was on his way home on leave. On the way, he was told by a friend of the arrest of his brother-in-law Kishan Singh and his wife Sharan Kaur. No newspapers were allowed in the army cantonment area. When his carriage stopped at the door of his house, Laj was standing in the doorway. She ran inside to inform her aunt of her uncle's arrival, then rushed back to greet him. Veeranwali first rushed to the door to greet her husband with a formal 'Sat Sri Akal', then went back in to tidy her hair in front of the mirror, change the *dupatta* on her head before emerging again to help bring in her husband's bags. Laj also began to help her aunt in bringing in small bits and pieces. Neighbours and friends soon began to pour in to welcome Hushnaak Singh on his return, and Veeranwali was busy making tea for everyone. After the visitors left, she asked, stirring sugar into his tea, 'Ji. I hope you have been well'.

'I have been well so far, but it seems you are not going to let me stay that way for too long now', he retorted. This was just the kind of reply she expected. She had already sensed rancour in her husband's expression, but had not been able to fathom the exact cause. She did not continue the conversation any further. Hushnaak Singh swallowed his tea with obvious unwillingness. Veeranwali put off further discussion till it was time for their dinner. Hushnaak Singh ate his meal in sullen silence. Veeranwali had lost her appetite. Hushnaak Singh changed and lay down on his bed. After she had given Laj her dinner, Veeranwali wound up the kitchen, and then approached her husband. She sat by his side on the bed and began to press his legs. For a while, all was silence between husband and wife. Then Hushnaak Singh turned over on his side, yawned, as if he had dropped off to sleep and had just woken up to see Veeranwali siting near him. Veeranwali said to him, 'Ji, please, look here, don't show your displeasure like this; see, how we've been waiting for you, to talk to you, but you don't even glance at us. I hope you've been granted some days of leave?' Hushnaak Singh turned on his side, towards her, but covered his eyes with his hands in a gesture of despair. 'You may say this will be permanent leave for me! You can't bear that fortune should smile on me. I was so close to being promoted, but you'll make sure that doesn't happen.'

'Why? What's the matter?'

'Now, do I have to explain this to you? You know that these are days of unrest and the government does not tolerate anyone who has links with the revolutionaries. Can it be kept a secret, so that the government does not know that any of our relatives are among those revolutionaries? Even if they do come to know, we can tell that we are not on good terms with them. But why have you brought her into our house? Don't you understand this is a crime?'

Veeranwali felt herself begin to tremble on hearing these words. It hadn't occurred to her that bringing the sick child Laj to her house would displease her husband to such an extent. Her whole being filled with dread and she broke into a sweat. 'Why did you bring this girl into my house?' Hushnaaak Singh demanded a reply.

Somehow, Veeranwali gathered courage and narrated the events that had taken place, with a tone of deep humility and supplication towards her husband as if she were praying to a goddess for benevolence. But she realised that this god—her husband—was made of stone. She, who had looked forward so eagerly to her husband's return, found that her hopes were shattered and her dreams scattered and transformed into shadows that haunted her. She tossed sleeplessly the whole night. Her tears flowed like precious offerings, but the unmoving deity was unaffected. Her husband's accusations had made her feel that she was indeed guilty of a terrible crime.

The uneasy silence that lay between the couple became more evident the more they tried to hide it. Friends and neighbours came to hear of the matter. The advice and opinion of the wise neighbours and concerned people further convinced Hushnaak Singh that he was not in any way responsible for sheltering and nurturing his brother-in-law's daughter. He believed that Laj's presence in his home was responsible for the destruction of all his hopes. Else, he would definitely have been promoted to the rank of Subedar-Major during the current conflict. Some inkling of this talk might have reached Laj. Hushnaak Singh's leave came to an end, and he ordered the horse carriage to be brought to his door. He grabbed Veeranwali by the arm and dragged her out to the carriage, forcing her to sit in it. He locked the house and put the keys in his pocket. Laj, who was playing outside with other girls, watched helplessly as her aunt, whose eyes were filled with tears, looked back towards her. The horse carriage drove off.

4

'Brother, what happened to Laj?'

'But Veeran, we had left her in your keeping!'

The conversation between Kishan Singh and his sister Veeranwali took place in the meeting area of the Multan Central Jail, fourteen months later. The one hour that was allotted to them to converse was taken up by this question for which there was no answer, and the silence between them said it all. The emotion behind their thoughts could not be expressed in words, and perhaps only someone who understands the language of silence could interpret what the heart was trying to communicate. When the bell rang, the brother and sister parted in silence, their eyes still fastened on each other. Little did Kishan Singh realise that this was the last time he would see his sister.

There are constant comings and goings of prisoners to the jail. Kishan Singh hears that Laj has been admitted to the Lahore hospital but he has no way of knowing that Veeranwali is undergoing an even more strict imprisonment in the army cantonment. In there, even a fly can't enter or depart without permission. Who would have conveyed to Veeranwali any news about her revolutionary brother, his wife, or the daughter of that revolutionary? And how, and by what means Veeranwali had reached the jail to meet her brother, was not known to anyone. She put her life at risk to do this, and successfully kept it a secret from Hushnaak Singh; her guilt for her failure to protect her brother's legacy due to her compulsions weighed heavily on her and she could not bear the sorrow. In her agony, she fell ill. Hushnaak Singh did not care about finding out the cause of her illness, and medicines did not work. Before Sharan Kaur was released from prison, Veeranwali gave up her life rather than live to face the person whose trust she had not been able to honour.

On her release, Sharan Kaur went immediately to the Lahore hospital. The main door of the hospital was closed. The gatekeeper told her, 'This is the patients' rest hour.' She turned away towards the left of the doorway where there was an outhouse for sweepers. The sweeper looked at the Sharan in her homespun khadi, and asked, 'Who do you want to meet?' Sharan Kaur was waiting for someone to talk to, and replied at once, 'My daughter is ill in this hospital. Her name is Laj.' The sweeper asked her if she knew the ward number, and then added, 'We don't know that name. I go in every day and sweep all the wards.' Sharan Kaur told her, 'I don't know the number of the ward, or room number. I just heard that my Laj was in this hospital.'

'You heard? You mean, you did not admit her here yourself?' The woman asked in surprise.

'No, we were in jail. She got sick at the time I was in jail.'

'Oh, then she must be the revolutionary's daughter!' exclaimed the sweeper woman, hearing Sharan Kaur mention the jail. 'Over here, no-one knows her by the name of Laj. She's fair complexioned, thin...about twelve or thirteen years of age? She speaks very sweetly. Sometimes her talk makes us laugh, and sometimes it makes us cry. Was she living with her aunt?' Sharan Kaur nodded in assent.

'Yes, then, that's her. When she came here she asked, "What's the meaning of 'revolutionary'?" She said that her uncle had demanded from her aunt why she had brought home a revolutionary's daughter. From that day on, she is known as the revolutionary's daughter. When the doctor comes around, she always asks him, "Please can you take me to the jail to see my father?" The doctor just laughs'. Sharan Kaur stood transfixed, listening to the words of the sweeper.

The woman asked, 'Has Sardar ji not come with you?'

'He's still in jail. He has only served half the time—he got three years.' On hearing this, the sweeper sighed deeply and said, 'Your daughter is very sensible. She told us that she had seen her uncle take her aunt away. Then she had slept outside on the steps of the house and caught fever sleeping in the cold. When she became very ill, she was left here. She said she asked to be taken to the jail, but no-one listened to her.... Now, she is only waiting for you.'

Sharan Kaur understood. She had exhausted all her tears even before she reached the room where Laj lay. On seeing her mother, Laj's eyes brightened. It was the last flicker of the lamp that burns out at dawn.

Sant Singh Sekhon

Sant Singh Sekhon (1906–1997) was born in village Chak 70, district Lyallpur (now Faisalabad, in Pakistan). He received an MA in English and Economics, and in 1939 started a journal, *Northern Review*. He wrote plays and novels as well as short stories and is also highly regarded as a critic. He won the Sahitya Akademi award in 1972 for his play *Mittar Piyara* and the Padma Shri in 1987. Sekhon is well-known for his progressive vision; in addition to the depiction of social realities, his characters deeply reflect his understanding of human psychology.

The Ploughman

At eighteen years of age, Sahbo had grown into a beautiful strapping young woman. Almost every day her parents, who belonged to a nomadic tribe, and her relatives would deliberate upon the matter of her marriage; they had been trying to reach some agreement about it in some of these meetings. But Sahbo was not in the least interested in any of the young men in her family. The oldest son of her father's elder brother, Ameer, who had been imprisoned twice in cases of theft, was tall and good-looking, but Sahbo considered him to be a coward. Both times he had been caught during the buglary, and the boys belonging to that newly empowered clan of *jat*s had also beaten him up. Even if he was not an outright coward, he was a spineless fellow, the sort of person who would commit theft by breaking a hole in the rear wall of the house. In fact, those boys from well-established and affluent families also saw him as a weakling. They would say that he was all brawn, but had no heart. And it was the quality of heart that was valued by Sahbo, not bodily charm, of which she herself had plenty. She was tall too—all of five feet and six inches. And did she not herself possess a supple body, and fair complexion?

Another thing, Sahbo was quite impressed by the *jat* Sikhs. They had lands to their name. The British had carved out canals in this area of Sandal Bar, and given land to the *jat* around the place, even though Sahbo's entire clan had been living in the area of Bar for generations. And if her ancestors, the elder men in her family, had any guts, would they have allowed any one to settle on their land? However, Sahbo was not very concerned about these matters, though she had heard her father and his brothers complaining. It was also true that Sahbo's father had neither land nor a house in that village. He had plenty of cattle—and flocks of sheep and goats—and he was not a tenant ploughing someone else's fields; and he was able to sell milk and ghee, and trade some of the animals, which was good enough. But the house they lived in had been given to them by the resident on the land, Gurnam Singh. The *jats* had allowed her father to take half the space in his compound, and that in itself made Gurnam Singh entitled to all the dung fuel in the place. And while Sahbo's father and her brothers—Gaama, Sajada, Allu, Sooji—were not cowed down or the least servile, it was Gurnam Singh's wife, Har Kaur, who would speak in soft, humble tones to Sahbo's mother Ayesha, trying to flatter her. And though neither Har Kaur nor the *jats* of Gurnam Singh's family could even pronounce the name of her mother Ayesha properly—they would say 'Aisha'—Sahbo still felt compelled to think of them as superior, somehow.

And, of course, none of the women of the *jat*'s family—none of the daughters or wives—were as beautiful as Sahbo. It was not Sahbo who said this about herself out of vanity. Even the best looking among all the village women said this to Sahbo and her mother Ayesha. The girls of all the neighbouring houses were always praising Sahbo's beauty. It was quite clear that no one in the village matched up to the slim and tall Sahbo, but how could they know how beautiful she really was under her robes, but she herself? In spite of this, Sahbo was desirous of becoming a part of the *jat* families, and perhaps an exalted member of their clan.

From a village about five or six miles away, a handsome young man, from the nomadic tribes, used to visit Sahbo's home. His name was Shahabuddin, and he had a mare who appeared to Sahbo as sleek and lovely as herself. It was said that he also had a measure of land, as much as the land of one of the *jat*s, maybe as much as that of Gurnam Singh, Wadhwa Singh, Ishar Singh or Kishan Singh, but Sahbo found this hard to believe. If the British had indeed given the land to a nomad like Shahabuddin, wouldn't they also have done the same in the case of her father and other men of the clan? He was ordinary in the eyes of the *jat*—maybe the *jat* of his own village called him 'Saaba' for short, the way the people of her village called Sahbo as 'Saabo'. Whatever it may be, Sahbo's father and brothers had never considered Shahabuddin a suitable match worthy of her. He, however, would frequently cast glances at her. Sahbo would feel as though he was looking at her right through her clothes and sizing her up. This made her uncomfortable in his presence, and so she did not really think well of him. She suspected that she was the reason why Shahabuddin made so many appearances at their house. Once on the way back from Lyallpur, Allu, Sahbo's brother, had happened to meet him, and brought him home. That day, she remembered, she had been standing at the door when they arrived. Perhaps Shahabuddin had been attracted to her since that day. But she was certainly not appreciative of the way in which he would land up at their house every few days after that first visit. If he was so interested, why did he not declare his intentions and ask Sahbo's father to give consent to *nikaah* with her? What was stopping him? Maybe, he had already done so, and her father has refused. However, Sahbo would have heard something about this from her mother, but she had not been told anything. It could be that her parents were so set against any idea of Shahabuddin marrying their daughter that they did not think it proper to even mention it to her, for fear that she might begin to think about him as a prospective husband. And why would they need to do this, Sahbo thought to herself. If at all she wanted to, she could easily run away with him. He had a mare that could gallop at a fast pace. Couldn't they both ride away on that faster than on a train. Hadn't Shahabuddin suggested to her, Sahbo, don't you want to try riding the mare? Sahbo had not given him any reply, but—she had smiled to herself. It was true she was veiled, but Shahabuddin might have seen the trace of a smile in her eyes. Whatever it may be, it was clear that Sahbo was not prepared to run away with him.

If Gurnam Singh had had a grown-up son, would he not have fallen in love with Sahbo, despite the fact that the *jat* women of the household did not allow the nomad women to come into their kitchens, and were particular that their food should not be contaminated by contact with those people. Sahbo was sure that she would have been accepted as a daughter-in-law in Gurnam Singh's family. But then she would also have doubts whether these *jats* would have that kind of courage. Besides, Gurnam Singh's son was barely eight years old. Once, Gurnam Singh's twelve-year-old daughter had jokingly conveyed a message from him to Sahbo, saying that when he grew up, he wanted to marry Sahbo. But this was just a joke, after all. Sahbo was neither a child, nor so foolish as to mistake it for anything other than that.

Around this time, a new situation arose, in which it seemed that there would be signs of the fulfilment of Sahbo's wishes. This was in the form of a nephew of Gurnam Singh, who belonged to the area near Ludhiana, arriving there to stay with his maternal uncle. He was about eighteen years of age. He wore a turban of cream-coloured muslin and a length of white cloth around his waist. Sahbo liked his appearance, and also liked the sound of his name, Niranjan.

Gurnam Singh was in no hurry to send his nephew back to his own home for a few months, at least. It was monsoon, when the fields needed to be ploughed and made ready for planting the wheat crop, and where would he find a ready help in this area, but his nephew Niranjan? At first, Niranjan was like a guest, enjoying his uncle's hospitality. After some days, he began to go with his uncle to plough the fields, just as a way of occupying himself. This suited his uncle, who did not want to hire another hand for the field, and thought he would save money for a month or two if Niranjan worked for him—he was quite a calculating man, that Gurnam Singh!

Niranjan also took a fancy to Sahbo. He would catch sight of her while entering or leaving the compound, and she would meet his eyes without being shy. Niranjan became quite fascinated with looking at Sahbo and exchanging glances with her, and so did not hesitate to extend his visit. Gurnam Singh did not have to persuade him, he agreed to stay on for some more time at his uncle's place.

In a few days, however, Niranjan got tired of having to get up early in the morning to plough the fields. In the Bar area, the custom was to plough very early in the morning. The ploughmen would start out shortly after the middle of the night, and they would finish ploughing a few acres by the time they returned, at seven or eight in the morning. These were nights when *kabaddi* matches would be held in the village, particularly in the moonlit phase of the month. The village boys would play *kabaddi* in the open grounds till late at night, and Niranjan would often join them, playing the game and returning home very late at night. On some nights Niranjan would hardly get an hour's sleep before Gurnam Singh would shake him awake to go out and plough the fields. Niranjan would try to ignore him, but eventually would have to get up and get to work. Poor Niranjan was exhausted. His cream-coloured turban lost its lustre and was never starched. The folds of fabric could not keep their crispness any more, and the plume of the turban could not keep itself perfectly sharp and stiff. Gurnam Singh's daughter-in-law would wash it every few days, but a turban does not retain its stiff, regal contours by washing alone. Niranjan would try to stretch and fold the material to give the end of his turban the required shape but it would only stay up for a few hours before collapsing and the unstarched cloth would go limp. Niranjan's smart, pointed shoes became grubby with dirt, but he somehow managed to protect them from losing their shape. His waistcloth did not rustle as it used to when it was crisp. The villagers would laugh at him, and tease him, 'Oye, you stupid fellow, why are you becoming a slave? You think your uncle is going to leave his lands to you?'

Niranjan did not think he was badly off. He knew well enough that back in his own Majri village he would not get a better deal than this. Here in the Bar, at his uncle's, he had to go out to plough once a day, and could eat well; butter and milk was available to him; in Majri he had to plough twice a day and eat the same frugal diet that his father ate. They did not have land vast enough to employ more hands; nor did they have the capacity to manage other farmers' fields. As it was, they had only one pair of bullocks for ploughing; either he or his father could use it at a time. His father was impatiently waiting for Niranjan to come back, and had sent letters asking Niranjan to return and do the ploughing, while he attended to other tasks, such as cutting the grass for fodder. But Niranjan was aware that this task was not very important. During the monsoon, there was no urgent need to get a lot of fodder for their two bullocks and one buffalo—the bulls would feed themselves on the grass growing abundantly in the fields when they were taken out for ploughing. Niranjan's mother had actually sent word to him to say that it was quite all right for him to stay at his uncle's place for longer. She knew that in living in the Bar area Niranjan could build up his health partaking of plenty of ghee and milk. Maybe the availability of such abundant ghee and milk was not such as Niranjan could benefit from, but it was a good reason for him to make up his mind to stay on longer with his uncle. And the truth really was that he was quite happy to exchange glances with Sahbo every now and then, going in and out of the house, and he was not prepared to forego this pleasure just yet. So he stayed on.

His appearance was not as good as it had been, and he was often the butt of jokes, but Sahbo found him attractive enough and in her mind, she saw in the ploughman the same Niranjan of the starched cream turban and crisp waistcloth that she had first seen.

Finally one day Sahbo did talk to him, on the pretext of helping to lift up a basket-load of cow dung. That night it had been raining and they had not gone out for ploughing, so he was free in the morning.

'Well, I will soon be leaving, Sahbo,' Niranjan said to her after a few days of their meeting.

'So take me with you then,' she spoke up, having gathered the courage to make her decision.

It was in this way their relationship had deepened from flirtation to a more serious level. Then it happened that they decided one night that they would run away together. There was a railway station about two miles away, from where a train left every morning at four. They planned to take the train. Sahbo was to go to the rooftop where Niranjan slept, wake him up without anyone in the family noticing.

As decided, Sahbo went to Niranjan in the night and shook him gently to wake him. Niranjan mumbled to himself in his sleep and turned over. Sahbo crossed to the other side of the bed and shook him again to awaken him as quietly as she could. Niranjan rolled over to the other side and slept on. Sahbo tried a few more times to rouse him from his sleep, but he did not wake up. At last, she gave up in despair and returned to her own bed.

In a few days a rumour spread in the village that Sahbo had run away with someone. Then it became clear that she had indeed gone away, with one Shahabuddin from the Chak 34 area, riding with him on the back of his mare. Some days later it was heard that with the consent of the family Sahbo and Shahabuddin were married in a *nikaah* ceremony over in the Chak 34 area.

'I thought my Uncle was trying to wake me up to plough the fields!' When his close friends asked about the event, that was the explanation of the shamefaced Niranjan.

Jaswant Singh Kanwal

Jaswant Singh Kanwal (1919–2020) was born in village Dudhike in district Moga. He was a stalwart among Punjabi litterateurs. He was a novelist, short story writer and an essayist. Rural culture is foregrounded in his works, which centre around the villages of Malwa region, with themes of social diversity and romantic relationships. There is an idealistic aspect to his vision. He wrote about the events in the time of militancy in Punjab and the injustices suffered by the Punjabis are often the focus of his work. Some writers have commented on the variability and contradictions they see in his ideas, but many recognise his unwavering sympathy for the Punjabi people through all the trials the state has been through. He was awarded the Sahitya Akademi prize in 1997 for his work *Toshali di Hanso*.

Honesty

I had reached Wolverhampton on the express train from London. Even though there was a blizzard raging outside, I felt no need to keep my overcoat on inside the train, and so I took it off. The white man who sat opposite me was absorbed in reading his newspaper, while his cup of tea waited beside him. We Punjabis are very different in this matter. We always borrow a newspaper—we never have our own. Or worse, we often look over the shoulder of the person with the newspaper, and read the headlines surreptitiously, as if we were entitled to share the newspaper. True to my Punjabi nature, I also glanced stealthily at the man's paper, and noticed what he was so deeply absorbed in, the results of the dog races.

I had the presence of mind to quickly suppress a smile. I was also a little ashamed of my behaviour, but I still thought that in every way—be it hard work, responsibility and good fortune, I was on higher ground than this white man. With this thought, I ordered a coffee to recover my sense of dignity. We Punjabis associate a man's dignity with the state of his mustache, and so I thought I would perk up my own mustache to show my pride. However, my white co-passenger did not show any interest at all in my air of self-importance. I began to indulge in some introspection.

'Look here, Kanwal Singh,' I said to myself. 'The reality is that even after becoming free, your people are still working as slaves in the smoky factories of this country. No surprise that our false pride does not impress anyone!'

When the train stopped in Birmingham, the white man stepped off, leaving the paper on the table. It was a thirty-page paper, and many pages of it were plastered with photographs. Back in Punjab, we even grab discarded newspapers when we alight from a train. The thought made my remaining pride melt away, and the coffee was no help in restoring the drooping of my mustache. It was in this reflective frame of mind, pondering about the contrasts between English and Punjabi attitudes, that I got off the train at Wolverhampton. At the gate, as I handed my ticket to the collector, a blast of chilly air blew on my forehead through my turban. And then I realised that I had left my overcoat behind on the train. That coat belonged to my friend Gurdial. I turned to look back, but the train had already left the platform. It had hardly stopped for a minute at the station.

In a distracted state, I made my exit from the station. My condition was as pathetic as that of an opium addict who had been beaten up and robbed of his drug dose, and did not even have the cash to buy another fix. In all my travels through England and Europe, this was the worst day for me. Trying to forget the episode of the coat, I threw myself into a taxi. I could not take pleasure in any of the sights now. I hadn't come sightseeing, I had come for a get-together at my friend's house. I cheered up at the thought.

On reaching his house, I found Gurdial at home. Even though I hadn't told him that I was going to visit, he was utterly delighted to see me.

'This is wonderful, Kanwal! It's great that you've come! You know, I just won thirteen pounds at the pools, so let's celebrate—we'll spend it all tonight. He was jumping about like the waves tossing on the shore of Liverpool. 'Coffee, perhaps?' he suggested. 'I know you won't have whisky or brandy, but it's cold.'

Somehow, I still could not bring myself to be cheerful. I thought I might tell him about the loss of the coat and that would dampen his spirits too. But I kept my mouth shut.

'What's the matter? Why are you looking so gloomy?' He searched my face to find the reason for the serious look I had.

'So you've won thirteen pounds at the pools, and you now need at least four pounds more,' I said calmly, scratching my ear.

'Oh, don't bother about pounds, we can manage, you tell me what it is.'

'I have to pay for the coat.'

At first he did not understand what I was trying to say. But when he realised what I was so worried about, he laughed heartily. This made me even more perplexed than I was already. He picked up the phone and got busy dialing a number.

'Hello? Railway enquiry?'

'Yes sir'.

'I'm sorry, but a person newly arrived from India had forgotten his coat on the train.'

'Which train was it?'

'The express to Liverpool'.

'Where was his seat?'

'Next to the pantry car.'

'Where had he placed the coat?'

'On the shelf.'

'Can you describe the coat?'

'Sir, it was a black coat and it has checks.'

'We'll try to find it for you.'

My understanding of this reply was that it was negative, since 'to try' in the Punjabi sense of the phrase meant that it was not a definite yes, and so meant nothing. All of that night, I was not able to enjoy myself, though I was in the company of friends. Despite the brightly lit place and the warmth of whisky, I was listless and disturbed. When we were coming out of a pub or club, the cold sharp wind pierced through me unsparingly, even though I had a new coat. I kept feeling annoyed with that white passenger on the train who had not only caused my self-respect to droop, but also caused the loss of my coat. At night, I was so restless that I knocked over the flask of warm water kept near my couch. I was still upset, and I felt my hands had become numb with cold, such was my condition.

The next evening, there was a call from the railway office.

'Your coat has been retrieved. Please come to the office and bring three shillings as payment for the packing.'

The news came as a blow to me. I had nourished the desire that the coat should not be found. It would have confirmed that England was no better than Punjab; that would help me retain that Punjabi pride that our stiff mustache is a symbol of. On the other hand, the news was so good that the depressing cold seemed to have lessened, and the warmth of sunshine made the day beautiful. When I recovered from the surprise that the return of the coat had sprung on me, I realised that I felt smaller than before. I had prided myself on something that didn't exist—because in Punjab, I had never got back anything that I had lost—not even a handkerchief. But here, in the UK, that coat costing four hundred rupees had found its way across four hundred miles and was now covering my back. I reasoned to myself, this is how things change, how people who were poor once, become rich, and those who were kings once have become paupers in every way...I was trying to reconcile with this truth.

'Kanwal Singh, do understand that Rome was not built in a day, a nation also takes centuries to evolve.'

'So where do I stand, and my pride, my "mustache"?'

'My dear, it has not even begun to sprout!'

I therefore conclude, whether I, Kanwal, like it or not, I have no choice but to raise my arm in a salute to that display of white man's honesty that I have witnessed.

Sujaan Singh

Sujaan Singh (1909–93) achieved fame as a short story writer, though he was also known as a writer of prose. He was born in Dera Baba Nanak, district Amritsar. Though he retired as the principal of a college, he faced severe hardship in his early life. Sujaan Singh depicted the lives of the poor, the labourers, the working class and the farmers from a socialist perspective, repeatedly presenting the issues of class struggle to his readers. He received the Sahitya Akademi award in 1986 for his book *Shehar Te Graan*.

Kulfi

Though it was nearly the end of the month, it seemed as though the month would never end. I was reflecting on this, how the first fifteen days of the month pass by so swiftly, and the month's salary dwindles steadily over these fifteen days, till it vanishes into thin air. As I lay, I felt the mattress dig into my back, and when I turned over and ran my hand on my back, I felt the pattern on my skin.

'Kulfi! Creamy, cold kulfi!' called out the vendor from the street in a voice that also held the promise of a delicious chill. That voice echoed in my head for a long while. I could see that white creamy kulfi very clearly with my mind's eye. My mouth watered at the thought. But there was nothing I could do. The restriction that lack of money brings is worse than physical restriction inside a jail. Just so that I could take my mind off the thought of the kulfi, I began to ponder over the origin of the word itself. Where did the word 'kulfi' come from? 'Kufal' is a word that means 'to lock', and the goldsmiths say this about pouring the gold into a mould so that it gets 'locked' into that shape. From this, is seems, comes the word 'kulfi', as the cream is also poured into a mould and locked—or frozen...and so, all the while thinking about this, I drifted off to sleep, getting some relief from the desire for kulfi that was tormenting me.

Kaka, my little boy, shook me awake before I was done with my afternoon nap. He had grabbed my arm and was shaking it. I was irritated, but his sweet lisping voice managed to soothe me.

'Daaji! I called you so many times, why don't you wake up!'

'Yes, yes, what do you want? Tell me.' I answered, a little impatiently.

'Daaji, I want a *taka*, Daaji!'

But of course I did not have a taka for him. I was completely out of pocket. It was the 26th of June, and even the daily expenses of the household were somehow being met by means of credit from the nearby shop.

'Daaji, come on, give me a taka!'

Right outside our door, a vendor was calling out, selling sweet rice candy.

Just to buy some time to think of a reply, I said, 'Kaka! What do you need a taka for?'

'To spend it, what else? What else do you do with a taka?'

After the Great War, when everything had become very dear, we used to get a half-penny as pocket money. With that, the amount of roasted gram we could get from Masti Ram's shop was so generous that we could hardly finish it all. But now we did not get as much as we did then even if we paid more. And as for income—my own income was far less than my father's, though I had more educational qualifications than he had. I began to ponder over the economic situation of the world and the effect of the practices of all its capitalists.

Again the vendor called out his wares, and again Kaka demanded, 'Daaji, give me a taka, come on!'

'A taka is no good, my dear.' I said, with despair born out of the circumstances.

'Huh? No, no. Taka is good. I can buy candy with a taka.'

'Candy is no good.' I had hardly uttered these words that Kaka interrupted me. 'Candy is sweet.' He said firmly.

I had no answer to this argument. I too am fond of sweets, but I had to keep up my defense.

'Sweets will make you cough, my child.'

'Just give me a taka. I won't get a cough', he insisted.

It looked like the boy was going to throw a tantrum. But I did not have a taka to give him. Perhaps it was to distract him, by promising him some bigger reward, I blurted out, 'This rice candy is not good. We will go to the market in the evening and have kulfi.'

By this time, that vendor had gone away. Contrary to my expectation, Kaka agreed to wait till the evening to eat kulfi. I thought, fine, at least for a while I would get some relief. I got dressed, and even though it was still quite sunny, went out of the house. I wandered around aimlessly in the streets, just killing time. How ironic it is, that simply for the want of a taka I should have to waste all this precious time.

Why do I not tell my boss that I really cannot manage with the current salary, and ask for a raise? But will anyone listen to my request? No one hears the voice of a lone individual, and it is not to be expected that all the employees will unite for their demands. Even if they were to think of it, they would not be allowed to gather and press their demands—they would be dispersed. Some might even be dismissed from the job. I was afraid this might happen to me. The terrible spectre of unemployment hovered over me and I trembled with fear. I admit I have always been quite cowardly, and in the current circumstances, I decided to keep quiet.

As evening came, I hoped Kaka would have gone to bed. I approached the house on tiptoe. I did not call out, but knocked gently on the door. At once, a voice called out, 'I'm coming, Daaji!' and in a moment Kaka ran up to open the door for me.

'Daaji, are we going out to eat kulfi?' he asked, eagerly.

'Go upstairs, go now', I said.

The boy turned away, walking off in a dispirited way. On the terrace, I sat down on the bed and took him in my lap. I spoke gently to him, 'It is very late now, we will have kulfi tomorrow.'

I did not expect it, but he quietly accepted my words. He lay down and stared up at the sky for a long time. 'Daaji, the stars are really rupee coins, are they not? Elder cousin says that they are coins, so, Daaji, why do the coins not rain on our roof?'

I dismissed his question with a short reply 'No, stars are not rupees.' He kept looking at the stars, lying on his cot, and at long last, fell into sleep.

The next day I thought of borrowing some money from my colleagues at work, but somehow could not summon up courage to do so. It is very hard to beg. It is demeaning to be a beggar—one would rather die than beg.

In the end, I did yield to my need, and borrowed a sum of three rupees from a friend. On reaching home, I saw that Kaka was taking his afternoon nap. No sooner had I been served my lunch than my wife took the three rupees away from me. And soon, all three rupees were spent—some wood for fuel, vegetables for the next meal, salt, oil and other things—even before Kaka woke up. I put up a struggle, 'I have to buy some kulfi for the boy,' but she said, 'He's not going to remember anything about kulfi. Let it be. I'll give him a taka to get rice candy.'

As soon as Kaka awoke, he asked for kulfi. He threw a tantrum. Why would yesterday's taka be acceptable now in place of kulfi?

I finally promised him that we would go out to buy kulfi in the evening, and he gave in, trusting me with his taka to be kept safe till then. In the early evening, I made an excuse of getting some exercise and slipped out of the house, returning quite late at night. I was relieved to find Kaka fast asleep. Over the meal, my wife informed me that the boy had been waiting for me all evening. I lay down next to him, but was very restless. I could not get to sleep for a long time, but ultimately, I did fall asleep. As it is said, sleep can come even when one is lying on thorns.

Kaka too was restless as the night wore on. He tossed around on the bed, and even kicked me several times in his sleep. When he flung out an arm onto my face, I was jolted awake, though I had been partially awake already. He muttered something that I did not hear, but when he mumbled more audibly, I heard the words 'Kulfi... Daaji...kulfi'. My wife called out to me 'Sardarji, are you listening?' And, seeing that I was awake, she continued to speak. 'Look at him, the wretch, demanding kulfi even in his sleep!' I felt as if I had been struck with lightning, but what could I say? I did not reply, and Kaka also fell silent.

When he woke up the next morning, Kaka did not ask for kulfi. Even after I returned from work, he did not ask for anything. I had my lunch, and lay down on my bed for my afternoon nap. The prickly mattress and the inability to get any more credit, both bothered me. After a while, I dozed off. I was not fully asleep, though, when a familiar call from the street fell on my ears. 'Kulfi! Cold-cold kulfi! Creamy kulfi!' I awoke at once. Kaka had been sitting near me playing with an old rubber duck. The vendor's call, when it came the second time, alerted him. He threw the toy aside and got up. He went near the door and stood at the doorway, looking out. I thought he would come back to wake me up, but he continued to stand there in silence. Then he slipped out. I too got up and quietly walked to the doorway, watching him from behind the door. I saw that the kulfi vendor was taking out kulfi to give to the son of the Shah ji, the merchant who lived opposite our house. That boy was known as the 'bully' of our street, always out to beat up boys smaller than him. He was around eight years old, older than our Kaka by about three years. Kaka stood there, his legs held apart and straight, his arms behind him, in the stance of a soldier. His eyes were riveted on the kulfi held in the hand of the vendor, but he did not ask the vendor to give him any. But just as the vendor put the plate of kulfi in the hands of the Shah's boy, Kaka leapt towards him and punched the bully in the face. The plate of kulfi went flying, so did the *faluda*, the spoon, and everything, and the Shah's boy fell, tumbling into the gutter. Kaka stood above him, looking at him in triumph. Quickly, the Shah's boy got up in fury. He was bursting with rage at the wasted kulfi and the insult to his pride. He had hardly found his feet when Kaka gave him a forceful kick and sent the bully reeling back into the gutter, screaming. The kulfi vendor advanced towards Kaka to strike him, but I rushed out and picked up the boy. The vendor helped the Shah's boy to get up. The Shah's wife, who rarely put up with such things, came to our house to complain. The energy of his actions had made Kaka's face and body burn. His mother began to scold him. 'Come here, you ruffian! Because of you we have to listen to complaints from people!' She even raised her hand to slap him. But I stopped her. 'Don't be foolish. Rather you should be thankful that a brave son is born of a cowardly father!'

Kartar Singh Duggal

Kartar Singh Duggal (1917–2012) was born in village Dhamiaal in the district of Rawalpindi. He held many distinguished positions which included those of Director, All India Radio; Secretary, National Book Trust and Advisor in the Ministry of Information and Broadcasting. He was also a nominated member of the Rajya Sabha, the Upper House of the Indian parliament. He is known primarily as a short story writer, though he also wrote novels, poetry and non-fiction. He was a sharp observer of psychological states and human sexuality, and perhaps for this reason some critics regard his writings as as too explicit in the treatment of such issues. Duggal probed deeply into the psyche of his characters, and the subtlety of his thought is reflected evocatively through the Pothohari dialect of Punjabi. Duggal was awarded the Sahitya Akademi award in 1965 for his collection of stories *Ek Chhit Chanan Di*. In 1988, he was honoured with Padma Bhushan and in 2007 he was awarded the Sahitya Akademi Fellowship.

Neeli

Neeli was fair-skinned. In fact, she was whiter than white, as if a ball of white butter had been washed with milk to make it whiter.

Lovely she was, and healthy. The milk from a healthy cow is bound to be wholesome. My wife had chosen Neeli from several other animals owned by the cattle-owner, and it was decided that we would buy Neeli's milk.

Every morning, the owner would bring Neeli to our compound, stand her under the mehndi tree, and she would be milked, a whole milk can full, before she was taken back.

Every morning, Neeli would arrive, her owner following, carrying on his head a basket full of fodder. He would place the basket in front of her. Then he would slowly stroke her back. While she munched the fodder, he would squat and start milking her. The milk squirted into the can in a steady rhythm.

All the while that she was being milked, Neeli would continue to munch on the nutritious mixture of fodder and cottonseed. When we had settled the rate for the milk with the milkman, we had insisted that the cow should be fed the best of fodder and grain. That was included in the bargain. Now and then, my wife would go to examine the basket and check the quality of the cow's feed and to make sure that the milkman was keeping his promise. Naturally, if the cow got such nutritious fodder, her milk would be rich and creamy, and a good amount of butter can be obtained from it.

Every morning Neeli would arrive at our gate, very eager and excited. I wondered whether she was eager to munch on her delicious fodder or whether she was eager to relieve herself of the heaviness of the milk she was carrying.

And so Neeli would arrive on days when we were still asleep. Or on days when we had just woken up, or we were in the midst of getting ready—she would be there, quietly, and her milk would sing into the brass can in a musical rhythm, and she would leave.

Many months passed. Then suddenly, Neeli refused to be milked. She was due to give birth.

We did not have to wait many days for her to return. Now Neeli would come followed by a female calf, who resembled her—the same white, soft skin, tail with a pretty bushy tip, shy and dew-eyed.

My wife had come to depend on the supply of milk from Neeli. We would purchase all the milk that Neeli gave in the morning, and we could not think of having milk from anywhere else in our house. My wife would often remind the milkman, Neeli's owner, 'Oh, you rogue, mind that you let her calf suckle some of the milk, will you? She'll grow up into a fine cow one day.' But that fellow would not pay attention. Whenever he was reminded of the calf, he would look away and mutter under his breath.

It was natural that as soon as her calf would begin to suck at her teats, Neeli would let down the milk, so the milkman did not bother to fill up her basket with nutritious fodder. When we reminded him that he must feed her the same rich fodder he had been giving her earlier, he would say that, yes, he was doing so, just that he had changed the timing, and he gave it to her in the evening rather than in the morning, along with the straw feed that was usually given at that time.

My wife was disturbed by this. She would repeatedly lament that the milk had become watery, and that the milkman was not allowing the calf to drink even a small amount of milk. She would say again and again that the poor calf was getting weak and her bones were sticking out. How could he deprive the poor animal like that? But to no avail. He paid no heed to all her remonstrations. He would reply, 'This Neeli, she saves up her milk and allows her calf to drink it later!', gesturing to the calf who would be trying to push its head towards her mother's teats as if to prove that he was right and our complaint was baseless.

Finally, the inevitable happened. The calf died.

The next day, the milkman arrived looking downcast. The calf had died that night and Neeli had not eaten a single morsel, nor had she drunk any water. There would be no milk that day.

My wife ground her teeth in frustration. She had felt that the man had deliberately been withholding milk from the calf, leading to her death. Neeli had no earlier offspring either who had survived. But we were silent, because nothing could be done, the cow's owner had already suffered a loss, and was showing his misery in his tears, and we were afraid that that there would be no more milk from Neeli.

'The stupid fellow has lost a good calf just for the sake of a little bit of milk,' my wife spoke in an undertone as the milkman turned away.

The next day we got up to see that Neeli was at our gate. The milkman followed after her. He was carrying a basket of fodder on his head. Earlier, Neeli would sometimes open the gate herself with her horns, and entering, would make her way to her place under the mehndi tree. But that day she just stood at the gate, unmoving. Her eyes full of an indescribable sadness, she stayed there.

The milkman also followed at a slow pace behind her, and opened the gate. She walked slowly into the compound, taking each step as if with difficulty.

I stood in the veranda and watched her. My wife stood next to me holding our little daughter in her arms, The baby wriggled and laughed in childish glee as her mother carried her.

The milkman set the basket of mixed fodder on the ground under the mehndi tree, and mixed it around with his hands. The fragrance of the fresh fodder spread through the air. Neeli was still walking very slowly and had not reached the spot. She appeared pensive, taking halting steps as if unwilling to go any further. At last she reached the shade of the tree and stood beneath it. The milkman made the gesture of spreading the fodder in the basket to entice her to eat, showing her the fragrant cottonseed and grain mixture. Neeli stepped forward, then back, then forward again, and then turned away from the basket. No mistaking, there was indeed delicious soft grain fodder in the basket that she would find appetising. But that day, Neeli found it impossible to eat. The milkman began to stroke Neeli's head gently. Then he stirred the fodder in the basket again to attract her attention. The fragrance rose. Neeli's head turned instinctively towards it, and as if impelled by nature, she stepped towards the basket and lowered her snout into the feed. She stuck her mouth into the basket of fodder for some time, but could not bring herself to start munching. She did not begin eating, and after a while, she lifted her nose out of the basket and turned her head away from it, as if rejecting the food.

The milkman was distraught. He picked up the basket and placing it on his head, walked off, with Neeli following him slowly.

Again my wife lamented the loss of the calf. 'This greedy man lost the precious calf just to save a bit of milk!' she muttered in despair, and then went in to tell a servant to go to the dairy to buy some milk.

Now my little girl snuggled in my arms, and holding her, I paced up and down the veranda, watching the milkman walk away on the road with the basket on his head, and Neeli stumbling along behind him, as if she was completely unaware of the direction she was going.

My wife was inside, still issuing instructions to the servant, '...also, get some cow dung from the dairy, it is *sankrant* tomorrow, the first of the month, and the kitchen has to be wiped with it.'

But I was still absorbed in watching Neeli recede slowly in the distance, as a small object thrown into the swirling waters disappears, or as an unconscious tear is absorbed in the eye, or a kite cut from its string flutters aimlessly away into the sky. Finally, she vanished in the distance, lost among the coming and going of people hurrying on the road. I really wonder at the rush and haste with which people move about on the roads.

The next morning, I was barely awake, when I looked out and saw the gate of the compound being opened. The milkman entered first, with his basket of mixed fodder on his head, and just behind him, Neeli followed. Her head raised, she appeared to be sniffing the tangy scent of the food in the basket. I thought the milkman had finally succeeded in persuading her to eat, and this turned out to be right. No sooner had he set down the basket under the mehndi tree that Neeli stepped forward and began to nibble the fodder. The milkman watched her eat for a while, and then picked up the milk can and sat down near her for milking.

Neeli stepped away.

The milkman looked up at her again. She still had her nose in the basket and was eating the fodder. He shifted his position to get nearer. Neeli withdrew again.

The milkman had no choice but to get up. Neeli had her nose buried in the food and continued to munch slowly. She had not eaten for three days.

The milkman began to stroke her back. For a while he kept stroking her gently and lovingly, murmuring softly to her from time to time. He kept on calling her with affection, 'Neel, Neel...' and went on stroking her for several minutes.

Then, very cautiously, he sat down near Neeli again. She was now eating at a faster rate, gobbling her food. She stood motionless, and casting a quick glance at her, the milkman stretched out his hand towards her teats. Neeli kicked her back leg and moved away.

The milkman stood up, crestfallen. She was eating her food all right, but she was in no mood to be milked. He began to stroke her head, and her little horns, and her long, beautiful neck and continued doing so for some time. Slowly, he advanced his hand on her back, still stroking gently, playing with her tail, and then, very carefully, sat down again under her. He kept stroking her while sitting there, and cleaning bits of dung off her back legs with his fingers. Then, uttering a prayer, he advanced his hand again towards her teats. Neeli jumped back, startled, and kicked her leg with force before moving away.

The milkman got up in anger. He glared at Neeli for a moment. He was beside himself, as if he would do something awful. Meanwhile, Neeli was gobbling down the fodder, as if nothing had happened.

He leapt forward and snatched away the basket of fodder. Placing it on his head, he started to walk away quickly. Neeli stood as if surprised, staring at him as he walked off. As he reached the gate,

Neeli mooed as if to call him back. He did not turn. He opened the gate to go out and again Neeli called out to him. In his anger, the milkman did not listen to her and left the compound.

For a long time, Neeli stood under the mehndi tree, her face turned towards the gate where her master had gone, as if she were waiting for him to come back. Now and then she would moo loudly as if she were calling out to him. Was she telling him something? 'O my master, why don't you understand that only two days have passed since my child died? My dearest one born of my womb, has been snatched from me. O, how can her memory fade from my heart? But my hunger is too much to bear now. For three days I did not eat, and feeling weak, I must eat. Can you not understand a mother's feeling, how, when my darling would touch my teats with her soft lips, my milk would pour down by itself? How she would nudge my body lovingly with her body? Do you not know what is the bond of a mother with her child? Maybe I will forget her one day...yes, I will surely forget her. I will not refuse to give milk. I will give you milk. But can you not be patient for some time? Maybe for just one or two more days? Then I will forget my little one, I will not feel so empty, I will not feel this darkness around me...Then, as I eat the fodder given to me, I will yield my milk to you. What do I need this milk for now? My child, who needed it most, is gone now. My master, come back, do not leave me to starve. See, how much injustice has already been done to me. Come back, master...'

For a long time, Neeli stood under the mehndi tree, her face turned towards the gate where her master had gone, watching and waiting for him to come back. The milkman did not return.

Santokh Singh Dheer

Santokh Singh Dheer (1920–2010) was born in Bassi Pathana in the district of Patiala. He was a versatile writer, poet, essayist, novelist, translator and editor. He contributed to the field of progressive literature, and was concerned with presenting the realities of the lives of farmers, labourers and the poor. He was awarded the Sahitya Akademi prize in 1996 for his short story collection *Pakhhi*.

A Shared Wall

When, at last, after months of running around, poor Kapur Singh was able to gather the wherewithal to build his house, a big obstacle confronted him. It was regarding a shared wall between his house and that of his younger uncle's son, his cousin Darbara.

Kapur Singh's house had collapsed during the heavy rains of the previous season. Many houses had been swept away in the flood, but the damage that befell Kapur Singh's house was the worst in the village. No part of it had remained standing.

Kapur Singh was already in dire straits, financially. It was difficult for him to manage his household. First he went around the offices of the district administration trying to get a loan from the government. The officials there practised the usual favouritism. Kapur Singh had to make many efforts to persuade someone to help. He had to mortgage his land. His family was temporarily staying with some people and he could wait no longer. Finally, he managed to buy the bricks and stack them, arranged for the cement to be delivered, but could not start the work until he had had a talk with Darbara about the construction of the shared wall.

The front of the plot faced a lane. There was no problem on that side. On the right, was shared Chachi Ram Kaur, Kapur's aunt. This wall and a part of her house had also been damaged along with Kapur's, and she too needed this wall to be repaired. At the back of the plot was the dwelling of the family of Chanan Singh Chiniaan. He too had to construct a roof from the support of a wall on that side, to extend his dwelling, so he had agreed to share half of the expenses for that part. If there was any problem, it was the wall on the left, on Darbara's side. And this problem did not seem that it would be solved all that easily.

Kapur Singh made attempts to speak to Darbara about it but each time he met with a non-committal response from Darbara. Worse,

Darbara would remark, 'We'll see when the time comes; we can build the wall some other time.' But Kapur Singh could not afford to wait—how long could he and his family remain homeless?

That wall had been weak and broken in places since the time the plots had been carved out. There were gaps and missing bricks all around. It seemed weak and patchy, like rags. The gaps in the wall were a few fingers wide in some places. Thus there was an urgent need for Darbara to repair the wall just as much as it was necessary for Kapur Singh. A new wall would suit everyone. But Darbara could afford to ignore the need for repair to the wall because he didn't use that part of his property to live in—it served to store materials and house the livestock. His own family lived in the house next door, which was in a good condition for habitation, having sufficient space for the whole family. But Kapur Singh could not do without a new wall. He had to build the whole house afresh and he could not do so with one side of it being weak and unstable. All three sides of the house would have good walls and the fourth could not be left unrepaired—it would make the whole frame lopsided. If the fourth wall was made, a room could be built on the roof, but a weak wall was useless for any purpose.

Kapur Singh was utterly at his wits' end. He would find himself filling up with helpless rage, for it is believed that even a mild adversary can prove to be a dangerous one. But he also knew that rage was not going to be helpful in dealing with this matter. He had asked several neighbours, including Chachi Ram Kaur and Channan Singh Chiniaan, to speak to Darbara and persuade him, but Darbara remained stubborn as ever. When all efforts by friends, relatives and neighbours failed to convince him to agree, Kapur Singh thought that he would try once more and speak to Darbara himself. Perhaps there was some chance that the man would see sense.

The next day he stood at Darbara's doorstep and, somewhat hesitantly, called out his name. The girl inside told him that he had gone to visit the Patwari, a village elder who was responsible for keeping land records. Kapur Singh started out after him. It might be a good idea to discuss the matter in the presence of others rather than alone. On reaching the Patwari's place, he found that there were several people sitting there on the *charpais*—Ratan the Patwari, Dhamma Singh the Sarpanch of the village council, Tunda the Lambardar, one or two others and Darbara himself. Darbara sat close to the Patwari, and looked as if he was dictating something to him. Considering the other men present there as participants, Kapur Singh spoke to Darbara in a calm, reconciliatory manner. 'So, Darbara Singh, what shall we do about the wall?'

'What wall?' Darbara feigned complete ignorance of the subject.

'Surely you have not forgotten? Our shared wall, of course.'

'I have no need to do anything about that wall!' retorted Darbara, looking away into the distance.

'All right, you don't need it, but I really need to build it.' Kapur Singh spoke humbly, as if pleading. But this did not have the slightest effect on Darbara. 'You need it, you build it.'

'How can I make it on my own—it is a long wall—forty feet in length, fourteen feet high, one and a half feet thick?'

'What favour are you doing to me by this?'

'No favour, it's just that work on building my house can't start without it'.

'Am I responsible for your house? If the work can't start, so what?' Darbara shot back.

The Patwari, sitting nearby, spoke mildly to both of them, 'Why prolong the question? Make a compromise now.'

But the Sarpanch interrupted to sharply cut off the Patwari's intervention. 'Patwariji, why should we be involved in their dispute? They're brothers—let them sort it out with each other!'

Kapur Singh well understood what the Sarpanch's words indicated about his attitude. On many earlier occasions, the Sarpanch had displayed hostility towards him. It suited him that now that Darbara was being hostile towards his cousin—the Sarpanch had no qualm about using this hostility against Kapur Singh.

Knowing this, Kapur Singh spoke patiently to Darbara, 'Darbara, see, I'm humbly requesting you, we are both householders, why should we quarrel, let's join together in building the wall. Whatever terms suit you, I'll accept them. The wall is quite weak, it'll be good for both of us if we make it strong. I wouldn't have insisted if the condition had not been so bad. It's difficult for me to bear all the expenses, but I'll bear most of the cost and you can give less amount if you wish.'

Kapur Singh's quiet pleading softened Darbara's resistance. He relaxed the frown on his face, and felt that he might agree to his cousin's proposal. But just then the Sarpanch muttered something in his ear, so softly and indistinctly that no one else but Darbara could guess what he said.

Darbara's frown, about to dissolve, turned into a scowl, furrowing his face and he exclaimed, 'Oye, am I crazy, why should I take up your burden?'

'But what's the reason for your disagreeing?' Kapur Singh was still trying to reconcile matters. After all, his need was urgent.

Darbara Singh stared into the distance again. 'I don't have the capacity to spend so much money. What do you want—I should sacrifice myself?'

'Fine, I'll spend the money for now, you can give it later when you are able to.'

'You want that I should be indebted to you?' There was no way that Darbara would accept anything. It is true that there is no greater friend than a brother, but also there is no greater enemy either.

Tunda Lambardar tried to step in and bring the discussion to an end. 'It's just a small thing, these money matters, a little here or there can be adjusted later,' he said, feeling sorry at Kapur Singh's desperate situation.

'Chacha, you don't know anything!' Darbara answered back at once. The Lambardar quietened down. He was not prepared to be insulted by such a blockhead.

Kapur Singh felt thoroughly disheartened. What should he do now? There was no way to persuade this insincere man. If he spent four hundred to pay for the wall, Darbara would be fine with it, but if asked to share the expense, he did not need the wall. He knew that Kapur would have to build the wall anyway, so there was no need to put in any money, and no-one could touch the construction on his side of the wall.

'Darbara! Look at my condition, how long I have been wandering homeless. Now please don't obstruct...whatever you agree to, I accept...' Kapur Singh was blubbering in his depair.

A soft whisper was heard again.

Darbara appeared to be acting under some malign influence. He did not look towards Kapur as he spoke unfeelingly, 'I don't have any spare money, my situation is bad too. How can I do anything for you...?'

The Patwari, Sarpanch, Lambardar and several others listened to this conversation in silence. Kapur Singh renewed his appeal with even more humility than before. 'All right, let's have the width of one brick only, not one and half.' He pleaded.

'Not a single brick!'

'Let it be half.'

'Not even half, none.'

'Then, just share half of the total bricks needed, forget about the labour.' He lowered his demand further. But Darbara did not yield an inch, as if he were made of immovable stone. 'I have said it plainly, I refuse; I don't want any wall, don't ask me!'

The fact was that even if Kapur Singh undertook to make the wall himself, the old structure had to be demolished before the new one could be built. Both of them needed to agree on this. On the other side, the attached structure had to be protected, the pillars raised to keep the roof beam up, and the rest of the wall could be demolished and built anew. So Kapur Singh explained with great patience, 'Darbara, I cannot demolish the old wall without your consent, you will have to be there. And you know that the new wall can only be made after demolishing the old one.'

'Sardarji, I am not going to let the wall be touched! I won't stand there, and watch. What do you think of me?'

'No, no, that's not fair!' Someone spoke up from among the listeners after Darbara spoke.

Now Kapur Singh became inflamed. 'That's who you call an enemy!' he thought to himself. How long could a person be patient?

Even so, he suppressed his annoyance, and spoke, a little assertively,' So when I make the wall, will you still take the support of my wall to put your roof beams?'

'Who can stop me from building my beams on the wall? I am the owner of the wall!'

'Is it your wall alone? Are you the sole owner?' Kapur Singh had to express his anger about this.

'Even more so, Sardarji, I am going to lodge an appeal against you. If you demolish anything from your side and it brings the wall down, and then the room on my side will be exposed in the rains, and if my roof gets destroyed, you will be responsible.'

On hearing this, Kapur Singh flared up. 'Go and do whatever you want. I know why you are spouting all this legal jargon. You think I'll have to pay you a fine for your haveli? Let me see what appeal you make. I'm going to demolish the wall, let's see how you stop me!'

Darbara was younger than Kapur in age, and slighter of build. Moreover, he had never so far spoken rudely to his cousin. But another person's instigation can work a lot of mischief. Darbara stood and rolled up his sleeves, raising his voice. 'Come on, I dare you to go and touch that wall!' he threatened.

They had come close to blows, but Tunda Lambardar got up quickly and stood between them. He restrained Darbara, and pleaded with Kapur Singh to leave the scene.

Kapur Singh walked away, declaring, 'Come and see, I will pull down the wall, you try to stop me. You will see how I build the wall, whether you give your share or not.'

The village was united in blaming Darbara. 'It's not right on his part. He should accept some solution, not reject everything'.

The problem continued to bother Kapur Singh. Should he go ahead with building his house? Maybe it would be better to live outside the village. It seemed impossible that the wall would be built. It did not appear to be proper to make half of the house as a new construction, and keep the old crumbing wall on one side. If the wall could be made, all the rest of it would be solid, and the house would look good and well-proportioned from all sides. Finally, he made his decision. He would start work on the construction, and by the time the work got to the area adjoining the wall, they would find a way out. It was certainly better than remaining stuck in the same situation. If the wall could be made properly, well and good, otherwise temporary support could be provided on the corners of the house and one side would remain weaker than the rest. People advised him to approach the deputy commissioner, but this would have prolonged the matter. Soon the warm summer days, ideal for building, would be over. Once the short days of winter arrived, the masons would not be able to complete the work. If delayed, who knows when it could be resumed again?

The construction began. The wall on the boundary with Chachi Ram Kaur was torn down, and the labourer began to dig the foundation. In three days, the wall was completed. The back wall, verandah, kitchen—the foundations were laid. The walls of the front room came up. The frames of the doors and windows were fitted. In just a few days, the entire place began to look different. The solid new wall from Chachi Ram Kaur's side contrasted with the tumbledown wall on Darbara's side. Everyone who passed by remarked that it would be better that the dilapidated structure also be re-built.

But Darbara was still not willing to allow anything to be done.

The lintel above the doors and windows of the front room was fixed. The elevation at the entrance was filled in. The front room was on the side adjoining Ram Kaur's house, while the entrance and porch were on the side adjoining Darbara's. The roof of the porch had to be kept low, and a lintel put in place so that a small room could be built above it. To do this, it was necessary to resolve the matter of the wall on Darbara's side. Now there was no more time left to waste.

When no response came, Kapur Singh collected the village people at his door. A crowd gathered. The Panchayat came and Darbara was told to allow the wall to be built. At first, he made excuses, 'I can't afford it...I don't need it...I have to get my daughter married...' but finally the Panchayat was able to cajole him into accepting, and he had to bow to the opinion of the village people.

He was excused from paying for the labour. It was decided that he would pay half the cost of the bricks and other materials. Because his need of the wall was not urgent, he was told he could make the payment in two instalments, one to be paid that January, on Lohri, and the second to be paid the following January. The papers were duly drawn up.

Though all the labour cost, which was considerable, had fallen to Kapur Singh's share, he was satisfied. The construction could proceed. It was true that he had put up the other half of the labour cost—about forty thousand extra—to pay, but it was still all right. He had himself made similar suggestions earlier to Darbara.

The next day four men arrived from the Panchayat to supervise the demolition of the old wall and the digging of the foundation for the new one. The crowd that gathered seemed to be in a festive mood.

Darbara had not been pleased that that the work had been allowed to go ahead, but now he was even more furious because he felt he had lost some of his pride in the entire business.

When Dhamma Singh, the Patwari and Nahar Singh, the Akali, each took up the ends of the rope for measuring the straight length of the wall, Darbara shouted out angrily, 'Mind that you do an honest job, Akali, and don't favour the other!'

'You are both the same for us, Darbara,' said the Akali.

Everyone looked at the rope.

On his side, the Patwari put down the rope about a hand's width towards Kapur Singh's side.

At once, some people shouted, 'Oh that is not correct, the rope is not straight!'

Someone told the Patwari that the placement of the rope where the digging was to start must be marked a little to the other side. It was quite clear to everyone, so the Patwari had to shift the rope slightly.

'Now it is fine.' Everyone was satisfied.

The mason had made a cut on the spot and begun to dig, when Darbara suddenly shouted out, 'I don't like this, this is not right, the wall is four fingers on my side!'

'What do you mean on your side? Everyone present says it is correct,' Kapur Singh said.

Darbara uttered an abuse, and shouted, 'Who dares to make the wall on my side!'

However humble a person is, no one can tolerate being abused. Kapur Singh rolled up his fists and threatened Darbara, 'Wait, I'll bury you in this trench!' And at the same time, his younger brother brought out a pickaxe from inside the house. Each side began abusing the other. Darbara Singh's nephew brought a large axe. Darbara came down and with both hands, hit Kapur Singh with a lathi. 'Let me see how you bury me,' he said as blood flowed from Kapur Singh's head. He called out to his brother, who hit Darbara with the pickaxe first on his neck and then his forehead; Darbara tumbled into the trench dug for the foundation. The men who had held the rope stepped aside. Eventually, some people ventured to come forward and stop the fighting. The women rushed out of their houses and began to berate one another loudly, their arms flailing. For two hours, there was utter chaos; nothing could be heard clearly in the din; screams and shouts and abuses were hurled.

After the furore settled down in a few days, the wall came up as was decided on but the uneasiness stayed and life became unpleasant. Neither of the parties were on talking terms. The men involved got bail, but they were sworn enemies now. This is how the seeds of conflict are sown that can last for generations.

Two, four, sixth months passed and then a year. The time for payment came, but Kapur Singh could not bring himself to go around to Darbara's place and ask him to pay up. There was nothing to worry, he told himself. The agreement had been made in front of the whole village. Darbara could not back out.

Six months passed. The time for the second installment also came and passed. Kapur Singh was planning to go to the Panchayat one morning when all of a sudden Chachi Ram Kaur came to him, clutching at her heart. 'Kapur Singh, have you heard?'

Startled, Kapur Singh asked, 'No, Chachi, what is it?'

'What? Don't you know? That boy Darbara—he's on his deathbed, almost!'

'Darbara...?'

'Who else? He is laid up with severe pneumonia, he caught a bad cold this season; his wife was weeping so much last night that I couldn't bear it; and without any money, it is not easy to get treatment, you know that.'

'Chachi, I didn't know, you are the first to tell me.'

'You've become a stranger even though you are next door!'

'Because the other side of the wall may well be a foreign land when it comes to contact, Chachi.'

'You should know, flesh does not separate from the nail.' Chachi left with this veiled taunt.

Kapur Singh got up and went up hesitantly to Darbara's door.

In the courtyard, near the wall, Darbara's bed was placed in the sun. Kapur Singh was shocked to see his condition, he just stood there looking at him. Darbara's body was terribly emaciated. It had shrunk almost to the bone, his skin had grown dark, his eyes had sunk deep. His family was clearly distressed.

Darbara's wife brought out a stool and placed it at the bedside for Kapur Singh to sit on. But Kapur Singh sat down on Darbara's bed, very close, and asked him, 'How are you, my brother?'

Darbara lifted himself a little, leaning on his quilt, said, 'I am better now, brother...' He tried to speak with whatever strength he could muster.

'Don't trouble yourself; don't get up.'

'I am too... weak...' Darbara's voice and body trembled while speaking.

'You will be all right; once you recover, your weakness will also go,' said Kapur Singh, trying to reassure him.

Darbara's daughter, Harbans, came with a hot poultice, which she began to apply to Darbara's aching sides.

'Are you getting some treatment?' Kapur Singh asked.

'Treatment!' No, there was none. And nursing at home was hardly any treatment.

It was all very clear to Kapur Singh. He knew that the financial condition of both their families was the same. He took out a ten rupee note from his pocket and slipped it into Darbara's pocket, and said, 'I will fetch a doctor from the town.'

It was Darbara who reminded him. 'But I still have to pay you back...for the wall...'

'First you get well, then you can pay the money. What use is money without life?'

Darbara's eyes welled up. After a while he asked, his throat choked with emotion, 'Is the work on the house complete?'

'A little bit of plaster work remains, the cement fell short.'

'I didn't want to be so harsh. It was the Sarpanch who goaded me to oppose you.'

'Don't think of these things now. It's natural that some disagreement does take place in families.'

'Do you think that this summer we can arrange Banso's wedding?' Darbara spoke with some hope in his voice.

'Why not? It is better to finish one's responsibilities well in time'.

'Will you come?'

'As you wish.'

Darbara, with trembling hands, clasped the hands of Kapur Singh. 'My brother, I'm nothing without you.' His lips quivered, and rivers of tears streamed from his eyes down his cheeks.

'O brother, take heart, we are brothers not strangers ...' Kapur could hardly utter these words, for tears were pouring down his face too.

Kulwant Singh Virk

Kulwant Singh Virk (1921–1987) was born in village Phulwarn in Sheikhupura district of Pakistan. After an MA degree in English, he joined the army, and later served as a Public Relations Officer in the army. Virk was essentially a short story writer. He went to Pakistan after the partition of Punjab in connection with the return and rehabilitation of women. This experience lies behind his emotional narratives of the Partition. He is considered to be the chronicler of the ordinary people, and their everyday experiences. Virk was awarded the Sahitya Akademi award in 1968 for his work *Naven Lok*.

The Earth Stands On the Horns of a Bull

Beside the tar road just outside Amritsar was the village of Thathi Khaara. Not very far, and it seemed to Maan Singh that even if it were a faraway village, it would appear less distant, given his mood of expectation and elation. Indeed, that was the reason that, though evening was approaching and the weary and slow steps of the horse drawing the *tonga*, his mood remained buoyant.

Maan Singh was a soldier, on leave from the army. The village he was going to visit was the village of his friend and army colleague, Karam Singh. Everyone knows that the comradeship that men share in the army is unequalled in any other profession. Both of them had been together in their regimental center, and subsequently they had both been assigned to a battalion that was fighting on the Burma border. Karam Singh had been recruited earlier and had reached the rank of Havaldaar, while Maan Singh was as yet in the rank of Naik.

One of the special talents that Karam Singh possessed was a silver tongue. Many boys from the village had joined the army, and when home during their leave, would hardly talk to the young people in the village, other than offer the formal greeting 'Wahe Guru Ji Ki Fateh'. But when Karam Singh was home, there would be crowds of people going to the well to bathe, to meet him there. In the cold nights of winter, they would gather around the dying warmth of the mud furnace where grain was roasted, and listen to Karam Singh's stories through the night. He was famous in the entire regiment for being an excellent rifleman, with the most accurate aim. If there was a contest of marksmanship, Karam Singh's bullet would find its mark as surely as if it were being guided by an invisible and unwavering hand. Then, in the fighting, he had brought down many of the Japanese soldiers whose presence was hardly visible at this distance, when they might easily have been mistaken for the woods. With this great ability, he could take revenge for those men on his own side who had been felled by the Japanese snipers. The bursts of machine gun fire could not achieve what Karam Singh could accomplish with one bullet that would take down the enemy's gunman. He was physically fit even though he was getting older. In gymnastic exercises, he excelled on the bars to such an extent that onlookers were impressed by his almost supernatural control in handling the equipment.

But in the battle, all such exercises were forgotten. Many other activities were suspended, such as the dressing up for parades and playing of the brass band, or the strolling in nearby bazaars, dressed in mufti. There were no bazaars in that area anyway. They did not ever see anybody from their village, or even their region. For this reason, Karam Singh was quite annoyed when Maan Singh's leave came through. If they had both been given leave, they could have gone home together. They could have spent their vacation in each other's company, and returned together. Amritsar and Chuharkana were not so far apart—perhaps only fifty miles lay between the two places. The former was known as 'Majha' and the latter as 'Baar'. One was developed and had been so for a long time, but the other had just recently been inhabited. But these days it was nearly impossible to get much leave at this time. Very few got it and, very seldom was it granted. Just like medals for bravery.

So when Maan Singh got on to the army truck that was returning from the border, Karam Singh said to him, 'You must go and visit my home. When they see that you have just returned from here, it will be almost as if they are meeting me through you. And when you return, and I see you, I will get the same feeling—that I have met them. When I hear all about them from you, it will be the same as if I was there.'

Then he asked 'Have you ever been to the area where my village lies?' As if he wanted to persuade his friend to take an interest in visiting his home.

'No, I've only passed through Amritsar, never been to the other side.'

'There are many gurudwaras over there—Tarn Taran, Khadoor Sahib, Goindwal Sahib. You should go and pay respects at all these places. And meet my family. I will drop them a letter to tell them that you are coming.'

And that was why, almost towards the end of his leave, he was making his way towards Karam Singh's village in a hired *tonga*.

'Bapuji, I'm Maan Singh, from Chuharkana,' he greeted the elderly man sitting in the covered entrance of Karam Singh's house.

'Please come in. Welcome. Please come and sit.'

Maan Singh entered and sat down on the *charpai*. The elder seemed a little put off by Maan Singh's arrival. At first, he looked this way and that, then bowed his head and continued to look down.

Maan Singh was not an intemperate man, but he was somewhat surprised at this cool reception. Perhaps this was someone who was not a family member?

'Are you the father of Karam Singh?' he asked, to make sure, and expectant of a better welcome.

'Yes, this is his house.'

'Perhaps he wrote to you about me?'

'Yes, he had written to say that you would be coming to visit us.' On saying this, the old man abruptly got up and went into the courtyard. He untied a calf from one pole and tethered it to another pole. Then he began to stroke the calf and allowed it to lick his fingers. Then he went in and could be heard announcing the arrival of Maan Singh and asking for tea to be brought. Then, as if hesitant to re-enter the entrance hall, he went to the courtyard again, and stood near the horse that was tied there. He brought some more gram and mixed them into the horse's feed. At last, he turned and came back to where they were sitting. He seemed lost in his own thoughts. He looked around vacantly sometimes towards Maan Singh and at other times, into the air.

'Where is Jaswant Singh?' Maan Singh, asking about Karam Singh's younger brother.

'He will be here soon with the fodder.' Just then, Karam Singh's mother entered, carrying tea. Maan Singh stood up and greeted her with a smile. 'Bebeji, Sat Sri Akaal'.

The old lady appeared as if she would say something, but no words escaped her lips. Maan Singh took the tea from her hands and she turned around silently.

'What kind of people are these Majhi folk?' Maan Singh thought to himself, surprised. He was very uncomfortable, but now that he was here, he could not leave abruptly. 'I will stay one night and leave', he decided.

That night, Jaswant Singh returned and in the warmth of his meeting with him, Maan Singh found someone to talk to.

'Karam Singh's feats are very famous in the fight going on at the Burma border. His accuracy in rifle shooting is remarkable. No sooner does he press the trigger, than the Japanese soldiers fall, before the rest of us can even spot them.'

Maan Singh paused in his narration, hoping that he would be asked to further elaborate, in more detail, all the stories of the war in Burma. He was full of stories that he wanted to tell the listeners, but no-one seemed to be interested in hearing them. There was silence for a while, then the old man spoke, 'Jaswant, when is the water for the fields to be released?'

'It is day after tomorrow, at three in the morning', he replied.

At the mention of the time, three in the morning, Maan Singh again picked up the subject. He wanted to talk at length about his dear friend Karam Singh.

'Well, at least, being in the army saved Karam Singh from getting up so early! He is always reluctant to get up early; he gets up last, after everyone is up.'

This remark also did not evoke any response from the others.

Then the evening meal was served. They had tried to provide a substantial dinner. Jaswant engaged himself in fanning the visitor while he ate. Maan Singh felt that perhaps he was mistaken in his impression that he was not welcome in the house.

While they ate, Karam Singh's little boy came toddling up to where Maan Singh sat on his charpai. He felt that even if he could not talk about Karam Singh to the others, surely he could talk to this little boy. Maan Singh picked him up.

'Do you want to visit your father? Come with me if you want. It is a place where there is a lot of rain, you will like to play in the rain!'

This appeared to affect the old man as if he were being stabbed. He spoke sharply, 'Here, take this boy away. Let's have our meal in peace!' Hearing his voice raised, the old lady came out and took the boy away.

Now the very air in the house seemed oppressive to Maan Singh. All he wanted was to conclude his trip quickly and make his way back. He brought up the subject of his plans for the next day.

'How far is Tarn Taran from here?' he asked.

'It's about four miles.'

'Is it possible to get a tonga from here in the morning?'

'What is the need for a tonga? We will send Jaswant with you tomorrow. Both of you can go together to pay respects.'

The offer pleased Maan Singh. Jaswant was an easy companion to spend time with, he felt.

But when they left together, even Jaswant became tight-lipped. Whenever they met any acquaintance on the way, he would not stop, but greet them from a distance, and go on his way. Maan Singh would have liked to stop and speak to a few people there. It was not every other day that he got a chance to travel in this area.

Along the way, Maan Singh mentioned Karam Singh again. 'Karam Singh has done so well in the army, he has really given distinguished service. Why did you not join the army?' he asked Jaswant.

Immediately, Jaswant recoiled, as if some guilty secret of his had been revealed. After a pause, he replied, 'One son is enough for the army'.

Then he asked, changing the subject, 'What is the state of the crops of fodder and sugarcane in your area?'

'The crops stand as tall as a man', he replied. But his heart was not in this kind of conversation. He really wanted only to dwell on the subject of his dear friend.

When they returned to the village, Maan Singh wanted to get back home. He could take the night train from Amritsar and would reach home by early morning. In their own way, each person of the household had taken good care of him, but the visit has disappointed him. Even now, tea had been prepared for him in the kitchen, while he sat alone in the entrance hall.

Just then, he saw that the postman was walking down the street, carrying his postbag. It seemed as though he was going to pass by, but then he entered and sat down on the charpai.

'What have you brought?'

'What shall I say, it's only the pension. Poor Karam Singh's pension.'

'Karam Singh's pension? Has Karam Singh been killed?'

'Sir, the whole district is in agony at the news. And you are sitting in his house, and you still ask whether Karam Singh has been killed? It is now fifteen days since the letter came.'

Maan Singh struggled to breathe. He was shocked, his face and throat numb, and then the tears began to flow unchecked, till the numbness dissolved. All the people inside the house, Karam Singh's father and his little son were weeping along with him.

Seeing the postman, Karam Singh's father, realized that the truth had been revealed. Now there was no need for him to bear the burden of concealment. He could weep freely. Both sat for a long time near each other, joined in their grief.

Finally Maan Singh spoke, 'But why did you not tell me this as soon as I came here?'

'Oye, we thought the boy has come home on leave, we must not spoil his few days of relaxation. When you go back to his battalion, you will find out. The leave period is precious for a military man. Just as Karam Singh looked forward to his leave, so do you, in fact, more so, as the people from Bar are fond of an easy life and are not used to much hardship. But we were not successful in hiding the facts from you. We could not give you much happiness.'

As he left the village, Maan Singh looked around at the village of which this old man was a native. All around, the boundary walls of the land were dilapidated, and there were many memorial spots and graveyards that spoke of the sacrifices made by people in this area to defend it from the invaders and attackers of the country. This was the reason why the old man was so strong in his forbearance. He was bearing the burden of the world by himself, in order to save others the pain. Maan Singh had heard the myth that there is a bull on whose horns the weight of the earth stands. He remembered this on seeing how Karam Singh's father, like that bull, who even when himself weighed by a heavy burden, wanted to carry the burdens of all others.

Ram Saroop Ankhi

Ram Saroop Ankhi (1932–2010) was a novelist and story writer, and also wrote poetry and essays. He was born in Dhaula, in Sangrur district. He edited a quarterly journal *Kahani Punjab*. His characters are drawn from ordinary rural folk, the vagrants, the lovelorn, the petty criminals and philanderers. He tried to write in the form of epic narrative. He was given the Sahitya Akademi award in 1987 for *Kothe Kharak Singh*.

The Cycle Race

The milk vendors were on strike that day, but Hakam Singh still came to the town. He needed money. His younger brother had to purchase some bags of manure for the cotton field. The hotel owners had promised to pay him today. Even if two of them paid up, he would be able to manage.

His cycle carrier did not have any milk cans on it that day. Only the tube of an old tyre lay strapped on it. Without the usual load of the milk cans, his cycle was sailing on the street like a bird skimming over the village pond. He took good care of it, scrubbing and polishing it every day. Not a screw rattled. One could ride it effortlessly.

The sweltering heat of summer was beating down on the earth, though the strong blast of the summer *loo*, that hot wind, had not yet gained force. The afternoons would be baking hot. People were waiting expectantly for the cooling rains to descend but so far the monsoon gave no signs of arriving.

He got off his cycle to drink some water at the hand-pump near the railway barrier. The water at this pump was always cool and sweet, being fed from the channel of a canal flowing nearby. One's teeth felt pleasantly numb and a delicious sensation swept over the tongue. He drank his fill contentedly from the water spouting out in full flow and then set off again. Glancing sideways, he noticed a young man and his new bride get off their cycle to take a drink as well. The youth was working the handle of the pump while the bride bent down, cupping her hands and bringing her mouth close to the spout to drink.

Hakam Singh was cycling along absorbed in his thoughts when a cycle shot past him. He realised that it was the couple on their cycle. Vividly coloured braided tassels hung from its handles. The bride was seated on the carrier at the back of the cycle, one of her hands wrapped around the youth's waist. She looked towards Hakam Singh, face aglow with happiness. Oh, the thrill of speed, the pride in her husband's strength, and the celebration of victoriously overtaking Hakam Singh's cycle!

It was terribly hot. Even after drinking that cooling water, it seemed he was thirsty as ever. His stomach felt bloated, his lips parched. After covering a distance of about four and a half miles, they reached a crossing. He saw that they had stopped to drink water again and take a breather. He too stopped and drank some water. His eyes darted towards them again. Laughing to himself, he mocked, 'Skinny fellow! Imagines himself to be strong as a wrestler. Pedalled with his spindly legs and cycled past me. Now try! Now I'll see what you can do!'

Hakam Singh was over forty. He possessed little land. He was also partially blind in one eye. He wasn't fortunate enough to get a bride, but had managed to get his younger brother married through his earnings by selling milk. He was an obedient young man. Though their mother was still living, Hakam had his meals with this younger brother. After his early morning round of delivering milk, he used to join his brother in the fields. They had also managed to purchase some land by mortgaging some jewellery. Hakam Singh was large boned, muscular and sturdy. He could take physical labour in his stride. Even with the load of heavy milk cans he could spin his cycle as lightly as a top. And today, without the encumbrance of the milk cans, his cycle seemed to have grown wings, on which he soared across the sky.

About half a mile ahead of the crossing, the youth with his bride attempted to overtake him. He was straining hard, but for Hakam Singh it was a breeze. He kept abreast of the young fellow, sometimes getting ahead, then slowing down. It was as if he was testing the youth's stamina. At one point he felt like racing a mile or two ahead so that the boy wouldn't have the nerve to try to get past him again. A taunt sprung to his mind. 'That fancy girl sitting on the carrier behind him thinks *her* man is the strongest in the world. Hah!'

Then Hakam Singh began to feel as if the youth was his own younger brother. His feelings softened and he thought that if he were to speed ahead, it might create a bad impression on the bride. She would think that her husband was weak. What respect would she have for his manhood then? What good would be his own little victory in cycling if it were to result in the downfall of that young fellow and the death of romance? If that youth were to become the victor, it would at least result in some benefit for him. He even began to feel sorry for the fellow.

The crossing was left behind, approximately two miles. Whenever Hakam Singh tried to move ahead, the bride would begin to look anxious. It was as if she was expecting something untoward to happen. Sometimes Hakam Singh cycled to their left, and then to their right. But the bride's face always turned in his direction. When he lagged behind them, her face took on a happy glow. Even her eyes seemed to be laughing with delight. She sat erect, and her posture on the carrier took on a proud stance.

Let's see how much strength this fellow has! A mischievous thought arose in Hakam Singh's mind. But seeing the beads of sweat dripping from the youth's forehead, he realised that the young man was quite tired. He might just collapse from the exertion and his bride with him. Two buses had passed them by, one coming and the other going in the opposite direction. A number of trucks had also trundled past. The road wasn't very wide. At times both cycles had to get off the road to distance themselves from the oncoming traffic.

Now the road was free. There was no vehicle behind them either. Hakam Singh came abreast of the youth's cycle. He pretended to wipe off some sweat from his forehead. He pressed his left hand to his waist as if he was extremely exhausted. He then bent over and started cycling as if mustering up all his strength. He looked stealthily at the bride. She was smiling. The youth was expending all his might, determined not to let his cycle lag behind.

Hakam Singh gradually slowed down. Then he stopped. By this time, they had gone far ahead. But Hakam Singh could see the bride's happy face quite clearly. He saw her appreciatively patting her husband on his back. He dropped his eyes and looked away.

Manmohan Bawa

Manmohan Bawa (b. 1932) was born in village Verowaal, district Amritsar. He is primarily a mountaineer, traveller and painter, and has travelled widely around the world. He has travelled to places of historical and mythical significance in remote areas and mountainous regions. This has added to his vast and in-depth knowledge of these places. Bawa entered the field of literature late in life and wrote travel books and stories for children. His forte is historical fiction and mythological tales but he addresses many contemporary issues: women's liberation, oppression of Dalits, differences between non-tribal and tribal cultures, and the day-to-day lives of people. His novel *Kaal Katha* was joint winner (with Kirpal Kazaak) of the Kusumanjali award, and the Odia translation of his novel *Ajaat Sundari* was awarded the Odisha State Sahitya Akademi award.

Neelma

Background:

The years, 1300–1310

The story has a historical background, and is set in the districts around Sunam, Sangrur, Barnala, Samana and Deepalpur (now in Pakistan). The main historical character in this story is Ghiyaas-ud-din Tughlaq, who later became the Sultan of Delhi, and was the father of the well-known Sultan Mohammad Tughlaq.

These events took place at the time when Malik Ghiyas-ud-din was the Subedar, army commander in the area of Deepalpur, and was known among the people as Malik Tughlaq. Neelma was a princess of the state of Samana, and when he first saw her, she reminded Malik Tughlaq of Rani Padmini of Chittor, Rajasthan. However, he himself was certainly no Ala-ud-din Khilji, nor was Neelma Rani Padmini. When Khilji had attacked the Chittorgarh Fort to vanquish it and win Padmini, Malik Tughlaq had been there, and the sight of the flames of Rani Padmini's pyre had sickened him. The queen threw herself alive on the pyre to save her honour, he thought; that was what the Rajput sense of honour meant. Only a Rajput could be so brave, but bravery is not all. His opinion was that if the Rajputs set aside their attachment to their personal honour and grandeur, and fought with their head rather than their heart, no Turk invaders could ever have conquered them. Instead, they still fought according to ancient rules of conduct and tradition, utterly ignorant of modern and effective methods of warfare.

Neelma was the daughter of Raja Surjan Mal Bhatti of Samana. She had two other sisters who were just as beautiful as she was. But her deep dark eyes, her magnificent bearing, her intelligence—all these characteristics set her apart from her sisters.

Malik Tughlaq had heard much about her, but only once did he have a chance to meet her and talk to her. This was on an occasion when, without his military regalia, he was on a tour of the district to survey the digging of a canal in the area. While he stood on the site, talking to the superintendent about the progress of the work, he saw a Rajput lady, accompanied by some soldiers, riding towards them. He knew that this lady was no other than Neelma, more likely because the place where they stood was the state of Samana of which she was a princess.

She did not glance towards him as she came near and dismounted, and all the persons there bowed towards her with deference, except for Malik Tughlaq. She spoke to the superintendent and asked him a few questions about the digging of the canal. She advised him that the canal should not be dug straight but turned towards the Sind-Sarovar lake, the waters of the canal would flow into the lake, and would increase the reservoir of water, from which other canals could carry the water further and people could use the water from the reservoir too. This would solve the problem of water shortage during periods of drought.

The superintendent threw a puzzled glance towards her, and then looked questioningly at Malik Tughlaq. Neelma's glance then fell on Tughlaq. She saw a tall, well-built man, with a high forehead and determined look. His demeanor was authoritative. Neelma bowed slightly and said, 'I beg your pardon; I did not see that Malik Tughlaq is here.'

'But how did you know I was Malik Tughlaq?'

'Just as you knew that I am Neelma Devi.'

* * *

She was more beautiful than the praises that he had heard of her. He saw a depth in her eyes that he had not seen before. Every night, the memory of her face floated into his mind. He would be lost in his thoughts, and would make frequent trips to Samana in the hope of seeing her.

Army commander Rajab Ali was his younger brother, three years younger, and like a friend to him. They had fought many battles together, faced many circumstances both favourable and adverse. On Rajab Ali's persistent questioning, Malik confessed to him.

'You know that five years have passed since my wife died. Now I am thinking of marrying again. I am tired of returning after the day's toil to an empty home, as there is no-one to come back to.'

'I have myself said this to you quite often. But you did not heed...'

'I now think that if we make marital alliances with the princes and princesses of this place, we will make our political and administrative base quite strong. Our own mother was a *jat* lady from Lahore.'

'Brother, come to the point now!' Rajab suppressed a smile, and said. He had an inkling that all this was about Neelma.

'I am considering the possibility of marriage with the daughter of Rana Surjan Singh of Samana. Her name is Neelma, and she is a very fine and beautiful lady. What do you think?'

'You have already made up your mind, so why do you ask? You have only to order me and I will take the message across.'

'It is not such an easy task, Rajab. You know what the Rajputs are like. What if the Rana refuses our proposal? And it's not just a matter of the Rana's consent.'

'What else?'

'Princess Neelma may herself refuse.'

'Neelma?'

'Yes, Neelma. She is a proud woman. The Rana does not have any sons. It is Neelma who takes care of most of the matters of state. Other than that, there are many rajas from principalites like Bikaner, who are interested in making this alliance.'

They were both silent for a while. Then Rajab said, 'My brother, I think you have no reason to be nervous. I have not seen you look so worried even when facing the Mongols in battle! Just send a proposal, and we'll see what happens.'

* * *

Rajab Ali decked himself up in the full military regalia of black garments, knee-length leather boots, thick leather breastplate, brass helmet over the black headgear with the end of the scarf flung around his neck. Accompanied by a faithful cohort of mounted soldiers, he rode off to Samana.

Malik Tughlaq waited impatiently for him to return from his mission.

Dusk was falling by the time Rajab returned, but not with the news Malik had hoped for. Rajab's face was dark with anger and there was an expression of defeat on his face.

'What was the Rana's response?'

'It amounted to a rejection of our proposal.'

'I want to hear exactly what he said. In his own words.' Malik prepared himself to hear the worst.

'This is what he said, "It is true that today you are our rulers, but we are still Rajputs. We can give our lives to protect our honour."' He stopped speaking.

'Carry on. Why did you stop? I know what he must have said, "Malik Tughlaq is not only a *malecha*, impure, but also a descendant of slaves."'

'Yes, something to that effect....'

'Well, let it be.' Malik interrupted him. 'I know what he must have said.' His voice did not have anger in it so much as despondency and helplessness.

'I am amazed at your reaction! We will have to do something about this. By now, the news of this must have spread from Samana to Lahore. Can we command the territories if our self-respect is damaged? What authority will we have?'

Malik Tughlaq looked at Rajab with piercing eyes, and spoke slowly and deliberately. 'If you propose that I should attack Rana and forcefully bring Neelma, then abandon this idea. Rana is under our subjugation, no doubt. His lands are ours, his men are ours. But on the other side, Tariq Beg and Targi are preparing to advance on Hindustan with their Mongol armies. At this time, we need the friendship and support of the Ranas, not their enmity. The Ranas have longstanding and close relations with the chieftains around the areas of Ravi and Chenab rivers. These are the same chieftains who have sent Mohammad Ghori packing, many a time. Remember, Rajab, the solid structure of peace and power in the kingdom is built on the foundation of wisdom.' Thus Malik explained to his brother the intricacies of the political situation in Punjab.

Rajab listened to these words with great attention.

Malik continued, 'However, even if circumstances were different, showing any kind of force in the matter is alien to my nature.'

For a long time, they discussed the issue and that of the impending attack by the Mongols, but could not reach any conclusion.

Seeing that his brother was upset, Rajab was upset too. He was in charge of tax collection in the district. There had been a drought for the last two years, and crops had been badly affected, and was why Malik was having the canal dug. Malik had given orders that tax collection should be eased till the conditions improved. Without telling Malik, Rajab began to squeeze the people of Samana for taxes. If someone could not pay, their stores and livestock would be taken away. If they had nothing, they would be imprisoned and whipped. Additional taxes and restrictions were imposed on the trading caravans passing through the area. The people suffered terribly under the burden. They knew the reason for these excesses. The Rana knew it too, and so did Neelma. But they could say nothing.

* * *

Seeing Neelma preparing to go out, Rana Surjan Mal said, gravely, 'It's true that our state is not as vast and great as it used to be, but I am still your father, and the Rana of Samana. Shouldn't you have asked for my permission before agreeing to go and meet Malik Tughlaq? I am still living, am I not?'

Neelma looked at him with some compassion, and replied, 'Wherever you have got your news from, it is not true.'

'So are you not going out to meet Malik Tughlaq? Remember, we are Rajputs...',.

'Malik Tughlaq will not dare to send word to command me to meet him,' declared Neelma.

'So, then what is it?'

'It is I who sent word to him to meet me.'

'*You* sent word to him?' her mother, listening to them, exclaimed in surprise. 'Do you not have any concern for Rajput honour? Have you lost all sense of pride?'

'Let me remind you of what happened some years ago across the Ravi river when the Mongols invaded. My sister's husband was brutally killed and my sister Gayatri Devi was carried away by them. Did anyone worry about the Rajput honour at that time?'

'That was during a war. We had no choice,' her mother said.

'And how it is different now?'

'It is impossible to win an argument with you,' her mother surrendered

* * *

It was under a banyan tree on the banks of the Sind-Sarovar, a short distance from the habitat of a holy man of that area, that Malik Tughlaq waited, in the full grandeur of his status, accompanied by a number of his loyal soldiers. He saw a palanquin approach from afar, escorted by Rajput horsemen. He had anticipated that this time too Neelma would arrive riding on a horse. The palanquin came to a halt about fifty feet away, and Neelma alighted from it. She instructed her soldiers to stay where they were, and advanced with slow steps to the point where Malik awaited her.

Malik also ordered his soldiers to stand back, and stood there, his heart beating fast.

On approaching him, Neelma bowed down in an exaggerated manner, thrice, to salute him, and then stood before him, her head lowered.

'You sent for me. I am here.'

'It is strange that you came with so many of your guards, just to meet Neelma? What was the danger?'

'Not because of any danger, but out of respect for Princess Neelma.'

'Your subject is before you,' she said, her head still bowed.

'I am aware that I am in the presence of a princess, daughter of Rana Surjan Mal Bhatti, not any subject.'

'We are ruled by you, that makes us your subjects and the subjects of the Sultan of Delhi, Ala-ud-din Khilji. The same Sultan who brought death to so many Rajputs and Muslims, and was the reason for Rani Padmini sacrificing herself as *sati!*' It was clear that Neelma had prepared well for this encounter and was choosing her words with care.

Malik Tughlaq bent his head in a gesture of contrition and shame.

'I am an officer under the Sultan, but how can I be responsible for his actions?'

'You are overlords, you are powerful, you can do whatever you want. Why ask me?'

Malik suspected that this discussion was not the real reason for Neelma's arranging this meeting, but he kept his peace.

'With all regard, you know that tyrannical exercise of power is not my disposition; I do not act thus.'

'Maybe you don't directly, but indirectly you do the same.' She was referring to the excesses of the tax-collectors on the people.

'Whatever my brother Rajab did, was without my knowledge. As soon as I came to know, I stopped him.'

'I am obliged.'

'Now, Princess Neelma Devi,' he spoke with some impatience. 'Officially, I am merely in the position of a deputy, but I stand here before you as a human being. As such, may I ask whether you have seen anything at all in me that is worthy, any noble quality that I have?

'If I had not, I would not have thrown all convention and caution to the winds to stand here before you.'

'I admire your courage. Now, if we are done with the pleasantries, shall we come to the point? Please do me the favour of telling me what specific purpose brought you here. For what service can this slave be of some use to you? I will be grateful if you enlighten me.'

'I have some conditions to put down before you.'

'Command me. I am eager to know what they are. And I'll do whatever is in my power.' Malik replied at once.

'I cannot say whether it is in your power, but it is surely of benefit to you.'

'Do not test my patience, Princess.'

'Then, listen, Malik Ghiyas-ud-din Tughlaq! The Mongol generals Tariq Beg and Tarki Beg are advancing towards Deepalpur once again with their armies. You might be aware of this already.'

'I am well informed about it. And also, that they have crossed the Chenab river. I have sent messages to the Sultan's Amir to prepare for battle. The army from Delhi is also marching here for support.'

'The last time they invaded, Tariq and Tarki Beg's father Khutlag Khwaja killed my sister's husband by deceit, and carried away my sister.'

'I have heard of this too.'

'I want their heads. I want to see their heads displayed on the city walls of Samana and Deepalpur.' Neelma's eyes flashed with anger. 'Can you do this, Malik Tughlaq?'

He stared at her, speechless. He could not take his eyes away from her glowing, impassioned face, and his heart beat faster than ever. In that moment, he felt that he saw her in the role of his queen, his *begum*.

'What are you thinking? Perhaps it is too difficult a task for you.'

'Maybe, we'll see. But I am puzzled about one thing. There are many Rajput chiefs from Jaisalmer to Bathinda who would be quite keen to go ahead and battle the Mongols. Why did you not ask one of the Rajput chiefs to help?'

'Because I know you have the best chance of defeating the Mongols. The Mongols have dragged Rajput honour into the dust, and brought low the very pride of Punjab. I am very conscious of this, and also of the sad fact that even after the loss of their pride and honour, people like my father and our many Rajput relatives are content to live a life of ease and luxury, and they are not capable of fighting the Mongols.'

Both of them stood silently in contemplation. Then Malik spoke.

'Princess, I am grateful for the confidence you have placed in me, of which I do not think I am worthy. I often wonder why Allah has put people like the Mongols on this earth. They are a scourge.

Wherever they and their horses roam, the land becomes barren. It is my most ardent desire to remove them from the soil of Punjab so that not one of them survives to return here again.'

'Then you accept my condition?'

'No!'

'No?' It was Neelma's turn to be astonished.

'It is my duty to enter into battle with the Mongols, and to defeat them is my greatest desire.' Malik smiled as he spoke. 'I do not wish to bind you down to any condition. If my frankness can be excused, I would like to say that I have utmost regard for you in my heart. I will be satisfied only when you have the same feelings towards me and accept my deep love for you. I desire to win not the Princess Neelma, but her heart and mind.'

Neelma had always had great respect for Malik's bravery, sincerity and his personality, but after this conversation he seemed to her the finest man she could dream of or imagine. Whether he fulfils the condition or not, she thought, I will always be...

'May I ask what you are thinking?' Malik interrupted her reverie.

'I honour and respect your feelings.' Neelma bowed her head.

'How different is this manner of bowing from the earlier one!' Malik Tughlaq remarked to himself with happiness, as he looked at her.

* * *

A vast army stood in readiness to confront the oncoming Mongols. Khilji had sent a substantial Turkish battalion led by Malik Kafur to augment Malik Tughlaq's forces. Apart from the Turkish army, there were the Rajputs from Rajasthan, the Jats from the area between Bangar and Ravi, the Gujjars from Bharatpur, and the chieftains from the hill regions of Kullu and Kangra; this combined Hindustani army prepared to save the country from the ravages of the Mongols.

The armies were yet to engage, when Neelma summoned the *talukdaar* of Sunam, Qurbaan Ali, to her presence. He was the husband of one of her very close friends, Dulari Bai. An Ahir by caste, he had been appointed to the post by Malik Tughlaq himself.

The strapping, tall warrior stood humbly in front of Neelma, and said, 'It is an honour for a person like me to be remembered by your Highness. I am in you service.'

'I have given you the trouble to assign a very special task to you. You may have heard that the Sultan's Amir 'Mughlati' is annoyed with Malik Tughlaq, because the Sultan has entrusted the command of this army to Malik Tughlaq and not to him.'

'Yes, I have heard this rumour. The Amir feels that his rank as Amir is higher than that of a deputy. He takes it as an insult that he has to follow the instructions of a mere deputy.'

'There is information that he is secretly in league with the Mongols.'

'This is very bad news. Does Malik Tughlaq know of this?'

'Yes, indeed, he is well aware of it. But I want to speak to you about something that he does not know about.'

'What is that?'

'It is this, many of our own Rajput relatives are displeased with the relationship between me and Malik Tughlaq. I have information that some of them are conspiring to join up with the Amir to assassinate Malik Tughlaq,' Princess Neelma said.

'But do they not realise that by doing so they are putting themselves in danger? Tughlaq's death means victory for the Mongols, total destruction of all their people. The Mongols do not spare anyone.'

'They know this very well. This is why they planned the assassination after the battle, at the time when Malik will not be concerned about any danger to himself and will be returning from battle to celebrate the victory.'

'Oh, I see!' Qurbaan Ali exclaimed involuntarily. He thought for a moment, and then spoke, 'But how can I, your servant, help you in this matter?'

'I wish to entrust you with the job of protecting Malik Tughlaq when he returns from battle. But you must take care that no one, including Malik Tughlaq, has any suspicion of this conspiracy before the battle. Otherwise, it will create division in the ranks and it will weaken our armies.'

'I understand, Princess.' Qurbaan Ali replied. He considered awhile, and added, 'However, there is a flaw in your plan.'

'What is that?'

'No-one knows what the outcome of a battle will be. Suppose I am killed in the battle?'

'You can decide at some time in the course of the battle, or just before it starts, to tell Malik about this. That is for you to decide. But I have full faith that you will return alive and victorious.'

* * *

More than a month had passed since Malik Tughlaq's army had taken position at Deepalpur. The news from the field was sometimes in favour of the Hindustani forces winning, and sometimes the other side. Both sides suffered heavy losses. Then news came that Tariq Beg and Tarki Beg had sent a proposal to negotiate a truce.

Malik Tughlaq was pleased to receive the proposal because it was a sign that his spies had succeeded in their mission. The two commanders met on the field at Naharkot, near Multan. Tariq Beg presented the point that it was not in anyone's interest to prolong the battle, as it would only lead to more casualties on both sides. He proposed that if a certain amount of cash, a certain number of men and horses were given to them, they would turn back.

Malik Tughlaq said in reply, 'In the first place, I do not accept your proposal. But even if it were possible, what is the surety that you will go back quietly? And that you will not return again to attack?'

'Do you not take us at our word? Do you not trust us? This is an insult to us Mongols.'

'I am compelled to take this view based on your previous actions. Did your father not deceive the Raja of Multan in the same way?'

'Let it be so, then. I was only saying this for your benefit. If you want to see your defeat at our hands, so be it!'

'Let me propose something else,' Malik Tughlaq looked straight at Tariq Beg in the face. 'I hope the gallant Tariq Beg will not hesitate to accept it.'

'All right. Let us hear what you propose.'

'Why should we not settle the matter of victory or defeat by one-to-one combat? I am sure Tariq Beg has full confidence in his own might and strength?'

All the gathering held their breath at this turn of events. Tariq Beg glared at Malik Tughlaq and then at his brother Tarki Beg.

'Well? What do you say? If I am killed, then all the money, weapons, men and horses will be yours, as you have said. If I win, the Mongol army will have to go back empty-handed.' Malik Tughlaq made his stance clear to all.

Tariq Beg could not back away from this frank challenge in front of soldiers and generals from both sides. He was also proud of his expert swordsmanship, famous all through Afghanistan, Persia and Turkistan as having wreaked havoc in many battles; many great warriors had been vanquished by his fearsome sword.

On the other hand, Malik Tughlaq had received training in swordsmanship from his father, who had been the most faithful and brave acolyte of Sultan Iltumash. He was of that slave heritage, in which loyalty to the master till death was the essential teaching, and who struck terror in the hearts of kings and rulers of many lands.

Then the swords of both the warriors were unsheathed. Malik Tughlaq was happy that he had a chance to fulfil his promise to Neelma. The soldiers of both armies encircled the two combatants as the fight began. The clashing of metal on metal was heard. The force of each strike dented the other's sword. It was a battle of equals. Each tried his utmost, both were drenched in sweat. The furious combat continued for over half an hour. Malik Tughlaq had one or two secret feints up his sleeve, but he was waiting till his opponent was tired, when his arm would show signs of weakness and he would begin to stagger a little. Such an opportunity came and he took full advantage of it. He made a sudden strategic turn, and swung his sword with such force that Tariq Beg's head was separated clean from his body, and like a large melon, it fell and rolled in the dust.

Victorious, Malik Tughlaq was staring at the dust-covered head of Tariq Beg, when his brother Tarqi Beg, shocked and enraged, rushed at Malik Tughlaq with his sword drawn. But Qurbaan Ali was standing between them, and swiftly intercepted the attacker, and in a flash, Tarqi's head too rolled in the dust along with that of his brother.

The Hindustani forces lost no time. They bore down on the Mongols, and pursuing the fleeing Mongol army, cut them down in large numbers. Their heads were hoisted on to the walls of the Sultan's fort.

The triumphant Hindustani army was returning to Deeplapur, their flags waving. The conspirators—the Sultan's Amir Mughlati, in cahoots with some Rajput chieftains—moved to accomplish their pre-planned assassination of Malik Tughlaq. But they were not successful. Qurbaan Ali had forewarned Malik Tughlaq about their plans. Amir Mughlati and the Rajput princes were caught and thrown into prison.

* * *

A soldier arrived to give Princess Neelma the message that Malik Tughlaq desired to present the heads of Tariq Beg and Tarqi Beg before her.

'Let the heads of both be strung up on poles on the top of the city walls of Samana, and convey to Malik Tughlaq that the Princess herself will be there to welcome him.'

Her sister and her father approached her. Her father looked grief-stricken, and her sister wore a look of jealous condemnation.

Neelma noticed the expression on her father's face, and stood before him, head bowed. She thought to herself, 'Can a human being never get rid of false pride and narrow-mindedness?' She did not know what to say to them.

'What I want to say, they are not prepared to hear.' She kept her gaze lowered at the feet of her father, and spoke softly, 'You will remember that the Mongols had carried away your eldest daughter. If you are not able to understand me, or accept my actions, you may console yourself that this daughter of yours faced the same fate and was carried away by the Turks.'

Her words were spoken simply and humbly but its underlying meaning was clear.

Gurdial Singh

Gurdial Singh (1933–2016) was born in village Bhaini near Jaito in Faridkot, Punjab. A prolific writer, he wrote novels, short stories, children's books and plays. He is one of the three great novelists in Punjabi, along with Nanak Singh and J.S. Kanwal, who gave new direction to the Punjabi novel. In his fiction, he has traced with great empathy, the suffering, fortitude and resilience of the peasants and the downtrodden in rural areas, caught in the transition from feudalism to capitalism. Through simplicity of style and language, accuracy of description and honesty of purpose, Gurdial Singh turn his progressive beliefs into imaginative storytelling that has a powerful impact on the readers. He was awarded the Sahitya Akademi prize in 1975 for his novel *Adh Chaanani Raat*, Soviet Land Nehru award in 1986, Padma Shri in 1999, and the Jnanpith Award jointly with Nirmal Verma.

Common Ground

A woman who had alighted from the train stood looking around, undecided. Bantu craned his neck to one side and squinted at her (he had poor eyesight so he could not recognise people from a distance). He moved closer and looked more carefully; then it appeared he knew who she was, Jai Kaur.

'Who are you?'

'I am Jai Kaur.'

'Oh, what brings you here?'

As he said this, Bantu's face broke into a smile. For a moment, Jai Kaur hesitated. Then she spoke, in a very low voice, 'I have come to my in-laws. The younger daughter-in-law is in hospital.'

'Oh, is all well?'

'She is to give birth.'

'Let us go then.'

Jai Kaur could not think of a reply. She was in a quandary. The day was fading rapidly and it would be late by the time she reached the village. No other person had got off the train along with her. The train was generally not as late as it had been that day. Usually it would reach well in time, when much of the day remained; but today it was unusually late. It occurred to her that she could stop nearby at her niece's house for the night, but she had to return by the next day's train. She stood there uncertain, thinking, and took another careful look at the man, Bantu, who stood before her. She saw a friendly gleam in his eyes; his demeanor seemed to be quite harmless.

'Fine. Let us go'. She braced herself and agreed to accompany him.

Bantu immediately set off taking such long strides that the bale of provisions he carried wobbled on his head. He clutched it fiercely as if he were trying to control some wayward creature. At the same time he was muttering and smiling to himself.

'So, tell me, Jai Kaur. Is all well at home?' He was quite jovial as they started on their way.

'Yes, by the Guru's grace.'

'That is good, that is good.'

Bantu sighed. He saw that the sunlight was fading, and the rays of the sun had reddened, and he experienced a feeling of ecstasy within. But he also saw that the sun still shone brightly on the fields of *bajra*, and so lowered his gaze and walked on.

It was very quiet at that time of evening, but as they walked through the tall trees, the sound of their footsteps made the birds roosting in the branches raise such a racket that the quiet was shattered. After a while, the birds settled down, and all was silent once again. Bantu could hear the sound of Jai Kaur's footsteps behind him, and it seemed to him that their rhythmic movement was like the sound made by musical instruments in the gurudwara when devotional hymns were sung.

'It is many years since we last met, isn't that so, Jai Kaur?'

'Yes,' said Jai Kaur, in a small voice, as if scared to reply.

'So you have been living with your younger nephew for the last six or seven years?' he inquired.

'Yes'.

Jai Kaur lifted her eyes to look at Bantu, and felt apprehensive.

He had stopped and, looking back at her, was shaking the loose dirt from his footwear. She saw a gleam of redness in his eyes just like the red light of the sun. But she also saw that his beard was discoloured and grey, and that made her feel less nervous. She felt that she no longer felt afraid or hesitant in talking to Bantu, for she had not realised earlier that he had become much older. As they continued to walk on, the distance between them shrank, and, walking just a step behind him, she could now observe him from top to toe at very close quarters. Bantu's calves were as thin as sticks, and the skin on his neck sagged. His spine was bent, and bones of his emaciated shoulders protruded sharply. His clothes were grimy with dust.

Suddenly, the vision of the young Bantu of earlier times sprang up before her eyes. This Bantu had a noble bearing, a tall straight figure, soft features and eyes glowing with an indescribable radiance. The Bantu who...

Jai Kaur felt a shiver run through her. She was again gripped with some kind of nervousness, before she regained her calm, and even felt some laughter escape her lips.

'How did you manage to get into this state?' she asked, with some pity, and trace of sympathy in her voice. 'Have you been ill or unwell?'

Bantu drew a deep sigh and replied, 'Jai Kaur, now what can I tell you...don't ask.'

'Come on, you cannot lose heart in this way.' She tried to reassure him. 'Everywhere it is the same...this is the way of the world...it is difficult for everyone.'

'It is the way of the world, yes. But the world now has come to such a dreadful state...no-one bothers about anyone else. See, should I be wandering around at this age? It is ten years since I gave away my property to my sons. After that, they turned their backs on me. Both their wives turned out to be so mean that after they got everything, they declared that the old man is not of any use to them. No-one wants to serve the old man food on time, offer him water, or wash his clothes…now what can one say, Jai Kaur, one has to bear these things, maybe as results of one's past deeds.'

Jai Kaur felt very sorry for Bantu, who was being given such a hard time in his house.

'Do not worry, do not feel so bad.' Jai Kaur was emphatic in her reply. 'Think of people like me, who don't have any place of their own anywhere. God hasn't been kind to me either. All my life I'm at the mercy of relatives, having to stay at my nieces' house. It's different for men. Everyone has these problems…as Nanak says, everywhere there is suffering…is there anything we can do? As we sow, so we reap…it is the way of our karma, our past actions.'

Bantu felt a sense of comfort as he heard her speak, just as a dejected person finds solace in the story of another dejected person. In a way, Jai Kaur, who seemed as miserable as him, was one with whom he felt a deep affinity, as though they were on common ground.

He glanced towards the left, and saw that the red glow of the setting sun had almost disappeared, and some stars could be seen twinkling in the sky. It was quite humid, since there was no breeze, and there was not even any sound of rustling of leaves among the standing crop in the fields. The path had become even more narrow. Jai Kaur walked unafraid behind him. He felt quite drawn to her, and wanted to stop and have a good look at her—her fair complexion, high forehead, deep voice, her mature features and body as yet unaffected by age—in all, she still appeared to possess some womanly attractiveness.

'Jai Kaur, this is 'our' field,' he pointed out the land and the full crop around, stopping and shaking the dirt out of his shoes. All of this, he told her, had been sown this year, right up to the tall tree at the very far corner.

Jai Kaur also stopped in her tracks. She felt suddenly breathless and her heart was beating fast. The tree that Bantu had indicated was the same tree, under which, thirty-five years ago, he had come near her and grasped her arm. Now she felt nervous, but at the same time, she also wished that he might grasp her hand in the same way…

at the thought, she began to shiver. All this while, Bantu did not move forward, but stood there, dusting his shoes, with his gaze fixed steadily on her. Jai Kaur stared back at him with some hostility, and then lowered her gaze. She was now genuinely fearful of the man, and did not appreciate his steady stare.

It seemed Bantu was deliberately drawing attention to the tree, in a playful way. 'See, we have planted *bajra* here. I had wanted some other crop here, but you know, nobody listens to an old man, they do what they want.'

'It's all right…'

'This tree was going to be cut and sold around the time of my marriage, but I told my father that it could not be done. The tree will remain even if the land is sold, I told him.'

Jai Kaur felt very uncomfortable. Why was Bantu raising the subject of that tree again and again? Then he resumed walking forward, with Jai Kaur following him slowly several steps behind, keeping distance between them. So much so that Bantu could no longer hear the sound of her footsteps, and stopped again, to look back at her.

'Come on now, come, it is quite close now.' He spoke encouragingly. 'This is the village path, now we are not walking on the edge of the fields.'

Jai Kaur looked up, and found that the village was indeed a few hundred meters away. She hurried forward to come up level with Bantu again.

'Jai Kaur, since "your sister" passed away, I too am waiting for death.'

Because Bantu had emphasized the words 'your sister', Jai could not suppress a smile. He was referring to his wife.

'Jai Kaur, there was a time when we were strapping young men. We never thought about god, or death. Today, it is different. Now it is as if we are just waiting for death, life is not worth living any more. But death does not come when we want it.'

'Oh, why do you talk of dying just yet? You will have time to see your grandchildren married, your great grandchildren playing in your lap...and it is the great grandchildren who will do the rites to help you on the way to heaven.'

These words, uttered by Jai Kaur, threw Bantu into some kind of frenzy. He was like one who at the same time, had an intense desire to live, but also a desire to die.

'Yes, you're right, but who wants to live such a life, so miserably hard? Who knows what heaven is? All one knows is this hard life. I'm treated like a dog by the rest of the family, and made to bark for a few pieces of bread, that's my condition.'

Jai Kaur understood Bantu's feelings. She could very well feel the sense of one-ness with him that she had felt thirty-five years ago, when they were both young and unattached. It was the same now—dependency on others. She herself had longed for a child for more than twenty years, but no prayers to the gods, or appeals to saints had yielded any results, and finally, her husband's sudden demise had put an end to all hopes. Now seven years had passed, and she would spend some of her days in her in-law's house, and some of her time with her nieces at her parental home. Just for her bread and upkeep, she had to put up with whatever treatment was meted out.

'It is for these children's and grandchildren's sake that all this has to be tolerated, Jai Kaur; if we don't, we're thrown out, to sleep under the stars, in the company of dogs...'

Bantu walked on, narrating his tales of woe, becoming agitated again as he spoke, as before.

'This is no way to live! And no way to die—all alone. When there is no one to mourn, no one to remember, even that death is meaningless, Jai Kaur.'

Bantu continued talking, but Jai Kaur's attention was no longer held by his talk. She was drawn to the flickering lamps in the village, which seemed to her like radiant flames in the darkness. She looked towards Bantu to see his fading form, his stick-like figure hovering around her, and she felt a great sympathy with him.

'All right, I will take this outer path,' she said to him, adding, 'Do not lose heart. Whatever time we have, let us live contented, for even if we spend the time weeping, it's not going to make our lives a luxury, or change our destiny.'

'That is true...true...' he murmured, and turned away on the path towards his own house.

Ajeet Kaur

Ajeet Kaur (b. 1934) was born in Lahore, Pakistan. Her most memorable work is in the genre of short story writing, though she also wrote prose and autobiography. Ajeet Kaur wrote significant fiction around the themes of political and bureaucratic corruption. However, her chief concern is the exploration of the complexities of man–woman relationships, and it is these that she goes into most incisively and evocatively. In 1985, she was awarded the Sahitya Akademi award for her book *Khanabadosh* and the Padma Shri in 2006.

Gulbano

Guard Khushdil Khan's wife Gulbano was such an extraordinary beauty that her fame spread over twenty or more villages around. A tall Pathan woman, with creamy complexion, soft and nubile limbs, Gulbano was an ethereal, fairy-like beauty.

And just as every beautiful fairy is guarded by a monster who imprisons her behind stone walls in a fortress, so did Khushdil Khan keep her hidden from the eyes of the world.

Of course, the convention among Pathans is to keep their women hidden away, as though they have not married them in a legitimate way, but have brought the woman by force or loot, to live with them. However, Guard Khushdil Khan had kept his wife under such strict watch, that no-one had ever had a chance to catch even a glimpse of her.

When the long summer days came around, the women of the village would go down to the town market to buy provisions. Every one of them would look forward to this trip with eagerness, as if they were going to a fair. They would wear the *burqa,* but under the *burqa*, they would wear make up. The loud beating of the *dhol* would precede them, so that, on hearing the sound from a distance, the Pathan men would move off the streets, and the way would be open for the women. When they reached the edge of the town, and there was no-one to look upon them, these Pathani women would throw back their *burqas*, and allow their *heena* adorned feet, with their silver anklets, to dance to the rhythmic beat of the *dhol* to their hearts' content. That dance, held back for days, weeks and months, finally found expression; and it burst from their feet like bubbling water from a fountain, flowing and free. And thus the wives would gather, from this village, and in large numbers.

But when the groups reached the village of Garhi Mawaaz Khan where Guard Khushdil Khan lived, a great sigh would pass their lips, and a great ache would arise in the depths of Gulbano's body. All the women of Garhi Mawaz Khan would join the group in the street, but Guard Khushdil would never permit his wife to join them.

Then all the women would enter the courtyard of Guard Khushdil Khan's house…the very house which was also a prison for a woman. The *dhol* would be played. The women would dance. Fruit and delicacies—pomegranate, apple, guava, apricots, corn, jaggery, sugar candy—would be distributed, and enjoyed.

Gulbano's beauty would amaze the gathered women, and at the same time, strike at their very hearts. The *dhol* would sound, but its rhythm spoke of an intense pain. The women would dance, but movement of their ankles and feet would exude an agony that rose like a long scream. And what was it like for Gulbano? Her feelings were those of a person, who stumbling in the dark night, has a bowl of precious milk knocked out of her hands, the milk spilt. And it was as if all the stars in the sky were smouldering with the fire in the heart.

The women would eventually return to their own homes. And Gulbano would be left within the sweltering heat of her passion's prison, and feel as if she would shrivel up and die.

Occasionally, the friends and well-wishers of Guard Khushdil Khan would suggest to him that he let his wife join the other women in their activities. 'Even cows and buffaloes have to be let out sometimes to bathe and drink, and walk around,' it was said.

But he would not respond to any such suggestions.

On the days when the groups of women would descend on his house, he would go wild with rage. He would yell at his servants, at the colleagues from the station, at the children and at his wife. He would go around smashing things—it was as if a desert whirlwind had blown into the place and was tearing it up.

Then the days would pass, and the storm would subside. Life would carry on. Gulbano would again begin to accept her life within the four walls as her natural habitat, and live with it as before.

But one day...

Chandan had just brought in the large milk-pan and set it in the courtyard, when Gulbano passed through the yard. She did not look towards him. But Chandan threw a glance in her direction just for a moment. In that moment, it appeared to him that he had seen the beauty of a delicate, milky white and bright sea shell, as if a fragile shape reflected in a rainbow prism of translucent light had been revealed to him. And Chandan felt like a king.

Wherever he went, whenever he talked to anyone, Chandan would speak of Gulbano...he would describe how she walked, her clothes, her jewels, her hands, her face and her feet.

He had seen Gulbano walk through the courtyard...Gulbano herself...and for Chandan, it was as if a radiant light had passed through the dreary night of his life.

No word was spoken. Gulbano had not even looked at him. But for Chandan it was like a dream that had spread its wings and alighted in his heart, and from within its folds, a hundred hopes had raised their heads, like tiny creatures emerging into the light to see a world that was fresh and new and wonderful, though it might have existed for centuries, it was revealed for the very first time, upon which they looked with infinite amazement.

That one glimpse made a royal out of Chandan. At that moment, he was a king.

Here was Chandan, whose heart was expanded and transformed with that single revelation which opened up the universe for him.

Here was Guard Khushdil Khan whose heart, even after years of proximity to Gulbano, stayed stone-like and ash-dark like the cinders from a spent volcano.

Here was that Gulbano, who was physically close to Khushdil Khan, and yet so far away.

Here was that Gulbano who was physically so far from Chandan, and yet so close to his heart.

One of Gulbano's friends came to see her, and told her that the man who came to deliver milk to their house, the man called Chandan, would speak of her, Gulbano, to everyone—in an ecstatic tone, he would talk of her beauty, her hands and hair, her face and lips.

The next day, Gulbano stood behind the doorway, unseen, and watched Chandan as he poured the milk from his pan into theirs. The pure milk, as it flowed into the pan, seemed to flow as a life-giving force might flow, into the desert of her heart.

Each step in the courtyard was like a dance. Each moment a song bubbled up from within her body, as if her soul had begun to hum in ecstasy. She was lost in its melodious murmur.

Spring entered her heart. It flowered into a tree—Chandan—full of fragrant blossoms, the scent of which spread and overcame its emptiness. Her beautiful body, which had been barren of feeling, experienced the stirring of love, just as a drop of rain falls into the heart of an oyster and transforms a grain of sand into a pearl.

This time, when the village women came visiting, and the beat of the *dhol* was heard in her courtyard, everyone was filled with happiness, and so was Gulbano. Seeing her so happy, the rhythm of the *dhol* was joyous, and so were all the wives, and so was Chandan, far away from the village, tending to his cattle at the riverside.

The one unhappy person was Guard Khushdil Khan.

Eventually, the stories about Chandan and his talk about Gulbano reached him on the wings of rumours. An uncontrollable fury took hold of him. In a blind rage, he returned to his house.

Gulbano was washing clothes, beating them with the large flat stick used for washing, and she was singing as she worked.

Khushdil Khan grabbed the stick from her hands and struck her on her back. 'You dare to sing—defying the religion!'

He then grabbed her arm and dragged her out to the courtyard. 'Now tell me, is the talk about Chandan true?'

Gulbano was silent. The one truth of her life—how could she deny it? She could not lie.

Khushdil Khan dragged her up to the roof of the house.

'Let me unite you with your Chandan. Here, go—go to your Chandan...'

And he threw Gulbano off the roof with all his force. One scream, and then...nothing.

People heard the scream, and came running to the scene. Khushdil Khan realised that his wife lay on the ground in full view of all the people and they were looking at her body.

He hurried down and out of his house carrying a thick sheet and ran into the street. He quickly threw the sheet on Gulbano, and covered her face.

Raghubir Dhand

Raghubir Dhand (1934–1990) was born in village Jandali, district Sangrur. He migrated to England in the 1960s, and was one of the first progressive Punjabi writers in England, who inspired many other writers to join the progressive literature movement. The Cambodian government awarded him with an honorary doctorate for his services to Cambodia.

Raghubir Dhand was a committed Marxist writer and wielded his pen in support of the have-nots and exploited classes. He delineated with great detail the issues of racial discrimination in England and in Punjab, and also the dilemmas of the Punjabi immigrants under the impact of Western culture. His mastery of psychological nuances, fast-paced narration of events and actions and effective use of Malwai dialect are the most impressive features of his work.

On The Other Side

There was snow all around, as far as the eye could see, white as the teeth on a black man's face. The sky was covered with clouds. It was around ten o'clock in the morning, and silence prevailed all around. It was an eerie kind of silence—like the moonlight in a graveyard, like the sullen faces of people standing in a queue, a sad tune floating around in a confined space.

A procession was drawing near...

In the large front garden of the club stood a gathering of about a hundred men and women, dressed in elegant clothes, staring at the oncoming procession. They had their pet dogs with them—almost as many in number as the people—tiny dogs, like little lambs; massive dogs, like lions; black and brown and white. The people in the gathering held mugs of dark ale in their hands.

Pamela was accompanying her mother for the inauguration of the club that day. She was ten, had a slightly oval face, and her soft curly hair, under a hat, fell to her shoulders. She wore a new yellow embroidered coat, light brown skirt and white socks.

She too had been staring at the procession for some time now, with much curiosity but no aversion. She would have continued to do so had not her mother said, with anger and hatred, 'Huh! Bastards and beggars, these niggers!'

Hearing her mother's words, Pamela felt a sudden shock run through her. She took her eyes off the procession and looked up straight into her mother's eyes. 'Who, Mamma? Who are you so angry with?'

'Them! Those dirty coloured ones in the procession!' she replied, still staring angrily at the crowd.

Pamela was astonished. Her astonishment gave rise to many questions, as astonishment always does. She wanted to bombard her mother with these questions, one after another, 'Mamma, who are these people in the procession? Why are they doing it? And

Mamma, why are you so angry with them? Why do you call them by these names—niggers, dirty coloureds...and why call them bastards? Mamma, these are terrible words to say!'

But she could not muster the courage to ask any of these questions. She was afraid to look at her mother's angry expression. It was strange to her—she had rarely seen such unkindness in her mother before.

She looked towards her mother again, into her eyes, to see if she could also understand that her child wanted to ask her something, that she was bursting with questions...and she would sense it and give her some answer. Then Pamela could be calm and quiet, like the snow lying silently in the fields. But her mother showed no sign of calmness or relaxation—she was angry and tense as before. Pamela, brought up in English society, was not used to such signs of tension in people around her in everyday life.

A girl in the procession, with long brown hair, was holding a placard aloft in her hands, and as she did, she shouted a slogan, 'Black and white!' And at once, four hundred arms with clenched fists were raised, and they shouted in unison, 'Unite and fight!'

Pamela's mother moved away, towards the group of assembled people in the club, and joined them.

'Today our country needs a man like Enoch Powell!' proclaimed Councillor Merrick, removing his glass of dark Guinness from his lips for a moment.

'These black people should be driven out of here as soon as possible. They have taken away our jobs!' said the van driver Malcolm, who, like the majority of English workers, did not fully understand the state of affairs.

'All the beds in hospitals are occupied by black women! Where do we go to deliver our infants?' the shrill voice of the pub owner Mr Cruikshank's wife, rang out. A devout Christian. She had not had a child of her own so far, and was not likely to have one now.

'These black people have smelly mouths!' Pamela's mother added her own two bits to this parliament of free-minded people.

Pamela was watching the procession, but all the while, she was listening to this conversation. She had never heard this kind of talk.

She might even have believed some of the things they were saying had her mother not said that black people had smelly mouths. This was something she could never believe, never!

She wanted to go up to her mother and shake her shoulders, and tell her, 'Mamma, you are totally wrong. Their mouths do not stink. Afza and I sit together in school and there is no smell from her mouth or from her—she bathes several times a week!'

This time, she did not feel afraid to speak. She even took a couple of steps towards her mother. But somehow her feet froze and she couldn't move. In frustration, she took off her hat, shook her hair, and put the hat on again.

In the procession, a white girl intertwined her arm with that of a black girl, and both waved their arms together in the air, 'Black and white?' The reply came, with the joining and waving of many black and white arms, 'Unite and fight!'

The optician Mr Marshall looped the dog's leash round his hand and tried to express some of his thoughts, 'Well, I understand that the blacks have an objection to not being admitted as members of the club. But I don't understand why white boys and girls have to be so stupid as to join them.'

Mr Ross, the officer who looked after public education, who had been silent till now, simply smiled and said, 'Such is today's wayward youth—our young generation!' The officers in England are wont to smile in this way when expressing an opinion.

All the men and women gathered continued their conversation as they walked into the club to drink beer.

The clouds towards the south and west had cleared. The tall trees seemed to be recovering from the ravages of the cold season and the snow was a little unsettled. Maybe it was the spirit of the protestors in the street that had brought life to the surrounding nature. The procession had approached the club and now the faces in the crowd could be seen distinctly.

Pamela felt isolated and alone. She drifted away from the group in the club, and went up to the low wall that formed the boundary of the club. She stood, resting her hands on the wall, and watched the people in the procession intently. The procession continued to advance...it would reach the end of the road in front of the club, then come back and pass the club again.

There was a hubbub at the gate. It seemed an argument had started there. Pamela rushed to the spot.

'Why the hell did you ever come to our country?' yelled a white Englishman from within the gate, twisting his face with disgust and scorn.

'Because your factories needed cheap labour. They begged us to come and get their industries going,' a handsome tall Negro answered, in a level tone.

From among the crowd on the other side of the gate a girl marched up and said boldly, 'For your information, when this question was asked in Hyde Park of an American, he said, we have come here to impregnate your women to make sure you have children!'

All the people on that side roared with laughter and someone said, 'Absolutely right!'

'Because of you, ten lakh native English people are unemployed,' said one middle-aged woman with thick glasses, quoting official figures to defend her statement.

A white man with a brown beard was about to reply to her when another white man, with one arm, came forward and said, 'Do you know that in the Great Depression of 1930, there were no blacks in this country and even so two million (twenty lakh) were unemployed. How do you explain that?'

An infuriated white Englishwoman rushed out of the club. She pushed aside the other people standing inside the gate and stood face to face with the people opposite, glaring at them as if she wanted to kill them all. She spat out her words with venom, and extreme arrogance, 'You are filthy! Smelly-mouthed! All of you should be taken to the English Channel and...'

At once many voices shouted, 'Shut up! Fascist! Dirty bitch... stupid...' and the rest of her words were lost in the uproar.

A beautiful blonde English girl turned to the black youth standing next to her and gave him a big kiss, in full view of the crowd. Then she called out to the woman inside the gate, 'Hey, there is no smell in his mouth. Come on, kiss him and see for yourself!'

A young Indian girl wearing a hand-woven sari wrinkled her lovely nose and tossed back her long plait, saying, 'Even if someone gives me a hundred pounds, I wouldn't kiss that woman's dried-up lips smelling of cigarettes! I would throw up, I would!'

And she turned her head, pouted and made a sound of spitting. 'Thoo!'

The woman inside the gate was incensed. 'Shut up', she screamed. 'I'll pull out your tongue!'

The beautiful blonde girl put her arm around the waist of the young Indian girl and waved her other arm in defiance, 'Come on then!' she challenged.

The Indian girl stepped forward, her arms outstretched. 'Just try and lay your hands on me. You'll see!'

May Allen, the black wife of the English professor Frank Allen, spoke out in a determined voice, 'The time has gone when you used to cut up our ancestor's bodies into pieces and feed them to your dogs. This will never happen again.'

'Yes, send all the dogs out from the club. The're also black!' a voice added.

'And send us all the ale that you are drinking—that's also black!' said another voice.

The pretty Indian girl still had her arm raised. Arms held limply on the side do not have the force that can challenge and attack, or the courage to face attack. The upraised arm with a fist has even more power than the vote. History can be changed with the vote, but slowly. When the arm is raised, history itself is challenged.

A policeman standing a few metres away saw the upraised arm. His sense of 'duty' aroused he took hold of the girl's arm firmly, admonishing her, 'Madam, you can only speak, not raise your arm!'

The man with the brown beard who was standing near them, said laughingly to the Indian girl, 'Reena! In a free country, one's only allowed to bark!'

Laughter rippled through the crowd.

Reena and Aileen linked their arms. They raised their joined arms and shouted loudly in unison, 'Black and white?'

All arms were raised. 'Unite and fight.'

Pamela continued to watch keenly. A little while back, her mind had been full of questions and she had been feeling oppressed by these unanswered questions. But now she was elated, joyful; she felt refreshed and energetic—like a river flowing calmly, or a sky having just been washed clean by rain. A new book had opened before her. A momentary event can be very powerful in its impact. Life reveals itself with a force and clarity, such that all the doubt and confusion is swept away, and the answers to all our questions are immediately revealed.

Pamela looked around her and at the club with a slow, deliberate glance. The ale was frothing in their glasses, and the black dogs were licking the hands of their white masters with their red tongues.

A smile of contempt came to her girlish lips.

Then she looked out on the other side of the club. The marching crowd had turned back and was now approaching the place where she stood. Hundreds of black and white arms were raised and slogans rent the air.

A smile of admiration came to her girlish lips.

The clouds in the sky had completely cleared away. The protestors were near her. The lovely young Indian girl and her long-haired white companion were leading, their hands intertwined, their arms held up. The sun had just come out to greet them, and its rays illuminated the whole scene.

Pamela's face was wreathed in smiles as she saw them. Her body was full of energy. She looked over the wall, and saw that it was very high on the other side.

Now the procession was very close to her. The frontrunners, the two girls, were parallel to her. She put one foot on the wall. Then she asked one tall black man walking along the wall who was nearest to her, 'Please, can you help me get over the wall?'

Instead of stretching out his hands, the young man put his shoulders to the wall. And the next moment, astride his shoulders, she raised her arm, and shouted at the top of her voice, 'Black and white!'

Many arms waved and many voices offered the spirited response, 'Unite and fight!'

The glass of beer dropped from the hands of a middle-aged woman standing inside the club...

Gulzar Singh Sandhu

Gulzar Singh Sandhu (b. 1935) was born in village Kotla Badla near Samrala in Punjab. He was editor of the daily *Punjabi Tribune*, and *Desh Sevak*, and taught at Punjabi University, Patiala. His writing reveals a deep interest in the emotions of ordinary people and how people change when faced with conflict or driven by their aspirations. He adopts a humanistic view of life. Sandhu was awarded the Sahitya Akademi prize in 1982 for his collection *Amar Katha*.

Disgraced

When he was released from army service, Baksha came back to his village, bought some land and bullocks, and began farming. But his very first crop was devastated by the floods. He then bought a bicycle and began to ferry milk from the village to the town. But then he unwittingly got involved in a murder case. After that, he joined up with a friend and took a license for a liquor shop, but did not make a profit as most of his own friends frequented the place and freely consumed all the stock. He left the village and moved to Patna, where he drove trucks in a company owned by his brother-in-law.

But the truck met with an accident.

Finally, he landed up in Delhi. One of his close friends from the army was a taxi driver in the city. He had, of course, learnt how to drive while in the army; in fact, he even had a license for driving heavy vehicles. He needed to pass a first aid test to earn a badge as a taxi driver, then he could be a driver for anyone who had a taxi for hire, for a hundred rupees a month. Drivers can usually manage their meals and small expenses from tips and extras, so that meant that the hundred rupees could be saved. In two months, he had familiarised himself with the layout of Delhi by travelling around in his friend's car. Shortly thereafter, he took the test and earned his badge at 5, Rajpur Road.

To pay back his friend Shera for his help, he drove Shera's car for free for one month, and after that, Shera borrowed a friend's car for him to drive. Why was Shera so helpful? Both men had joined the army together, and were also distantly related to each other. The truth was that Baksha's father, who had been a commissioned officer in the cavalry, facilitated Shera's induction in the army at the time, and without his help, Shera would not have been selected. Shera could never forget this favour and helping Baksha in turn was just a small way of repaying the tremendous help rendered to him by Baksha's father. In fact, it was better to have a companion—together they could earn more and do much better for themselves. Baksha's father had blessed the duo, saying that 'two together are always lucky'. Shera thought the same, and felt that their unity strengthened their position among the other taxi drivers at the Regal Taxi Stand.

Baksha and Shera together also made arrangements to find a place where they could stay. They did not eat together as they had different work hours and were in different parts of the city at a given time. If Shera was driving in the Ridgeway camp area, Baksha might be somewhere in Mehrauli; if Shera was in Shahdara, Baksha might be picking up passengers in Rajouri Garden. Wherever they were sent according to their number in the taxi rank, they would go. Someone going to Chawri Bazaar, fond of a night of entertainment; a businessman who was desperate to make more money, a clever middleman, a Brahmin from Madras or a Marwari from Rajasthan or a *jat* from Haryana, a tall good-looking young fellow or a well-dressed and made-up young girl—all kinds and class of passengers would ride in their taxis. At night, when they returned, they would share the stories of people they had driven, and have a lot of fun in talking about them. Occasionally, they would go to see a film, or have a drink, and take turns to pay, or help each other out. Usually they never kept account of a few rupees spent here or there—what did that matter when there was such good understanding between them?

The two of them were not particularly prone to the usual bad habits that many drivers have. Rather, Shera had advised Baksha that if they were prudent, they could save a couple of hundred rupees every month. They did just that, and began to put aside money in savings. Back home in the village, their families were able to sustain themselves, more or less. They both had wives, and not many other family responsibilities—the wives would stay for six months at their parents' homes, and for six months at their in-law's. In such situations, when the husband is working away from home, the wife does not worry too much, even if they are recently married. For it was true that Shera and Baksha were working hard to earn money. Soon they would get permits and after that they could buy their own cars on the basis of loan instalments. No need for a Baby Austin, a Hindustan would be good enough. Even allowing for extras, like taxes, it was possible to buy a car in the range of ten thousand rupees. They had informed their families at home of their plan, and it was taken as quite acceptable.

Shera and Baksha bought a car. Once the loan instalments for that were paid of, they bought another car, again on loan. Now both had their own cars. They were comfortable working and living as friends. They were not dependent on the owner of the taxi stand to give them their salaries, but were working for themselves. When the second loan was paid off, they became free of liabilities and so they took two rooms in Lajpat Nagar where rentals were cheap. Each one in turn went home and brought their wives to the city. Both couples would cook in one kitchen and share the household expenses. But Baksha's father warned Shera, 'Even real brothers cannot keep up a joint household, so be careful you don't end up quarrelling', he said. 'Oh, there is a greater chance that brothers may fight, but friends will remain friends', both of them protested in unison.

There is a saying that it takes a long time to build something, but only a short time to destroy it. Inevitably, one day Shera and Baksha fell out. Despite much effort, their wives did not get along. Shera's wife would claim that her husband was more thrifty and sensible in handling money, while Baksha's wife would say that Baksha worked much harder and came home later. Both of them would play up their own husband's roles in the running of the household and managing the income. Both tried to outdo one another in extolling the extent of hard work each of their husbands did. And each said to the other, 'We can manage alone much better without you', and decided to go their own way. The two men also consented to this because it was better than having arguments every day.

Now all the loan instalments had been paid. Shera had the new car, and the older one was taken by Baksha after paying off the small amount remaining. But the day they split up, they were rueful. 'Let's accept it, yaar! We will survive this!' Baksha said, laughing it off. 'How does it matter? We live next door, we just have separate kitchens, that's all!' Thus comforting each other, they walked off to their vehicles at the taxi stand. In trying to justify the move, or perhaps to find a rational reason for it, Shera commented, 'See, if we both had to spend the whole day together as our wives do, we too would be fed up in no time!' And Baksha agreed. 'It makes no difference; as it is, we are so busy, we hardly have time to meet each other, sometimes for days at a time.' This conversation helped them to reconcile with the separation.

But it was never the same again. Shera was ambitious and wished to own more cars; Baksha's desire was to accumulate money. They were outwardly civil to one another, but inwardly felt bitter. Even the other drivers at the stand saw this, and were no longer intimidated by them as they had been earlier. In fact, they saw the internal division as an opportunity to further alienate them from each other, and instigated them. When Baksha suggested installing a telephone at the stands, the idea was rejected by Shera and a few of his supporters. Then if Shera organised a call to strike work, Baksha would willfully disobey the call, driving his taxi as usual.

The elections for the taxi drivers' union came around. Both contested the elections egged on by their respective supporters. While campaigning, each spoke against the other. Since they had been close and knew everything about each other, they took out all the dirty linen to wash in public. Both were of *jat* blood, neither would retract or step down. Both cultivated their own group of supporters. Their animosity grew. It came to the point when, at first there were arguments, then fisticuffs, and then weapons. Shera got hurt in one such encounter, before people could intervene to break up the fight. Dreading further attacks, neither came home that night. Shera could not sleep, nor could Baksha, as each plotted on how to entrap and defeat the other. The pair who has been once inseparable were now poles apart—blood had thinned out and turned to water. Shera engaged a few henchmen, and so did Bakhsa. These musclemen took Shera's car out of the city and damaged it, while the other's men drove off with Baksha's car, damaged it in retaliation, and broke Baksha's arm in the bargain. Shera's car was repaired, and Baksha's arm healed, but both suffered a loss of around eight hundred rupees each. There was tension in both households. The wives were constantly fearful of an increase in hostility, worried that something may happen to their husbands. So they tried to calm down and resolve the situation, but by now the differences between the two men had become irreconcilable.

The matter became so serious that Shera initiated a court petition against Baksha under Section 307, 'Intent to Murder', taking the help of a few policemen and witnesses arranged for the purpose. Everyone at the stand was aghast when the summons arrived for Baksha's arrest. Seeing this terrible outcome of what they had thought were trivial squabbles, the petty mischief-makers felt sorry, but it was too late. The arguments and minor scuffles which they had enjoyed were one thing, but being sent to jail and suffering for life was another. They set about trying to get the two parties to reach a settlement. Some would explain to Baksha that it was better to ask for Shera's forgiveness, reminding him that it was Shera who had supported him in his initial years in the city, due to which he was so well settled now. They said that they accepted Shera's foolishness, but Baksha must realise that his position was weaker, and he should not forget Shera's earlier benevolence. The arguments of these peacemakers had no effect whatsoever on each other; they were not willing to even meet face to face. Shera had erred, and could not acknowledge that he had, so he did not yield. Baksha felt he had not done any wrong, so he did not yield. They had been friends, companions and co-workers, they had helped each other, shared their finances, equally; this very equality stopped them from bowing down to the other. This was the core of the issue—and the problem seemed insoluble. They were persuaded to appear before some reputed persons to help them find reconciliation. They returned without even speaking to each other. People accompanied them to the sacred Gurudwara Sis Ganj, but even there neither admitted to any fault. They seemed impervious to the destruction they had unleashed on themselves and their families.

The date of the court hearing drew near. Both of them prepared their witnesses for the day, and tried to engage the cleverest lawyers. They tried to make sure that their witnesses would be steadfast in their statements. Shera was nervous, if any of his witnesses defaulted, the case would turn out against him, and on his part. Baksha was afraid that if his witnesses did not speak up, he would be condemned. The irony was lost on them that in this madness, they were destroying the very wealth and prosperity that both had built together.

The date of the hearing was nigh. They had written back to their village for support, but no-one turned up. The first hearing was critical, and whatever the witnesses said that day would be more or less final.

A telegram was sent to Baksha's father that he should come and express regrets in the court on behalf of his son and thus save his skin, but he did not arrive.

Three days remained. No sign of Baksha's father. Then two days to go. Still no-one came. On the day before the hearing Baksha's father arrived. People gathered to witness the spectacle of the humiliation of the old, white-bearded father of Baksha in front of Shera.

The day of the hearing arrived. Even as they were being persuaded to make amends, they continued to hurl abuses at each other. Just before they were to leave for the court, the old cavalry officer, Baksha's father, walked to the taxi stand. He had a milk-white beard, and walked with the help of a cane. He stood there, still as a statue. Neither Shera nor Baksha approached him. He too did not glance at either of them, but stood motionless. It was not clear whether he did not wish to speak, or whether he was unable to speak. But his whole body, from head to foot, was trembling with emotion. Baksha did not look at him. Shera, it seemed, could not dare to look at him. The men at the taxi stand brought out a chair for him to sit, but he pushed it away with the tip of his cane.

Suddenly, something came over Shera. He rushed forward and fell at the old man's feet. This was the same man, the cavalry officer, who had made it possible for the desperate, starving Shera to be recruited in the army in spite of Shera's having been declared medically unfit. How could Shera forget his immense obligation to this old man? Shera got up and, then touched his knees and his white beard. The old man was silent. When Shera looked at him, he saw that there were tears in his eyes. He tried to say something to him, but did not speak.

Then Shera turned to Baksha, who had been standing there in sullen and angry silence, and touched his feet too. But the old officer stepped forward and caught Shera by the shoulders, pulling him up. Then he addressed Baksha, 'You are a disgrace! Were you not ashamed to give trouble to this boy?' Then he confronted both of them together. 'Have you evil fellows no shame? Have you no respect for this white beard of mine? Did you not think of the trouble you have caused me in my old age? Is it right to drag me around like this, shaming me, lowering my dignity, you rascals?'

The onlookers gathered at the taxi stand could not understand what exactly had happened. It was time to go to the court. Shera and Baksha collected their witnesses and proceeded to the court—not to present the plea that had been prepared, but to reverse it.

Dalip Kaur Tiwana

Dalip Kaur Tiwana (1935-2020) was born in village Rabbo in Patiala district. She received a PhD degree in Punjabi Literature, and engaged in research at Punjabi University. She is first and foremost a novelist, although she has done extensive work in the areas of children's literature, translation, stories, autobiography and criticism. She is chiefly credited with giving voice to two kinds of women in her novels. The first are the traditional set of women, who live within the male-oriented society, and the second are the educated women who are attempting to carve out their own independent path. The tension between traditional and modern values is very sensitively presented in Tiwana's novels. The Sahitya Akademi awarded her novel *Eh Hamara Jeewna* in 1971. She was honoured with the Saraswati Samman in 2001, and the Padma Shri in 2004. Many of her works have been translated into English and other languages.

The Confession

Every single day she would say to herself that this would be the day. She would tell her father everything, and she would beg him to forgive her. But when she was in her father's presence, she could not utter a word. Many were the times when she resolved she would tell all, but then she would stop herself because she was afraid her father would be angry with her. He might stop loving her as he used to. Maybe...she suffered deep pangs of regret and repentance—but what could be done about it now? Daadi—her grandmother—was long dead. Her last words had been, 'Jeeti, write to your father at once. I am not going to live much longer now.' These words echoed in Jeeti's ears.

Jeeti would feel anger surging in her towards her mother. It was her mother who used to exclaim with bitterness, 'The old woman is not going to die. Oh no, she would rather see us all go before she does. She was born with evil powers. All this while she has been raising false alarms so that your father leaves his job and comes back on hearing about her health, but she doesn't die! She won't vacate that bed of hers!'

So Jeeti thought that, indeed, her father would have to leave his work, lose his job, spend money—perhaps five rupees—on the fare in coming and going to and fro, so why write to him, calling him back? Daadi is not being serious when she says she will die soon.

Jeeti did have great affection for her grandmother. Whenever her mother was not looking, she would slip a milk sweet or two to her Daadi, because her father had told her that elderly people are like children, they like little treats; her mother would scoff at this, saying, 'Does the old hag need extra energy? Does she have to go to the fields and harness the bulls for ploughing? All she does is lie in that bed, she is so useless.'

Jeeti felt quite sorry for her granny. She would quietly and secretly crumple up some sweet *roti*, or mix *roti* into the *daal* so that Daadi would find it easy to chew and enjoy the food. She would wash Daadi's clothes, and mix some medicinal oil to rub on Daadi's temples. Her mother would always interject, 'Look, child, this bag of bones gave me enough trouble—much trouble—every day, she would raise some matter to cause quarrels between your father and me. I could never dare to do anything without her permission. She would even lock up the kitchen cupboard. And if I dressed neatly in clean clothes, she would taunt me, saying, 'Oho, where do you think you're going all decked up? I did all the work at home, but there was no pleasing her. Instead, she would say to me that I'm from a mean stock, I come from a low-down family...all this she would say, and more....' When Jeeti heard these words, she too would begin to regard her Daadi in a different way, and did not like her as much. Because of this, she would often get irritated at Daadi's frequent requests for water or something else and shout, 'Daadi, stop, don't interfere, don't talk nonsense. You don't know anything. Sit quietly.'

But after a while, Jeeti would forget about it, and gaze with affection at her grandmother's wrinkled face. She would notice how her grandmother's hands trembled, and would feel really sorry for her. A thought would come into her mind, '*it* may be that by next year

Daadi will no longer be with us...how sad!' and she would sit near her Daadi and give her many hugs. Then Daadi would say to her', Go, now, my dear, do your chores or your mother will get angry...'

And when Jeeti's mother would scold Jeeti, Daadi would protest, 'Stop this, daughter, why do you torment the child?'

'Amma, it is you who have spoilt her. Even if I ask her to do a minor task, you can't bear it. You always jump up to defend her!'

Her mother would often refuse to buy Jeeti trinkets that the vendors brought around to their home. Jeeti would go to her grandmother with a woeful expression, and this would evoke Daadi's protest, 'Why can't you buy her something she wants? Children set their hearts on such little things. It won't ruin your household budget, will it?'

Her mother would retort, 'Amma, you will surely spoil this girl. Am I to fulfil every single demand that she makes?'

Daadi would persist. 'Little ones like to have these treats. There's no harm in agreeing to their small wishes. May her father live long who provides for her!'

Jeeti felt happy when Daadi spoke up for her. But Daadi would also be very firm in not allowing her to go to see the *Teej* fair, as she believed that girls were not safe when they went there. There were bad people, from unknown places, even from faraway Moga or somewhere else, and they would kidnap girls, take them away. Jeeti was exasperated by this. So many girls went to the fair. Why would anyone carry them off?

Another habit of Daadi's often irritated Jeeti. She did not like it when, on wearing a new dress, Jeeti would admire the dress and herself. Daadi would say cuttingly, 'Girl, there'll be enough time to dress up like that when you grow up. For now, be sensible, and listen to your elders.' Jeeti was filled with resentment. 'Just listen to her!' she thought. 'As if she did not wear nice clothes when she was young! She only wants an excuse to get after me!'

Gradually, over six months or so, Daadi began to get weaker and weaker. And so it was that Jeeti's father took her aside on one of his visits home and told her. 'See, you know how your mother is, Jeeti. It is your job to look after Amma and see that she does not suffer much. And you must promise to write to me regularly about her condition.'

Daadi became more and more difficult to look after as her health worsened. She would call out to them to give her water, and after having a sip, would call out again. At times she would begin to wail and whimper without reason, and at other times she would speak quite clearly. Jeeti's mother would comment, 'This is just her way. She will not die all that easily. Because of her evil deeds, her illness is going to linger for many more months. Good people depart from this world peacefully, without suffering. But who knows what hell is destined for this one!'

Daadi's illness was indeed lingering, and her release seemed distant. Jeeti was exhausted with attending constantly upon her grandmother, pressing her head, giving her medicine. She was disgusted at her Daadi's constant coughing, and felt a sense of loathing when she had to wash Daadi's clothes reeking of sickness. She hated the way the elderly Brahmin woman who visited them would advise her, 'Child, parents are precious, like the fading season, they will not come again. You must serve them, it is the equivalent of making the holiest of pilgrimages...'

Several times Jeeti wrote a postcard to her father, to ask him to come home, but each time Daadi would suddenly recover. But one day, when Daadi said to her, 'Child, call your father home. It's time now', Jeeti did not pay much attention to her. Her mother too, was quick to declare, 'Oh, she's all right. Why must your father leave his work and come back again and again? There is no need to send a postcard...' and so Jeeti did not write.

After two days, Daadi again asked, 'Girl, did you send the card or not? I am not going to live much longer now. Last night I saw your grandfather in my dream. He seemed to be saying he knows what the situation here is like for me...dreams like this are not good...'

'No, Daadi, nothing will happen to you, you're all right. I just thought why give Father the trouble, Mother also said the same, and so I did not send a card...'

'What? You didn't...?' so saying, Daadi looked at Jeeti, agitated. She did not say another word. That evening she did not have her tea, or her medicine; at around midnight she awoke and asked for some water. In the very early hours of the morning, she died.

Daadi died. Jeeti cried and cried. She could not forget that in her last moments how much Daadi must have wanted to see her son. Stupid me! She lamented to herself. Why did I not write to my father? She felt anger towards her mother who had insisted that nothing would happen to Daadi. But what could be done now? It was too late. She remembered how good her Daadi had been to her. How hard she had worked all day, spinning the cotton, swabbing floors, washing utensils…would she now never return? 'Daadi, forgive me…I did not write to my father as you had asked…I am very bad.'

Whenever she saw an old woman, she would be reminded of her grandmother, and she would think that if now her Daadi were to be here, she would never speak rudely to her, nor would she allow her mother to quarrel with Daadi, and she would really look after her. She repented that she did not understand during Daadi's life that there was such a short time left for her to live, that she would be swept away like a twig from the banks of a stream. Now she remembered her all the time. She carefully put away the stick that Daadi had used for walking, and she also kept Daadi's prayer beads in a box, taking them out and looking at them often. She had not allowed Daadi's embroidered long skirt to be given away.

Her father arrived as soon as he heard of Daadi's death. He wept inconsolably. Jeeti was again filled with repentance for not having written to him earlier. She decided that now she would certainly tell her father that his mother had wanted him to be called earlier, but she thought, 'Father will only be more sad when he hears that his mother was waiting for him and calling for him just before she died, and he might also be angry with me for not writing to him in time… but no, even if he gets angry, I must tell him…I *will* tell him.' But each time she was in her father's presence, she grew silent, unable to utter a single word.

Having heard about the arrival of Jeeti's father, the neighbours and other friends came to offer their condolences. One old woman who had been coming to visit Daadi off and on, said to him, 'My son, your mother would say that she only wanted to see you once so that she could die in peace.' As Jeeti's father began to sob loudly on hearing this, Jeeti felt terrible.

'Son, parents are here in this world for only a short time...one can give value to so many other things in life, go and earn money, but serving one's parents is the most sacred action one can perform—it is no less than making a pilgrimage!'

'How was I to know that Mother would pass away so soon? If I had known I would never have stayed away. I knew Jeeti was looking after her grandmother very well, so I went away for work.'

Jeeti felt as if she had been indirectly blamed. Her face fell and she was about to say, 'Daadi had...'

'Jeeti, did Mother suffer a lot when she was nearing the end?'

'No, Father...' Jeeti answered in confusion.

She understood the grief in her father's expression, and felt great pity, and regret...if only she had written!

Her father would go through Daadi's belongings and touch them—Daadi's small snuff box, her bangle, her earrings—and he would put them away carefully. He would often ask her, 'Jeeti, Mother must have said something at the end, did she say anything?'

Jeeti was tempted very often to tell him, 'Before Daadi breathed her last she asked for you to be called, but I did not write the letter to you.' But the words again stuck in her throat and she only shook her head to indicate the nothing was said.

'Jeeti, I hope you were not rude to her the way your mother used to be?' her father asked.

'Father, I...' she began to cry.

'All right, don't cry...I just asked...I know very well that you took very good care of her...better than I would have, I know.' Her father consoled her.

Jeeti could bear it no longer. She decided, I will surely tell him...

'Father, Daadi...' And she could say no more.

'Don't cry Jeeti, these things are not in our control, what can we do now...' and Jeeti's father's eyes filled up with tears.

Jeeti was tormented and her sense of guilt was suffocating—Daadi would appear in her thoughts again and again, and each time she would resolve that she would tell her father. But at the last minute she would hesitate to do so.

Her mother would say, 'What is to be expected—are the old ones supposed to live forever? One day, they have to go...and she had lived a long life as it is. Look at how this girl is behaving, going around with a long face all the time, just to avoid getting down to work.'

Jeeti hated this habit of her mother's and thought bitterly that it was her mother after all who had stopped her from writing—but now there was nothing to be done about it.

'Father...'

'Yes, my girl?'

'Why did Daadi die?' She changed the question even as she tried to speak. She was torn with guilt.

'Father, Daadi...'

Her father interrupted her, 'It is all right, child. Try not to think about your Daadi so much. You know she is not going to come back.'

She would stay silent, and think, how can I tell him that Daadi... she could never find words to complete the sentence, and she would weep, and say, 'Daadi, how could you die just like that? Why did you ask me to write the letter? Why?'

Gurbachan Singh Bhullar

Gurbachan Singh Bhullar (b. 1937) was born in village Pikho in the Bathinda district. He served as a journalist at the Russian embassy for several years before becoming the editor of the *Punjabi Tribune*. He was primarily a short story writer, but he also contributed to the fields of lexicography, translation, children's literature and editing. In his earlier stories, there is a depiction of the rural way of life and culture of Malwa region, but in his later fiction, he depicts urban culture in the metropolis, possibly because he had become a resident of Delhi. In 2003, he was honoured with the Sahitya Akademi award for his collection of short stories *Agni Kalash*.

The Toy Car

'Chhoti! What are you up to?' A voice, sharp with anger, is heard from the kitchen. It belongs to my wife. In the same moment, Meet comes running and rushes into my arms. The very fact that my wife addressed her as *Chhoti*, and not by her name, signals that the little girl must have been up to some mischief. Now, seeing the toy car in her hands, I recall that I had heard the soft sound of the glass screen of the showcase in the drawing room being slid open slowly. It often happens that, when occupied in deep thought, a sound does not immediately penetrate the consciousness, but circulates at the back of the mind. As soon as the mind switches back into awareness, that same sound is heard. The sound of the glass screen of the showcase sliding back was heard by my wife a while back, but to me, it seemed as if I heard it just now.

'You've taken it out again!' Abandoning her work in the kitchen, my wife runs out after Meet, holding out her hand to take the toy car back from the girl. 'Give it to me! Let me now finish with it once for all. I will give it away to Koko-bird!'

Meet shrinks further into the shelter of my lap, looking up at me with terrified eyes. I am in a dilemma. I surely do not want her to damage the little toy car. But I am also not ready to take it away from the child and watch her as she cries and screams. She will scream, my wife will get even more angry, and the creative mood that I'm trying so hard to create, will disintegrate.

'She has become so naughty!' my wife complains. 'Look how she quietly brought a stool and put it next to the showcase, climbed up, without making a sound. Just by chance, I happened to hear the sound of the glass being moved. She tries to be so clever!'

'Give it back, my dear,' I try to coax the child. 'This car is meant for decoration in the showcase, to be looked at, not to be played with. Doesn't it look nice in the showcase?'

She does not speak. She continues to clutch the toy tightly in her hands, clinging to me all the while more and more as if to protect herself. This seems to be her answer to my question. She seems to indicate that she expects me to shield her, and not to say anything other than to defend her.

'Ok, what I'll do is, I'll get you another toy car, bigger than this one,' I promise her.

'You're lying!' she protests vehemently. 'You always say that, but you never bring anything!'

'Now *you* are lying!' I answered back, slapping her cheek softly, with affection. 'Did I not bring you a car for you, the red one, which was bigger than this? So I'll get you another one—a big, lovely one, all right? It will be for you and you alone—no-one else can take it. Your mother will not dare to snatch it from you!'

'That red car was nothing like this car! It was a silly car!' she pouted. 'It did not wind up—the key was broken. It had to be pulled with a string. And it would just turn over while moving, it was all crooked!'

'You broke its machinery, remember?' Trying to distract her from the toy car, I engaged her in this verbal play. 'When I brought it home, it was brand new. It used to run quite smoothly, it never turned over. You fiddled with it, and broke it, naughty girl!'

'It broke by itself, the very next day.' She did not give up. 'It was not a nice car. It was a stupid car and I don't want a car like that! I hate that car!'

'All right, all right! It was a stupid car. It was also not a nice colour. It was broken. Maybe when they made it, they made it badly. It had to be pulled with a string—it couldn't run. You win. I lose.' I pinch my earlobes as a gesture of apology. 'This time I'll get you a car exactly like this one, in a beautiful colour. It'll be an automatic one—it'll run on its own. No string, no pulling!'

'No, you will still get a silly one, I know!' She is almost tearful. She realises that perhaps I am taking sides with her mother in this confrontation between her mother and herself. She is sure that, in carrying on the argument, I will succeed, and she will be defeated.

'Oh, dear God, of course not! I will get a proper car, just like this one. If you don't believe me, look.' I take out a twenty-rupee-note from my pocket and hold it out to her. 'Keep this carefully. It is for your car. Remind me tomorrow when I go to college, that on my way back, I must stop and buy a car for you like this one.'

With utmost reluctance, she hands over the toy car to her mother. Perhaps she has figured out that since she is not going to be allowed to play with the toy car anyway, she may as well keep the possibility open of having a new toy. After all, every dispute necessarily ends in a compromise. Meet also accepts that she can get a new toy car if she gives up this one. Her mother carries away the toy car, saying, 'If you even touch this again, I'll dispose of it. Forever. I'll give it away to the Koko-bird.' She places it back on the shelf in the showcase, closes the glass door, and, picking up the stool, takes it to another room and puts it away.

'Okay, my dear, now go and play. Let me sit by myself. Will you do as I ask?' She sits on my lap and stares at me silently.

'Come on, you're a very good girl, aren't you?' I give her a gentle kiss on her forehead and take her off my lap. 'Go now, first you can put away this money, and then you can play with your blocks. Let's see if you can make a Taj Mahal with your blocks! Go on, I have to think about something and do my work.'

The toy car in dispute had been gifted to us many years ago by a relative in England, who had sent, through someone, the following: a beautiful pen for me, expensive perfume for my wife and the toy car for my son. The car was quite small, not more than six inches in length and open on the top, like a sports car. But it was extremely well designed, with details that made it look just like a real car, only in a miniature size. The seats at the back were vacant, but in the front seat were the figures of a very good-looking English couple, the man at the steering wheel and the lady beside him. They looked life-like, with happy expressions on their faces. The man had his hands on the steering wheel. It was possible to open the doors of the car and take them out. There was a dashboard near the steering wheel, just the same as in a real car. The car had tiny wheels, with black tyres, exactly like the tyres of a car, and there was a boot at the back. The hood of the boot could be opened, revealing a spare tyre of the same size as the other tyres; a jackscrew lay beside it. There was a small battery hidden under the back seat, connected to a switch near the steering wheel, which, when pressed, set the car in motion. Another switch could be pressed which would light up the front headlights of the car.

At the time it arrived, my son was very small. He was too young to play with a toy such as this. My wife packed up the toy car in a box and tucked it away safely under some clothes in a trunk. Our minds were quite made up that such a unique toy was not a thing to be given to little children to play with, as they would only damage it. There was also no place in our home at that time to display it. We left it lying safely in its box, hidden away under the clothes in the trunk.

After a while we had to move out from our rented accommodation. We then moved to a house on the outskirts of the city, in a newly developed locality, where rents were still fairly reasonable. In this house, by a stroke of good luck, there was a display cabinet, a showcase, in the drawing room.

We placed, on the shelves of this cabinet, a few books, a pair of wooden elephants, some artificial flowers, and also the toy car. Our two older children were quite surprised at the sudden appearance of this treasured piece from a mysterious place of hiding. But by then they were too old to play with a toy like this, so after examining it and admiring it, they left it alone. It was the youngest, Meet, who wanted to grab it and put it in her own toy box along with her other toys.

On being told that the car looked much nicer when displayed in the cabinet, she would understand that this was the correct thing to do, but she still wanted to assert her own claim on this fascinating toy. She was torn between these two impulses. On the one hand, she knew she was not going to be given the toy, so she would forget about it for a while. She would accept the situation she knew would not change, and pretend that the car did not matter to her, it could stay on the shelf for all she cared. But the other impulse was that she wanted the toy car to belong to her alone. Toys were not supposed to be displayed behind glass, she would think, and she would then become desperate to have it. Then she would wait for a time when her mother was not looking, and take the car out, and dance around with glee, having obtained what she most wanted.

Seeing her with the car, my wife would snatch it away and put it back in its place in the showcase, and would warn Meet strictly that if she did not leave the car where it was, it would be given away to the Koko-bird, that creature who could take away anything. Meet would restrain herself, afraid that if the car was given to the Koko-bird, it would disappear for ever. At least now it lay within sight on the shelf. At some time or the other she might still get her hands on it. So she would leave it alone for some time.

Anyway, Meet has returned the toy car to her mother today without too much fuss. There have been many times when she has created a huge fuss over it. I am relieved. If she had kicked up a fuss today, my whole day would have been lost in pacifying her. For several days now, the plot of a story that I wanted to write was taking shape in my mind. I hadn't been able to find the quiet time I needed for thinking about it that Sunday, and today I have specially taken leave from college for this purpose. Now I am trying to put myself in the right frame of mind. The two older children are away at school. I pull up my chair in the front yard, near the row of flower pots, and make an effort to sketch out the entire story in my mind, and to visualise it as if it were a film unfolding before my eyes. Meanwhile, my wife makes breakfast in the kitchen; after I eat, I will go up to the terrace and begin to write.

These days, when I actually think of penning down ideas for my story that have been circulating in my mind for weeks, I find that the links and threads of many other stories begin to appear in my mind and they all intermingle. I am experiencing a kind of creative ferment, and gradually, I am able to visualise the outlines of three or four stories. I am filled with an eagerness to write down each one of them as quickly as possible, without any delay.

But this matter of Meet and the toy car has disrupted my thoughts.

My wife returns to the kitchen after replacing the toy car back in the showcase, and resumes her work. Meet takes the money I have given her for the new car and goes away. Soon she gets busy with playing with her bricks and trying to make her Taj Mahal. I lean back in my chair and resting my head, I close my eyes and begin to try to resolve the tangle of the stories in my mind. I aim to choose one story from the intertwined ones, and work it out first. Which story will it be? I have to keep other stories in the background, and try to focus on a single one, the one which is most ripe for harvesting, the one which will take shape as soon as I pick up my pen, one which flows effortlessly towards completion, taking its reader with it in one sweep, without the least difficulty.

Just then, there is heard the blast of a car horn somewhere in the street. I am startled and get up from my chair—I hope it is not someone who has turned up at our house, to put a sudden halt to my writing! No, I see that the horn blaring is that of the car standing in front of the house on the corner, the one that belongs to Gujjar Seth, the businessman. They have recently bought that newly constructed house, and sold their old car for this new one, worth eighty thousand rupees.

The head of that household, the businessman Gujjar Seth, is illiterate. Even his two sons, who run the business along with him, are illiterate. But the sons and daughters of these sons attend English-medium schools. The family has a shop on Panchkuian Road, which sells snacks and fast food like *samosa* and *chhole bhature*. They do such a good job of it, that their shop has become the most popular one in the area, such that people queue up outside. The shop begins preparing the food early in the morning. Customers drop in all day; however, it is in the evening that the crowds throng outside their shop in such numbers that it is impossible to pass through the street. People drive in on cars and scooters, or walk to the shop, whether in groups, with families and friends, or singly, in hordes. This only shows that popularity grows once the word is spread, and in this way they have profited in lakhs of rupees from simply selling the humble *samosa* and *chhole bhature* in their shop.

I am glad that the car is that of Gujjar Seth's, and not that of a visitor to our house, which would have ripped up all the delicate threads of the story I was so laboriously trying to put together. I settle back into my chair, contented. But very soon, the noise of the car is heard distinctly quite nearby, indicating that the car is coming down our street.

This is a street which is still being laid, and sand and gravel is piled up on both sides. These sliding piles have now spread out along the sides and unevenly cover the centre of the street, so that now it has become difficult to walk in the street. The bits of gravel poke the soles of shoes. They damage the tyres of cars and scooters. For this reason most people who drive in on their scooters or cars, leave their vehicles at the end of the street and walk down.

I get up again from my seat and glance up the street. I am astonished to see that Gujjar Seth's car is rolling down the street, driverless and at high speed, riding roughly over the piles of stone and gravel. I can hardly believe my eyes. One has heard that at some place an engine standing at a railway station started to roll on the tracks by itself, or that in some town a stationary bus had started moving without any driver at the wheel. On reading the reports of such incidents in newspapers, such news often sounds quite incredible. But now I see with my own eyes that Gujjar Seth's car is running down over the piles of gravel on its own. It seems that this expensive car, costing eighty thousand rupees, is going to crash into the wall at the end of the street at great speed and will be destroyed.

While I am still trying to understand this situation and think of how I can prevent the disaster, I notice that the car has come nearer, and that, framed within the circle of the steering wheel of the car is the face of a small boy. The face is barely visible. I see that it belongs to the young grandson of Gujjar Seth, who is no more than eight or nine years old. As he is very small and cannot look over the steering wheel, he is peeping from within its frame. I am both astounded at the sight of such a young child driving a car, and relieved that at least the car is not without a driver.

Suddenly, Meet appears at my side, and questions me. 'Papa, the Koko-bird is not real, is it?' It is clear that even though she returned the toy car, she has not forgotten about it.

By this time, the speeding car has passed our house and Gujjar Seth's grandson has succeeded in turning it into a vacant plot of land nearby. It has narrowly missed hitting the wall of another house.

Then the boy tries to drive the car over a mound of sand piled up on the side. The car wheels are stuck and the car cannot move forward, but the wheels keep revolving as the machine makes an effort to move. The boy is treating it as a sort of game, and enjoying revving up the car's engine. He reverses the car and revs it up to take it over the mound, again and again. Each time the wheels remain stuck in the heap of sand and revolve furiously at the same place making an awful noise. This goes on for some time.

Seeing me so absorbed, Meet gets impatient and tugs at my arm again, persisting in her question, 'Papa, Koko-bird is not real, is it?'

In reply, I blurt out, without thinking, 'The Koko-bird is real, my girl!'

Meet is stunned with my reply. 'But…you always used to say that there is no such thing as Koko-bird—it is not real!'

I pat her head and say, 'Child, I used to say that without thinking, it was not true. The Koko-bird is definitely real.'

Gujjar Seth's grandson accelerates the car again, attempting to drive it over the mound of sand. This time too, the car stops, its engine making a loud noise, unable to go over the mound.

Meet is still obsessed with the Koko-bird, 'Does that mean that Koko-bird will really take my car away? What if Mama gives my car to it—will Koko take it?'

I stroke her head to calm her down. 'No, my child. Koko has already taken away my car. Don't believe that I will allow it to take away your car as well. I will beat that Koko, really I will!'

She is delighted that I have said that I will punish the Koko, but she is puzzled by my statement that Koko has taken my car. 'Where was your car? When did you have it? When was it taken away?'

Not being able to drive the car up the mound of sand, Gujjar Seth's grandson decides to reverse the car, turn it aside and skirts the edge of the mound to drive it away. He goes back the way he came, driving roughly over the uneven piles of gravel, passing in front of our house, and disappears.

Meet is still puzzling over the news of my car being taken away by the Koko. It is beyond her understanding. I get up without saying anything, and tip-toe to the drawing room. Very silently, and slowly, I slide the glass on the cabinet in which the toy car is kept, and remove it from the shelf. I hand it over to Meet.

Afzal Ahsan Randhawa

Afzal Ahsan Randhawa (1937–2017) is a celebrated writer of Pakistan. He was born in Amritsar. In addition to writing short fiction, he has also written poetry and novels and is also a translator. A lawyer by profession, he was inclined to politics. He represented the Pakistan People's Party in the Assembly elections, in which he contested and won from the Lyallpur (now Faisalabad) constituency in 1972. However, in 1977, Zia-ul-Haq placed a restriction on his participation in politics for eight years. Randhawa's stories create a distinctive atmosphere as he portrays a world in which the feudal order prevails, with all its rivalries, family feuds, passions and enmities. A number of Sikh characters are included in these stories. In 2013, he was awarded with the 'Kamaal-e-fun' award by the Pakistan Academy of Letters.

The Generous Elder

The flowers of the ridge-gourd that are wilting a little, catching the light of the sun on their yellow petals just as it warms and dissolves the dew on them—this beautiful glow is what I love. But when the sun grows hotter, these delicate flowers begin to droop. The freshness of flowers and then their wilting are the two extremes of their existence, and I am fascinated by the short life they lead between these two extremes. Our lives are the same, perhaps. Or perhaps it is not the same; but that night when Rattan Singh and I had faced each other for the last time, I had seen the reflection of the same pale yellow glow on his countenance that told the same story as that of these wilting *tori* blossoms. Now seven years have passed since I last saw that sickly reflection on the naturally robust and rosy complexion of Rattan Singh, and it still stays in my memory. Roaming around in this big city, I see someone who resembles him slightly and I catch my breath. I experience a constriction in my chest as though my heart has been squeezed tight. I swear by the Guru, brothers born of the same womb are an immeasurable wealth, no matter if they are good or bad. And other than that fatal night, Rattan Singh had always been a good brother, the most loving and respectful brother in every possible way. How a few terrible moments can change a whole lifetime! I have heard that since then Rattan Singh has not been seen to smile. As for me, I feel that my very soul has been transformed, and my heart has turned to stone.

Even so, my stone-like heart turns to soft butter when I remember Rattan Singh's pale face on that night. But what is the use of thinking about these things now? Now the city is my life, not the village, with its *tori* flowers and its fragrant earth-scented breeze. Nothing has remained of that time. My life is different now—rather, it has changed utterly. Rattan Singh, too, must have changed. Chando must also have changed. The little girls in the village must have grown up. The grown-up ones might have got married. The married ones might have their own children. Everything will have changed. Only God knows.

Indeed, there is not much difference now between village and city life.

Perhaps this is the reason that even in the city I am not able to forget the pale yellow colour of those *tori* flowers. The girls here are seen to favour this colour in the dresses they wear, and even those who don't, have complexions that have the same hue. When I enter the Kachehri Bazaar, it is as if I have entered a field of *tori* plants. On the other hand, just as the lines on the *tori* leaves are seen to resemble the faces of people, I see the same look reflected in the sad expression on Sameena's face. When she sits close to me, I have often felt the need to raise her tear-stained face up towards mine, to meet my own eyes and see my tears flowing so that her own tears could dry up. I have wanted many a time to kneel down before this nervous and scared-looking girl and say to her, 'Come now, give a smile', and when she smiles, I will be so grateful. Sometimes, she puts her hand on my heart, and asks,, 'Is this made of stone?', I should be able to tell her, 'No, it is soft, it is like melted wax'. But I cannot understand why I don't say anything, or express anything, and when she comes to meet me, I just keep staring at her silently; she weeps to herself, or she sits near me looking at me continuously as if she were trying to pry open the secret that troubles my heart, with her constant scrutiny. Finally one day, she says to me, 'You really have no feelings at all.'

She is a college-educated girl, so she must be right. But it is not so long ago that I was full of such passionate energy that it almost radiated from me and overpowered anyone who was near me. I was full of the exuberance of youth—that proud mustache that adorned my face, that turban neatly folded, low on my forehead, the long polished cane in my hand, and in my head that intense intoxication of the liquor that Rattan Singh used to brew. I was a fine specimen of youth, but Rattan Singh used to say, 'Oh, brother of mine, have you any idea at all about when one becomes a real youth?'

'No, when?'

'Not only when you have this staff in your hand, and a bottle of liquor with you, but when you have the image of a young lass in your heart—that is the time you feel you are young, my dear Bachan Singh!'

'Oh, really?' I would laugh at this, and so would he.

Rattan Singh was a little younger than me. He must have been about twenty three years old at that time. We were true brothers, regardless of the animosity of the entire village against us. That was why our father, a stalwart who was one of the most respected figures of his time, always used to say, 'I consider both Rattan Singh and Bachan Singh as the light of my eyes, and as long as this light is there, I am not afraid of anyone.' He was certainly right. But we only remember that a day came when he did not wake up from sleep.

I was away studying in college at that time. After our Bapu died, Rattan Singh was left alone in the village. No other uncles or senior relatives. Other than God and myself, there was no one for Rattan Singh to turn to. So I left my studies at college and returned to the village. Though he always had a swagger, Rattan Singh would walk around with even more of a swagger after my return, he was so thrilled with himself. He would repeat, 'Brother! One and one don't make two, they are equal to eleven! Let the whole village rise against us, we can overcome all of them. But it would be very hard if we are alone!'

This was the truth. We were both strong and able-bodied, we ate well, we drank well. We had an equal share of everything and we did not need to do any hard work. We had the ability to deal with any difficulty, strengthened as we were with each other's complete support. We enjoyed our life together.

It was a day in the cold month of January that I had first set eyes on Chando in the bright light of the winter sun. She was the only daughter of Harbans Singh of Baliyan village which was just about three miles from ours. My black mare was swift, and I would easily cover this distance in minutes to reach the banks of the river near their village where Chando would be waiting for me. Having left my village late in the evening, I would return in the early hours. I would eat at home and go to the *haveli* to sleep, while Rattan Singh would sleep at home.

Spring arrived. It was in those days, I think, that Rattan Singh went off for a few days with some of his friends to a fair. One evening, I was leading my black mare out of the haveli quarters, dusting off the saddle with a cloth, holding my staff in one hand. As I was about to mount the horse, Rattan Singh turned up. He was looking downcast and seemed tired, perhaps from the exertions of travel.

'Rattu! When did you arrive?' I was the first to speak.

'Just a while back, brother. I've just eaten.' By the tone of his voice, he sounded a little disturbed

'I've come to see you, but you appear to be leaving. Going somewhere?'

I could not think of a fit answer to his question. How could I tell him about my late evening sojourn? As I hesitated, he said,, 'Look, if you are going out to meet some fellows, you can go, but if you are going out to meet a woman, I will not let you go.' He stepped forward and grabbed the reins of my horse.

'Why not?' I asked, surprised.

'You ask me why? Brother, you know we have many enemies around. Can't trust a woman not to betray you. I will not let you go anywhere alone, I swear!'

'Oh, don't be so silly!' I laughed. 'All right, come along with me then! Today let us go together. Let me show you the one who will be your brother's wife. But hurry up, she must be waiting since long'. Then Rattan grasped his own staff, and jumped on the back of my horse. 'Let's go then'.

The moon shone brightly that night, so brightly that it seemed to be day. We rode to the end of the village and I turned the horse towards Baliyan. At once he spoke quickly, 'Brother, we are going to Baliyan?'

'Yes,' I affirmed.

There was no other village on the way. So Rattan Singh was right to make sure. Then he asked, 'Who is she?'

'Wait and see when we get there,' I replied.

'But, tell me'.

'Just wait awhile!'

'But, brother, who is she? You must tell me!' He was bent on extracting the girl's name.

'Chando'. I finally told him.

'Chando? Who is she?' he asked immediately.

'What do you mean, you don't know? Harnam Singh's daughter, who else?'

'Do you swear to it?'

'Yes,' I said, quite taken aback. 'Is she not the right girl for me? Why are you so shocked to hear her name?' Rattan did not reply. I looked back at him, but I could not see his expression clearly in the light of the moon. He was staring somewhere in the distance, and then, as if he had suddenly remembered something, he said, 'Brother, just stop the horse.'

'Why?' I asked, but I did rein in the horse.

The horse stopped and Rattan Singh jumped off. I stared at him in great surprise, while he wiped his sweaty face with his scarf and said, 'Get down from the horse.'

We had reached the deserted area in between our village and Baliyan by this time. 'What is it?' I was still astride the horse and turned it to circle around to see if there was some danger lurking by.

'What is it, Ratta?' And then I too dismounted from the horse. Rattan came and stood very close to me. I could see that his face had a pale, yellowish hue, like that of *tori* flowers, but his eyes were glittering brighter than the metal knob on his staff. He was looking at me sharply and searchingly with those eyes, I could not guess why.

The next thing, he tied up his scarf on his head, and, stepping back from me a few paces, he strengthened the hold of his lance in his land. And he said, 'Bachna, only one of us will see the dawn of tomorrow morning. So prepare yourself.'

At that moment, I saw that my dear brother, born of the same mother, the brother who I had carried on my shoulders, had become a stranger. I let go of the reins of the horse that I had been holding in one hand, took up my own staff, and took some steps back.

Only the sky above was our witness, and the black mare who stood beside us. Other than that there was no one for miles around. And Rattan Singh had suddenly become a mystery to me.

'But, why?' That was all I was able to say.

'Why?' he shouted out, and laughed in such a way that I, who had never known fear, began to tremble. Cold shivers ran down my body even though it was a warm evening.

Rattan shouted, 'There is one Chando—and there are two of us!'

'But Rattan, listen to me, don't be foolish', I tried to speak to him as I had always done, as an affectionate brother, to placate him. 'Listen to you!' he laughed wildly as he had done before. It was not really laughter, it was more like a frightening howl.

'This is it. Only one of us shall see Chando's face! Better get ready to die!' He took up the lance and attacked me. I dodged him. A cold shiver ran through my body. I was the son of the same father, I had been suckled at the breast of the same mother. I too had as much passion, as much strength as him, to combat him. Even so, at that moment I shrank away from confronting Rattan Singh. Or maybe I shrank away not from fear of Rattan Singh, but from myself. And from the spirit of our Bapu, which was perhaps watching us here, and whose voice I heard within me, saying 'You two—Bachan and Rattan—are like my two eyes.'

When Rattan advanced towards me with his lance raised, I threw away my own stick and uttering only one sentence, 'You win, Rattan Singh', and I sat down on the ground. I did not have the strength to remain standing.

This was our last meeting. I have not returned to the village since that night. I left it the very next day. I went to the city and was recruited into the army, and was posted far away. After completing seven years, I came to this distant city, and took up a job. In all the nights and days since that last meeting, there was no night or day when I did not think of Rattan. For better or worse, he had been my brother, my flesh and blood, and on that night, that close connection was gone, and I had lost all that was vital in me.

I have heard that Rattan Singh has given the name of Bachan Singh to his son with Chando. I have heard that no-one has ever seen Rattan Singh smile. And Chando's face has that pale hue of *tori* flowers. Those *tori* flowers that do not grow in cities. Those *tori* flowers that I love so much.

Mohan Bhandari

Mohan Bhandari (1937–2021) was born in village Banbhaura in Sangrur district. Subsequent to his obtaining an MA degree in Punjabi and in legal studies, he worked at a senior level with the Department of School Education. He is recognized as a short story writer though he has also done work in translation and editing. Bhandari's early stories portray the realities of people's lives in rural settings, but his later writing focuses on the vagaries and events in the lives of the middle class and bureaucrats. The rhythm of speech, the lively dialogues and the use of Malwai dialect are qualities that make his stories enjoyable. Mohan Bhandari was awarded the Sahitya Akademi Award in 1998 (which he returned in 2015) for his collection of stories titled *Moon di Akh*.

The Wooden Pestle

That day, Kishna Carpenter was sad...very sad. He wanted to cry his heart out. To keep crying. Keep crying.

It was a holiday.

Kishna Carpenter and his son-in-law had been drinking since morning, but the liquor seemed to be having no effect.

So he quietly stepped out of the house. His son-in-law didn't try to hold him back. He knew that Kishna wouldn't be deterred. He would go to the liquor vend. Bring back another bottle. He had done this earlier as well. Whenever the drink could not take hold of their senses, Kishna would go off to get another bottle. The two of them would again resume drinking late into the night. And another holiday would be spent in that manner.

Kishna's son-in-law waited, kept waiting and finally drifted off to sleep. Kishna had not yet returned with the drink.

And on that day, Kishna was very sad. He had never been so sad in all his life. He felt as if a boil was festering, throbbing inside him. His son-in-law had enough money to buy whatever pleasures they wanted. But he hadn't been able to buy even a second's worth of peace for his father-in-law.

His son-in-law was perturbed.

His daughter was distressed.

And on that day, Kishna was sad...very sad. He wanted to cry his heart out. To keep crying. Keep crying.

He remembered his son.

He remembered his wife.

She had died five years ago. His only son had passed away when still a child.

Who else was his own in this whole wide world?

Only this one daughter was left.

Only this one son-in-law was left.

His son-in-law had brought him to the city. Dressed him in new clothes. It was a new city, full of life. Its dazzling lights pierced through his eyes. The peace of the village was missing. The restful calm of the village was missing. People hurled themselves around, in whirls of activity. Huffing and panting. Tense, anxious, as if the place was on fire.

He was wearing brand new clothes. He could feel their starched stiffness rustling on his body. A harsh scraping stiffness as if someone was driving an abrasive tool over his head. He felt as if any moment those starched clothes would fall off. He would be left standing naked, on the street. In front of everybody.

He stumbled. He was drenched in sweat from head to toe. Rivulets of sweat began dripping down his legs.

His first day in this big city was one he would never forget.

But he had been living in the city for five years now. In these five years he had won his son-in-law's heart. He looked after the work of the entire workshop himself. So far, he had not suffered a loss in any of the transactions he had managed.

He was made for success.

His daughter said so.

His son-in-law said so.

He would win the biggest business deals. That was why his son-in-law didn't want to let go of him. There are all sorts of secret deals in business which cannot be divulged to everybody. And Kishna was his father-in-law. Why would he think of harming his son-in-law? That was why he tried his level best to keep him happy. Never did he hesitate to loosen his purse strings for him, never did he contradict or oppose him.

He could purchase for him every pleasure that could be bought, but what about obtaining for him peace of mind, satisfaction, contentment in life? These could not be bought with money. He was helpless in the matter. Perhaps that ineffable moment of peace was denied even to him. Though he was the city's biggest manufacturer. Number One in riches.

Yes,...that day, Kishna was very sad. Each moment, each incident of his life replayed itself in his mind.

Back in the village, he used to fabricate wooden pestles. His home was nearby. A small courtyard in front, with a leafy mulberry tree, its shade cooling, refreshing. Sitting beneath the cool shade, a coarse khadi cloth wrapped around his head, bare-chested and barefoot, wiping the sweat off his forehead, he would remain busy making pestles.

If someone remarked, 'Oye Kishna! What do you work so hard for, day and night? Give yourself some rest, at least in this sweltering heat. Look how you're drenched in sweat!' Kishna would reply, laughing, 'My good fellow, work is man's "karma". This toil not only gives me peace of mind, it also keeps my body in good shape. A man's true labour is known only by his sweat. Haven't you heard the story?'

And he would begin telling the tale.

Once upon a time, a god descended from the heavens to the earth. He felt very hot there. The oppressive heat tormented him. Fairies collected some cooling nectar from plants, but it did nothing to ease his discomfort. The fairies then went in search of water. But the sap from plants and the dew had dried out in the sun. There was no well nearby. The heat had sucked out the water from ponds and pools. Scouting around, the fairies finally came upon a pile of wet clothes. They wrung out the clothes in a vessel and took it to the thirsty god. The god drank it contentedly. He told the fairies, 'This water has quenched my thirst of many lives. It tastes like ambrosia. Take me to the place where you got it from.'

When they reached the spot, the clothes could not be found.

The woodcutter, whose clothes they were, had left for the town.

The clothes had been drenched in the sweat of his labour.

On listening to this story the hearer would avert his gaze, Kishna would shake him by the shoulder and say, 'Son! The honest sweat that makes you wrinkle your nose is what the gods thirst for! They love those who toil!'

And the listener would realise the truth of this, and nod to show agreement.

And Kishna Carpenter would again resume making his pestle. When done, he used to do other odd jobs. Repairing joints of wooden beds. Fashioning the *gulli-dandas* that kids played with. Those kids lost the *gullies* every day, smartly tapping at them with their sticks. He chiselled out some more for them. And so, kept himself busy.

He was content.

When he got tired of sitting in his little courtyard, he would set off for a stroll in the village. There he would hammer at the loose joints in someone's wooden stool, sharpen the worn edges of the spindles on spinning wheels. Sharing some banter with the passersby, he would return home. Some woman would give him grain, another would hand him some *gur* (molasses), yet another would give him a glass of milk and some would get by with simply addressing him affectionately, as *deora*, our brother-in-law.

He would relish each such gift.

If at some time he looked at himself in the mirror, his mind would rise up in waves of emotion on seeing the crescent-shaped scar on his forehead. As if something had pierced his heart. The whole incident would come back to him in all its intensity.

He had been sitting in his courtyard, making a pestle. Bachna's son, Mehlu, who was playing *gulli-danda* nearby, knocked at a *gulli* with such force that it spun into the air and its sharp edge hit his forehead.

Blood spilled out in a gush.

Mehlu's mother Kartaro came rushing out. She quickly tore off a strip from her new muslin *dupatta*, dipped it in cold water and tied it to his forehead. That eased his pain a little bit. He was quite stunned by what had happened all of a sudden.

Even now, Kishna could feel the impression of Kartaro's trembling hands as she held the wet bandage to his bleeding forehead.

He sat in his courtyard every day, making pestles. Pestles with flowers carved on them, so smooth to the touch that the hand would slide off them. Their fame was spreading far and wide, to other villages as well. Village folk would stop by at his house, take a breather under the cool shade of the mulberry tree and chat with him for a while. Then they would buy a pestle and set off, talking about him along the way, commending his craftsmanship and skill at making pestles.

If newlywed brides saw no pestle among their wedding gifts, they would go into a sulk and refuse to eat. Women who had come to inspect the gifts would turn up their noses, chins wagging, and say scornfully, 'What rubbish they have given to the girl! They haven't even given a pestle, pride of the kitchen and the adornment of their *daaj*, their dowry!'

Once the daughter of a Brahmin sulked in this manner. The village was rife with gossip. No sooner had the villagers finished their daily chores than they sat down to chatter about this incident. Each one spun a yarn wilder than the other's. People were relishing every morsel of this gossip. Gajjan theatrically put his hand to his ear, closed his eyes and lustily started singing a *boli*,

> *Sour is the Brahman's daughter*
> *Not ready to go to in-laws*
> *Without the pestle in the daaj*
> *Unhappy with anything to carry*
> *But the pestle of the neem tree*
> *Where is the pestle to admire?*
> *How to admire the pestle?*

Kishna almost swooned with delight on hearing the *boli* Gajjan had coined. He went up to the boy, slapped him heartily on the back, pulled out a rupee from the folds of his *khakhi* turban and handed it to him.

The people cheered even more.

Kishna's life coursed through the swirls and eddies of such small, nondescript pleasures and annoyances. Little waves gently touched his boat of life without rocking or drowning it. But then one day Kishna felt his life's boat lurching dangerously. His wife suddenly fell ill. Kishna did his utmost to get her medical treatment. He tended to her day and night. But one day she departed, leaving Kishna alone to deal with the whole wide world. Kishna had to accept it as God's will and stifled his grief. Work brought him solace. He began to keep himself absorbed in his work.

His life picked up again.

Finally his son-in-law brought him to the city and now he had been here almost five years. In these five years he had won over his son-in-law. After all, he was his father-in-law and would never think ill of his son-in-law.

He used to be lost in his thoughts.

He sat all day on his cushion, talking to the traders and businessmen who had come from other places. He kept an eye on the factory workers as well.

This was the responsibility assigned to him.

'What sort of work is this? To watch others at work! If this is considered work, then I pray that God frees me from such work. I am amazed...how can these people continue to live and thrive, who think that their work is simply looking at others' work!'

These thoughts began to plague him.

He began to turn sad.

His bones ached. His head spun and he was dizzy. He yawned all day. His eyes watered. He would shudder all over.

His son-in-law spent money like water, trying to get him to feel happy. But Kishna remained sad. The baubles and objects of pleasure bought with money could not please him. He longed for a moment of peace.

Finally his son-in-law took him to a doctor. The doctor checked his pulse, his tongue. When he couldn't diagnose anything, he asked Kishna,

'What ails you?'

Kishna answered, 'My heart is sad...as if there is a vacuum, something lacking inside.'

'Understood, understood', the doctor said. 'You are suffering from a deficiency of Vitamin B. You need to take B Complex tablets'.

Kishna kept quiet. But when they came out of the clinic, Kishna laughed and said, 'I have just learnt that one can obtain ease with medicines!' Now his son-in-law was left with only one remedy, 'Drink'. Man drinks and becomes a lord and master for those moments. Liquor dissolves away the grief of many such afflicted.

He reasoned that Kishna will also forget all his troubles and sorrows under the influence of liquor. He will descend into a pleasurable world.

That's what his son-in-law thought.

That day was a holiday. Kishna Carpenter, and his son-in-law sat drinking away their sorrows when suddenly Kishna got up and quietly went out. Perhaps to get another bottle.

His son-in-law was pleased.

Kishna Carpenter, had not yet returned with the liquor. His son-in-law lay on his bed, waiting impatiently for him.

The urge to drink was assailing him.

He heard a knocking at the door. Kishna's son-in-law turned over on his side. The knocking resumed.

It must be his father-in-law knocking at the door, back with a bottle. He quickly got up to open the door.

He was left speechless.

Outside, in the courtyard, sat Kishna Carpenter, sated with drink. A full bottle of liquor lay next to him. He was holding a tool in one hand. In the other, he had a piece of wood.

He was trying to make a pestle.

Jasbir Bhullar

Jasbir Bhullar (b. 1941) was born in village Sahinsra in district Amritsar. He wrote children's books, novels and stories. After a Master's degree in Punjabi, he joined the Armed Forces, and reached the rank of Colonel in the army. Then he decided to take early retirement and become a full time writer. Bhullar draws from many significant moments and experiences in military life, and portrays them from a humanist angle. The focus on human rather than nationalistic concerns is prominent in his writing. He was given the Sahitya Akademi award in 2010 for his novel *Pataal de Gith Muthiye* in the children's literature category.

The Snow Demon

The snowstorm raged in full fury.

Clouds of snow spread through the sky.

Nothing seemed real there. The only reality was the hillock of icy white snow that seemed to be heaving with deep breaths.

Suddenly the hillock shifted and a gloved white hand emerged. The hand flexed and closed its fingers as if grasping at the air. It was hard to determine whether its attempts were effectual or not. However, in a while the other gloved hand also appeared and spread its fingers to the sky.

A large body freed itself from the imprisoning snow. For a while it lay there in a heap, taking long deep gasps of air. As the breathing gradually evened out, the form lifted, slapped itself vigorously to get the blood circulating and then stood up, dusting off piles of snow from its body. It looked as if a huge snowman had got up to survey its snowy empire.

Clad in thick thermal clothing made to withstand the freezing temperatures of the glacier, the large body looked even more overpowering.

Aadam boa...

The screaming blizzard was a painful assault on the ears.

Sugar-like particles of snow brushed past the figure, some of them settling on the large frame. Shards of ice were pricking its face like sharp needles. The force of the gale seemed to almost sweep the body off its feet. Had he been a leaf broken off a branch, he would have been blown far off by now. But he was no helpless leaf. He was a soldier.

He quickly turned his back to the snowstorm and sat down. He let his head fall over his closed fists in a movement that showed a sense of defeat, and remained like that for some time. Then, as if a fog was slowly lifting from his consciousness, he looked around dazed...anxiously.

Where were they?

When setting off, there were exactly twelve of them, ten plus two, twelve, he was sure. And now?

He looked around but could hardly see anything. His head was bent down against the onslaught of the blizzard, his hands shielding his eyes.

His thick goggles were clouded by snow. With his gloved hand he scrubbed the snow off.

What he saw made him almost reel with shock.

A crow was lying dead near him.

The glacier was snow, all snow. It wasn't mud; there was no mud even to a depth of four to five thousand feet. No plants grew there. No buds blossomed there. Nothing could remain alive there. It was only the Ladakhi crow that could survive those impossibly harsh conditions. In the minus thirty to forty degree centigrade temperature of the glacier, men froze. Their dreams froze, their blood froze.

The soldiers often left behind empty cans of food. Jet-black crows could often be seen, pecking at the crumbs of food sticking to the cans.

The crows were slowly increasing in number.

The dead crow lay half buried in the snow. Subedar Puran Singh's befuddled brain slowly began to awaken to the sound of gunshots. This wasn't anything unusual. He was accustomed to the heat of battle, where bullets flew in every direction. But no crow had ever died of bullets there. The death of the crow certainly made it clear that it was not only the crow that had died.

The change of the battalions of soldiers had been continuing routinely. Subedar Puran Singh had gazed at the returning soldiers with astonishment. They all seemed to look the same! Straggly unkempt beards, sad fatigued faces, dull eyes through which death glimmered. Even though they were returning from the glacier alive, they didn't seem to believe that they were actually alive. The murderous cold of the glacier had frozen their happiness, settling itself in a grim layer of death on their faces.

Full battalions of soldiers used to routinely arrive on the glacier, but none ever returned complete. There the eyes of the soldiers always held an unnerving question, would they return from the glacier alive?

The glacier was a mighty demon, a snow demon. It seemed to be in meditation for thousands of years in quest of attaining divine powers.

For some years now, soldiers had been audaciously trying to thwart its meditation and they were paying a heavy price for enraging it.

The Jat Light Infantry was presently guarding Bilafond La (the Pass of the Butterflies, at the end of the LOC between Pak and India), The Alpha Company of the Dogra Light Regiment was to take over from them. Three groups of the Alpha Company had already done that with assistance from guides of the Jat Light Infantry.

Subedar Puran Singh had been standing there, having seen them off.

There was snow all around, as far as the eye could see. No possibility of a road or track being built there. Snow could not be turned into stones and gravel.

The first two groups of soldiers had gone beyond his line of vision, far into the cavernous white mountains. Some of the last group were still dotted across the snowy expanse, like a straggly line of ants in search of food. They were carefully treading over the trodden snow. It seemed the safest thing to do, considering the dangers of the treacherous glacier. But there was no certainty that this chosen path would be acceptable to the glacier every time. Knowing that frightening prospect, no one dared to walk through the glacier alone.

In that group too there were five soldiers. Each one linked to the other with a sturdy rope tied round the waist. Thus, even if they were far apart, they were still held together. They could help each other if the need arose.

At that time, the glacier was very silent, very still. Suddenly Puran Singh shuddered. He could hear muffled screams.

The bosom of the glacier had developed another deep fissure. The snow gave way under the middle soldier's feet and the crack quickly widened to trap the last two men, pulling them into the gap before they could act to save themselves.

This crack in the glacier was hundreds of feet deep.

This was not the first time something like this had happened. The snow would break away like this innumerable times. Soldiers would get buried in the avalanche. Their special thermal clothing could keep them warm and alive for many days. But ultimately they would have to succumb to the eternal sleep of death there itself.

Countless soldiers had been swallowed by the glacier in this manner. Neither the warmth of their bodies nor the intensity of their emotions could melt the snow or appease the hunger of the glacier.

Puran Singh rubbed his eyes in astonishment. The expanse of snow had blended seamlessly into the grey horizon. Not a trace remained of the small black blotches of the soldiers.

Among the dead was also the Commander of the Alpha Company. But this was not the time to sit back and mourn. This was only the beginning. In a few days, such incidents would seem like ordinary events. The empty slots would be filled by others. Life would have to continue as usual.

More than the concern for the dead soldiers was the worrisome question about the command of Bilafond La. The Commanding Officer of the battalion had no one whom he could spare to take on that responsibility. All the officers were already stationed at their posts. Now there was no option but to send Subedar Puran Singh to take over command of the company at Bilafond La.

When Subedar Puran Singh started out, stars were glimmering dimly in the sky. The moonlight reflected the snow so intensely that it hurt the eyes, veritably turning the night into broad daylight. But this dazzling whiteness was dark with gloom.

They kept walking steadily onward. The snow kept flying up like whirls of white dust under their heavy boots.

Gradually the stars and moon faded away and then vanished.

The wail rose on the chill wind, like cats mourning. The weather was getting rough.

Before they could think of combating the rising storm, a ball of mortar fire from the enemy camp landed near them. The snow flew up, triggering panic and alarm among the men. This was an unprovoked attack. They had come within the range of enemy fire.

They immediately fell on the snow and desperately crawled around for shelter. Staccato bursts of smaller weapons were now accompanying the mortar shells.

The fierce wind had now taken on the aspect of a blizzard. Tufts of snow began to rise up in spiralling whirls. Puran Singh strained his eyes towards the enemy camp and noticed a slight movement through the haze of the whirling clouds of snow. But his Sten gun wouldn't fire. The sub-zero temperatures had jammed it. Even if one bullet had been fired, the barrel would have warmed up. The gunfire would have continued and the barrel would have remained warm. But now how was he to warm up his gun? He looked towards his soldiers. Some were bravely holding up against the enemy fire. Some were crouching over their weapons. And some lay lifeless on the snow. They had given up the battle of life.

Subedar Puran Singh then pulled at a grenade pin with his mouth and threw it with full force towards the stealthily advancing enemy soldiers. Simultaneously there was a deafening roar that drowned out the burst of the grenade. He looked back and saw the mountain of snow behind him sliding forward threateningly. He tried to turn aside and run but the snow rushed over him with deathly speed.

Everything became still.

They could give a fitting retort to the enemy guns with their own gunfire, but were helpless before the glacier's enmity. They could only plead to be saved. Buried under the snow, Puran Singh flailed his arms desperately, like a man drowning under water. He somehow managed to carve out some breathing space for himself under the snow. His desperate gasps slowly brought him back to life. His agonized gasps became regular breathing as air returned to his lungs.

Emerging from the snowy grave, he lay in a motionless heap for a long time. When consciousness slowly returned, he cast a look around.

It was snowing heavily. The intensity of the blizzard had not lessened. The sounds of gunfire had died out on both sides. But the roar of the storm had intensified.

And darkness had added its gloom to the noise.

He once again cleared his goggles with his gloved hands. His searching eyes took him beyond the corpse of the crow.

His breath stuck in his throat.

The bodies of his comrades lay scattered, almost buried under the falling snow. They looked like randomly placed graves.

The glacier was not merely snow. It sprouted. Yielded a harvest of corpses.

There were many like them, buried earlier in the snow. In a while a thick layer of snow would settle on their bodies. They too would become a part of the snow. How many more would suffer the same fate after them, no one knew. The bodies would remain there forever, blanketed under the snow.

He would not let them die so quickly.

He went up to the nearest body. Gently wiped off the snow from its frozen face and bent close to it, as if whispering to it. Then stood up and dug a rifle upright behind its head.

Puran Singh wanted to utter a prayer for the peace of soldier's soul before he gave it the final salute. But he couldn't remember the soldier's name.

'It doesn't matter! Whatever be his name, his ID number, he fought bravely without asking what or why, and he died.' Though he hadn't seen him actually fighting, this much of a prayer was due to him.

He thought of digging a grave to bury the soldier, then rejected the idea. It was now the responsibility of the snow to take care of its dead.

He gave the soldier a final farewell salute and turned towards the corpse of the next soldier. He repeated the process with each of them. And then...

And then he froze, became immobile in front of the corpse. Half of its head had been blown off. The shrapnel from the burst of mortar had ripped off a part of his body. Yet he managed to recognise the face.

He was sure it was no one else.

It was Jinder.

At the same time that he had been issued the command to go to the glacier, he had gone home to his village for a brief holiday. His daughter was not so little anymore, but not old enough to wipe off her anxiety from her brow like a drop of sweat. Subedar Puran Singh had tried to allay his daughter's fears. 'What is there to worry about? Snow is not fire. And I won't be sitting far from Jinder anyway!'

That was the truth. At the time he was so close to Jinder that he could feel the corpse of his daughter's husband, her *suhaag*, within him.

Those soldiers' hands, which could wield artillery and guns, now hung limply by their sides, and felt as if they were detached from their bodies.

Frustrated at his helplessness, he hurled a howl of abuse that rent the sky. But who was there to listen to his cry?

He climbed up to a hillock of snow and let loose a continuous torrent of abuse.

His curses were lost in the din of the blizzard.

He turned to look back. The sacrificial harvest still lay inert and buried under the snow. The upturned rifles too would gradually sink into the gathering snow.

Snow! Snow! Snow!

There was no account of how much snow each side wanted. There was also no account of how much snow lay on each side. Yet they were fighting, and continued fighting for their share of snow.

The blizzard was raging as fiercely as ever. But the storm that was blazing inside his heart was far stronger than the one outside. He screamed loudly, 'Gluttons! How much snow do you want?'

For a split second it seemed as if the blizzard had stopped to listen.

He bent down and started throwing up handfuls of the sugary particles of snow in front of him. 'Here! Take this! And this! And this! Take more! More! More!'

He suddenly seemed to remember something. His hands stopped flailing. He stood quietly for a few seconds and then began to throw snow on the other side, behind him. 'You too! Take this! You greedy gluttons! Here, take this! And this!'

Standing on the hillock of snow, he kept shovelling the snow with his bare hands like one gone mad, throwing it on either side of him. He continued shouting, but his words seemed to freeze as they spilled out of him. His voice was reaching nowhere.

Thishoon! A bullet shot by the last dying breath of a soldier pierced the snow and tore through him. He fell. He made an effort to get up, but then collapsed on the snow.

Who knows if it was the conscience of a human or some restless soul? It was only death that could render the homeless to their eternal homes…and so he died.

Singing their funeral dirge, the screaming winds of the glacier gradually quietened.

The snow slowly settled on his body and covered it.

Suddenly the snow caved in. The lifeless body on the hillock tilted and slowly slipped towards the enemy side.

Had it slipped and come to this side, it still wouldn't have made any difference. It was merely a utilitarian object now, and had been made use of. It had fulfilled its purpose.

Kirpal Kazak

Kirpal Kazak (b. 1943) was born in village Bandhoke in Sheikhupura district in Pakistan. Apart from stories he also wrote novels, and conducted research on tribal culture. He wrote stories which were full of critical realism, and described movingly the lives of the Dalit and other oppressed people. His narrative is hard-hitting, and through his satirical style and sharp delineation of characters, he creates many layers of meaning in his work that add to its authenticity and multi-dimensionality. In 2017, he was given the Kusumanjali award for his story collection *Ant-heen,* along with Manmohan Bawa. He was recognised by the Sahitya Akademi in 2019 for the same book.

Roots

At every single station that the train halted, Ma would perk up and ask eagerly, 'Now where have we reached, son?' And each time I would tell her the name of the station, though unable to prevent myself from getting rather irritated with her.

When we had started from home, I had been in a buoyant mood, but Ma's persistent questions had caused a surge of irritability within me. And then, a while ago, my exasperation had reached its limit. A couple of uppity young girls had sat down in the seats opposite us, and their incessant chattering in a kind of slang with pretensions of speaking English, made my mother quite uncomfortable. She had shrunk into herself, and then asked me in a whisper, 'Son, are they from the same town as your wife?'

This question had a devastating effect on me; I could hardly breathe. Before things could get worse, I though it best to give my mother her sleeping pill, drew a blanket around her and let her drift off to sleep. I knew that it was not so easy for my mother to submit to this, but she did turn her back and lay as though she had indeed fallen asleep.

Over the last few years, this had become a pattern. My mother's behaviour had changed. When the two of us needed her to sleep, she would do so, and when we needed her to wake, she would comply. This quiet acquiescence on her part to our demands pleased my wife Shellie very much, but it left me disturbed and saddened. This was why, I, who had earlier brought her to the city, decided with a heavy heart, to take her back to the village again.

My mother's humility moved me immensely. And now, though she had turned on her side, away from me, I felt she was still looking at me. I choked and felt tears well up in my eyes, which I tried to hide by taking off my glasses and wiping them, brushing my moist eyes.

My wife Shellie would react adversely to my deeply felt sentiment for my mother, and say, 'Look at you, how you shed tears for your mother, but for me, you can't spare a single thought, can you?'

She would speak at a high pitch, almost as if screaming, and march off upstairs in a huff.

To be frank, I admit that her complaint was not without some justification. I too felt that I must try to restrain myself from being so sentimental in regard to my mother. But because Shellie tended to measure these tender feelings in purely material terms, I would seriously doubt the kind of upbringing that made her think in this way. I would even feel pity for her. Of course she did not take kindly to any suggestion of pity on anyone's part. She would raise the roof with her uncontrollable raving. I was at a loss as to how to manage her, but when the growing tension between both of us began to affect my mother, I began to realize that there was much else in my life that was beyond my control.

If indeed I could have had control over anything in my life, I would probably not have chosen to get married to Shellie. Even if I had done so, I need not have accepted the job that I had got as an act of charity on her father's part. I had done so despite the fact that my mother had done all she could to provide me with education, even though she had little means, and had gone hungry to make sure I had all I needed. Here I was, a man who had married a wealthy woman and on her behest, had moved to the city for work, excusing myself by saying that 'we must go wherever our fortune takes us'. It was because of Shellie's insistence. I had to do exactly what she wanted.

'It is not possible to expand our roots in the restricted soil of the village. Those low roofs and shaky walls are not going to be a strong base for taking a flight upwards. They can't take us to a great height.'

What place did my mother's wishes have in the face of such logic? What was to be the place of her vision of the future, which she talked of in all those years when I was growing up? She would repeat the same words again and again.

'My son will become an officer. He will make his mother proud, proud as a queen. He is human, after all. He knows that fulfilling his mother's wishes will give her peace and give peace to his father's soul, too. It is said that ancestors' souls cannot be at peace if their descendents are unworthy.'

It troubled me that my mother had stopped saying things like this now.

One day, I expressed this resentment to her. 'Ma, look, I did my studies, I got a job, I am married—don't you think I am like an officer now?'

'Of course, my dear son. You are right. For me, you will always be an officer. Wait and see—when the people of our village stand up and salute you. But you have left for the city and uprooted yourself from the village. Otherwise, my son, you know that for all parents, their children are always the best. When a child is born it is already a great person in the eyes of his parents!' Even without wanting to show her emotions, she would hide her face in her shawl and shed a few tears.

But it was difficult for me to spare even a sigh for my mother's feelings, far less shed any tears. Anyway what was the use of these tears and sighs, of which my mother already had an abundance? It often occurred to me that after my father's death and my departure for the city, my mother had only these sighs of loneliness for company. What had she got in return for the life she had spent in service and devotion? Some clothes given to her every few months? Some false assurances? Or the continually rising tension between my wife and me...was this all?

This uneasy state of affairs might have continued, or got worse, had something not happened to change Shellie's attitude towards my mother suddenly. This was very surprising, as it had always been very clear that there was no love lost between them. And not only was I surprised, but also pleased, when I came to know that the reason for this change was Shellie's pregnancy. She had always been averse to the idea of becoming a mother. She would argue, 'How strange it is that a woman gives birth to a child, but it is the father's family name that is taken forward! And on top of it, it is the woman's body and figure that are ruined!' Now I was happy that she changed her tune, to say, 'It's very important to set down roots. For this, a woman must become a mother.'

I would have liked to take this change in her attitude with some element of doubt. However, I was hopeful. I thought it possible that the coming of a child into our family might amend the fraught relationships between me, Shellie and my mother.

What happened was exaclty the opposite of this. With the blossoming of the flower of Shellie's womb, the roots of Ma's existence were uprooted.

'Look, if you are so keen to have a child, call your mother from the village, bring her here—or else, engage a servant to help!'

Just three months into the pregnancy, Shellie laid down an ultimatum.

To hire a servant would mean becoming further obligated to her moneyed father. And what of my mother? She would have no problem. Anyway it was her duty, too. So I had no qualms about asking her to move to the city to live with us, and to this purpose, I reached the village and put my request before her. Her reaction to it was immediate. How could she even think of such a thing? Then I told her about the situation, and on knowing the reason, she said nothing further. In a flash, she gathered up her meagre bundle of clothes, and stood ready at the door. She reproached me, asking why I had not told her about all this sooner.

Her eyes moist with tears, she said, 'My son, you know that only when a tree grows new branches and leaves will the roots have some value! And who is there for me here, but you and your family!' I believed her when she said this. For it was most remarkable how easily she abandoned her life in the village.

My mother adapted herself completely to living with us in the city. She did not complain, nor did she ask for anything. She neither offered an opinion, nor commented on anything. For some reason, it was disturbing to me to see her bending herself to all Shellie's requirements and whims, without demur.

For Shellie, it was a moment of triumph. She did not hesitate to point this out. One day, she went to a nursery and brought back a few potted plants. The pots contained the small versions of trees like banyan and *peepal*—which, in their natural form, would grow to be very large, but remained small and stunted when in pots, growing to only a few inches in height. She was quick to make a comment, 'Who says that roots need to be deep? If a tree like banyan or peepal can grow in a pot, why not a human?' This was targeted towards challenging my mother's constant talk about roots.

I wanted to protest loudly that it was a terrible injustice to stunt the roots of a plant so that it remains small. But I was mute. Somehow, I forced myself to silently swallow those poisonous words spewed out by Shellie.

My mother understood, and met it with a quiet patience. She did something that all artificial ways of tampering with plants could not achieve—she herself pruned and cut down her own roots. She did this while tolerating all kinds of taunts and remarks directed towards her. When she spoke to Shellie, she would do so in the kindest way possible. Chores such as crossing the road to bargain with vendors and to buy vegetables became everyday tasks for her. She became used to taking care of the housework to such a degree that she could easily have been taken to be a servant.

In my heart of hearts, I felt relieved. It seemed my mother had begun to put down her roots in city life. I thanked God for this. Shellie on her part was also happy in her 'victory', and took advantage of it by spending all her time in bed, though she was only six months into her pregnancy. We both thought that Ma would not cling to her attachment to the village for much longer.

But one day, all this optimism came to nought.

That night, sudden loud screams rent the air from the direction of house number 237. Ma was extraordinarily sensitive to the sounds of grief, and it was in the dead of night when the shrieks were heard. She got up at once and ran in the the direction of the house where the noise had come. I too started up to follow her, but Shellie entreated me, 'Don't go, please. Don't get involved in anything over there.'

The neighbourhood had gathered to witness a tragic scene. The elderly man in the house, Deen Dayal, was no more. 'Hai, o my brother! A good man, such a good man!' My mother wailed in grief that welled up from deep within her.

He too had, like Ma, come from the village to live with his son and family, and often when buying vegetables, playing with the children or walking the dog, he would meet Ma and share some of his feelings with her. The sorrow that rankled him was that both his sons had already divided up their parents' property, and also divided up the responsibility of care for the parents—the mother with one son, the father with the other. Before Deen Dayal had had time to adjust to the life in the city, he passed away. I was worried about the effect his sudden demise would have on my mother.

Ma was crying, trying to express her grief in tearful words.

'That's enough! Ma ji, please stop crying.' She was chided, as the children in the house were in the midst of preparing for their examinations, and were not to be disturbed. Ma quietened down. She shrank into a corner, hid her face and continued to sob softly, while a few other neighbourhood women joined her in mourning.

'Look here. If you are going to be weeping and wailing like this, I will have to take my children somewhere else!' Deen Dayal's son warned them more sternly this time.

At this, Ma fell into complete silence.

Amongst all the philosophical talk going on, such as, 'All of us have to die some day' or 'this world is but a temporary home', were the comments, 'See how things have turned out. Deen Dayal came from the village to live with his son so that the family could have some support. Both son and daughter-in-law are working, so they needed someone to look after the children. But shortly after coming here, his health deteriorated. Instead of being a help, he became a burden. With all the cost of living in the city, his medical treatment became a bigger drain on the family. It must be said that these poor people really had to bear quite a lot of trouble due to him.'

'Of course, that is true. It's so expensive to run a household in the city, the children's education is so costly and imagine adding to that the burden of treatment of an old man's illness.'

'The illness was his own fault!' Deen Dayal's son retorted. 'He was never happy—always criticising everything...the place is so dirty... there is corruption...there is noise...the toilets are built inside the house...he should not expect that the buildings and houses in the city can be changed just to suit him.'

Said another, 'Oh well, he was a simple man. He did not do anything to offend anyone. Whatever food and dress was given to him, he accepted without any fuss.'

This last remark seemed to give my mother some satisfaction. She looked attentively at the person who has spoken. She seemed eager to say something, but could not, as if her throat was constricted. I thought it was time for us to leave the gathering and go back to our house, as the other neighbours too were leaving, after making inquiries about the cremation which was to take place the following day. Yet I hesitated. I softly nudged Ma to indicate that we should leave, thinking she would resist. I thought she would say, 'How do you think we can leave a dead person lying here before his last rites are done?' But to my amazement, she got up immediately and without uttering a single word, accompanied me down the stairs.

The next morning, the funeral van drew up in the open courtyard in our locality. I stepped out of my house, and heard our neighbour Mrs Basu explaining to my mother that in the city there was an electric crematorium in which the dead were cremated.

'Ma ji', she was saying, 'It is so quick that in twenty minutes the body is burnt, and the packet of bones and ash are handed over to you. No bother, no doing this or that, none of that nonsense.'

I was alarmed on hearing this. Surely now Ma would turn to me and ask a hundred questions.

'What does this mean? If there is no fire, how can the sacred ritual be done? Who will go round the pyre and give it the holy flame? How will the soul be released from the world....?' But my mother said nothing, asked no question at all. She just stood in the balcony upstairs, and watched the body being carried to the van and taken away. She kept watching as a few people followed the van, but she did not express any need to join the crowd, nor did she request me to do so.

From that day onwards, Ma stayed absolutely silent.

One day, she put a question to me, 'My son, can you tell me where the roots of a human being are to be found?' I lowered my gaze and did not reply, but after that it seemed as if every moment of her being with my wife and me was irksome. Each action of hers seemed to be somehow contrary to us. It seemed as though everything she did was affected by the event of Deen Dayal's death. Both of us thought it best that she should go back to the village.

On the way back to the village however, I thought it a little unfair that my mother should leave us at the time of Shellie's pregnancy.

As we approached the village, she perked up immediately.

The women cutting fodder in the fields saw her and jumped up in joy. They ran up and embraced her. Back home, the entire village turned up to meet her and all those who heard of her arrival crowded around to talk to her. As for me, it appeared she had completely forgotten about my existence.

A few times, I tried to impress the fact of my presence on people. But no one paid any attention to me. A casual word, 'So how is our officer...?' was flung at me now and then. This was how I was treated generally by the people of the village. This situation left me deeply pained.

Even one glance at my mother's happy animated face, surrounded by the women of the village, told me that this was a different person from the silent one who had come with me from the city. Rather, it seemed she had never gone to the city at all. Then I remembered something that I had once read.

'There are many sides to a human being...' But as soon as this thought came, I realised that it was not the entire explanation. The next thought was that there is a time in life when it is possible for a person's roots to grow. Perhaps this was why my mother could not strike down roots in the city. But then I discarded this thought too, and was struck by a very painful question. What about me? Where did I belong—unable to feel at home and have roots in the city, and so separated from the soil of the village that my roots could not spread there. Not thinking any further thoughts, I was filled with the realisation that my roots had disappeared completely. Nothing was left of them...

BALDEV SINGH MOGA

Baldev Singh Moga (b. 1942) was born in village Anchariki in Bikaner district of Rajasthan. Though he had a Master's degree and a BEd, he took up the occupation of a transporter. As a result, he travelled widely over the length and breadth of the country and had an opportunity to observe places and people. He wrote stories and accounts of the truck drivers on the road, which were published in Amrita Pritam's journal *Naagmani*. These were so popular that he was given the sobriquet 'Baldev Sadaknaama'. He is a progressive and realistic writer, and writes on a vast range of subjects. The extract given below is from his novel *Lal Batti*, where he portrays the lives of prostitutes in the red light area of Kolkata. Though he wrote stories, travelogues, memoirs and plays, he has been recognised primarily as a novelist. The Sahitya Akademi bestowed the National Award on him in 2011 for his novel *Dhahwan Dilli de Kingre*.

The Business of Life

Have you heard: Devki Mausi has gone back to her village again? This time she will bring back the most tender young girls. These are the ones in demand in most of the establishments. Also, do you know where Kanchan has gone? Devki has gone to look for her—that is her secret agenda. If Kanchan is alive, it's all right, but if she has gone and killed herself, it could create a problem for Devki.

There are many such worries. Devki wishes she had not pressurised Kanchan about the rent for her room, when she has been living off Kanchan's earnings for so long. But then she assures herself—this is how business is done in this place, I have to survive. Besides, I have been more indulgent than many of the others—the owners of the other establishments always say 'Devki is too easy on the girls'. But still one girl has disappeared from her house. How could that be?

See Maya's little son Raju running up the stairs, wailing. Mantu has snatched two rupees from him and run away. Maya is so enraged that she wants to take a knife and kill Mantu or his mother. That Mantu beats up her boy everyday. Helpless in her anger, she slaps Raju. 'Why did you go near those people? If you had money with you, why did you show it to him? Bastards! Robbers! Beggars! They don't let us live in peace!' Raju cries and cries, and Maya takes him onto her lap and begins to cry herself

'I'll write to the Prime Minister, like Deesa has written', Raju sobs. 'I'll tell him that Mantu is very bad. Ma, he calls Suman Didi names. Khokha is also bad. Ma, all the people here are horrible. Why can't we go somewhere else, Ma?'

She wipes his eyes, and looks at the little child's innocent face.

'We'll go, my child, we'll go very far away.'

'Mantu and Khokha will not come there?'

'No, they can't reach there.'

'Has Kanchan aunty also gone there?'

'I don't know, maybe she's there. Now, you don't go out to play with Mantu and Khokha. I'll buy you a large slab of chocolate today,' saying this, Maya kisses her son's forehead.

On the footpath below, the urchins toss around one of Beena's metal utensils like a football, but Beena does not have the energy to stop them.

Suman does not play with the younger children now. Her mother does not allow her to. It has been heard that Suman's mother has taken a large sum of money to push her into the business, and now Suman wears red lipstick and white powder on her face.

Mantu has been teasing her. 'I told you, didn't I, that doctors will come to see you one day?'

Sure enough. And then there was a huge fight between Suman's mother and Mantu's mother.

Evening comes, and all the girls get ready—Hema, Madhu, Rekha, Maya, Sameena, Guddi, Chanda, Shama, and others. The music being played on the tape-players and radios at the *paan* shops, gets louder and louder.

Tonight, again, Hema wears a white sari. Her make-up is light, not garish. She has red *sindhoor* in the parting of her hair. A taxi waits below, with the pimp who will accompany her in it. Devki Mausi is not here today, so her commission of five hundred rupees can be kept by Hema. It has been arranged between her and the pimp, Devki is not to be told about tonight's assignment.

Hema loves wearing these kinds of elegant clothes, and she loves to play the role of a respectable married woman. Ah, the dinner invitations, the fine liquor! And above all, knowing that she is making a fool of the men!

Hema gives final touches to her appearance, and checks herself in the mirror. Just then, Rekha comes in with a morose expression.

'Hema, do you know, I'm in the same state as Kanchan?'

'How? Really?' Hema is shocked.

'I had suspected it for some days…but now…'

These words turn Hema's lively countenance to a dark hue. Her enthusiasm for the evening's pleasures dies down. She can hear Rekha's despondent voice going on, and she says, 'Most of us here are in such a condition, Rekha. Some of us speak of it, and some, like me, just struggle with it quietly.'

'What—you?' It is Rekha's turn to be surprised.

'We all have this sickness, more or less, Rekha. But can we hide it for long? Just like Beena Mausi, and then Kanchan, one of these days, our real condition will be evident on our very faces, we'll not even need to say anything.'

'So we're living in a fool's paradise!'

'It would be so, if we did not know the reality. But we all know what the end of all this will be. We know how we're going to die. So, it is okay to live this way and enjoy this hell we're living in. That's what we're doing.'

The hasty steps of the pimp are heard and he rushes in, agitated. 'Listen! There's a police raid going on in the neighbouring lane. Quick—we have to get out of here quick!'

'Raid? Now?' Hema is startled. Rekha runs out at once to warn all the other girls.

'A raid can happen at any time, ok? It is better to get out right now. We will escape being questioned by the police and make good earnings for the night.'

Both of them scramble down the stairs, into the taxi, and are off.

The rest of the women lock up their rooms and disappear into other hiding places. Some of them do not have identification cards. Some have not renewed their medical certificates of fitness after the due date. Even if they do, the police will always find some reason or the other to haul them up. So if it can be avoided, so much the better. Some who stay here may think that it will be all right—who can harm us? They are mistaken, for it is like a red rag to a bull, asking for trouble.

Tomorrow, the members of a political organisation and social workers are going to come around to collect contributions, and in an open area or nearby square, they will make long speeches. They will talk about all that needs to be done for sex workers, about social stigma, about how they will make sure they have all the facilities that every citizen has. Their children will get education and care, and equal social standing with all the children in society, like other children. They will arrange the marriages of their daughters with young men who need wives, and give them a chance to have their own homes and families. At night, the political leaders will get drunk from the proceeds of the charity drive, and land up at the brothels. They will laugh, and tell the women, 'If it were not for you, there would be rape in the streets and colleges every day! If it were not for you, men would hang themselves in frustration!'

With the encouragement and promises of these social workers, there will be more children born of the sex workers. They will grow up scrounging around in the streets like pariahs, and become citizens of the country, to contribute to the lists of voters. The government and non-government agencies will continue to busily collect all the statistics of the population of these woman and children.

It is night. Like all nights, this night too will pass. The girls will go to sleep, some in their rooms, some in the balcony, or roof—wherever there is space—in whatever state they are in—naked or half-naked, sick or simply exhausted. They will wake up after a while, their hair disheveled, the smell of stale liquor in their mouths, scratching their itchy thighs, and they will queue up at the latrines. Even to be near them at this time would fill anyone with revulsion and shame.

But the evening comes, the night falls, drink-sodden clients arrive, and they do not mind their bodies and fluids merging with the women's bodies, and business goes on as usual.

It is the same business that the gods and goddesses were always involved in; the same business that went on in temples with the *devadasis*, the women of the gods. It was the same business that went on in the palaces of kings, as in the establishments of sex workers, and in the streets, in the parks and in hotels and clubs.

And this business will always go on.

Waryam Singh Sandhu

Waryam Sandhu (b. 1945) was born in village Chavinda Kalan in district Amritsar. He writes poetry, criticism and prose, but his outstanding contribution and fame is in the field of the short story. He is considered to be the advocate of new progressive thinking. An in-depth and multi-layered exploration of subjects, and artistically complex descriptive style are hallmarks of his writing. Sandhu is the most important chronicler of the wave of Naxalite movement, Dalit consciousness and turbulence in Punjab. In 2000, the national Sahitya Akademi award was bestowed on him for his collection of stories *Chauthi Koot*, that he returned in 2015. He currently lives in Canada.

Each One Must Have Their Share

Ghudhu moved the buffalo from where it was tied, and mixed the straw and fodder in its trough. His eye on the buffalo, feeling its warm and odorous breath, he prepared for the milking and called out for a milk bucket to be brought. He spread the dung encrusted cloth on the buffalo's back, and tried to stop his own limbs from shivering with cold, while looking up at the pale sun glistening weakly through the winter mist that surrounded the landscape. It seemed as though, in the battle between the sun and the mist, the mist was winning. It held the sun in a deathly embrace, as if it were choking the life out of it, as a hefty wrestler puts his knee on the chest and chokes the throat of his opponent to keep him down. Ghudhu's hand instinctively flew to his own throat. Years ago, he had felt the same force on his own throat, when he used to be a wrestler and had to take the onslaught of his instructor's attack, or that of some more accomplished wrestlers. It was his nature to be more defensive rather than an attacker in wrestling. This was why the master of wrestling in their village had berated him, with his customary curses, 'Oye, Dharam-eya, you wretched fellow, look at your hefty body! If all you can do every day is lie down and surrender, then, idiot, why did you take to wrestling? Better use of your bulk would have been to make two of you, use one for ploughing the field and the other to tend to the animals! Then it would have been of some use, seeing that anyway you don't have any sense!' He, the youngest of three brothers, thus continued to be referred to gracelessly as 'Ghudhu', a childhood name. Now, he had left wrestling, and there was no fear of the strong knees of wrestlers pressing on his neck and holding him down. Still, he often felt a pain in his neck, with the memory—always, it was as though someone had him choked and pinned down.

His sister Bachno walked up with the milk bucket and pan. She had stayed on since the day she had arrived from her in-laws house on the day of their mother's demise. She handed the bucket to Ghudhu, and began to mix some flour in the buffalo's feed.

Ghudhu stroked the buffalo's back, and sat down for milking.

'See na, Veera. Our two elder brothers are coming today. Elder one must have reached last night at the bus stop, at Karam's house, see...so you settle everything with them, see...service and ceremony after mother's death has to be arranged, also ashes have to be taken to Hardwar, see...mother-daughter are special, wise people say, see...'

Ghudhu felt his irritation grow.

'Who are you to tell me what I have to do?'

He wanted to say some cutting words to this younger sister, but he swallowed his bitterness, muttering, '*Bhootni*, witch...'

Bachno did not stop making her insinuating remarks. 'See...I know you don't have much money but this also must be done. I told the elder ones also, "you have a lot, you don't need anything", but, see... we'll need some grain soon...you're getting to plough the land for free...see, everyone is not like our father...see, all daughters can have their share, but he doesn't even talk about it...'

Ghudhu, who had till now restrained himself, exploded. 'So you take your share, let the others take it too...as if tilling the land has made me some kind of maharaja, the king!'

The buffalo was startled on hearing his loud voice, and feeling the pain of his hands squeezing her teats too tightly, jumped back in agitation. Ghudhu fell on his behind, and though he managed to save the milk, a little did spill. He got up, picked up a shovel and rained blows on the hapless animal.

'See...look how he reacts to a simple thing', Bachno mumbled, picked up the bucket and walked away.

'Oh, what harm did this mute creature do?' screamed Ratno, Ghudhu's wife, coming out from the kitchen. 'Why are you venting your anger at other people on the poor animal?'

The frightened buffalo backed away to the wall of the shed, its eyes wide with fear, as if pleading, her body trembling.

The sound of a motorcycle could be heard, at a distance. Ghudhu began to mess around with his hands deep in the troughs. The motorcycle approached the compound, accompanied by the sound of barking dogs, and stopped at their doorstep. It was Ghudhu's brothers—Swaran Singh and Karam Singh. They rode the motorcycle through the entrance and parked it inside the compound, in the yard. Ratno covered her head with her scarf and went to open the door. The elder brother, Swaran Singh, took off his dark glasses, and wiped them with a cloth. Then he wiped some of the damp off his overcoat with his gloved hands, and walked forward to the *charpai* where his father Bishan Singh was sitting. The younger Karam Singh wrapped his warm shawl around himself and, seeing that his embellished footwear had been somewhat muddied with dung, tried to scrape it off on the doorstep frame, and turned to his sister, Bachno.

'Where is Ghudhu?'

Bachno slipped her arm out of her shawl and pointed towards the area of the cattle yard, where Ghudhu was trying to catch hold of a cow that had worked itself free because of the sound of the motor cycle.

'O, *pahalwana*, come over here. Let's have a chat about some things. *Bhaji* here can't take leave everyday and come to the village... I also have lots of work. Let's decide who will take the ashes of our mother to the Ganga—you or I?'

'Coming', Ghudhu replied casually, still doing some straightening of the tethers and pegs of the animal. Then he told his boy, 'Kaku, go and get a *charpai* and lay it out in the room.'

Before the boy could comply, old Bishan Singh called him. 'Kaku, bring a chair.' He sat up and moved aside to one corner of his charpai, making place for Swaran Singh to sit down on the other side till the chair was brought. But Swaran Singh remained standing, setting right his turban, and then smoothing his beard as he stood.

Swaran Singh was the eldest of the three brothers and the best educated. He had put himself through college and was now an overseer, making good money one way or the other. He lived in the town, in a house he had built for himself and his family. His daughter had been married off into a respectable family, and his two sons were also doing quite well in their jobs. They had a circle of friends among the well-to-do people in the town and they enjoyed their social life among these people, to the extent that they rarely visited the village. His share of the land was being cultivated and harvested by Ghudhu, and he would take some of the harvested grain from it. But he would tell his friends and acquaintances in the town that he had given his share of the land free to Ghudhu to use.

Kaku brought the chair. It was a steel chair which had been in their house for many years.

'Son! Just wipe the chair with a cloth', old Bishan Singh told the child, and folded his old quilt with its cover of faded cotton. He pulled up his wispy hair into a knot and rolled the strip of his soiled turban around his head. Whenever he was in the company of Swaran Singh, he felt as supplicatory and humble as a *jat* does before a *tehsildar*, a poor farmer facing a powerful official. Swaran Singh appeared to him to be made of some other stuff, not from his own weak self, stuff that was smooth and shiny and solid, the kind that wax statues are made of. Swaran Singh's sophisticated way of life made him feel as if he himself was rough and rustic. That was why he did not feel comfortable in the refined environment of his elder son's town house. He was nervous even walking around the place. He had the impression that his daughter-in-law and grandchildren were staring at him or ridiculing him. It was like someone had taken a creature living in the mud, and made it inhabit a marble palace.

Kaku had wiped the chair. Bishan Singh was still wondering if he should address Swaran Singh in a polite and formal manner, by which time Swaran Singh sat down on the chair. Bishan Singh began to think that maybe he should not feel so intimidated by his son. He is not a son of a viceroy, is he, he is my son, so what...he thought.

Karam Singh went over to carry a *charpai* out to the entrance room. He was two years older than Ghudhu. Always an absconder from school, careless about studies, he used to leave for school in the morning, but never get there. Hiding his satchel in the wood pile outside, he would go and play with his friends all day, and when it was time for school to be over, he'd pick up the satchel and go home. Being the youngest, Ghudhu would accompany him. That was how they grew up together, and together they dropped out of school, and began to help their father with work at home.

As a young man, Karma began to ferry smuggled goods, and Ghudhu, being of hefty build, with strong arms and legs, chose to become a wrestler. Karma succeeded in doing the work of a middleman, and gradually, he was able to transact deals in 'black' in which he would get his share. There would be swings in prices which he would profit from. He too built a house near the centre of the village, and lived in style. He had a dairy and a poultry farm, and did brisk business.

But the pehalwan, the wrestler Ghudhu, remained where he was. His father's struggle with farming was Ghudhu's legacy. What had been a joke by the master that Ghudhu could do the work of two men—one ploughing the fields, the other tending to the livestock—actually came true, as Ghudhu found himself doing both, with a lot of effort. He would try to work very hard, but he stayed in the same place, just like a man in a dream, who, in fear, tries to run as fast as he can, but finds his feet rooted to the same spot. Some malevolent force seemed to be pulling him back all the time.

He stood at the same place still, knocking the post into the ground with a hammer, and the blows resounded in his head. With each blow he felt as if he was being buried into the ground. All this while, though, his mind was on the talk going on between his two brothers. He was aggravated by their behaviour and that third one—sister Bachno. What were these so-called relationships worth?

His grudge against his elder brother was that the man presented him, Ghudhu, to his relatives and friends as a poor village yokel. He would take his share of the crop, but he behaved as though he had done a favour to his brother and given him the land to farm. Ghudhu of course could not leave the land, nor was it possible for him to survive without it. But he resented being looked upon as if his brother was doing him some great favour. The other one, Karam Singh, also took his share of the crop, but was never happy about it and would say that Ghudhu was not producing enough, and it was not sufficient. It was only yesterday that he was heard saying to his brother-in-law, 'Brother! Don't you think I should myself take a tractor and grow fodder on my share of two acres of the land for my cattle? That will be better than grain—the production of grain is not enough.'

'Oh, yes, yes,' agreed the brother-in-law, Bachno's husband. 'No harm in that!'

Ghudhu had heard this and knew they were intending that he should hear it. He was boiling within. There was not enough land to divide in this way, and if these two acres were taken out, it would really be difficult for him. He was worried about this, but he did not speak.

He did not want to bring the matter out into the open. He would have liked to talk to his father, his sister or his brother-in-law, who were the only people with whom he could share his anxiety, and ask for their help. But now he had heard that same brother-in-law instigating his brother to divide the land. And what could he expect of that sister, Bachno? She was already disappointed that he did not give her regard in the way the elder brother did. The elder one and his wife would come to visit her and ask after her welfare, help out when needed, and now and then, gift her some clothes. But Ghudhu much less visit her or help her out, would not even give anything to her son. She would say, 'Now see, when my boy goes to his house once in a while, he doesn't even care to give him a set of clothes! When did he last give us anything? Just on the occasion that the boy was born, he spared a few rags, nothing else! Not as if we are depending on what he gives us—but see, brother and sister should have these small tokens of affection, see...' and she would wipe an artificial tear from her eye.

Ghudhu was fuming at his sister's behaviour. The day his mother died and her body was to be bathed and prepared for cremation, he had taken her gold earrings and handed them to the wife of his younger brother as if she had the right over them.

For a moment he felt some anger towards his mother too. But the very next minute, the memory of her wrinkled face and her deep-set flashing eyes arose before his eyes, and he was filled with affection for her. She was the only one who had really loved him truly, the only one who had always spoken up for him. Rather, anything he had in his heart that he wanted to speak about, she would be the one to say just loud and clear for anyone to hear. She was the one who would declare, 'He is my innocent little boy, my *bhola*. He is like Shiva. The others are rascals.'

Ghudhu regretted his not being present at the time of her death. All his life, his mother had been near him, but when she died, he was not with her. She had been taken to the city by Swaran Singh for treatment after she had a sudden stroke and was paralysed. Swaran Singh had come to see her, and despite her objections, took her away with him and admitted her in a large hospital. That was two months ago. And after six weeks of treatment, her frail old body gave up the struggle for life.

Old Bishan Singh was left behind. As a father, he understood Ghudhu's difficulties. He knew what it was to be a farmer, and so Ghudhu's problems were familiar to him as much as his own. He had by nature a mild temperament, quiet and non-assertive; moreover, he was so overwhelmed by his two elder sons, their affluence and their manner that he could not put up any argument before them.

'O, come here now, mother's boy! What, you are still hammering away, what's the matter? We too have work to do...' Karam Singh called out.

Ghudhu got up, wiped his dirty hands on the cotton wrap and slowly walked up to the place where they were sitting, and stood there.

'Sit down.' said Karam Singh, indicating a place on the charpai. Bachno also arranged her shawl around her and sat down on the edge of the *charpai* where her father sat.

'Well, with respect, let me tell you that *bhaji* (indicating Swaran Singh) came to my house last night. We have come to discuss something...'

'What is it? Alright, discuss what you want...' Bishan Singh replied, in a low voice, scratching his beard.

'Yes, it's better we talk frankly among ourselves. We are all family members here, we should decide everything together...' began Karam Singh, looking at each person in turn. Then he gave a deep sigh, and said, 'We have to do this duty for our mother—arrange a proper ceremony, call all our relatives and well-wishers. We all know that the old lady passed at a ripe age, after living a long life, blessed with grandchildren, and so a grand celebration in her honour must be arranged...so do you agree?'

Bishan Singh replied sadly, with a break in his voice, 'We are small people, what sense in celebrating for people like us?'

'I also told Karam Singh that there is no need to go to such expense...it's a waste of money...'

'O, *bhaji*. What will people say? With such well-placed sons, they will say, it is very miserly not to arrange a good function. It's not important for you, maybe, because you live in the town, but we will have to listen to all kinds of talk from people...'

He was still speaking when Bachno interrupted him.

'Yes, *bhaji*. You should not talk like this. Our brother Karam Singh is quite right. My in-laws are already expecting an invitation, and are waiting—my sisters-in-law will have cutting things to say to me...I know', she spoke sharply, addressing Swaran Singh and her father.

Ghudhu was well aware that she was directing these remarks at him, in the guise of speaking to her father and elder brother. He had an urge to give the woman a tight slap. He thought Swaran Singh was right to say that such expense was unnecessary; he was concerned about his own financial condition.

'Look here, brother. I will be willing to contribute whatever my share is, you can decide...but I...' Swaran Singh said.

Ghudhu was disappointed. He had hoped that his elder brother would stick to his previous objection and save him from his worries, but the hope was dashed—he could see that there was no support forthcoming. He was seething within himself, hardly able to control his rising anger.

'Five to seven thousand is a reasonable estimate. Also *bhaji* has been saying that he has spent twenty seven hundred on mother's treatment. We can each contribute nine hundred for that...' this was Karam Singh's calculation of the money required.

Hearing about the mention of the amount spent on mother's treatment, Ghudhu felt a shock. He bit his lips: he did not know what to say, what to do.

'So you spent on mother's treatment? So what? Did not the poor woman spend her whole life looking after you?' Bishan Singh gathered up all the courage he had to speak up.

'See, Bapu, this is not right!', Bachno spoke with indignation, waving her arms about, gesturing specially towards Ghudhu. 'If she looked after him, did she not look after the others? Raise their children? And see, is he not controlling the whole property?'

'You keep quiet,' Ghudhu burst out. 'Who do you think you are, a lawyer?' His nostrils flared, his forehead burning in spite of the cold.

'Fine, I will not stay here now. See, my words are poison for him... I will not stay...' She flounced off angrily, waving her arms.

Now that the atmosphere had grown tense, Karam Singh tried to defuse the matter, but Bachno turned back and let flow, 'See, I have a share in the land too. What do you think...if you call me a lawyer, I'll show you!'

'Ok, let's leave it, we'll talk about it later,' said Karam Singh, and now he spoke directly to Ghudhu. '*Bhaji* doesn't have time, so tell me, will you be going to immerse mother's ashes in Ganga, or me?'

For two minutes, Ghudhu did not reply. He sat there silently. Thoughts raced round his head, or rather, they wrestled with each other. And, that same mist that surrounded the land in the winter, had descended on his mind. He was feeling numb, and so he sat, motionless. Then all at once, the fire within him leapt up, and with that, he too got up suddenly.

'Listen, do you hear? There is nothing hidden here between us... you know the condition of my household is not good. I cannot afford this Ganga business...' He stopped to take a breath, swallowed his spittle, then spoke rapidly, 'If you are very eager, you can take the old lady's ashes to the Ganga; and this old man you see before you still living (he indicated Bishan Singh) I'll do whatever I have to do for him...'

All the three—the father and the two sons—stared at him, astonished. He went on... 'The truth is...just now I have no money for this...so if you can't do it, let it be, sardarji! You can give me my share of mother's ashes and leave them here. Whenever I can, I'll go and immerse them...'

He left them gazing at him in amazement, and went indoors.

Khalid Hussain

Khalid Hussain (b. 1945) was born in Udhampur in Jammu and Kashmir. Because he has served as deputy commissioner in several districts of the state, he had the opportunity to observe people at close quarters. Apart from the travails of the common people, Hussain has also portrayed the agony of partition powerfully and sensitively in his writing, particularly the manner in which the cataclysmic event tore the lives of communities and individuals. Hussain's writing reflects the influence of the Pothohaari dialect, which imbues it with a gentleness and gentility. Though he usually adopts a realistic style, some of his stories are replete with striking imagery and symbolism. He writes in both Punjabi and Urdu, and is a successful writer in both Pakistan and India.

Eye Witness

In my pockets I have many pairs of eyes, which scrape painfully at my insides all the time. These eyes pierce my mind and heart. My right pocket contains the pair of eyes that belonged to my childhood friend Rajnath Razdan. He was my dearest friend and was killed in 1947, when the tribals pumped a number of bullets into his body. His head was split in two. Though he died, his eyes remained alive, and they were glaring at me. I was terrified—of myself, and of the fearful tribals...but I could do nothing. What can a child of nine do? All I could do was to carefully carve the eyes of my friend out of their sockets and place them in the pocket of my coat as a precious reminder of our love. Witnessing the tragedy of his death with my own eyes I would feel scorpions stinging my body and I would groan and writhe in pain.

That event in which Rajnath was killed took place in the village Anjar, which was once a peaceful happy village in the Bandipur area. The real culprit behind it was Ahmed Sheikh, whose land lay adjoining the lands of Sansar Chand Razdan and there was a dispute between them over the land. Sansar Chand, who was a money-lender and trader, had an eye on Ahmed Sheikh's land. The latter had also borrowed money from Sansar Chand, and had put up his land as collateral when he needed funds for his daughter's marriage. Ahmed Sheikh did not have the money to pay back the principal amount or the loan instalments. Sansar Chand then began to farm that land. This dispute became the reason for the murder of Sansar Chand and his son, my dear friend, Rajnath. Ahmed Sheikh had betrayed them to the tribal warriors, who did the killing. The villagers, most of whom were owed money to Sansar Chand and did not like him, on this occasion, put the blame on Ahmed Sheikh, and berated him for his cowardly action. They cut off all neighbourly ties and obligations with him and ostracised him from the community. Finally, Ahmed

Sheikh left the village. He crossed the border into Pakistani occupied Kashmir, and did not return.

I passed my school leaving exam from Baramulla's St Joseph School, and then joined Shri Pratap Singh College in Srinagar from where I passed the B.A. examination. After that, I went to the Aligarh Muslim University to study law. I was very studious and I loved to study. I was also fond of poetry and was inspired to pen my own verses. Quite soon I was recognised in the literary circles in Kashmir as one of the most talented poets. My father too had been a prominent poet, and had been a member of the Kashmiri wing of the Urdu academy of letters, and I think I inherited my flair for versification from him. Perhaps it was this unconscious absorption of this influence that made me a poet. On my own, I applied for and obtained a job at Radio Kashmir as a programme producer, and put my heart and soul into my work. Here too, I was able to make a name for myself. I went on to work at all the major radio stations in India, and then in Doordarshan television, where I became director. By the time of my retirement, I had reached the position of Deputy Director General of Doordarshan. All through my career and while travelling on assignments, I could not forget my friend Rajnath. Everyone tries their best to perform their duties in office, but it gave me particular satisfaction to do whatever I could for any Kashmiri Pandit whose application file crossed my desk. Rajnath's eyes guided my pen in approving and forwarding these files. I can say with complete confidence and honesty that I have never obstructed any files pertaining to the Kashmiri Pandits. I tried to help wherever I could, in any way, or get help for them from others. They were of the same blood and soil as mine as I was one of them. Every Kashmiri Pandit appeared to me like my friend Rajnath, for whose death I somehow felt myself responsible.

In my other pocket there is a second pair of eyes, which belong to my friend, companion and drinking buddy Lassa Koul. He was director of All India Radio Srinagar. We used to sit for hours over drinks, discussing the Kashmir situation, analysing the errors made from 1947 onwards by the Indian state, trying to understand why, after all these years, India had not succeeded in winning over the hearts of the Kashmiri people, what the government should do to mend matters and resolve the issue. I was the Director of Doordarshan in Srinagar at the time. We had a mission to keep the Kashmiri youth out of the net of terrorism through making relevant and interesting programmes for them to listen to and view. Lassa Koul was a shining example of who a Kashmiri is and of 'Kashmiriyat'—the essence of Kashmiri identity. A very handsome man, he was always cheerful and the life of every party. He had close and warm relationships with Hindus, Mussalmans, and Sikhs, and was on friendly terms with many of the leading personalities of Srinagar, including the bureaucracy of Kashmir. He was gunned down by the terrorists who suspected him of being an agent of the Indian government. His eyes always ask me the question, 'What was my fault?' How can I tell you, my friend, that this is the fate of most humans on this earth—the innocent die, by no fault of theirs. I was filled with helpless anger—at myself. The fire of rage burnt within me, and I would close my eyes in shame and pain.

Mohammad Azam Sagar was the warden of the Pahari Hostel in Poonch. His son Nishat Azam had done his MSc in Agriculture from the Agriculture University in Lucknow, and had returned home after completing his studies. One day Sagar sahib asked him to go to their village Naka Majari and supervise the harvesting of the crop. He was sleeping at night in the farmhouse there, when some army men in pursuit of terrorists, barged into the house. They saw that Nishat was alone, and woke him up to question him. He explained to them repeatedly and gave them proof of his identity that showed he was not a terrorist and that he had just finished his studies at the Agricultural University and was home in Poonch for some time, but the soldiers did not believe a word of it, and decided that he was a terrorist. They killed him mercilessly. There was an uproar in the village, and a protest march was taken out against the army. The army stuck to its version that they had killed a terrorist. I, who was deeply stricken by Nishat's death, put this news up on Doordarshan. After this, the government set up an inquiry into the matter. The report of that inquiry was never made public. All of Poonch turned up at the funeral of Nishat. Sagar sahib had been a friend of mine, and I made a special effort to reach Poonch from Kashmir. When

Nishat's body was being lowered into the ground, his eyes flew out of the shroud and came close to me. They were glaring at me and demanding to know why I had not broadcast the truth on my channel. I could not forget the unforgiving anger in Nishat's eyes. I kept his eyes carefully in the top pocket of my coat, and tried to be calm, but the agony of Nishat's death torments me still.

In the inside pocket of my coat, there is another pair of eyes. They belong to Ghulam Hussain, who lived in Tota Gali and was an informant for the army. He was an extremely patriotic Indian Muslim, and he strongly opposed the terrorists and their tactics. For this reason, he would, from time to time, give information to the army on the locations and the activities planned by the terrorists. Eventually, they found out that Ghulam Hussain was a secret informer and assisted the police. At first they warned him and then they threatened him that if he did not stop, he and his while family would be killed, but Ghulam Hussain was not intimidated by their threats and carried on his work as before. Finally, one night, the terrorists attacked his house, and pumped bullets into Ghulam Hussain and every member of the family. No one expressed any sorrow at this sacrifice by a patriot, nor was there any crowd to mourn his courage—neither the defenders of nationalism, nor the relatives or neighbours—as if it was not human beings who had died, but dogs. This callousness filled the eyes of Ghulam Sheikh with terrible sadness. They stared at me with reproach, and asked, 'Is this the kind of reward you get for being a patriot?' What could I reply to this? I had seen the charade of the government's indifference enacted too many times. All I could do was to take Ghulam Hussain's eyes and keep them in the inside pocket of my coat.

In Harni village, the terrorists had shot four innocent Hindus in broad daylight, and the whole village was enraged at this incident. Mendhar, Poonch, Surankot and Rajouri—people from all these places reached Harni when they heard the terrible news. There was much slogan-shouting against the government, and burning of effigies. I too reached Harni so that I could see with my own eyes and report on the scene. People from there told me that some days ago, some soldiers from the army battalion based in Balnoi had got over-excited, perhaps drunk, and they had crossed the border in dead of night. There they had struck upon a house where people from a wedding party lay asleep, and brought back the decapitated heads of some of the men. Then revenge was taken for this by the terrorists by butchering the blameless members of the Hindu family. With his dying breath, the elder man of the Hindu family Kishan Lal presented his eyes to me, and left me with the question, 'How long are we going to keep hating one another and cutting off each other's heads?' I put Kishan Lal's eyes in the other inner pocket of my coat to keep them safe so that when they meet the eyes of the people who were killed across the border, I could help them to share their pain with each other.

Small pockets here and there in my coat also hold eyes, like those of the Sikhs in Chitti Singhpura, or those of the innocents in Pathribal who were killed by the army after being named as terrorists, but when there was an agitation and it was proved by the people that these martyred innocents had nothing whatsoever to do with terrorists, the government of that time instituted a commission of enquiry to find out the truth. The bodies of the dead were exhumed and DNA tests were carried out, and finally the government accepted that an error had been made. The army men at fault were subjected to a trial by court-martial, but no one was punished. And as for the innocents killed in Chitti Singhpura, there was not even a commission of inquiry. The eyes saw the manner in which court authorities dealt with these tragedies, and they exuded tears of blood. I wiped the blood from them, and kept them in my pockets, close to me, so that they might feel somewhat reassured. But these eyes ask me repeatedly, 'Will the scales of justice be always tilted in this country? When will justice look equally upon all?' How do I tell them that I have been seeing this since my early childhood that both sides are infected with the same morbid disease. The propaganda of terrorists on the one hand and the governments on the other has strangled the human soul, and destroyed the human capabilities of head and heart. Even the balm of the scriptures cannot cure this, for these people refuse to understand. Instead, they cover everything with trappings of words and empty rhetoric. What threatens them?

Can a mouse swallow a snake? Can ants break down a mountain? Or a deer hunt a lion? I see that my friends, wise as any Socrates, Mansoor and Sarmad, have lost heart, and my world was dead. There are no takers for their poetic visions, Lal Ded, Nund Rishi, Waris, Hashim and Bulle Shah are mad, they say. So I made a decision that I will not let these eyes stew in misery any more—I will release them. I dug a deep grave and took all the eyes out of my coat and buried them in the grave. Then I turned homewards, and on getting home, I made sure that I tore up all the scraps of my conscience. I nailed shut the door of my mind and heart, and I closed my eyes and waited for sleep.

In the morning when I opened my eyes, I was utterly amazed to see all the eyes that had been buried were fixed on the walls of my room. They were staring intently at me as if to prove that they were still very much alive.

Mitter Sen Meet

Mitter Sen Meet (b. 1952) was born in the village Botna in Sangrur district of Punjab. He studied law and became a public prosecutor in government service where he served till his retirement. His profession became the perspective from which he viewed society, to describe it realistically. While his earlier work is dominated by facts, in his later work, there is a mixture of both fact and fiction. His novels are prescribed reading for the training of police personnel. Meet's novels give a new breadth and range to the fictional world of Punjabi literature. He won the Sahitya Akademi award in 2008 for his novel *Sudhaar Ghar*.

The Investigation
(extract from the novel *Tafteesh*)

No one likes to suffer an indignity or an insult, not even the humblest of persons. Far less the police, who are certainly not used to such words. When they, who are used to hearing 'Sir',

'*Huzoor*', face such a situation, that someone should come to the station, be openly rude, free a prisoner and take him away, is hard to swallow.

Also, it was not just a matter of putting up with an affront; it was also a cause for action. This time, the Baba had succeeded in taking away a man from jail, next another religious leader would come, and after that, maybe some political ideologue would turn up. If this kind of thing carried on, it would not be long before the authority of the police lies in tatters.

Fearing a revolt, Lal Singh let all the suspects go. He did not even retain those men—Pala and Meeta. The previous station clerk insisted on it; he would not hand over charge to the new one till it was done. Pala and Meeta were familiar with all the secrets of the station, they had been detained there so often. They had become some sort of assistants to the clerk. When they were released, due to the clerk's constant pleading that Lal Singh could not refuse, they were safe in the knowledge that no one would pursue them outside, nor harm them when they were in the station.

The first two days, Lal Singh did little other than stretch his legs on his table and read the newspaper.

If the government is not in any hurry to apprehend the murderers, why the hell did he need to exert himself? What do the politicians care? If they sense their position is under threat or under political compulsion, they will make a scapegoat of someone or other. On the one hand, there was pressure on him to bring the murderers to book before the funeral ceremony took place; on the other hand, nothing was being done about the kingpin himself, the one who was not just a stumbling block, but the biggest obstacle in the investigation.

It was only logical that Lal Singh would adopt the same attitude towards the investigation as the higher officials. He put the investigation relating to Bunty aside, and began to deal with matters of petty crimes. The pace and frequency of such crimes had increased since the time the police had been concentrating on the murder cases. There were reports of drugs being sold openly, the distillation of illicit liquor had increased. The number of organisers of gambling and betting had also grown. Some brawls and scuffles had taken place.

Lal Singh's indifference lead to some peace and quiet in the city. There were no detentions, no inquiries, no processions, no unrest. The city went about its normal business, without trouble.

The new chief of police did not seem to want to let sleeping dogs lie. He demanded daily reports on the progress of the investigation. He was worried that there were only a few days left for the funeral ceremony, which the Chief Minister wanted to attend. But he could attend that function only if the murderers were found and booked, so that he would have something to tell the public.

The government was trying to show that it was serious. A reward of fifty thousand rupees for each apprehended assassin, was announced as an incentive to the police. It was even promised that the successful personnel would be promoted to the next rank. What would it cost the Chief Minister to do something like giving a higher rank? All he had to do was sign an order.

Lal Singh was content to wait and watch. The police did not have a magic lamp like that of Aladin, from which a genie could be conjured up and ordered to bring the murderers! It was the standard procedure of calling in suspects, and investigating them, that might yield results. Moreover, the investigation had to be quite thorough, as it was not possible to judge from appearances about anyone's guilt or innocence. There might even be some excesses committed during an investigation—that was part of it. It was pretty clear that until the kingpin, the Baba, who was the main hurdle, was not removed as an influence in the matter, Lal Singh had no freedom to bring in suspects and interrogate them.

Lal Singh had submitted the required report to the chief of police. He had mentioned that the Baba was not a small fry. He was well-known, and recognised even at the international level. As a mere police officer, if Lal Singh attempted to confront him, there would be an outcry which would spread throughout the country. No less a person than the Chief Minister could take the decision to arrest the Baba.

The Baba's network of supporters was not limited to the city. It spread out, covering the entire state, and included everyone of note. What was more, his supporters, unlike the Lala's, were not the wealthy, the businessmen, the industrialists or the marketers of religion, but the hot-blooded and impetuous young students studying in universities and colleges, hefty musclemen in the city, innocent farmers and the oppressed classes—all were devoted to him. The Baba had devoted his whole life to them and for their benefit, and they, in turn, were ready to lay down their lives for him.

Lal Singh had given this background to the chief of police, so that the latter would understand the kind of difficulty that faced the police, and Lal Singh's helplessness in the matter. But it appeared to Lal Singh that the chief was worried about saving his own skin Just as he was about to sign the order he hesitated, and finally did not commit himself.

Lal Singh was ordered to first establish a case against the Baba, present it in court, and get a court warrant for the Baba's arrest. In the meantime, the chief would try to get the Chief Minister's nod to proceed further.

This was not a difficult task for Lal Singh. Returning to the station, he immediately set to work and built up a hefty FIR (First Information Report). The charges were not baseless—he had obstructed the police, that is, government, in their duty. He had forcefully obtained a release for the suspects detained in the police station. He had entered the station and intimidated the policemen. Lal Singh cited a number of penal code violations in the report.

The Chief was not satisfied with this. He remarked that the whole thing looked false and unconvincing. Worse, it showed the police itself in a poor light. What kind of image did it reflect—a police force that could not restrain an old man from entering a police station and getting men released? A police force that could not even protect itself? What this report did was to make the Baba seem like some sort of hero who could mock the police with impunity, who could, even at his age, challenge the police and make it look weak and helpless.

Revise this report, he was told. The basis of the allegations should be a real event, not an obvious cook-up. The event that he should be implicated in should show the Baba in a bad light so that his support weakens, and people turn away from him.

There were two ways in which this could be done, which are the easiest ways to frame a person. Either brand him as a womaniser, rapist etc., or prove that he had embezzled funds. The Baba was too old to be convincingly labelled a womaniser. His organisation had not collected any funds which he could be accused of misappropriating. On the contrary, this was a man who had given away all that he owned, all his property, to the needy, and had worked for the welfare of many without thought of himself or of money, so no one would believe that he was guilty of illegally amassing wealth. Instead, those who tried to make such allegations stick, would themselves be laughed at, with contempt.

Lal Singh could think of just one strategy. A protest march against the Baba could be engineered. There would be trouble during the march. The Baba would be shown as responsible for the disorder, and it would be easy to arrest him. However, the problem was, who would organise the march? This question vexed him.

The Union was a group that was quite fed up with the police and its lackadaisical approach to the investigation. Every day, when they came to the police station to inquire about the progress of the investigation, Lal Singh had ready answers prepared for them.

'What do we have to gain from delaying? Will we get promoted for delay? But it is your Baba who does not allow anything to go forward. Any suspect that we call in for investigation has to be released because of the Baba's intervention. The Chief is also quiet—maybe he is also terrified of the Baba!'

Was the Union supposed to have an answer to this? If the suspects had to be released, it must have been due to their innocence. The Baba was not one to support acts of terror—why should he protect them?

Lal Singh sat with them in an inner room and spoke to them confidentially. 'Look, the Baba's record is not flawless. In the past, he has been a patron of many hot-headed militant youth groups.

Even today, these groups are part of his following. The crime we are talking about might actually have been committed by some of his men. They are after the intellectuals and the rationalists. They feel they are threatened because the rationalists question their pseudo-religious rituals. It may also be that Baba's men are jealous of Lalaji's influence. We surely have to do something about the Baba.'

The Union were convinced by Lal Singh's argument. It seemed the Baba wanted to put down Lalaji, or why would he go to all this trouble?

Lal Singh pushed ahead. If the union had understood the situation, they must help the police. (The Union would be useful in arranging the protest march—that was his plan).

The Union has no objection to helping the police. In fact, they wanted to, so that the murderers could be caught. The Union was ready to make any sacrifice for that.

It is the police who will make the sacrifice. The Union only needs to help.

To erode the Baba's position, it was necessary that a large number of people gather for the protest march. At that time, people would be told about the Baba's exploits. If the people became agitated, the Baba would not dare to start an encounter with the police.

But the Union did not have the ability to organise the march against the Baba. Firstly, because the Baba's supporters were many more in number than the members of the Union. Secondly, many within the ranks of the Union had sympathies for the Baba. And, to cap it all, some of the Baba's men were underground. They could come up at a moment's notice and open fire at the workers.

But Lal Singh did not really need many workers. He could do with as many as could participate. It was his responsibility to collect the other people to make up the crowd. The police only needed some younger people to raise slogans.

The Union need not be afraid of the undercover goons. The police would be accompanying the marchers, and he, Lal Singh, would be with them at every step. No one could do harm to any Union worker.

This must happen soon, before the Baba got wind of the plans through his informants. The march must take place as soon as possible.

If all the leaders of the Union have to do is to raise slogans, it can be done anytime.

They decided to hold the march that evening at four o'clock. It would start from the square where Bhagat Singh's statue stood, and end at the gate of the Baba's residence. The Union would keep it a low key affair. A few slogans would be raised—that was all. On reaching the Baba's residence, they would put a petition to him to refrain from hindering the police investigation into the murders. The Union was confident, that on their request, the Baba would agree to their demand which was quite a reasonable one.

When the march started off from the statue, there were about thirty people in the crowd. There were more policemen present than workers.

Darshan was concerned about the low strength. He feared that by the time they reached the Baba's residence, there would only be a few marchers left.

But as the march progressed, the number of supporters increased. At every street they crossed, a few more people joined the crowd. Seeing the crowd get larger, Darshan felt relieved. His slogan-shouting became louder. From the response he got, he could make out that people in the city were not happy with the Baba and were keen to see the murderers convicted.

Almost imperceptibly, the complexion of the crowd began to change. Hardly anyone was paying attention to Darshan's slogans now. Someone else was raising slogans, from amidst the crowd, and these were not the slogans that had been planned by the Union group. They were wild and abusive.

'Baba...Murderer of Bunty...dog...'

'Hang the Baba...'

'Protector of murderers...arrest him...'

'Burn, burn...burn the murderer...'

At the end of the market street, several unsavory characters joined the march. They had weapons—some were armed with sticks, some with axes, and some even had swords. Some had bricks and stones in their hands. Some of them even carried canisters of kerosene. Their shouts were heard over the noise, 'Kill him…kill the murderer, the traitor…burn him…'

Darshan was alarmed, and was dragging his feet, but Lal Singh seemed to be in a hurry. For Darshan, the turn of events was incomprehensible—he could not figure out who these people were. They were not the workers, nor did any of them belong to the city. But somehow they looked familiar.

Seeing Darshan wavering, a new leader scrambled on to the rickshaw. He grabbed the mike from Darshan, and began to shout slogans in favour of the youth organisation, the Lala and the police.

Darshan got off the rickshaw and breathed relief. Someone had also pulled down Ram Saroop from the rickshaw. He joined Darshan in the street. They were now simply onlookers—they were no longer in control, others had taken over. It was impossible to say what the outcome of all this would be.

Lal Singh whispered something to the new youth leaders. They march to the front of the Baba's house.

Lal Singh's informants had told him that the news of the march against the Baba had reached not only all parts of the city, but also the neighboring villages. And from there, many groups were gathering and preparing to come to the Baba's support. From near the slums, a group led by the leader Shamu of the Punjab Students' union had already started out, and they had some scythes, trowels and other tools in their hands. Informed of this, a contingent of policemen had been detailed to stop them in the way.

The workers at the thread mill had struck work, and led by Ashok, they too were on the way, making a hubbub as they approached.

One group of the Revolutionary Front had reached the gate of the Baba's house.

The rationalists' party was gathering at the Agarwal Dharamshala, which was near the Baba's house. At any moment there could be a confrontation.

In several villages, the news had been broadcast on loudspeakers amongst the villagers, and a call had gone out for them to come to the city. Some truckloads of villagers had already set forth for the city.

All the shops in the market had downed their shutters.

Lal Singh realised that things were getting out of control. There was a real possibility that a violent confrontation might take place. If this occurred, Lal Singh would have to pay.

He circulated among the crowd, and gave instructions to some of the men who were participating in the sloganeering.

Very soon, the marchers had covered the remaining distance and within minutes, were near their goal. As they reached the gates of the Baba's house, brickbats and stones began to rain on to the front doors. There were attempts to break down the doors with sticks and axes.

'O you fraud, come out. Come out if you dare..,'

'Let us see how you escape. Bring out the murderers you are hiding inside!'

'Destroy the traitor! Destroy his family!' The shouts grew louder along with the pelting of stones and bricks.

The men carrying the canisters of kerosene rushed forward and began to sprinkle the kerosene on the doors. Someone was about to light the flame, when the Baba roared from atop the roof of the house.

'Men from Union, where are you? Are you stupid? Can't you see that all these men are from the police and are paid troublemakers? Come to your senses, you fools! This is the plot of the police to make us fight one another!'

The Baba's powerful voice subdued the crowd. The raised arms with sticks and axes were lowered and some of the crowd tried to slink away out of sight. The Baba stood defiantly on the rooftop. A few armed young men stood around him, protecting him. They had trained their guns on particular persons in the crowd.

'If anybody tries to move ahead, we will shoot everyone,' an armed youth shouted, and at this, the man with the canister of kerosene dropped it, spilling most of the kerosene on himself.

From the other side of the marchers, the advancing rationalists' group could hear the noise of the ruckus. Before they reached the spot, there was the sound of a gunshot from someone in the crowd who had fired into the air.

Immediately, there were rapid gunshots fired into the air from the rooftop. The crowd scattered in all directions. The marchers fled, leaving behind here or there, a shoe, or a turban, or a scarf, in their haste.

A few more gunshots were heard, and then all was quiet from both sides.

The action that Lal Singh had wanted was over. He was now able to slap watertight charges, citing the penal code, on the Baba—disruption of peace, attempt to cause discord between two communities, shielding criminals and instigating violence, firing into the crowd with intent to cause deaths, obstructing the police in their action and sedition against the state.

But the Chief of Police was not terribly pleased at the turn of events. Even though the event actually happened, it was not cooked up, the whole city had been a witness to it, photographers had taken pictures, reporters had covered the event and given their reports. The general public was quite angry at the Baba's behavior. His men should not have fired at unarmed people.

The Chief fobbed off Lal Singh with nothing more than an assurance. Of course, the government will take action in this case—why should it not take heed when the case against the Baba was so solid?

By this time, it was the second day after the march. The Baba's supporters had lost no time in stepping up propaganda to defend him. Within a couple of days, they succeeded in convincing the people that the march had been contrived by the police. The entire plan had been made by the police and the men involved were also engaged by the police. The supporters got the photographic records enlarged and circulated them through the city, in which some of the familiar faces from the police could be seen quite clearly.

The Baba's organization reached out to Darshan and Ram Saroop and were able to co-opt them. The two of them accepted their role in the matter, and also confessed that they had initiated the march on the suggestion of the police.

Since the government was still keeping mum about it, Lal Singh anticipated a reversal awaiting him. He vowed he would have nothing more to do with the case. Let the investigation take its course! Let the Chief Minister's promise go to hell! If the CM was not bothered, why should the police care?

Sensing the rumble of agitation among the public, Lal Singh applied for leave for ten days. He would return after that function at the funeral was over.

But instead of the acceptance of his leave application, the consent for the Baba's arrest was issued, and Lal Singh was vastly relieved.

The Chief Minister gave full power to Lal Singh. He was allowed to arrest the Baba as well as his supporters. If they applied for bail, he could invoke the National Security Act.

Lal Singh was satisfied. Finally, he had had a chance to show what he could do.

6
Drama

I. C. Nanda

I. C. Nanda (1892–1965) was born in village Gandhian in Gurdaspur district. He was a professor of English and retired as Principal, Government College, Lahore in 1947. As a playwright, Nanda was cast in Henrik Ibsen's mould and is known as the father of Punjabi stage drama. The Irish drama artist Norah Richards influenced and inspired him. He took up themes such as child marriage, love marriage, widow remarriage and mismatched marriages. He favoured a liberal attitude towards life and supported the change in social values. However, despite his social commitment, Nanda did not look for radical and constructive solutions to social problems; rather, he looked for solutions that were mysterious and indirect.

The Bride
(An excerpt from the closing scene)

Characters

Lajo:	A six or seven-year-old girl
Melo:	Lajo's elder sister, about seventeen or eighteen years of age
Hushiar Chand:	Lajo and Melo's father
Kauran:	Lajo and Melo's mother
Basanto:	Melo's friend
Bhulli:	A *nain*, the barber's wife
Pandha:	A Brahmin priest or teacher; astrologer who performs wedding rituals

[*Hushiar Chand, wretchedly poor and struggling to make ends meet, arranges his young daughter Melo's marriage with a widower, who is old enough to have grandchildren. The marriage procession is about to arrive at their doorstep but Melo is unaware of it.*]

Melo:	*(Alone)* I don't understand. Wedding! Tonight! Whose wedding? The *baraat* is about to arrive! Who were they talking about? Us? No, no! Money? From where? Why was father getting so angry? Well, let Bebe come, everything will become clear. It's very surprising indeed!
A voice:	*(From outside)* Melo, O Melo!
Melo:	*(Recognising the voice)* Basanto, why're you calling me from outside? Why don't you come in? *(Basanto comes in)*
Basanto:	*(In a teasing manner)* Congratulations, girl!
Melo:	You shouldn't tease me all the time.
Basanto:	Is that so? Do you think I'm teasing you? As if I don't know that you're getting married! Girl, you will forget us completely once you go to your in-laws' house.
Melo:	Whether anybody is getting married or not, you have to tease.
Basanto:	Well, however one may try, do such things ever remain hidden? You may or may not tell me, but I know it already.
Melo:	What! What're you saying?
Basanto:	As if you aren't aware of it? Bhulli *nain*, the barber's wife left your house just now. I heard everything from her. She says that your in-laws live near her parents' house.
Melo:	You're making it all up just to fool me!
Basanto:	No Melo, I'm telling you the truth. Your in-laws are very rich. You're very lucky; you don't even have a mother-in-law, which is rather good as there's nobody to quarrel with you.

Melo:	Still teasing me! You're always joking, making fun ... well, since you're married yourself, you tease others!
Basanto:	Don't you worry; you're also getting married very soon. Your husband, may God bless him, is an old man. They say he's ten years older than even your father.
Melo:	Keep quiet; don't bark so much. God willing, you'll also get such a son-in-law!
Basanto:	But, Melo, I'm telling the truth. I'm not joking. He has sons and grandsons and then Bhulli was saying that just last year he had married off his daughter, she's your age.
Melo:	That's enough! Stop joking!
Basanto:	I'm not joking, my friend. That's the truth.
Melo:	I don't believe you.
Basanto:	*(Earnestly)* I swear in the name of the goddess, I'm not joking. Why should I lie? Rather, I felt very sad when I heard about it.
Melo:	Is that really true? Oh my God! *(She sighs, sits on the ground and covers her face with her chunni)* Oh! Now I understand everything! *(Holding her head in both her hands, she sways forwards and backwards)* How unfortunate I am! My luck has deserted me! What do I do now?
Basanto:	You *(sympathetically, putting an arm around her)* ... no, no, don't cry like this. My sister, stop crying!
Melo:	*(Weeping)* Go away, leave me alone! Oh my God! I wish I wasn't born! My own parents have turned my enemies! I'll commit suicide! Now what's there for me to live for!
Basanto:	Why, but why? May your enemies die, why you?
Melo:	I'll consume opium, hang myself, jump into a well! A moment's pain is better than a whole life of suffering. Please go away; just leave me alone!

Basanto:	Don't lose heart! May I suggest something to you?
Melo:	What can you suggest to me, my friend? Whatever is my fate will happen! Very soon, I'll be damned!
Basanto:	Listen to me Melo, get up, cover your face with a *chunni* and run away to your masi's village ... nobody will come to know. Go away this very moment; we'll see what happens later. Just go, hurry up!
Melo:	No, no, this isn't possible. Let me die, my redemption lies in that!
Basanto:	*(Taking her in her arms)* Melo! Melo! Get up. *(She forces her to get up.)*
Voice:	*(From outside, off the stage)* Melo's mother!
Basanto:	Melo, Melo, hurry up! Don't let this opportunity slip away. *(She drags her.)*
Melo:	*(Sighing)* I'll jump into a well! I'll jump into a well ... no I won't ... *(Basanto drags her away forcibly.)*
Melo:	*(Offstage)* I'll kill myself; I'll kill myself.
Voice:	*(From outside, near the stage)* Melo's mother, O Melo's mother!
Hushiar Chand:	Melo's mother? *(Peers into the room)* She must've gone out. The elders have rightly said that women have no brains. There're so many things to be done, she shouldn't have gone out. But women can't stay home. They can't rest till they haven't been to seven houses like a cat. *(Kauran and Lajo come jumping and dancing. Lajo goes to her dolls and sits there.)*
Hushiar Chand:	Why did you go out? Will you ever listen to me or not?
Kauran:	I was going to *nain* Bhulli's house for a minute when I met Karmo's mother on the way and got a little late talking to her.

Hushiar Chand:	Women don't stop gossiping and gossip doesn't leave them. Dealing with fools is always a loss-making proposition.
Kauran:	Well, you always talk like that. Now tell me about the *baraat*.
Hushiar Chand:	It has arrived and all arrangements are made. They're almost next door *(Sound of drums and trumpets is heard from a distance)*. See, they're already there. They'll be here in a moment.
Kauran:	Then let me bring the *salu*. *(Takes out the red salu from a suitcase and drapes it over her head and shoulders).*
Pandha:	*(From outside)* Maharaj, hurry up. Why're you late?
Hushiar Chand:	There's no delay, Pandha ji. You go, we're coming. *(To Kauran)* Call the girl, dress her up in new clothes and be quick.
Kauran:	The girl isn't here; she must be inside. *(Goes towards the inner room)* Melo, O Melo! Why're you hiding girl? Hurry up! This is no time to feel shy. Be quick, my precious daughter.
Hushiar Chand:	Girl, where're you hiding? Why don't you come out? Hurry up!
Pandha:	*(From outside)* Maharaj, the time is running out, they're asking for you.
Hushiar Chand:	Pandha ji, you go, we'll join you soon. We're getting her ready. *(To Kauran)* Why don't you do something? Go inside and lead her out. Is this the time to be bashful?
Kauran:	*(Goes into the room)* Melo, please come out, my love! Why're you scared? Please come, Melo, my daughter Melo. *(Kauran comes out, rubbing her hands)* The girl isn't here, what shall we do now? Oh! What shall we do now?
Hushiar Chand:	No, no, she must be there, call her! *(Authoritatively)* Call her!

Kauran:	Melo, O Melo! Where've you gone at this moment! *(Hushiar Chand also looks around and calls out to her)* Oh! We've been disgraced; the girl isn't here, what shall we do now? She might've run away somewhere. Oh! We stand disgraced!
Hushiar Chand:	Didn't I tell you not to leave the house! Now sit here and repent!
Kauran:	O girl, O girl! Oh! We'll have to face public disgrace! Who shall we take to the *laavaan*? Oh my God! What do I do now?
Pandha:	*(From outside)* O Maharaj, Maharaj! I've already come here thrice, why don't you come? The auspicious time for the wedding is running out. The priest from the groom's side is getting impatient.
Hushiar Chand:	*(In a defeated voice)* You go, Pandha ji, we're coming. *(To Kauran)* Now tell me, what's to be done? How're we going get through this difficult situation?
Kauran:	Oh! I wish I hadn't given birth to a daughter! What can I say? I can't think of anything.
Hushiar Chand:	Be quick. Put the wedding *chunni* on Lajo, otherwise we won't be able to raise our heads.
Kauran:	*(She moves away from him with a start and holds the chunni tightly)* Oh! No, no, no ... Oh! This is injustice, this is injustice!
Hushiar Chand:	What injustice? *(He snatches the chunni from Kauran, puts it on Lajo who's playing with her dolls, picks her up in his arms and takes her away.)*
Kauran:	*(Running after him, shrieking and beating her thighs with both her hands)* Oh God! Injustice has been done, grave injustice!
Lajo:	*(Arms and legs flailing to free herself from her father's grip)* My dolls, my dolls! Let me play with my dolls!

—Curtain—

Harcharan Singh

Harcharan Singh (1915–2006) was born in Chak No. 576, District Shekhupura (now in Pakistan). He taught Punjabi literature and retired from Punjabi University, Patiala. . He won the Sahitya Akademi award in 1973 for his play *Kall, Ajj te Bhalak*. He is one of the pioneers of Punjabi drama. He deals with the problems of common people in his plays. After I. C. Nanda, he carried forward Henrik Ibsen's realism and foregrounded social issues in his plays. Like Nanda, he addressed contemporary issues; hence his plays retain their social relevance. Working in Sikh history into his plays, deft construction of the plot structure of the plays, writing plays regularly and making efforts to present them on the stage, and striking an alliance with an able theatre artist Harpal Tiwana, are his other shining achievements.

Unfulfilled Desire

Characters:

Ambo (Amar Kaur)
Sheru
Karmo
Lambardar
Karma
Raja

Scene: A dilapidated house facing east in the middle of a village; its door opens into a narrow, dirty street. Under the neem tree in the courtyard, a beautiful, tall woman, about 30, is sitting on a low cot applying kohl to her eyes. Almost all her clothes are new. She appears ecstatic but sometimes, sorrow casts a gloomy shadow on her face. She picks up the mirror and is very happy to gaze at her reflection. The door is pushed from outside. She immediately places the phial of kohl and the mirror on the floor and gets up to open the door.

From outside: Ambo, Ambo! Are you ready or not?

Ambo:	*(Covers her head and face and then opens the door)* Yes, what else? Did I have to harness the horses? *(Sheru can be seen in the door. He is a young man of about thirty. Wearing a string of black beads, loose loincloth made of coarse material, he sports a dark brown turban with a plume. His moustache and face are smeared with attar.)*
Sheru:	*(Twirling his moustache)* How beautiful you look; I can't even describe it!
Ambo:	Come in, why've you stopped at the door?
Sheru:	*(Smiling)* I thought, perhaps you haven't recognised me.
Ambo:	If I don't recognise you, then who else will I recognise?
Sheru:	Then why did you cover your face? Your own people don't cast an evil eye. Lift the veil a little. Let me have a glimpse of your face.
Ambo:	*(Lifting the veil and laughing)* I feel very shy of you today.
Sheru:	*(Gazing at her face)* Ambo, look at me for a moment.
Ambo:	Why, tell me!
Sheru:	I thought I should remove all my doubts about you being someone else. I swear you look totally different today. You're bright and beautiful like the Naina Devi Temple after the rains!
Ambo:	*(Turning around as she laughs)* Really?
Sheru:	I say you're some fairy from the skies, a fairy.
Ambo:	Just leave it now; don't go on embarrassing me like that.
Sheru:	It isn't a lie. It's the first time I've seen you so happy.
Ambo:	I don't know what has happened to me after meeting you. It appears as if fourteen years of sorrow have turned into joy in a moment.

Sheru:	Ambo, you haven't seen anything yet! *(Lovingly)* You fool, you've been living in a hell till now.
Ambo:	*(Drawing a deep breath)* There's no doubt about it, a veritable hell.
Sheru:	Well, earrings, bangles, pump shoes and clothes, is everything alright?
Ambo:	Everything that you've brought is very good!
Sheru:	Is there anything missing? Tell me, what's this thing called 'watch chain'?
Ambo:	When did you come to know about it?
Sheru:	Yesterday when I was going to the city, two city women were sitting in my tonga. One of them said, 'I've made a watch chain for my daughter-in-law.' She was praising to the skies the goldsmith who had made it.
Ambo:	*(Smiling)* It's an ornament to be worn on the wrist, but it's very costly.
Sheru:	Don't worry about money. I may have to mortgage two fields, but I'll definitely get you a watch chain. Don't forget that you're dealing with a *Jat*!
Ambo:	I need nothing more. Now that you're with me, I've got everything.
Sheru:	Ambo, we're here not to merely pass time; living well and enjoying life, only these two things matter to me. I know how to keep myself fit and happy. This life is to be enjoyed; who's seen the next one? We don't have to waste our life, my dear. We're on this earth for a short time, we have to live life to the hilt; we aren't born again and again.
Ambo:	*(Pushing the cot towards him)* Sit down, just for a while.
Sheru:	We'll sit under the shade of the *tahli* at the well when I'll be working in the fields and you'll bring me my food.
Ambo:	*(Drawing a deep breath)* Where I used to pick the wheat stalks?

Sheru:	Forget about the past now, you'll be the queen of these fields, the queen!
Ambo:	And you, the king!
Sheru:	But I'm king only if you're there. I only know that life has no meaning if you don't get the woman of your choice. *(Looking at her and laughing ecstatically)* There are very few well-matched couples in this world; others, yoked to each other, just waste away.
Ambo:	*(Laughing and holding his hand)* Are you serious or are you saying this just to make me happy?
Sheru:	Ambo, since my childhood I've cherished only one wish.
Ambo:	What?
Sheru:	Well, one must have a life partner of one's liking, otherwise it's better to have none. And now ultimately God has granted me my wish.
Ambo:	But the desires of girls remain buried in their hearts. Parents yoke them with anyone they like and then it's survival!
Sheru:	Actually, God had made you my partner; it was luck that took a different turn, but that's over now. You should thank God.
Ambo:	*(With tears in her eyes)* I'm really very angry with my parents who spoiled my youth by tying me to a drunkard.
Sheru:	*(Consoling her)* Nothing is lost even now Ambo; you're now in the place where you truly belong.
Ambo:	I worry that I may end up in the gutter once again.
Sheru:	Forget about it, dear. *(Looking up towards the neem tree)* Look, the way new leaves have sprouted on this *neem*, you too are born anew.
Ambo:	*(With a deep sigh)* These sprout every year. But my desires haven't sprouted even once in the last fourteen years.

Sheru:	May God bless you! Now they'll sprout every year! *(They laugh uninhibitedly)*
Ambo:	You seem to be very happy today, like you were on that day.
Sheru:	Which day? Tell me; please tell me, for my sake.
Ambo:	There was a fair that day when you were feeding water to your cattle at the well and I'd gone there to fill my pitcher.
Sheru:	Believe me Ambo, from that day onwards I began thinking about you. You'd left with your pitcher but I stood there for quite a while thinking of your lot and crying over it. I didn't even go to the fair. Don't ask me how sad I was!
Ambo:	*(Surprised)* Is it true?
Sheru:	On that very day I resolved that, come what may, I'll end all your sorrows. I gave up all my arrogant ways and turned into a person of extremely modest means. I begged and entreated everyone; only then did I succeed in persuading the villagers to permit me to marry you.
Ambo:	*(With great sympathy)* That means you had to suffer so much for my sake!
Sheru:	But how I enjoyed this suffering, only I know. It was like the strong kick that foreshots give a drinker, and the days passed in a state of heady intoxication.
From outside:	Chowdhry ji!
Sheru:	Who's it? Are you Raja?
From outside:	Chowdhry! I've been round the entire village looking for you.
Sheru:	Well, how long will it take now?
From outside:	The *Panch* are just waiting for you. Everyone is there.
Sheru:	Well, then, go on, I'm coming. *(Looking at Ambo)* Why're you so disturbed?

Ambo:	He knocked at the door and I almost died with fear; I thought it was my sister-in-law. My heart is pounding even now.
Sheru:	Let her come; we aren't afraid of anyone.
Ambo:	You don't know; she's the devil.
Sheru:	When the bride and the groom have agreed, then no magistrate can interfere. We've sealed our love by exchanging our hearts.
Ambo:	Take at least my clothes to your home; she might actually come here.
Sheru:	We aren't taking anything from here. I'll fill the home with everything. *(Leaving)* Now, get ready soon; we need to leave.
Ambo:	I just have to wear a *ghagra*!
Sheru:	Then do so now, we'll go together.
Ambo:	You go; I feel shy wearing it in front of you.
Sheru:	Is that so? Your shyness will vanish in a few days. *(She goes in. A moment later, a woman hurries in. She appears to be greatly agitated.)*
Karmo:	*(Looking around)* Bhabhi Amar Kaur! *(Ambo comes out holding the ghagra and she begins to tremble on seeing Karmo)*
Ambo:	Bibi, what brings you here?
Karmo:	Bhabhi, I can't tell you; last night I heard a rumour, it could be true or false, but I couldn't eat anything afterwards.
Ambo:	*(Fearlessly)* Why false? It's true.
Karmo:	Oh! What have you done!
Ambo:	Go to the panchayat and ask those who've done all this!
Karmo:	Tell me what your problem is.
Ambo:	Bibi, if you were a widow like me, only then could I tell you my problem!
Karmo:	*(Beating her thighs with her hands)* Oh! You must be happy now; having killed my brother even when he is alive! You slut!

Ambo:	The one who left home twelve years ago, didn't send a letter, no news, not even a penny; for me, he's dead and gone.
Karmo:	You bitch, tell me what you lack in this house? What's it that you don't have?
Ambo:	Do I have my father's estate to live on? Only I know how I've been living the life of privation. Today you've come because of your brother, to assert your proprietary rights on me! Where were you when I was keeping myself alive by grinding grains for others and cleaning cattle sheds?
Karmo:	*(Looking inside the room)* You eloper, which lover of yours have you given this house to?
Ambo:	What was there in this house? Dirt and dross of the whole neighbourhood! He had gone away only after squandering on liquor whatever little there was.
Karmo:	Look at that! What's happening to this world! Women in the past spent their entire life waiting for their men!
Ambo:	I did no less; I've spent twelve years counting each day! It's easier said than done, *bibi*; a person realises it only when one has to pass time like I did!
Raja:	*(From outside)* You're late, everyone's waiting for you.
Ambo:	I'm coming. *(Holding the ghagra)* Let go of my *ghagra*, the *laagi* has come calling again; what will people say?
Karmo:	*(Softening)* Bhabhi, do as I tell you. You've spent a long time like that; wait for a few days more. I received a card from him the day before yesterday. He has written, 'I'm boarding a plane.' I think he should be here in a day or two.
Ambo:	Patience too has certain limits. I've wasted my golden youth waiting for him. Moreover, even if he does come back he won't put me on a throne; there'll be the same bullying and beating again!

Karmo:	From the first day I could see that you had dissolute habits. This isn't a new thing!
Ambo:	Had I been of this type, I wouldn't have lived in this hut for fourteen years! I'd have done something disgraceful and eloped with someone long ago!
Karmo:	(*Screaming and cursing Ambo*) Ambo, you're bringing disgrace to us by getting married to one of our relatives; they're our rivals. May you never find solace even in the next world! I'll go and plead in front of the wicked panchayat and see how they allow you to remarry. With my brother alive, who has the guts to do such an immoral thing? (*She starts moving. Lambardar enters*)
Lambardar:	(*A bit angry*) Girl, what're you doing here? The entire village is waiting for you!
Ambo:	Taiya ji, *bibi* didn't allow me to come. Tell me, what could I do?
Karmo:	(*Wailing loudly*) Ambo, the way you're dragging the good name of the family in dust, may you never find peace in either world!
Lambardar:	Bibi, why're you making such a fuss? Let go of her *ghagra*. Don't be a fool; everything has been settled.
Ambo:	Taiya, she's a pervert, but you didn't think about that either?
Lambardar:	Oh God! There isn't a noble daughter like her in the whole world. The fortitude with which she endured a life of privation, nobody can do that. She could've managed even if she had two fields of her own; I don't know how she has been managing to survive! The village took pity on her to bring her sufferings to an end. That braggart may not even have realised it, but this poor girl is almost starving to death.
Karmo:	He has been away for so long; the day he comes back he'll fill the entire house with everything. What do you think of my brother?

Lambardar:	We jolly well know what a breadwinner he is! Besides this, who knows if he'll come at all?
Karmo:	Taiya, he's boarded the plane. Just wait for a few days more.
	(Sheru returns)
Sheru:	What're you doing Ambo? The *laagi* was sent so many times to fetch you. *(Seeing the Lambardar)* And we gave so much trouble to *Taiya* also.
Lambardar:	What could she do, Karmo didn't allow her to go.
Sheru:	Who's Karmo to stop her?
Lambardar:	Boy, keep quiet! Let me talk to her myself.
Karmo:	*(To Sheru)* Go away and get lost. Lord it over your mother or sister! Be warned, don't dare say anything to me!
Sheru:	What have I got to do with you? A big queen, you think you are!
Karmo:	You rascal, now that you're bent upon spoiling our reputation, you're going to be in trouble!
Lambardar:	Keep quiet Karmo! Don't go on like that!
Sheru:	Then why don't we move now? Why this delay?
Lambardar:	Don't be in a hurry, we'll go; let me convince her. Karmo, move aside, let the daughter-in-law go.
One Person:	Lambardara! Karma has come back.
Everyone:	What? Where?
Lambardar:	Where has he come from at this moment, to spoil everything?
	(Someone coughs at the door. Everyone looks in that direction. A weak, emaciated and sickly person comes in.)
Karma:	*(Greeting everyone)* Wah-e-Guru ji ki fateh! How are you Lambardara?
Lambardar:	Karmeya, is it you? I can't believe my eyes!
Karma:	Are you alright Karmo? *(Seeing her in tears)* You fool, you shouldn't cry like that.
Karmo:	*(Hugging him)* Thank God you've come back, my brother. We've waited so long for you!

Karma:	I didn't want to come now either, but my disease gets worse each day. I'd written a letter to you.
Karmo:	But you didn't write anything about your disease.
Lambardar:	*(Addressing Karma)* Tell me gentleman; shouldn't you have informed us about your whereabouts? It's been a long time since you left this place.
Karma:	Lambardara, you know me, I haven't changed at all.
	(He coughs very loudly)
Karmo:	Brother, hasn't your asthma been cured yet?
Lambardar:	He mustn't have given up drinking.
Karma:	I may come back after going round the whole world, but I remain the same.
Karmo:	Is your luggage in the tonga?
Karma:	*(Laughing)* What luggage do I have except the clothes I'm wearing?
Lambardar:	He's returned empty-handed just the way he went. What could this worthless fellow have earned!
Karmo:	*(With a sigh)* Well, I've got everything now that my brother is back.
Karma:	Well, Lambardara, tell me about the village? Anything new?
Lambardar:	Everything is fine. *(Understanding the situation)* Karmo, first give him some water and only thereafter talk about anything else.
Karma:	Karmo, when did you come here?
Karmo:	I came just now; I haven't even taken off my *jutti*.
Karma:	Good that you've come; you must've been expecting my arrival.
Karmo:	Sit down on this cot, brother.
Karma:	*(Looking at the new clothes and other adornments lying there)* What beautiful things are here!
Karmo:	Bhabhi Amar Kaur, come out, bring water and serve it with the grace of God.

Karma:	Amar Kaur? Is she still alive? I thought she must've been dead by now. I was also wondering about this lady who went in!
Karmo:	*(Looking into the room)* Come brother, quick.
Karma:	What happened?
Karmo:	God knows what's happened to Bhabhi; she's fallen prostrate on the ground.
	(Holding her in her arms, Karmo brings Ambo to the door)
Karma:	*(Seeing her)* She's wearing such beautiful clothes waiting for me! Where did she get all this treasure from?
Karmo:	No, brother, it's a different story. Hold her, let me pour water into her mouth.
Karma:	Ambo, look, I've come back.
	(Ambo opens her eyes once and loses consciousness again on seeing Karma. Karma trembles on seeing her; momentarily his entire past flashes in front of him. On seeing her face, he looks frightened like a guilty person. Karmo pours water into Ambo's mouth. The curtain falls.)

Balwant Gargi

Balwant Gargi (1916–2003) was born in village Sehna, district Bathinda. He did his Masters in English and Political Science in Lahore. He later retired from the Indian Theatre Department at Punjab University, Chandigarh. Initially he wrote in English and Urdu, but after meeting Rabindranath Tagore, Gargi took to writing full length and one-act plays in Punjabi. He also wrote pen-portraits, novels and research papers. He received the 1962 Sahitya Akademi Award for his well-researched book *Rangmanch*. He was honoured with Padma Shri in 1972 and the Sangeet Natak Akademi award in 1998. He ushered in a new wave in the field of Punjabi drama, exploring the subtleties and nuances of human relationships and social oppressions. His plays are well-knit and his stagecraft remarkable.

The Night of the Tempest

Characters:

Surjeet:	A boatman
Deepo:	His wife
Lajo:	His sister
Sundar:	His friend
Bhua:	Aunt (father's sister)

(A hut near the banks of a river. Oars, ropes and fishing nets lie strewn. Towards the back of the stage, a sick Bhua is lying on a low cot. Deepo and Lajo are talking to each other. Deepo is blowing into the hearth to stoke the fire.)

Lajo: Deepo!

Deepo: Yes.

Lajo: Bhua is dying and she has a cough; maybe she's choking. Once she starts choking, she regains her breath with great difficulty. Has the concoction come to a boil?

Deepo: No, not yet. I've been trying my best to stoke the fire by blowing into it, but there's no heat in the hearth today, as it were.

Lajo: We've been giving her this concoction for two days but there's no relief; rather her breathlessness is getting worse. Go and bring the same medicine from Kansi *vaid* which he gave earlier.

Deepo: The night is very wet, the river is in spate; how can I go?

Lajo: After giving her this concoction, massage her chest. The massage may perhaps give her some warmth. I'll look for someone outside. *(Looking out)* Oh my God! The water in the river has risen very high; the waves are reaching the thatch of our hut. You pulled the boat out and tied it to the tree, right?

Deepo: It has been securely tied. No harm will come to it.

[*A song is heard:*
Steer my boat to the bank
Tired are the questing feet
Agonized, the hoping eyes
Unknown yet is the journey's end
Steer my boat to the bank]

Lajo: Who is singing at this hour?
Deepo: I don't know who it is.
Lajo: Do you hear the splash of oars?
Deepo: Yes.
Lajo: All boatmen of the village have dragged their boats to the bank. Who could this be?
Deepo: Can't say; the river is badly swollen.
Lajo: Yes. Look how the winds are howling, as if they'll blow everything away!
Deepo: Lajo, I've always dreaded the storm.
Lajo: The storm reminds me of the day when my brother went away leaving you behind.
Deepo: Don't remind me of that day, Lajo.
Lajo: I can't forget it. I've told you so many times that this hut is unlucky, we should've left it. But you didn't agree.
Deepo: How can I leave this hut? I've spent full six years in it. Your brother brought me here as a bride in a palanquin. In the light of this very lantern you had lifted my bridal veil and seen my face. You had led me into this very hut. I love it. So many memories lie buried here.
Lajo: Your son died in this ill-omened hut!
Deepo: Yes, my little one was born here and died here. The sun had set. Lamps had been lit. Lifting him in my hands I had only walked ten steps away to bury him. How can I leave this hut?
Lajo: I am very scared. My own self is out to devour me.

Deepo:	Often I go to his small grave. A portion of my entrails lies buried there. My mind too is a grave where countless desires and memories lie buried.
Lajo:	Stop talking about all these things now! Take the lantern and get the medicine from Kansi *vaid*. I'll attend to Bhua in the meantime.
Deepo:	The light of the lantern is unsteady. Look, how the wind is howling! The shadows on the wall are trembling. There're shadows of many memories in this hut. I'm weighed down by the burden of these shadows. This net, these ropes and this broken oar; using this oar, your brother crossed to the other side of the river many a time.
Lajo:	He left because he was sick of your bad ways.
Deepo:	My bad ways?
Lajo:	Yes! You were besotted with Sundar even when you knew that my brother loved you to no end! All the boatmen of the village were on one side, and my brother on the other! Despite everyone advising him to the contrary, he still brought you here.
Deepo:	I too gave up everyone, left all the handsome young men of the village and came with him.
Lajo:	This is why he was ready to die for you. He would've forgiven you for everything, but you fell in love with his friend Sundar. As they say, even a witch spares the near ones.
Deepo:	Lajo, Lajo, please, please keep quiet for God's sake!
Lajo:	This one action of yours tore my brother apart from me forever.
Deepo:	Lajo, Lajo I swear by the boat, I swear by the river bank, I had no such love for Sundar.
Lajo:	Foolish woman, is love of different types? Is love like a flower or cloth that is available in different varieties? Love is love, just as the water of Sutlej is water. You did love Sundar.

Deepo: No! No!
Lajo: I know it.
Deepo: Don't insult me, Lajo. You're suffering from want of love in your life. Your lover died of a fever. You didn't marry anyone because of your love for him. In the name of love, don't say all that!
Lajo: Even now when you see Sundar, you start trembling. When you hear his voice from a distance your fingers stop kneading the flour. Your ears become alert like that of a frightened mare.
Deepo: Lajo! Lajo!!
Lajo: A woman must stay sincere to only one man.
Deepo: *(Sighing)* I know that.
Lajo: I've seen these tears of yours many times. And I also know for whom you're shedding them.
Deepo: Lajo!
Lajo: What I say is true.
Deepo: But Lajo, is it a sin to even think a little about some other person? A small eddy, a wave that rises spontaneously.
Lajo: Yes.
Deepo: Oh! What do I do with this mind of mine? I've kept it chained, very tightly, steering clear of storms, away from the tides. It's like a boat anchored in that part of the shallows where the waves of the sea can touch it but can't unmoor it. Even so, why was Surjeet so angry? He knew that I am his alone.
Lajo: In the matters of love, no man's mind can ever be deceived. You loved Sundar. Such love flows from your eyes as will make a man mad for the rest of his life. You did love Sundar.
Deepo: But what's my fault in this? My mind is of this type. God has made it like this. You tell me what's my fault if my ears resemble oyster shells, if my nose is small and if my neck is long? How do I rectify all these? My heart is also like this, brimming with passion.

	If I had a bigger nose, if I had smallpox marks on my face and if I had a black mark on my forehead, then nobody would love me, not even Sundar!
Lajo:	Don't talk nonsense.
Deepo:	I don't know what attracts me to Sundar. He is different from the others. He talks little, just stands and watches, innocently. Forgive me! Oh my God! What am I saying!
Lajo:	Have you never met Sundar?
Deepo:	No. Never. He passes by me. After I've pushed the boat from the ford, I pass by him. When I see him, I can feel my entire body quivering in excitement. My tongue gets stuck to the palate. Now I'll never talk to him. I am full of fear.
Lajo:	Are you scared of him?
Deepo:	No, I fear myself. I fear my passion, my fate!
Lajo:	Why?
Deepo:	Do you remember that night when Surjeet had gone to watch the acrobats, where torch-bearers holding big torches in their hands lighted the arena? I had stayed back home. In the meantime, Sundar came. That day, the river was in spate and he had gone to the other side of the river in his boat. He kept the oars and nets here. He stood near me. His biceps were glistening in the light of the lamp, and I felt them with my hand.
Lajo!	You fool!
Deepo:	I felt them just for the heck of it; they were hard like stone. I felt like biting into them.
Lajo:	Foolish woman, this is what love is!
Deepo:	I felt them for no reason. He touched with his fingers my neck, below my cheek, here *(pointing towards her neck)*—where a lock of my hair fell. That night the storm was raging as it is today, and the water in the river was rising in the same way. My entire

	being trembled at his touch, his first touch . . . and I closed my eyes and rested my head on his chest. At that very moment your brother entered and stood behind me. His eyes burned red with anger. He had an oar in his hand. On seeing me he lifted the oar; his entire body had become stiff. He yelled like a mad man and threw the oar at the wall. The oar broke into two.
Lajo:	And then he left.
Deepo:	I ran after him and held him by his shirt. I begged him, cried and told him that there was nothing between me and Sundar. But he didn't relent.
Lajo:	Where there's love, there's suspicion too!
Deepo:	He unmoored the boat and pushed it into the storm. I waited for him that night. The waves went on wailing as they struck the boulders, spewing froth. But nothing was known about him. When the water receded, his shoe, loincloth and turban smeared with mud were washed away to the bank. I picked up all the three, dried them up and put them in the trunk. This is the reason I don't leave this hut. I'd never allowed Sundar to enter the hut. I always wished and prayed that if Surjeet ever returned, he should see how true I've been to his memory!
Lajo:	Now only his memory remains; he'll never come back.
	(Bhua coughs loudly)
Lajo:	Please go and get the medicine from Kansi *vaid*. Else she might pass away this night! Only Kansi *vaid's* medicine suits her.
Deepo:	The river has risen very high. Kansi *vaid's* house is beyond that low-lying area and it's flooded with water. *(The song is heard again: 'Steer my boat to the bank.')* That's Sundar. He's pulling his boat and tying it to the tree.

Lajo:	Ask him to go to Kansi *vaid* and bring him here.
Deepo:	You tell him.
Lajo:	*(Calling him)* Sundra, oh Sundra!
Deepo:	I am feeling giddy; there is a quiver under my feet, as it were.
Lajo:	You go and put a bandage on Bhua. I will ask Sundar to bring Kansi *vaid*. He won't refuse me. There was lightning just now. Yes, it's surely Sundar coming from the bank.
Deepo:	Perhaps it's raining.
Lajo:	No, it's just a light drizzle. Maybe it's the spray from the tide. Give me the lantern; I'll open the door.
Deepo:	The upper edges of the glass have turned jet black with soot because of the sputtering flame; let me clean it a bit.
Lajo:	There's no need for that; it's pitch dark outside and its dim light'll be sufficient in this darkness.
Deepo:	Yes, I will look after Bhua.
	(Lajo opens the door. Sundar enters)
Sundar:	Uff... there are whirlpools in the river...! Water is driving everyone away.
Lajo:	Oh my God!
Sundar:	Yes, all the villagers are leaving along with their cattle with flood waters in the tow. They'll go to the neighbouring village which is on slightly higher ground.
Lajo:	Bootewal?
Sundar:	Yes, Bootewal.
Lajo:	Deepo's parents live there.
Sundar:	Crocodiles have come out of the river. They're crawling on mounds of sand. It's a deluge.
Lajo:	Your boat?
Sundar:	I've brought it back safe. I've tied it to the *jand* at the goddess's temple.

Lajo:	Bhua is very sick. Once she starts coughing, it's difficult for her to stop. Could you go to Kansi *vaid* and get the medicine from him?
Sundar:	Yes, I will. But perhaps he too may have left.
Lajo:	His house is on the hillock. He won't go anywhere out of fear of flood. When there was a flood twelve years ago and the entire village was deserted, he hadn't gone anywhere. He's a happy-go-lucky fellow. He loves to drink *bhang*. Even now he must be lying intoxicated in his house. You go to him and get the medicine. His medicine is very effective. He eradicates the disease from its roots. Nobody else's medicine suits Bhua except his.
Sundar:	Fine, let me bring my boat. Water is flowing everywhere in deep gullies. I'll be back soon. I'll take the boat and bring him.
Lajo:	If he himself doesn't come, then bring the medicine. He has known our family for the last twenty years. He knows which medicine is to be given. He had wrapped the medicine in small packets for Bhua, but we couldn't bring them because the river has been in spate for three days now. Whenever Bhua took his medicine in the past, she was cured immediately.
Sundar:	Okay, I'm going.
	(Sundar leaves. Lajo closes the door. Bhua coughs loudly)
Lajo:	*(Loudly)* Deepo! Take the stone from the fire and bring it; let's give Bhua hot fomentation. Look, don't tell Bhua that we've sent Sundar to get the medicine. If she comes to know this, she'll not take the medicine. She remains annoyed with Sundar.
	(Bhua coughs)
Bhua:	Who has gone to Kansi *vaid* for the medicine?
Lajo:	I've sent Nathha from our neighbourhood.

Bhua:	Nathha will throw the medicines somewhere along the way. That day when I told him to push the boat to the *jand* to tie it there, he broke an oar.
Lajo:	Don't worry, he'll bring it.
Bhua:	You could've asked Jeona, he would bring it.
Lajo:	Jeona left the village last evening with his bullocks and cart. His children, wife, entire family have gone to the other village. Now only a lame bullock is left behind. The poor fellow is now lowing in the enclosure.
Bhua:	Don't know what revenge God has to exact on this village! Every four years these floods arrive. There's no armour against water. May God help us!
Lajo:	*(To Deepo)* Have you buried the potatoes in hot ashes?
Deepo:	Yes.
Lajo:	How many?
Deepo:	Three. I am not hungry.
Lajo:	I am famished.
Deepo:	Perhaps Bhua has fallen asleep.
Lajo:	Thank God, she's relieved.
Deepo:	She's still wheezing.
Lajo:	Poor Bhua! She has had troubles all her life. I was very young when our mother passed away. Bhua brought up both of us. I remember when the glow worms twinkled on the grass in the night, Bhua used to narrate the story of a king and queen to us. And sometimes she narrated stories of magicians, or of the sea and fishermen. When Surjeet went to the other side of the river to catch fish, he came back with baskets full of fish. Bhua roasted fish. Have you roasted the fish?
Deepo:	No, it's lying in the pitcher as it is.
Lajo:	I learnt how to roast fish from Bhua. Sometimes when Surjeet went into the river for a swim and went out of sight, Bhua took the boat, followed him

	and brought him back. Now the poor soul can't even stir!
Deepo:	This is because she doesn't eat anything! Yesterday I made porridge and gave it to her, but she pushed the bowl away.
	(Knocking on the door)
Lajo:	Perhaps Sundar is back. *(Lajo opens the door and Sundar can be seen fully drenched in the rain)* Have you brought the medicine?
Sundar:	Yes, there're three doses, one dose every three hours.
Lajo:	How're they to be taken?
Sundar:	With lukewarm water or with concoction.
Lajo:	Give these to me! May God bless you! *(Sundar goes away and Lajo goes to Bhua and then turning towards Deepo)* Deepo, has the concoction come to a boil?
Deepo:	Yes, it has been simmering for a long time.
Bhua:	*(Groaning)* May God be merciful!
Deepo:	Well, Bhua, do you have stitches?
Bhua:	*(Coughing)* I'm a wretched woman, lying in this room, suffering from cough and pain. The days and nights never seem to end. They keep coming and going like the tidal waves of the river.
Deepo:	Bhua turn on your side. I have to apply fomentation.
Lajo:	Is the stone very hot, Deepo?
Deepo:	I have brought it here after sprinkling water over it and it is wrapped in flannel.
Lajo:	Well, Bhua, has the pain subsided a little?
Bhua:	They're like what they were.
Lajo:	Kansi *vaid* has sent the medicine, take it.
Bhua:	Perhaps it would relieve the pain a bit.
Lajo:	These're three doses, each to be taken every three hours.
Deepo:	How?

Lajo:	With lukewarm water.
Deepo:	We should keep applying hot fomentation also to her chest with the stone. It'll keep her warm. Now let's give her one dose, the rest later on.
Lajo:	I'll give the medicine to Bhua.
Deepo:	Perhaps you haven't closed the door. The spray from the waves is coming in through the door.
Lajo:	Go and close the door.
	(Lajo goes to the inner room to prepare the medicine. Deepo goes to close the door and peers outside)
Deepo:	*(In a low, tremulous voice)* Sundar, you're still standing here?
Sundar:	Yes, I'm just about to leave.
Deepo:	Where's your boat?
Sundar:	Outside. I just lingered to have one glimpse of you.
Deepo:	Well, go now!
Sundar:	I'm going.
Deepo:	*(Suddenly)* This, what's this mark on your forehead?
Sundar:	It was very dark. I slipped and fell somewhere. A tree trunk lying in the way hit my head.
Deepo:	Well, now you must leave quickly.
Sundar:	After that night I've never come to your house. I just watch you from a distance when you go out and come in.
Deepo:	Where did you go in this storm?
Sundar:	Dheru, the water carrier's horse was swept away. I don't know where it went; it was swept away in a stream of water. I'd gone to look for him.
Deepo:	Was it found?
Sundar:	No.
Deepo:	Why did you go searching for the horse? If something unexpected had happened? Most people have left the village, why didn't you go? You don't have any cattle for whose safety you had to stay back.

Sundar:	I've no fear of the storm. I thought, perhaps I wouldn't be able to meet you as it is. Who knows if the storm came, someone should call me from this hut?
Deepo:	*(Staggering)* The last time . . . no, no, you go!
Sundar:	Yes, the last time . . . that night, that storm. That touch of yours that produced quivering sensations in my mind! That image of yours is etched permanently in my mind.
Deepo:	I'm scared of Surjeet. Since that day, I've started dreading him all the more.
Sundar:	You're superstitious.
Deepo:	Many times, I thought of calling you, but my voice stuck in my throat. I thought that if I called you, Surjeet would speak from the other side of the river.
Sundar:	You're stupid. How many years have passed since that night?
Deepo:	Four.
Sundar:	It appears as if it happened just yesterday, as if that moment was just a short while ago; as if there is no time gap between that night and this.
Deepo:	Don't say such things.
Sundar:	I went round this hut many times in the nights to see you. On wintry nights I used to stand on that mound of wet sand for hours together, unable to utter a word. As if thorns had grown on my tongue. My dreams were buried in this sand.
Deepo:	Sundra! Don't you fear either the darkness of the night or the rising flood?
Sundar:	Water drowns everything.
Deepo:	*(With a shudder)* I don't know what lies hidden under water; nothing is visible.
Sundar:	To me your eyes appear to glisten in the dark, your moist eyes!
Deepo:	Don't touch me. I haven't forgotten that night.

Sundar:	Surjeet won't come back now. You're obsessed with an idea; in being continuously troubled by the fear of his arrival you're merely wasting away under the shadow of this fear. It has been four years since he left. His turban, loincloth and shoes were found, drenched in water and smeared with mud. A crocodile must've eaten him. Why're your hands trembling?
Deepo:	With fear.
Sundar:	What are you afraid of?
Deepo:	Listen! What was that sound?
Sundar	*(Laughing)* That was the sound of the clanging of the boat chain anchored at the ford, and the splash of the flowing water rubbing against it.
Deepo:	It appears as if someone is wading through water; as if something is stuck in the mud and someone is hauling it. Strange thoughts arise in the mind!
Sundar:	All superstitions!
Deepo:	Who was it?
Sundar:	Nobody but your thought which sprang out of your mind.
Deepo:	Your flute gives me great solace.
Sundar:	I hear the pounding of your heart even here.
Deepo:	Sometimes I feel that my heart will beat very fast just once and then stop. Your touch has produced tingling sensations in my entire body . . . vibrations fast and furious which have no beginning, no end. *(With rising passion)* Sundra!
Sundar:	Yes!
Deepo:	Sundar, my head has become heavy; sparks are flying in front of my eyes. With my head resting on your chest, my heart is pounding faster still.
Sundar:	Deepo!
Deepo:	*(In a voice brimming with passion)* Someone is rowing a boat through my blood. Someone is producing eddies in my veins. Bhua's pains have

	subsided with Kansi *vaid's* medication. Is there no medicine to dry up the rising tides of the sea and to slacken the winds; a remedy to suppress the tempest rising in my mind?
Sundar:	I've been sipping winter and summer waiting for this storm.
Deepo:	This storm has inundated my four years of life-soil with water.
Sundar:	There's no difference between that night and this one. Time has shrunk like a small vortex. It's as if that night has expanded to touch the edge of this night. All my dreams have melted in your faltering words, in your warm touch, in your throbbing chest ... *(In the background, the sound of laughter rises like the noise of the waves, then it is heard very clearly. Deepo screams.)* Who's it? Deepo, why're you scared? Who's it?
Deepo:	Surjeet! When there was lightning, I saw him approach us from the bank.
Sundar:	It must've been an illusion.
	(Laughter is heard again)
Deepo:	No, it is Surjeet. Surjeet is standing behind you! Surjeet!
	(Surjeet, covered in mud, walks in)
Surjeet:	Yes, I am Surjeet. Why're you shocked to see me?
Deepo:	Surjeet!
Surjeet:	I knew that what I'd seen before I went away was true.
Deepo:	No, Surjeet, no! *(imploring)* No!
Surjeet:	Why've you lifted your head from Sundar's chest?
Deepo:	*(Sobbing)* No . . . no! Surjeet, no!
Surjeet:	I went away from here to the other bank. My turban, my shoes, my loincloth and all other clothes were taken by the river, dragged away by the waves. Having got rid of everything, I went to the other side, after casting away all thoughts and desires! But,

	what could I do? For four years your last cry, your tearful entreaties went on echoing in my ears.
Deepo:	*(Sobbing)* I....
Surjeet:	Your sobs swam in my mind like oyster shells. I thought perhaps you were right and I was wrong. You were telling the truth and I was lying. *(Laughs mockingly)* I didn't return for four years. I feared the verdict of my fate. I wanted to keep a small spark of hope in my heart glowing. If I had come earlier, this hope would've been extinguished. The echo of your last cry wouldn't go out of my mind. The farther I went, the louder it became—your cry, filled with your entreaties. For four years, whatever I did, your memory, your voice, your laughter, your touch stood between me and my work. I saw your shadow in the waters, in the fields. In the sound of the bells of the bulls I drove, I drove, I heard your sparkling laughter.... Why did I return, O my God!
Deepo:	*(Sobbing like before)* Just listen to me! Listen to me... listen! Whatever you've seen is a lie. Believe me!
Surjeet:	Should I believe you and not my eyes? shouldn't I believe my own fears expanding and shrinking in my mind? And not even Sundar?
Deepo:	Sundar had brought medicine for Bhua. He was returning now after handing over the medicine. I got up to close the door and started talking to him. Only once, after four years ...
Surjeet:	*(Laughs loudly)* Ha ha ha ..
Deepo:	Sundar is not to blame for all this. Lajo asked him to come here. He went only to get the medicine and ...
Surjeet:	Ha ha ha. Sundar, who was my childhood friend, who rowed the boat with me, who was the saviour of my boat, who saved my boat from every tide and storm, who was my friend ... in my absence he ...
Sundar:	But I ...

Surjeet:	(*Interrupting him*) Don't say anything, Sundar. There's no need for you to speak. You wouldn't raise your head in front of me, and don't do that even now.
Deepo:	(*With her eyes brimming with tears*) I feared this moment, which stood, as it were, behind these bushes waiting to entrap me.
Surjeet:	For four years I've been seeing your head resting on Sundar's chest. I couldn't erase that last frightened image of yours with the reflection of Sundar's love on it from my mind even after trying a million times. I've come to erase it now.
Deepo:	(*Beseeching*) Wait! Wait a minute! Listen to me! You'll have to listen to me. What you are saying is a lie, a lie! I swear by my waiting for you! I swear by your memory! (*Surjeet is leaving. Deepo holds him by his shirt. Hopelessly*) Where are you going again? O my God!
Surjeet:	Let go of my shirt. Go, go away!
Deepo:	(*In tears*) I waited for you in the dark nights. I waited for you with my eyes wide open. I measured out this entire river bank with my feet. And when I went to sleep for a while, you arrived!
Surjeet:	Let me go!
Deepo:	Where are you going? Where?
Surjeet:	Where my dreams are dying. The entire bank is covered with surf. I'll never come back now.
Deepo:	I've been looking after your little child in this hut, and your memory too. Don't go!
Surjeet:	Don't follow me. Go, go back. (*Tearing himself away from her, he leaves. Sound of hissing waves and howling winds.*)
Sundar:	(*Gravely*) He has gone away once again.
Deepo:	(*Crying and in anger*) Yes, and you go too. Go! Go now!
Sundar:	Deepo! Deepo! Listen to me, Deepo!

Deepo!	Go!
Sunder :	Deepo, why've you turned your face away from me?
Deepo:	Go, go away! This very moment! I have to shut the door. *(Shouting)* Go away!
	(Sundar leaves. Deepo closes the door and stands sobbing with her back resting against the door. The curtain falls)

HARSARAN SINGH

Harsaran Singh (1929–1994) was born in Gujjarkhan, district Rawalpindi (now in Pakistan). He retired from the Education Department of Punjab. He started his literary journey as an author of radio plays at All India Radio and then began writing one-act plays, and full-length plays for the stage. He wrote two types of plays: those in which he focuses on human relationships; and those in which he satirises political situations and circumstances. He was a champion of women's causes and dealt with gender issues in his plays.

A Helpless Mother

Characters

Rajo:	A woman abducted from Pakistan during the 1947 partition. About 30 years old, she has a weak constitution. Her name used to be Razia.
Nathha Singh:	An uneducated villager. Aged 35, who has kept Rajo as his wife.
Bebe:	Nathha Singh's mother. Aged 59.
Jamal:	A Pakistani officer whose job is to recover abducted Muslim women. He is also the son of Rajo's maternal aunt.
Shiv Singh:	A police informer

Dharma and Beera: Rajo and Nathha's sons, aged 7 and 9, respectively
Place: Nathha Singh's house in a village
Time: Afternoon, 1 PM

(When the curtain rises Rajo is sitting at the spinning wheel near the door that opens into the inner room. She is spinning. The door that leads outside and a part of the porch are clearly visible. The knick-knacks usually found in a simple village house can be seen. Nathha Singh comes through the porch. He stumbles on the threshold as he comes in)

Rajo: *(Stops spinning)* Be careful!
Nathha: *(Looking at the doorstep and cursing it)* It'll have to be hacked. It hinders coming in and going out. *(To Rajo)* Where's Bebe?
Rajo: *(Starts spinning again)* She's sleeping in the loft.
Nathha: *(Looking here and there)* I wanted to ask her about the bear tallow phial.
Rajo: *(Gesturing towards a recess in the wall)* It's there. *(Nathha Singh looks towards Rajo and then goes towards the recess)* Bebe doesn't take care of it. It was in the children's hands.
(Nathha picks up the phial and goes towards the courtyard)
Rajo: Who're you going to give it to?
Nathha: Lambar's labourer is standing outside. His Ammi's knees are aching.
(Nathha Singh goes out. Rajo stops her work. She appears crestfallen and becomes pensive.)
Rajo: *(In a low voice)* Ammi!
(Her eyes become moist. In the meantime, Nathha Singh comes back. As she wipes her tears Nathha Singh notices her action.)
Nathha: Has the spindle pricked you?
Rajo: *(Picking up the thread)* No.
Nathha: Did Bebe say something?
Rajo: No.
Nathha: Then what's happened all of a sudden?
Rajo: I remembered Asghar and Ghafoor.

Nathha:	Why all of a sudden today? *(He sits on the cot)*
Rajo:	They also called me 'Ammi'.
Nathha:	Bloody bitch, you haven't forgotten your Asghar and Ghafoor till now?
Rajo:	It happens very rarely now. When they were separated, I couldn't think of anything else except them, for months together.
Nathha:	*(Teasing her)* But the thought of cursing me kept occurring to you!
Rajo:	That too was also because of Ghafoor and Asghar. The thought that it was you who separated us ... *(Both remain quiet for some time)*
Nathha:	When I had dragged you from your cart, I should have brought your sons too. The rascals would have been driving my bullocks.
Rajo:	*(Leaving the thread)* You could've done whatever you liked, but you shouldn't have torn them away from me.
Nathha:	The fact, good woman, is that at that time I was obsessed with the idea of abducting a Muslim woman; I was oblivious of everything else.
Rajo:	*(In a choked voice)* But when you dragged me from the cart, you heard the shrieks of my sons. The way they had stretched out their hands towards me and had cried, 'Ammi, Ammi', you saw that too. The way I wailed and cried with my face turned towards them, you saw and heard that too.
Nathha:	Oye, who was bothered about the sufferings of the Muslims at that time!
Rajo:	I'd told you then that their father had already died and in my absence who'd look after those innocents? People were being slaughtered all around, who would've provided shelter to them! *(Crying)* They must've been butchered.

Nathha:	*(Irritably)* Oye, stop this whining and grieving over those swine! The Guru has rightly said that if a Muslim were to even dip his arm in oil, shove it into a sack full of sesame seeds and then swear as many times in the name of God as the number of seeds stuck to his arm, he still isn't reliable. *(Abusing her)* Bitch, you were baptised a Sikh ten years ago and two children also have been born to you, and you're still thinking about your sons from your previous marriage!
	(Rajo wipes her tears)
Rajo:	Since they too were born of my womb …
Nathha:	You can't be trusted at all. If the police come today, you'll go to the other side.
Rajo:	I've become the mother of your two sons, where'll I go now?
Nathha:	I think you'll take my children with you. Nobody knows what you may do.
Rajo:	I won't go to Pakistan now. People there will throw mud at me. Moreover, they'll call my Dharma and Beera bastards.
Nathha:	*(Enraged)* You bitch, how have Dharma and Beera become bastards? Had the Granthi not solemnised our wedding?
Rajo:	You've misunderstood what I said.
	(Bebe comes in from the porch. Rajo gets up and goes into inner room at the back.)
Bebe:	Son, are the children back from the school or not?
Nathha:	Not yet.
Bebe:	They're usually back by this time.
Nathha:	Yes.
Bebe:	Then go and find out where they are.
Nathha:	Bebe, they'll come back on their own.
Bebe:	Son, don't be so irresponsible. It's after a long and difficult wait that we had them. *(She moves on and*

	peers into the inner room and sees Rajo in tears.) What has happened to you, girl? Why're you crying?
Nathha:	The idiot wants to go to Pakistan.
Bebe:	Why is the wretch suddenly thinking of going to Pakistan after ten years? *(She walks towards Nathha Singh)* Look, don't lose her. Earlier when your first wife died, nobody was prepared to marry their daughter to you.
Nathha:	What do I do then? I too feel sad at the prospect of her going away.
Bebe:	Let me tell you; threaten her.
Nathha:	Bebe, she is incorrigible.
Bebe:	Don't worry. Just threaten her. It may work.
Nathha:	*(Pauses for some time and then loudly and intimidatingly)* If she thinks of going to Pakistan, I'll hack her to death.
Bebe:	*(Loudly)* Yes, in the past too, many were killed during the riots. *(Pauses for a while)* She isn't grateful to us for making her the queen of our house.
Nathha:	*(Loudly)* They say a blind man is no judge of colours.
Bebe:	*(Loudly)* Yes! Just as many people did with other Muslim women, it would have been better if she had been turned out after a few days or her dead body thrown into the river.
Nathha:	Bebe, my axe isn't rusted, is it!
Bebe:	Yes. *(In a low voice)* We are not going to kill her, my son. You are married to her. Let us just frighten her.
	(Both of them turn silent)
Bebe:	*(After some time)* I've thought of another way of threatening her.
Nathha:	What's that?
Bebe:	I'll tell you. *(Loudly)* You see, she'll languish in the rescue camps for the rest of her life. Nobody'll

	bother about her. Son, an abducted girl from my maternal village had come to a camp in Jalandhar. Her father came to take her away, but on seeing that she was big with child, he refused to accept her as his daughter. She begged and begged but he remained unmoved. Rajo will now take her two children with her. *(Addressing Nathha, in a low voice)* Son, we won't let the children go. We are thankful to God that they were born after a long, difficult wait and our family line will now continue, thanks to them. *(Beera comes running in from outside. His stumbles on the doorstep and falls)*
Nathha:	*(Rising)* Damn it!
Bebe:	*(Looking at Beera and with great concern)* Oh my God!
	(Beera cries. Rajo comes running and picks him up)
Nathha:	*(Looking for something to cut the doorstep with)* I'll cut it right away; otherwise it'll cause someone to topple over.
	(He goes inside)
Rajo:	*(Wiping Beera's face with her chunni)* You aren't hurt, are you, my son?
	(Examining his legs for possible signs of injury)
Bebe:	*(Lifting up his shirt)* You haven't hurt your back?
Rajo:	Don't cry, my jewel!
	(Beera stops crying)
Bebe:	Come to me, son. *(She spreads her arms towards him)* Where's Dharma?
Beera:	*(Wiping his tears)* He went in the police van.
Rajo :	*(Worried)* Where?
Beera:	Towards the police station.
Bebe:	*(Worried)* Where? To the police station? *(Turning towards Nathha Singh)* Come here, my son. See what Beera is saying. Come here quick!
	(Nathha Singh comes out with an axe in his hands)

Bebe:	Beera says that Dharma went towards the police station in a police van.
Nathha Singh:	*(Surprised)* In the police van? Towards the police station?
Bebe:	Oh my God! Some policeman may not have taken him to the police station!
Nathha:	But why would he take him?
Rajo:	This is not the time to think all this. Go to the police station immediately.
Nathha:	You just wait! *(To Beera)* Who took him to the police station in the police van?
Beera:	Nobody. He himself climbed behind it for a ride.
Rajo:	He may not fall!
Bebe:	Hurry up, my son, and find out! I'll distribute *parshad* if my grandson comes back safe!
Nathha:	*(To Beera)* Where was the van standing?
Beera:	In front of Shiv Singh's house.
Nathha:	Which Shiv Singh, Shiv Singh the gunner, or Shiv Singh the police informer?
Beera:	What? That one, whose house is situated near the *tahli*.
Nathha:	That means Shiv Singh, the police informer. The police must have taken him with them on a raid. He must have given a tip off to the police about a tavern being run by someone.
Bebe:	Vey, you just go! *(Nathha Singh puts the axe aside and goes out. To Rajo)* Have you seen it now? A house divided against itself cannot stand. *(To Rajo)* You tell me, why were you keening today?
Rajo:	Bebe, you have made a mountain of a molehill. When did I say that I'll go away?
Bebe:	*(Looking towards her and in a softer tone)* Then what happened?
Rajo:	I just remembered my Muslim sons. If a woman misses her children, won't she burst into tears?

Bebe:	*(Softening further)* Well, yes, you are right. This is unending grief. But let me tell you, you should understand that Waheguru gave you Beera and Dharma after taking your sons from you. *(With a faint smile)* He kept your two intact! *(Shiv Singh calls from outside)*
Shiv Singh:	Nathha Singh! O Sardara!
Bebe:	*(To Rajo)* Who's there? *(Aloud)* Who is it? *(Shiv Singh enters. Bebe becomes nervous on seeing him)* Shiv Singh, is everything alright? Where's my grandson? *(Rajo also advances towards Shiv Singh)*
Shiv Singh:	How do I know?
Bebe:	Vey, he had climbed into the police van.
Shiv Singh:	He must have jumped off somewhere. I don't know anything. Now listen, Bebe, the Pakistani police is outside.
Bebe:	*(Nervously)* Pakistani police!
Shiv Singh:	To take away your daughter-in-law. *(Rajo is thoroughly frightened)*
Bebe:	*(Beating her thighs with both her hands and wailing)* Vey Shiv Singh, may you be damned! You had to destroy our house!
Shiv Singh:	Bebe, I swear, I didn't give any tip off. Someone else must have informed on her; the entire village knows.
Bebe:	Vey, don't try to be clever! This is what you do . . . sinking the ships of others!
Shiv Singh:	*(Irritated)* You may go on saying whatever you want to. I'll go and bring the inspector. *(About to go out)*
Bebe:	*(With greater nervousness)* Shiv Singh, just listen to me. *(He stops and Bebe goes near him. Apologetically)* My son, I used harsh words in anger. Please don't mind. I'm like your mother. *(Looking angrily at Rajo)*

	This vixen must have sent the word ... that is why she has been sulking since morning ... *(crying and addressing Rajo)* ... you haven't been grateful to us for what we've done for you!
Rajo:	I swear in the name of God, I ...
Bebe:	What does your oath matter; it's our oath, the oath of the Sikhs that matters!
Rajo:	I swear in the name of the holy Allah ...
Bebe:	You hypocrite, you were just now saying that you don't want to go to Pakistan! You have been befooling us!
Rajo:	Bebe ji, I really won't go to Pakistan. Hide me somewhere, please ...
Bebe:	You're still pretending! Okay, go inside ...
Shiv Singh:	The police will take her.
	(Sounds of people marching into the house)
Shiv Singh:	They've come.
Bebe:	Oh! I'm damned! *(To Shiv Singh)* Let my son Nathha come back.
	(Jamal enters accompanied by some policemen. Bebe turns towards Rajo)
Jamal:	Shiv Singh, who is the Muslim woman here?
Bebe:	*(Pushing Rajo inside)* Go inside.
	(Jamal and Rajo look at each other)
Jamal:	*(Immediately)* Razia!
Rajo:	*(Stammering)* J-Jamal, my brother!
Jamal:	*(Moving towards her)* My sister!
	(He chokes on the words)
Bebe:	*(Pushes Rajo)* You accursed woman, go in!
	(Beera starts crying)
Jamal:	Mai ji, don't use force. We have to take her from here as per the law.
Bebe:	We'll see!
	(She pushes Rajo again into the inner room)
Jamal:	*(To the policemen)* Free Razia from this Mai and take her in your custody.

	(The policemen separate Razia from Bebe; in the meantime, some more villagers arrive)
Bebe:	*(To the villagers)* Vey, someone should call my son.
Jamal:	*(To a policeman)* Finish the paperwork soon. *(Gesturing towards Rajo)* She is my maternal aunt's daughter. *(Nathha Singh comes in running with Dharma. His foot catches in the doorframe and he almost falls.)*
Bebe:	*(Feeling relieved)* My son has arrived.
Nathha:	*(Looking at Jamal and Bebe)* What's going on?
Jamal:	Sardar Sahib, I'm an officer. My job is to restore those Muslim women to Pakistan who were left here during the riots. And I'm taking Razia with me.
Nathha:	Is Rajo ready to go?
Jamal:	*(A bit surprised at her Hindu name)* Rajo? Is it? *(Goes to Rajo and in choked voice)* Forgive me Razia that I couldn't even cry my heart out on seeing you.
Rajo:	*(Weeping)* Jamal, my brother!
Jamal:	And I couldn't even thank Allah! Thank you, Allah! *(Rajo is crying)* Razia, When I saw you, I choked with joy; but what'll happen to them when they see you?
Rajo:	*(Looking at Jamal)* Who, Jamal Bhai?
Jamal:	And what'll happen to you when you see them!
Rajo:	*(Excitedly)* When I see whom?
Jamal:	Asghar and Ghafoor.
Rajo:	*(Instantly in a happy voice)* Are they alive?
Jamal:	Yes.
Bebe:	*(To Nathha)* Now she'll go.
Rajo:	Where're they, Jamal?
Jamal:	In Lahore, with us.
Rajo:	*(In a heavy voice choked with emotion)* How're they, my jewels?

Jamal:	Handsome and young. But always depressed and soaked in grief from head to toe in your memory.
Rajo:	*(Weeping)* My children!
Jamal:	Wait, I'll show you a photograph of them. When I had first come to Hindustan, they had given me this photograph and told me to show it to you if I find you. *(Jamal takes a bag from a policeman and takes a photograph out of it and hands it over to Rajo. She looks very intently at it.)*
Rajo:	The same, exactly the same. I recognise them. This is Ghafoor and here is Asghar. *(Rajo presses the picture to her bosom. A few more people come in.)*
Rajo:	*(Weeping)* Curse be on me! Assuming that they had died in the riots, I had almost forgotten them after grieving over their loss.
Jamal:	Razia, you had to think that they were dead because when you were separated from them, massacres were still going on. When they saw people coming with swords and spears in their hands, they hid themselves behind other people in the cart. After some time, the army arrived and they were saved. Then they reached a rescue camp. There they waited for you every day. They tried to locate you among all those who arrived there. This is how they met us one day. Since then, they're with us. My Ammi has looked after them like her own children, but Razia, they're not contented without you.
Rajo:	*(She looks at the picture, sobbing bitterly)* My children!
Jamal:	Apart from this, there are many other things about your sons which make one cry. I think you should listen to all that Asghar and Ghafoor told us, after reaching Lahore. And you should tell them all that has happened with you. Now let's go from here.

(Rajo looks at her. Jamal addresses the policemen) I think the paperwork should be completed in the police station. (To Rajo) Now Razia sister, say your final goodbye to this house and come with us.
(Rajo is lost in thought. Bebe, Nathha, Dharma and Beera look at her.)

Jamal: What's going on in your mind, Razia? (Rajo doesn't answer; she starts crying) Razia, tell me what's it? (Rajo still does not answer. Insisting on an answer) Razia!

Bebe: (Turning towards Jamal, politely) My son, why are you taking her away forcibly?
(Jamal looks first towards Bebe and then towards Rajo)

Jamal: Razia, tell me! Why can't you go?
Rajo: (Weeping) What do I say, Jamal?
Jamal: Say something.
Rajo: (Turning her face away and weeping) Don't take me.
Jamal: (Surprised) Why?
Rajo: What do I say?
Bebe: My daughter, tell him clearly.
Jamal: (Insisting) Razia?
Rajo: (Weeping) People will throw mud at me, Jamal.
Bebe: (Sarcastically to Jamal) Yes, but do people let anyone be?
Jamal: Razia, you should not bother about any rogue. Let me tell you that this world is not bereft of slander. According to a sermon in the Holy Quran, some villagers once caught a woman of loose character and took her to an old man and asked, 'Old man, this woman was caught red-handed in an immoral act. According to the Law of Moses, this woman should be stoned. What have you to say about her?' When they repeated the question several times, the old man replied, 'Anyone among you who has

	never committed a sin should throw the first stone at her.' And Razia, not even one such person came forward. We should fear Allah alone, and not human beings!
Rajo:	Human beings are very tyrannical, Jamal. I'm scared of them.
Jamal:	Dogs keep barking and caravans keep moving on, Razia. You come with me; your children will be your sympathizers. You shouldn't care a hoot about others. Well, now, my sister, you must come with me. *(Rajo is in two minds for some time. Then she looks at her sons and advances towards them).*
Bebe:	*(Taking Dharma and Beera away from Rajo)* You stay away from them! We'll not allow you to take them with you. *(Jamal starts looking at Dharma and Beera).*
Beera:	*(To Rajo) Bibi*, where're you going?
Bebe:	Son, let her go where she wants to.
Dharma:	*Bibi*, where're you going?
Nathha:	*(Annoyed)* O keep quiet, both of you!
Rajo:	*(In a choked voice)* How can I leave them?
Bebe:	You may or may not go; but someone'll have to kill us before taking them away. *(Turning toward Nathha)* Isn't it, my son?
Nathha:	Yes.
Rajo:	*(Crying)* I won't be able to live without them.
Nathha:	I too won't be able to live without them. They are my sons too.
Rajo:	*(Cupping her mouth with her hand)* Oh! God! What do I do now?
Jamal:	*(Going to Rajo and in a choked voice)* May Allah be merciful to you, Razia!
Rajo:	*(Turning towards Jamal) Bhai jaan*, can't I take my sons with me?

Jamal:	No, Razia, you cannot take them without their father's consent.
Rajo:	But he just doesn't agree.
Jamal:	In that case you'll have to go alone, Razia.
Rajo:	*(Crying bitterly)* Bhai jaan!
Jamal:	*(In a choked voice)* Stop crying Razia; go ahead, shower your love on your dear ones and then entrusting them to Allah's care, go away from here.
Rajo:	*(Crying bitterly)* I ... I'll die without them.
Jamal:	May God bless you with a long life! *(Jamal wipes tears from his eyes with his handkerchief)* Come with me, my sister.
	(Rajo starts crying very loudly. Scared, Dharma and Beera look at her; sometimes they look at Nathha as well as at Bebe. Rajo goes to Dharma and Beera, hugs them and weeps.)
Beera:	*(Weeping)* I will also go with you.
Dharma:	*(Weeping)* Where are you going, Bibi?
Nathha:	She is going to Pakistan, where Muslims live. Do you also want to go there?
Dharma:	Bibi, I also want to go with you.
Nathha:	*(Dragging them away from Rajo and angrily)* What rubbish? Be warned if you say anything now!
Rajo:	*(To Nathha)* Let them come with me to the Wahga border at least!
Bebe:	No, my son! Who knows, she may insist on taking them with her once she reaches Wahga!
Nathha:	Do you think I'll do what she says?
	(Rajo is crying loudly)
Rajo:	*(With folded hands, entreating them)* Please allow them to accompany me up to the police station.
Nathha:	No!
Rajo:	*(Weeping)* What do I do?
Beera:	*(Weeping)* I'll go with you.

Rajo:	*(Caressing Beera's face)* You can't go with me, my son.
Dharma:	*(Grimacing)* Bibi, why?
Rajo:	*(She caresses Dharma's face)* Son, I'm going far away.
Dharma and Beera:	*(Holding her by her shirt)* We'll also go.
Rajo:	*(Extricating herself from them)* You should write letters to me about how you are, my sons.
Dharma and Beera:	No, we'll also go with you.
Rajo:	Send me your photograph too, a beautiful one with both of you standing next to each other. And when you are to get married, do write to me. …
Dharma and Beera:	*(Holding on to her shirt)* No, no!
Jamal:	Let's go Razia. *(Rajo takes Dharma and Beera in a tight embrace. Both of them are wailing. Then extricating herself from them with a final push, Rajo goes out immediately. Dharma and Beera try to follow her, wailing and shouting 'Bibi… Bibi…').*
Nathha:	*(Holding Dharma and Beera who are struggling to go out)* Oye, where are you going? *(Bebe also looks at the people outside who had started leaving. Her eyes are full of tears and she wipes her tears with her chunni. Beera bites Nathha on his hand)* Oye, son of a bitch! You've bitten me! *(He also starts looking at Rajo departing, sadness writ large on his face).*
Dharma and Beera:	*(Wailing very loudly)* Bibi! Bibi! *(They go on shouting and trying to free themselves from Nathha's grip. In the meantime, Rajo's loud voice is heard from outside).*
Rajo:	My sons!

	(Rajo rushes in from the porch. Jamal follows her. When she's about to cross the threshold, she stumbles against the doorstep and falls prostrate with great force. Leaving Dharma and Beera, Nathha Singh rushes towards her. Dharma and Beera also rush towards her. Jamal also makes a dash to her. Bebe reaches her side. Nathha turns her on her back. Rajo is unconscious and she is bleeding from her mouth. Asghar and Ghafoor's photo is nearby. Many other people rush in.)
Nathha:	*(Calling)* Rajo! *(She does not answer)*
Jamal:	Razia? *(Crying to Nathha Singh)* Get some water!
	(Nathha gets up and rushes in)
Jamal:	Razia! Razia! *(He tries to feel her pulse. In a trembling voice, full of fear)* Oh God! Be merciful!
Bebe:	*(Frightened)* Will she live, son?
	(Nathha brings water in a pot and pours it in her mouth. Rajo takes one last breath and then falls unconscious)
Jamal:	*(Wailing)* La Ilaha Illallah Muhammad Rasulallah!
Nathha:	*(Screams)* Rajo!
Bebe:	*(Starts lamenting, beating her chest)* Hai! My son is ruined!
Dharma and Beera:	*(Screaming)* Bibi! Bibi!
Jamal:	*(Wailing)* You have departed once again, Razia!
	(Nathha gets up all of a sudden and picks up the axe lying there)
Nathha:	*(Going towards the doorstep)* I will cut it to pieces!
	(He strikes at the doorstep. Everyone is looking at him).

—Curtain—

Editors' note: Nathha Singh misinterprets Guru Gobind Singh. Whatever Nathha is saying here, was said by the Guru for the Mughal king Aurangzeb. None of the Gurus ever said anything against the Muslims. They only criticised the rulers.

Gursharan Singh

Gursharan Singh (1929–2011) was born in Multan, Pakistan. As a professional, he was an expert in cement technology and played an important role in the construction of Bhakra dam. Starting his theatre career as producer of world famous classical drama and Punjabi literary drama, he established himself gradually as the messiah of Punjabi theatre. He wrote long plays such as *Dhamak Nagare Di* as well as very short plays through which he wanted to take his revolutionary message to the masses. His plays have minimal stage requirements and very few characters. He will always be remembered for his unswerving commitment to secular, progressive, egalitarian and people-centric ideals and also as an intrepid fighter against political establishment and regressive state policies. He was awarded the Sangeet Natak Akademi award in 1993 and the Kalidas Samman in 2004.

The Old Man Speaks

(The play is dedicated to those who consider it their duty to continue to fight against political corruption on the one side and religious fanaticism on the other.)

Characters

Baba: the old man
Congress (political party) member
Jathedar: Sikh leader
Newspaper Seller (NS): young boy
Other common folks

(The period following the assassination of Prime Minister Indira Gandhi. The subject of the play is the various violent incidents in Delhi and other places

in India after the Prime Minister's assassination when people belonging to a particular religion were murdered and raped, their homes looted and their properties torched.)

A newspaper seller (NS) enters the stage

NS: Today's breaking news … which will not be making headlines tomorrow, will turn stale day after and will be forgotten on the fourth day. … has been assassinated, killed.
(Three or four people buy the newspaper. Baba enters. He holds some things in his hand and a bag hangs from his shoulder. He seems to have come back from a long journey. His shoes are dusty.)

Baba: Has been assassinated?
Others: Yes, has been assassinated.
NS: Spend some money, buy a newspaper. A very big, well-known person has been assassinated.
Baba: A very well-known person?
NS: Yes, spend some money, buy a newspaper. A very well-known personality has been killed. The country was known by that person's name.
Baba: The country was known by that person's name!
NS: *(Aside)* Baba is very cheap. He doesn't want to spend any money, but likes to know all the news. *(To Baba)* Baba, a renowned personality has been killed in their own house.
Baba: Was killed in their own house, that's very bad!.
NS: What is bad about it?
Baba: Was killed in their own house!.
NS: Who was killed?
Baba: Whose name was known in the country.
NS: Whose name was known in the country?
Baba: The one who was a well-known person.
NS: Who was a well-known person?
Baba: The one who was killed.
NS: Who was killed?

Baba:	This is what I am asking, who has been killed? *(Others laugh)*
NS:	*(Aside)* Baba is a real rascal. He wants to know the news for free, but he's not buying anything from me. *(To Baba)* Baba, government flags have been lowered to fly at half-mast.
Baba:	Let them do whatever they want, how does it matter to us?
NS:	Mournful music is playing on the radio.
Baba:	Has some big man from the radio gone to heaven?
NS:	It's not a he, but a she that has gone to heaven. Television cameras are focused on her dead body.
Baba:	As if television cameras ever focus on living people!
NS:	The workers are on strike in the market.
Baba:	I don't need to buy anything in a hurry.
NS:	Distinguished dignitaries are coming from all over the world.
Baba:	Why? Is it their mother who has gone to heaven?
NS:	No, not their mother, the country has lost its mother.
Baba:	What happens when mother of the country dies?
NS:	The country becomes an orphan.
Baba:	The country is already an orphan.
NS:	What do you mean?
Baba:	This country has been an orphan for centuries. Is there anyone to take care of her? That's why the hungry and the homeless die in hundreds of thousands. Those who are not hungry, just read the newspapers and fight among themselves *(Newspapers readers frown at the Baba and leave the stage)*. There's only one news here. It was the same news yesterday, the same news today and it'll be the same news tomorrow. Now don't say, Baba is a miser, that he doesn't spend the money. Here take the money and put the newspaper in this bag.

NS:	*(While putting the newspaper in the bag)* Baba, there are many newspapers in this bag already.
Baba:	Not just newspapers, these are the essence of life, my boy. Now tell me what is your news? They say a murder has taken place. Murder of a well-known person. A person by whose name the country was known. She was killed in her own home. The flags have been lowered. The radio is playing mournful music continuously. Television cameras are focused on her dead body. The workers are on strike in the market. Distinguished dignitaries are arriving from around the globe.
NS:	*(Loudly)* Baba, the Prime Minister has been killed.
Baba:	*(Without showing any surprise)* So what? Now her son has become the Prime Minister.
NS:	He has asked the people to remain calm.
Baba:	And the people are indulging in arson.
NS:	Baba, you know all the news already …
Baba:	Because I know how to read between the lines.
NS:	How?
Baba:	Okay, you read your news and I'll tell you mine.
NS:	*(Reading the newspaper)* The Prime Minister has asked the people to remain peaceful in the country.
Baba:	It means that riots are taking place on a large scale in the country.
NS:	The government intends to start a campaign against poverty.
Baba:	It means that millions of people are dying due to poverty. *(Emphasising)* Listen to me, if the Prime Minister says that unemployment will be eradicated, then it means that the number of unemployed on the streets has increased. If the Prime Minister says that corruption will not be tolerated in the government then understand that corruption has peaked. If the Prime Minister says that the country's unity will be

	protected, then the country is ready to split into pieces. *(Walking away)* Now that is enough for today.
NS:	No, Baba. You have to tell me—what is in this bag?
Baba:	*Maa teri da sar* [your mother's head]. *(Changes his tone)* There is the history of 1947, 1964 and of 1984.
NS:	Forty-seven, sixty-four, eighty-four? Tell me what is their relationship?
Baba:	There were riots in '47. Houses were burned, innocents were killed, and children were orphaned, married women were widowed. There were riots in '84. Houses were burned, innocents were killed, and children were orphaned. married women were widowed. Those who ruled in '47 were white skinned. Those who are ruling in '84 wear the homespun white cloth. The wheel of time has come full circle. People are crushed, the rulers keep ruling.
NS:	Baba, what is the relationship between 1964 and 1984?
Baba:	In 1964 the father died and the daughter was enthroned. In 1984 the mother has died, the son is enthroned. A billion people ruled by one clan. All others are useless.
NS:	Baba is very clever. He says one thing but means something else.
Baba:	Son! I have suffered over and over again. In 1947, I lost my father. In 1984 I lost my son-in-law. My mother became a widow in 1947 and my daughter became a widow in 1984. In '47 a grandfather was orphaned, today a grandson has been orphaned. What a coincidence, then, a grandfather was ruling, today a grandson is ruling. Now don't say Baba makes up stories. Baba only narrates what he suffered. *(CHHUK, CHHUK. The sound of a train is heard. All characters line up as a train. CHHUK, CHHUK. Suddenly the train stops. Three passengers are pulled out and doused with petrol. Baba wants to extinguish*

	the fire but he is pulled and thrown away. While all this is being enacted the news keeps pouring in from behind).
1st News headline:	Today's breaking news. Three passengers belonging to a particular religion, travelling by Rajdhani Express were dragged out, sprayed with petrol and burnt at Tughlaqabad station, outside Delhi.
2nd News headline:	The railway minister claimed that there was no problem in railway operations. Everything was functioning normally as it should.
3rd News headline:	The railway minister has assured that all rail passengers will be given full protection by the police and the army.
Baba:	*(Picking up ashes from the burnt corpses)* Will be protected or turned to ash. *(A satirical laugh)* It'll be turned to ash. No, already turned to ash. Yes, the law of the land, the conscience of the country and the constitution of the country, everything turned to ash. In this country everyone has the right to live honorably. All turned to ash. *(Changes his tone)* Sprinkle this ash over the Himalaya mountain and immerse it in the river Ganges. Take this ash to the deep sea at Kanyakumari. *(Changes his tone again)* From Kashmir to Kanyakumari we all belong to one country. *(Rubbing it)* But we have become foreigners in our own country.
	(While Baba is speaking, the dead characters go out of the stage walking like zombies. They repeat: We have become foreigners in our own country.*)*
	(A Congressman [CM]—a member of the leading political party—enters the stage from the other end, followed by a lumpen bully Harichand [HC] who is mimicking his gestures)

CM:		So Harichand, what is the progress?
HC:		The progress is remarkable sir. Dragged three turbaned Sikhs off the train and sent them to hell. Burnt four taxis and turned them to ashes. Torched eight houses and taught the Sikhs an unforgettable lesson.
CM:		Well done. Now I can tell the Prime Minister that when a tree falls tremors are felt all around. Now what should we give you as a reward.
HC:		Sir, there is no need for any reward today. I have done well already. A lot of looted stuff has come my way.
CM:		What did you get? I would like to know that.
HC:		Silk sarees, transistors, VCRs, steel utensils, gold ornaments and ten thousand rupees in cash.
CM:		The policemen didn't stop you, did they?
HC:		Not really. Ostensibly, they told us to disperse. But very softly they told us to burn them all. We provided the fuel and they lit it up. Even though the army was all around, still we had great fun.
CM:		In other words, the army and police have done their duty as they were supposed to.
HC:		Yes sir, done their duty and also lent a helping hand in the looting.
CM:		That was expected of them.
HC:		Sir. What're the orders now?
CM:		Wait for the signal. The next programme will probably be to hold a peace march.
HC:		Peace march?
CM:		Yes, a peace procession.
HC:		How many people will be needed?
CM:		You're responsible to get around one hundred. But they should all be innocent-looking.
HC:		Sir, we're always waiting for a signal from you. It'll be the same people. Yesterday they took part in looting. Next, they'll participate in a peace march. Yesterday they were gangsters; today they'll be gentlemen.
CM:		How is that?

HC:	Like this: he takes off the scarf from his neck, buttons up his shirt up to the neck, combs his hair. Takes out a cap from his pocket and wears it. Shouts the slogan: 'Whoever incites a fight between Hindus and Sikhs will be called an enemy of the country. Hindus and Sikhs are brothers.' Sir, you'll lead the march and we'll follow you.
CM:	Very good. Okay, you may leave now.
	(Harichand prepares to leave but comes back)
HC:	Sir?
CM:	What's now?
HC:	Sir, the people of our constituency have come.
CM:	What people?
HC:	Those whose homes were looted yesterday.
CM:	Okay, you leave from the other side. Our next programme begins.
HC:	Yes sir.
	(He leaves. The Congressman acts as if making a phone call. Baba and two men stand at the door)
CM:	*(On the telephone)* What're you saying? The mob has torched the shops of the Sikhs? Where was the police? Inform the SSP to send more forces. Suspend the SHO. Sikhs are the pride of India. They have contributed immensely towards the Independence struggle. What did you say ... the mob is enraged that two Sikhs have assassinated our mother Indira Gandhi? But they were only two, the entire community can't be blamed for this? Yes, yes, take full action. Peace should prevail at any cost. Depute the forces. Enough is enough. Yes. Yes ... enough is enough. What has happened so far is enough. Nothing more should take place. A few hooligans tarnish the image of India and we just sit by and watch and do nothing. Impossible. We'll protect the people of our constituency at any cost. Even if we have to sacrifice our lives.

	(He puts the telephone down and addresses the people who have been waiting while he was talking on the phone. He speaks in a clever way to outsmart everything they say.)
CM:	Come in. I am extremely sorry that some social misfits have caused immense harm to people of your religion. Such wicked elements take advantage of every opportunity.
First:	But the police…
CM:	I know that the police didn't do anything. These people don't recognise their duty. They only know to live by cheating and deceiving. 'You bastards, homes of innocent people are being burnt in front of you. And you are just watching the fun. There has to be a limit to this wickedness.'
Second:	But even the people at the police station…
CM:	Even the people at the police station did'nt do anything. Yes, I have come to know that they took the phone off the hook at the police station. I called there many times. There was no reply or the line was busy. When I walked down to the police station myself, the SHO told me the phone was out of order but I could see that the phone was taken off the hook. Then I really took him to task. I'm sure he'll remember it for the rest of his life. Crooks, they play tricks with us, as if we are idiots. We ourselves commit such acts *(stumbling)*. I mean … let's see what we can do. Bloody young rogues think they can take us for a ride *(shifting)*. Well, tell me, what did you lose?
First:	The loss…
CM:	I know that enormous loss has occurred. They did'nt leave a single thing behind. They took silk sarees, transistors, VCRs, steel utensils, gold jewellery and cash worth thousands. First, they looted the houses, then torched them. But we'll not sit still, these criminals will be forced to return each and everything.

	What do they think? Each one of them will be sent to jail. There's still a government in control in this country. Isn't it? I'm meeting the Prime Minister soon today. I'll demand that everything should be returned, to a paisa.
Second:	But we're absolutely homeless now.
CM:	I know that you have become homeless. Your houses are no more. Winter is approaching. Where'll you go? The government is setting up camps for you. After all the government also has a responsibility. The PM is giving five lakhs from his fund.
Second:	Five lakhs? This amount is...
CM:	I know that five lakhs is not much. But this is the first instalment. More funds will flow from the Red Cross; you'll also get blankets. Tell me if there is any other issue.
First:	Issue? You did'nt...
CM:	I didn't leave any issue untouched, I know, this is what you want to say. Now if I do'nt understand your problems, who will? You people have elected me. I know that during the last election people of your religion were completely united and voted for me. You didn't vote for the Bharatiya Janta Party. We all know, that is a sectarian party which guards only the interests of the Hindus. Their slogan is Hindi... Hindu... Hindustan... But our party believes in secularism. Mahatma Gandhi taught us—Ishwar, Allah *tero naam, sub ko sanmati de bhagwan* [People call You Ishwar and Allah / Oh God, bless everyone with wisdom].
Baba:	*(He has reached a point where he can't control himself now)* What else did Mahatma Gandhi teach you?
CM:	*(Shaken)* What do you mean?
Baba:	He taught you to tell lies in front of people; fool them with your dramatic acts! We have'nt come to beg alms from you, because we know that all that

has happened, happened because of your intrigues and conspiracies. We have come to tell you that the PM has been assassinated. We're not happy about it. Some mean-spirited people distributed sweets, which is not a good thing. The same way some stupid people distributed sweets during the action on Darbar Sahib, when thousands of innocents were killed. Deception and stupidity have become supreme in our country. On the one side people are killed and on the other sweets are distributed. Those who distribute sweets have'nt lost their sons. Their daughters have'nt lost their husbands. Their kids have'nt been orphaned. *(Getting excited)* We condemn those who distribute sweets when others die. We despise the government, which is riddled with lies, killings and deceit. *(Saying this Baba turns away. The Congressman is enraged. Baba turns again and says)* Damn you.
(Saying this loudly he exits from one side.)

CM: *(The Congressman angry, exits from the other side, while saying)* They've killed our beloved mother and they're also damning us.
(Jathedar, Baba and two other Sikhs appear in the next scene.)

Jathedar: The Sikh community is in a crisis. The religious order is in danger.
Baba: What did you say Jathedar ji?
Jathedar: There is danger to the religious order.
Baba: *(Sarcastically)* The religious order has always been in danger.
Jathedar: What do you mean?
Baba: Jathedar ji, it has been 37 years since the country became independent. On the one hand the government kept saying that the country faces danger and on the other hand you kept saying that the religious order is in danger.

First man:	It isn't the faith that's in danger now; it's we people who are facing danger now. We have no good reason to stay in India.
Second man:	What sort of life is this? We're especially targeted and killed, our properties burnt. What have we not done for this country?
Baba:	What did you do? No one did anything for the country, everyone looked after their own interests.
First man:	Baba ji, you always take the opposite view. If we didn't contribute anything then who did?
Baba:	When did I say someone else did? No one did anything. Everyone looked after their own interests.
Second man:	What we need to think about is what should be done now.
Baba:	Ask the Jathedar. But, what'll he say? His politics all through the twentieth century has always revolved around religion.
Jathedar:	Politics and religion can never be a separate thing for the Sikhs. Our Gurus have said so and this is our history.
First man:	Jathedar ji is right.
Baba:	What's right? You and your Jathedar have become expert historians without reading or knowing a thing about history and are trying to fool people. Do you know why and when the Gurus gave this advice?
Jathedar:	When?
Baba:	At the time when Sikhs were selfless and fearless warriors. They were fighting against Mughal rulers' oppression and atrocities. Aurangzeb said that only Muslims would live in Hindostan. At that time the fight was between religions and that is why the response was from a religious perspective.
Jathedar:	So, should we go against the teachings of our Gurus now?
Baba:	The Gurus mandated us to stand firm against oppression and fight for your just rights. We need to

	follow that order. But tell me, what rights your wealthy Sikhs are going to fight for? They're the ones who rob others of their rights. What do they have common with ordinary Sikhs or other ordinary people?
Jathedar:	*(Irritated)* People like Baba are always willing to divide our religious community, the Panth.
Baba:	Yes, if someone suggests a sensible thing, it creates division in the Panth! As if the Panth is a group of fools. You should know that the government under which the Sikhs suffered a holocaust, is headed by a Sikh. The city in which all this happened has a Sikh as its Mayor. Now go ahead and say that they don't belong to the Panth.
Jathedar:	Yes, they're traitors to the Panth.
Baba:	Yet you're the ones who voted for these traitors. Why? Because they're Sikhs. You garlanded them. Invited them to your gurudwaras and honoured them. Didn't you do that?
First:	What's it that you really want to say?
Baba:	I want to say that the time has come to stop this refrain of Panth being a separate entity. Be part of the mainstream of the country and use the new political awareness of the twentieth century. Understand that the politics and the divisions are not based on religion but rather on classes. The wealthy classes of your Panth have been on friendly terms with the Congress Party leaders and on the other hand have been funding Sant Bhindranwale in Amritsar. Someone gave you a slogan that such a country should be created where Sikhs are in power. Those Sikh feudal lords rob the poor tenant farmers. Those Sikh factory owners live on the labour of poor workers. The capitalist Sikhs want to advance their own agenda by using you so that they can also grab a small portion of what the Birlas and Tatas of this land have. They want to see

	a place where they are the Birlas and Tatas. There is nothing more to it than that.
Jathedar:	But how can we live in this country now, where we have been treated like this and so much loss has been suffered by us?
Baba:	We should think about this. We need to think about it. We should have thought about it when the innocents were being killed in Punjab.
First man:	What should we do now?
Baba:	What should we do? Search within for answers. Change your thought process. Figure out who's your friend and who's your foe in this country?
Second man:	Who's our friend? No one.
Baba:	Well, if you keep thinking this way, then really no one will be your friend in this country. If you look to foreign countries for kindness, they'll sympathise with you superficially but will laugh at you in their hearts. What did America, Canada, England do when the Golden Temple was attacked and destroyed in the army action? No one did anything and it was in no way their responsibility either.
Jathedar:	But we don't have a friend even in this country.
Baba:	Why not? This is a country of seventy crore people and many people support you. When you were being attacked in Delhi or other parts of the country, who were the people who raised their voice in protest? They were printing and distributing leaflets all around. Open Maharashtra's newspapers and see how editorial after editorial was being written. They were saying that just because one Nathu Ram Godse killed Mahatma Gandhi, that didn't mean there was no place for Marathis in India. Who were those people who have risked their lives in Calcutta to save the Sikhs? Yes, there're many enemies here, but at the same time people who have faith in humanity and democratic values are not few either. Recognise them. But you'll

be able to recognise them only when you change your own view and have a more sensible approach to politics. This is the twentieth century, not the fifteenth or sixteenth. *(Taking out a newspaper from his bag)* Read this news: People's Union of Civil Liberties, People's Union for Democratic Rights, have called for a massive rally. For whom? For you? Why? Because they understand the character of the rulers. They know that the army boots that suppressed the Nagas and Mizos in the northeast yesterday are creating havoc in Punjab today. The only difference is that there the majority of army men were Sikhs and here they're non-Sikhs. They know that the forces that do'nt let the Assam issue to be solved, will' not allow the Punjab issue to be resolved either. They know that this country is ruled by plunderers who will never want people to stay united. These rulers will initiate riots and communal fights. But we should recognise the power of the people. They're rising up and are in the process of awakening others. Match your steps with them. Add your voices and words to theirs. Don't ask for a piece of land where Sikhs can rule, rather ask for the whole nation, where workers are recognised. The question is will you do so?

Jathedar: Leave it. What useless talk Baba has begun!
First man: But Baba speaks the truth.
Jathedar: What truth? It's a sin to stand here even for a minute. *(Angrily)* Waheguru ji ka khalsa waheguru ji ki fateh. Goodbye!
Baba: *(speaks after them)* Waheguru Ji ki Fateh. Go to the Singh Sahibs and have Baba chastised of religious misconduct.
(The newspaper seller enters the stage. Pauses a little. The same scene is repeated as in the first Act.)
Today's breaking news is ... which will not be making headlines tomorrow ... will turn stale day after and

	will be forgotten on the fourth day. (*Three people take the newspaper and start reading. The newspaper seller repeats 'today's breaking news'*).
Baba:	Stop this nonsense. What breaking news? There is no breaking news in this country. All news is stale. Hindu–Muslim quarrels. News of hatred among Hindus and Sikhs. Lok Sabha elections. Same old news, same old abuse. The games rich play involve millions. The poor are used only as tools. News about dalit colonies that were torched. News of jobless youth committing suicide. News of skyrocketing prices. News of the leaders switching political parties. All stale news.
Others:	(*looking up from the newspapers*) Yes, all stale news.
Baba:	O dear newspaper seller, get some fresh news, at least sometimes. Tell us of a new sunrise on this land.
Others:	New sun?
Baba:	Yes. When the hard-working people of this land will not be oppressed. There'll be Hindus, there'll be Sikhs, there'll be Muslims and there'll be those who don't wish to side with any religion. The news of that sun is awaited by millions of Indians.
	(*Baba utters these last words slowly. Then he looks to one side, as if seeing a sun in his imagination. Everyone looks to that side and turn still*).

Translated by Tajinder Kaur with inputs from Sadhu Binning

Charan Das Sidhu

Charan Das Sidhu (1938–2013) was born in village Bham in district Hoshiarpur. Despite poverty and humble beginnings, he went on to earn a PhD from Wisconsin University. He cleared the Indian Civil

Services exam securing tenth rank but preferred to teach at Hans Raj College in Delhi. He wrote about forty full-length plays in Punjabi, many of which depict characters and historical circumstances of the Doaba region in Punjab, and use the Doabi dialect. He tackled issues relating to the poor, Dalits, women and youth in his plays and wished to inspire these sections of society. He won the Sahitya Akademi award for his drama trilogy *Bhagat Singh Shaheed* in 2003.

Alexander's Victory
(An excerpt)

(Alexander's forces have refused to march ahead with him. Crestfallen, he is standing on the banks of the Beas, a river in Punjab. While he stands there, an ordinary looking person arrives and stands behind him, listening to what he is saying).

Alexander: I, Alexander, once a demi-god, immortal, limitless, unstoppable, mighty Alexander! Now? ... Helpless, weak and poor! I implore you! What should I do? Boundary? The boundary of the earth? Will man never be able to cross any boundary? Will the boundary always keep shifting and moving ahead? Will a person never be able to conquer everything? O Beas, bless me with victory once more! Or else, enfold me in your waves. Take me to the womb of the great ocean.
(Kalanaas approaches Alexander)
Kalanaas: Why, holy man, why're you standing on the banks of the river in the middle of the night? Is everything alright?
Alexander: Yes. Who're you?
Kalanaas: I'm a human being, a man of God, like you.
Alexander: Like me? ... Yes, at this moment every lowly insect is my equal.
Kalanaas: You appear to be very sad, likening yourself to insects! What happened? What's this victory and defeat you were muttering about? Have you run away from your home after quarrelling with your wife, like me? I've heard about your plays. I wanted to watch them, but

for the waspish tongue of Giano, my wife. She stopped me but I didn't listen to her and ran away.... Don't think of dying. Go away and sleep quietly. Tomorrow will be another day. It's Baisakhi tomorrow, New Year. Don't lose heart.

Alexander: What're you doing here, at this moment?

Kalanaas: O friend, what do I say now! It's a funny thing. The opening line of a song came to my mind, and it wouldn't let me sleep the whole night. I could only relax after the entire song was composed. Then I thought that I would sleep only after taking a holy dip in the Beas on the occasion of Baisakhi.

Alexander: You write songs?

Kalanaas: I didn't learn how to write anything. Those followers of mine who sing with me, they write sometimes. One of them is the son of a mirasi, and the other one that of a Jat. They haven't come with me here to watch your dramas. I've come alone.

Alexander: Then you're a dramatist, like Sophocles, and compose verses like Homer and Pindar!

Kalanaas: Yes, friend. I do make some noises once in a while. I've been at it since boyhood. My father tried hard to make me a shopkeeper who would weigh the wheat and millets for a chieftain, but I liked to sing. Acting is a difficult job. Everybody thinks I'm a useless fellow. My own wife keeps bawling at me the whole day. She says, 'You can't earn enough even to feed the family. All my five daughters crave for two square meals a day.' I think I shouldn't go back home: I'll build a small cottage here, on the banks of the Beas.

Alexander: Which village are you from?

Kalanaas: It must be about 30 odd miles from here, straight towards the east. ... Village Bham; District Hoshiarpur.

Alexander: You're from the other side of the Beas?

Kalanaas: Yes, brother. They call me Doabia, these people from Majha and Malwa. Fools! They make fun of me and

	call me 'stupid Doabia'. You appear to be a foreigner. You are a Greek soldier, aren't you?
Alexander:	What's your name?
Kalanaas:	Kalanaas Doabia.
Alexander:	Kaal... naas...?
Kalanaas:	Kala... naas!
Alexander:	Kaal... naas?
Kalanaas:	No, friend! I'm no conqueror of Time. Who has been able to vanquish Time till date? Time itself conquers everything. Even Ravana, the demon King of Lanka, who had tied Time to his bedpost, could not conquer it. How can a poor fellow like me become immortal by conquering Time? I sang badly. My acting skills were also poor. My father, my teacher and some resentful friends distorted my name, changed it from Kalidas to Kalanaas, 'a ruiner of art', and it became my nickname. I thought: how does the name matter? Let it be Kalanaas. If my family goes on performing dramas, generation after generation, then someday, down the line, a consummate artist like Kalidas will be born in my family too, who'll master all the art forms.
Alexander:	That means you're an actor, a humourist, a mimic and a mirasi!
Kalanaas:	Yes, I do a bit of acting too. Ah, now I recognise you. Aren't you the same person who was dressed as a king three or four days ago and made a speech from the stage? Greek Arjun's speech? What was his name? Achilles? You delivered it very well, that answer of Achilles to his mother. You're a very good actor; you mimicked the king so well.
Alexander:	I didn't mimic. I myself am King Alexander.
Kalanaas:	Just forget it! Don't boast like a *mirasi*!
Alexander:	No, brother Kalanaas Doabia, I really am Alexander.
Kalanaas:	If you were the real king, how could you come here alone? Your retinue would've followed you. Singing

	songs, wandering undressed, from one village to another, only carefree people like us can enjoy such pleasures. Coming out of your palaces at this unearthly hour, how can prisoners like you enjoy the whiff of fresh air on the banks of a river?
Alexander:	You talk very sensibly. In a way, I'm completely a prisoner. Thrice the conspiracy to murder me was unmasked, and that too, by my close friends and my servants. What's a king's life? You're apprehensive all the time! My father, Philip the Great, was stabbed to death by his own lover Pausanias in a theatre in front of everyone, at my sister's wedding. All of us together couldn't save my father from his assassins. Since that day, I too live under the shadow of this fear. And this night is the gloomiest night of my life.
Kalanaas:	Well, if you really are Alexander, then are you too afraid of death? You're the one who, with a single command put to death seventeen thousand Hindustanis after destroying the Sialkot fort? You're that trader in death who has been spilling the blood of innocents for the last ten years? What happened? Did someone attack you stealthily? Has the fear of death unnerved you?
Alexander:	It's not my death, but the death of my dreams! This is the first defeat of my life. And this defeat has come at the hands of my own comrades.
Kalanaas:	How?
Alexander:	They don't want to conquer the rest of Hindustan after crossing the Beas.
Kalanaas:	Wow, how wonderful! What a great hero you are! If you can't chop off a lakh more heads, you consider it your defeat!
Alexander:	An utter wag you are! A third-rate poet! How can you understand the desire to conquer the entire world? There's no power on this earth to stop Alexander.

Kalanaas: Great, Alexander! The Greeks too are as big fools as we are.
Alexander: Why're you laughing? What's made you so happy?
Kalanaas: It appears that your plays haven't had any impact on you. You don't learn anything from artists.
Aleander: How come?
Kalanaas: When acting in a play, each artist thinks that his play will have a positive impact on the world. It'll lead to greater love in the world. It'll bring peace to the world. But what happens is the exact opposite. I had imagined that the people of your country would be better judges of art. But it appears that you people are also also fools, like us.
Alexander: How come, Kalanaas Doabia?
Kalanaas: About four or five days ago, I watched a play of yours. A young son was counselling his father on how to rule. I felt very good. The son was trying to make his tyrannical father merciful.
Alexander: You mean... *Antigone*? Written by Sophocles? The scene between King Creon and his son Haemon?
Kalanaas: Yes, the King gets his niece murdered.
Alexander: Yes, that's the one. I'd learnt it by heart in my childhood ... My teacher Aristotle made us enact it. When my father married the second time and conspired to deprive me of the throne, my mother and I left the palace annoyed with him; I felt like murdering my father. Angry with him, I went to live with my maternal grandparents along with my mother. Philip sent my teacher Aristotle and he persuaded me and brought me back to the school. He made me act in *Antigone*. I played the part of Haemon. My friend Philotas became Creon in the play. Philotas was the son of Parmenion, who took my father's place. In a way, Philotas was my brother. He had saved my life in the Battle of Granicus. But look at the irony; I had to order Philotas to be stoned to death by my soldiers. His

father Parmenion was next in line to me as a successor to the throne. I had to get him murdered, otherwise he would've conspired to kill me. Creon was right in saying that the job of a king is not easy. He has to face traitors at each step. He has to save himself from murderous conspiracies of rebels. When I was young, I considered myself to be right; I endorsed Haemon's view. But now, as I get wiser, I consider Haemon was in the wrong. Now Creon seems to be right. My father Philip seems to be right. The job of a king is very difficult indeed. You cannot understand the helplessness of a king. He cannot do his duty as a king.

Kalanaas: What kind of duty is this, when one has to take the life of one's own people? But yes, you need to be congratulated for one thing; you Greeks have raised the level of stagecraft very high. Your actors are great.

Alexander: Naïve Doabia! Learning good acting is the foremost duty of a king or a leader; otherwise, how can I drive different sorts of people into the jaws of death in alien lands? The art of public speaking is taught very seriously in our schools. My victories are miracles made by my words; I encourage my soldiers with my speeches.

Kalanaas: Then why've your speeches failed now? Why've the Greeks deserted you?

Alexander: This is the first defeat of my life. This is what breaks my heart. I feel like beheading each one of the Greek soldiers, and have my generals stoned to death. They are betraying their king. The cowards! You come with me to Patliputra. I'll shower you with gold. You seem to be a nice person. You'll sing songs for me. If you know a bit of swordsmanship, even better. Well, I'll teach you swordsmanship too. I'll make you a general in command of ten thousand soldiers. I have no shortage of jobs for you. I have no shortage of gold. If you want. I can make you the king of all of Doaba after conquering it. In being friends with Alexander,

	nobody is ever at a loss. You can ask Porus. He has a bigger Sultanate now than he earlier had.
Kalanaas:	No, friend, no. I'm not such an idiot who would give up living a happy life to wander aimlessly like you from one country to another and to share my grief with canals and rivers! No, my brother, excuse me, I can't do it. What sort of king are you? I've never seen anyone as unhappy as you are.
Alexander:	Unhappy? Me? A person who conquers the whole world, who presides over the life and death of millions of people, who has inexhaustible treasures of gold and silver, can never be unhappy. You've proved yourself to be a worthless mimic after all, a mirasi! I just tried to lighten my heart by sharing some of my troubles with you and you now consider yourself my equal! You call me unhappy?
Kalanaas:	Equal? Why should I consider you my equal? You're far worse than me. You're an unhappy man.
Alexander:	Do I appear unhappy to you?
Kalanass:	Just go away, brother. Impress your Greeks with this imperious attitude of yours! I know one thing: nobody who is happy ever kills anyone; never does he lay waste flourishing cities! Having travelled thousands of miles, you're setting the earth on fire! How can you be happy? A person who is happy always seeks the happiness of others. He prays for the welfare of the entire humankind.
Alexander:	Do you see this fist, if I hit you with it, your skull will be smashed to smithereens!
Kalanaas:	Is that all you can do? This is just proof of your foolishness. Very powerful you are. There's great strength in you. You can make the impossible possible. Nobody can defeat you in armed combat. But what about wisdom? You're bereft of it; utterly devoid of it! Did no rascal ever teach you that if one has limitless strength and immense power, then this power and

	strength should be used to save lives, to establish peace? That it should be used to eradicate poverty and disease? Having power is one thing, its correct use is another. Learn from Gautama Buddha. Learn from Vardhamana Mahavira. Learn from our selfless *baba*s who worked for the welfare of others. Gautama Buddha didn't suffer less than you. For five years he wandered in jungles, hungry and thirsty. After renouncing his kingdom, his wife, his son, his father and after severing all bonds of love with his kith and kin, he left his home so that he could find a cure for sorrow, disease, old age and death. And you? You're prowling like a mad elephant, like a rabid dog, raising fires of hell on this earth! Rubbish! Haven't realised yet what real victory is?
Alexander:	What's the real victory?
Kalanaas:	Real victory is victory over one's self, over one's desires, cravings and wants. *(Chants)* 'Conquer your mind and conquer the world.'
Alexander:	'Conquer your mind and conquer the world,' you wrote this song?
Kalanaas:	Whether I wrote it or some kind-hearted *baba* of ours, this is a legacy of our vedas and shastras. The epics of your country also teach the same thing. You have listened to your body thus far; listen to your soul too sometime. A sinner like you is reborn as an insect. He is caught in the cycle of eighty-four lakh reincarnations.
Alexander:	What nonsense are you talking about? The riddle of birth and rebirth?
Kalanaas:	Have you no faith in the rebirth of soul? This philosophy of eighty-four lakh reincarnations is the basis of our religion.
Alexander:	Stuff and nonsense! Your priests have unnecessarily trapped people in the cycle of imaginary hells and heavens. These are superstitions. After learning all this from your country, our philosopher Pythagoras tried

	to spread these superstitions in Europe as well, but our people didn't listen to him at all. But you people have been dragging this muddle from generation to generation till date.
Kalanaas:	Granted that these may be superstitious, but your Homer also talks about souls. He talks about how souls dwell in Hades. That day I saw a tableau of yours depicting this.
Alexander:	I worship Homer. My teacher made a new copy of *Iliad* for me. I always keep it with me in a golden box near my pillow. I remember the entire *Iliad* by heart. Achilles is my ideal. I'll live like him: 'One may live for a short while, but one must earn a name.'
Kalanaas:	But you left with Achilles' partial blessings only!
Alexander:	How come?
Kalanaas:	Do you know Odysseus met the dead Achilles' soul in Hades?
Alexander:	Yes.
Kalanaas:	What did Achilles' soul say to Odysseus? That there's a lot of difference between the live Achilles and the dead Achilles! Man should always try to preserve life by all means. Life is a great blessing. Learn to live! A man may be very poor, he may even be a slave, but a man alive is a million times better than a dead man. *(Chanting and repeating)* 'Three phases of life—beauty, youth and parents won't come back. These won't come back.'

Translated by: Swaraj Raj

Ajmer Singh Aulakh

Ajmer Singh Aulakh (1942–2017) was born in village Kumbharwal, district Sangrur. Initially, he wrote poetry and novels. He started his journey as a playwright with one-act plays and short plays; later he wrote full-length plays in which he focuses on the life of small farmers of the Malwa region. He portrays with great poignancy the struggles, agonised life and feelings of the rural poor owning very small landholdings. The cultural and psychological compulsions of the various characters contribute to the dramatic tension in his plays. He won the Sahitya Akademi award in 2006 for his book *Ishq Bajh Namaz Da Hajj Nahin* after receiving the Sangeet Natak Akademy Award in the year 2005. He returned the Sahitya Akademi award in 2015.

Satyr

Characters

Maatu (age 26 years): Rajo's son
Bhooti (age 8 years): Maatu's child bride
Rajo (age 45 years): Maatu's mother
Kailo (age 22 years): Leehlu's mother
Leehlu (age 9 years): Kailo's son
Darshan (age 20 years): Maatu's friend
Darshan's Bhabhi (age 20 years)
Darshan's Servant Jagga (any age)

[In Rajo's courtyard, Bhooti and Leehlu are playing the game of marbles. Leehlu has an upper hand in the game. Pleased at having won, he teases Bhooti by clanging all the marbles in his pocket]

Leehlu:	(*Teasing her*) See, have I won or not?
Bhooti:	You cheat! You cheated to win! Give back my marbles.
Leehlu:	Who cheated? I've won them by hitting the target! Now you want your marbles back!
Bhooti:	I'll tell my Bebe.
Leehlu:	Go, and tell her. Is your Bebe a police inspector? Do what you want to do; tell anyone you like.
Bhooti:	I'll tell Maatu. He'll pull your hair.
Leehlu:	Maatu, your husband? That druggie? He'll pull my hair only if I let him. Look, how she's threatening me by invoking her husband! As if he's a deputy collector somewhere!

Bhooti:	He must be your husband. How can Maatu be my husband?
Leehlu:	You're married to him, not I. You're his wife!
Bhooti:	Your mother is Maatu's wife *(cursing him)*, you devil!
Leehlu:	My mother is my father's wife. She's married to my father. You're married to Maatu, so you're Maatu's wife.
Bhooti:	What's marriage then? Marriage is good thing. One gets beautiful clothes, ornaments, *laddoos*... *jalebis*... *(pleading)* Leehlu, please be my brother and give me my marbles! Don't worry, I'll be your sister! Hunh!
Leehlu:	How can you be my sister? You're my Tayi! Maatu my Taiya, Bhooti my Tayi! *(Rajo comes in)*
Rajo:	You bastard! How can she be your Tayi? She's your Chachi. Maatu is younger than your father by two years.
Leehlu:	Two years! How wonderful, Ambo! What a bagful of lies you carry! You say Maatu is two years younger than my father?
Rajo:	What else, *vey*?
Leehlu:	Ambo Sahib ji! My Taiya Maatu is older than my father by six months. My Bebe has told me everything.
Rajo:	I gave birth to Maatu, bastard, not your mother! Go away and get lost! If you try any more tricks of yours, then be warned! *(Leehlu keeps standing there and laughs)* Will you go or not? Look how the scoundrel is grinning! Well, then, wait a minute. Bastard!
Leehlu:	*(While going out he teases them by twiddling his thumb at them)* Hey... hey... hey. *(Rajo picks up the broom and runs after him to hit him with it. Running out, he teases them by*

	mimicking the honking sound of an automobile) Teen... teen... teen....
Rajo:	A shameless clown like his father! Mirasi!
Bhooti:	Bebe, he cheated me of all my marbles.
Rajo:	Why do you play with this scoundrel? You should play with girls of your age.
Bhooti:	The girls also tease me, by calling me 'Tayi-Tayi, Chachi-Chachi!'
Rajo:	*(Spreading the cot)* Don't worry. You shouldn't get annoyed. Once you grow up, you'll understand everything. Come here, and sit with me. See, what I've brought you... sugar candy toys. *(Feeling very happy, Bhooti sits on the cot)* Eat as many as you like, my daughter. All these are for you. *(Bhooti eats them)* Are they tasty?
Bhooti:	Yes, they're very tasty. You bought them?
Rajo:	What else, my silly one! These are not to be had free of cost.
Bhooti:	*(Looking intently at a candy)* What's this? Boy or a girl?
Rajo:	It seems to be a doll, exactly like you, a little doll.
Bhooti:	Then I won't eat it. I'll keep it in my basket where I keep my dolls. I'll play with it.
Rajo:	It's a sugar candy shaped like a toy, my child. It's for eating not for playing with. If you play with it, it'll become dirty, or it'll break. Finish it off, my child.
Bhooti:	No, I won't. It's my friend.
Rajo:	Well, then do as you like... You haven't had your milk today? You must drink it. You know, I've bought the cow for you only. If you drink milk, you'll soon grow up big and strong.
Bhooti:	What'll I get by growing big soon, Bebe? As a grown up, I'll have to clean the cow shed. I'll have to help Maatu cut the fodder with the machine. Besides, a person becomes old also after growing up. He

	starts coughing, and then he dies. That is how my grandfather had died.
Rajo:	May your enemies die! Why should you? *(spits)* ... thoo ...
Bhooti:	Why did you spit?
Rajo:	*(Lovingly, caressing her head)* So that no evil eye may harm my queen of a daughter-in-law!
Bhooti:	*(Surprised and looking innocently at her)* Daughter-in-law?
Rajo:	Yes, daughter-in-law *(with greater love and longing)* a daughter-in-law. Bhooti, my child, you're my daughter-in-law, more loving than even daughters. You should now grow young quickly! Then all my desires will be fulfilled. There'll be hustle and bustle in my house, because of you! *(Bhooti does not understand all this. She's busy eating the candy).* Only I know how eagerly I'm waiting for that day! *(Kisses Bhooti on her head and prays)* O God, may that day arrive while I'm still alive, before I die!
Bhooti:	*(Innocently)* You shouldn't die, Bebe. I'll feel bad without you at home. You bring so many things for me. You're very nice, Bebe! My mother in my village used to beat me a lot. She always made me carry my little sister in my arms. If I didn't, then she abused me and also beat me up badly.
Rajo:	Oh no! The witch! Is this girl to be beaten?
Bhooti:	When I wanted to play, she asked me to look after my sister. But you don't stop me from doing anything.
Rajo:	Why should I stop you? This's your home, my child. Tomorrow, you'll be the mistress of this house!
Bhooti:	What's that, Bebe?
Rajo:	*(Laughing)* You'll learn about that too. Why ask that now! *(Getting up)* And if you're my daughter, then do one more thing that I ask of you. *(Goes into the low-roofed mud kitchen)*

Bhooti:	What?
Rajo:	*(From the kitchen)* I'll tell you. *(Comes out with a glass in her hand)* Take it, drink this glass of milk.
Bhooti:	The whole of it? It's a lot of milk.
Rajo:	It isn't much. Drink it, or I won't speak to you.
Bhooti:	Then I'll have it. *(After drinking half of it)* That's enough. I can't have more. My tummy is full.
Rajo:	Only this much! You didn't have even two sips. Be my daughter and have a little more.
Bhooti:	I swear, I can't have any more.
Rajo:	Well then, I'll keep it in the kitchen. Have it whenever you are hungry. *(Comes back after leaving the glass in the kitchen).* Now I'm going to the enclosure to make cow dung cakes. Look after the house. Don't leave it.
Bhooti:	Okay.
	(Rajo goes out. Left alone, Bhooti starts playing with small pebbles and starts humming a song). A traveller like Ranjha, Riding a horse An umbrella covering his head Whose door he knocks That maid is blessed. *(Kailo enters and she stands quietly, listening to Bhooti singing the song).*
Kailo:	Dear Jathaniye, you sing so well. Where did you learn this song?
Bhooti:	My elder sister used to sing it. I learned it from her.
Kailo:	Where's your mother-in-law? Where has she gone? You must keep a strict eye on her; she's always making rounds of the village for no reason.
Bhooti:	Bebe has gone to the enclosure to make cow dung cakes.
Kailo:	Did our Leehlu come to your house? Where have you hidden him?

Bhooti:	Your Leehlu cheated me and took away all my marbles. When my Bebe came, he ran away. Your Leehlu is a big cheat, Kailo.
Kailo:	So what? He is the son of your *Deor*. *(Noticing the remaining candy)* Kuriey, who brought this candy for you? Maatu?
Bhooti:	My Bebe brought them. *(She picks up her candy)* Don't eat this one; she's my friend.
Kailo:	*(Tasting a candy)* It's very tasty. You're lying Bhooti, Maatu must've brought them.
Bhooti:	Why should I lie? I'm telling you the truth. Do you know, Bebe brings so many things for me … laddoos, jalebis, sweets …
Kailo:	And Maatu, what does he bring?
Bhooti:	He brings other things.
Kailo:	*(Eagerly)* What other things?
Bhooti:	One day he brought some ash and said, 'Rub it on your body; you won't have bad dreams.'
Kailo:	You had bad dreams?
Bhooti:	Yes, you see Kailo, in my dream a big black giant takes me away forcibly. And then he enters into a big hole. I scream, but no sound escapes my mouth.
Kailo:	Really! Have you stopped having bad dreams now?
Bhooti:	Yes, now I rarely have them. Bebe keeps a small brass pot full of water near my pillow.
Kailo:	Good! What else does Maatu bring for you?
Bhooti:	What else will he bring? One day he brought this amulet and said, 'If you wear it, then you'll become beautiful like the school teacher.'
Kailo:	*(Laughing)* What nonsense! The rogue! Bhooti, be my sister, come here and sit with me. *(Bhooti goes to her and Kailo caresses her, making a show of her love.)* If I ask you something, will you tell me

	truthfully? *(Bhooti childishly nods her head)* Tell me, does Maatu love you?
Bhooti:	*(Nodding her head)* Yes.
Kailo:	How?
Bhooti:	In the same way as you're loving me now.
Kailo:	Does he put you in his lap?
Bhhoti:	Yes.
Kailo:	And then?
Bhooti:	And then he hugs me tight.
Kailo:	And then?
Bhooti:	But Kailo, he doesn't know how to love. He doesn't love me like Bebe. One day he bit me on the face.
Kailo:	The beast! Satyr! Let him come back, I'll teach him a lesson today. *(Expressing surprise and anger)* Is this the way? Moreover, at the time of finalising this marriage, I had made very clear that till the girl turned thirteen, he shouldn't go near her. But no! People are just interested in their own selfish motives. Well, rabid dog that he is, he should look at the child's age! *(To Bhooti)* Go and fetch your mother-in-law. I'll give her a piece of my mind! Go and tell her that Kailo sister is calling her! *(Bhooti goes out. Kailo drinks water from the brass pitcher. Maatu enters; he is intoxicated.)*
Maatu:	*(Greeting her with folded hands and speaking in the manner of a drug addict)* Bhabhi Sahib, Sat Sri Akal. How come have you descended today on the earth from Indra's abode? How fortunate for me! Sat Sri Akal!
Kailo:	What's all this Maatu? Did I arrange your marriage for all this?
Maatu:	What're you saying Bhabhi Sahib? What happened? *(Flirtatiously and in an exaggerated manner)* Why is the bejewelled Her Highness so angry?

Kailo:	Why did you touch Bhooti?
Maatu:	No, no Bhabhi Sahib! Are you saying that I'm a sinner! If this is what you mean, then I'm prepared to swear!
Kailo:	Bhooti herself told me. And you're talking about swearing!
Maatu:	She's just a child Bhabhi Sahib, she'll say anything! One day I tried to wipe her nose and she started screaming!
Kailo:	What nose! You should control your inner beast, let me tell you!
Maatu:	No, Bhabhi Sahib no! I never defy you. Moreover, if such a desire were to ever arise in my mind, I'll come straight to you and fall at your feet! Won't you oblige me even this much!
Kailo:	Won't I beat you black and blue? Try giving me a dirty look, and I'll gouge your eyes out!
Maatu:	Bhabhi Sahib, you have got angry over a joke. I'm just indulging in *deor-bhabhi* banter! You may get angry with me, but as long as Bhooti doesn't come of age, you shouldn't spurn me!
Kailo:	I'll hit you with my *jutti*, scoundrel! You're just going on and on …!
Maatu:	(*Feeling insulted*) Then who're you to me? Who're you to come between me and Bhooti? She's my wife; we've paid three thousand rupees!
Kailo:	Didn't I arrange the match? They gave their child on my word.
Maatu:	Didn't we give you a six-gram gold ring? Fodder for your cattle we've been giving you free! Should we go on slaving for you even now?
Kailo:	Is that so? Now you remember all that you've done for me! But when you had an axe to grind, you were pestering me day in and day out!
Maatu:	Did you then get me an eighteen-year-old in full bloom of her youth?

Kailo:	Are you a rich Sardar to deserve an eighteen-year-old! You don't own even three acres of land and you want to have a girl in full bloom! If you wanted such a girl, you should've been born in a rich family of a Seth or a Sardar! Get a girl in full bloom for this louse-eaten fellow! Look at your status!
Maatu:	*(Unable to find an answer)* Then what do I do with this kitten of yours?
Kailo:	Didn't we show the kitten to you then? Then you said, 'No problem. With time she'll grow up on her own! Five years isn't a long time! It'll pass in the blink of an eye!'
Maatu:	You said she was ten, when she wasn't even eight at the time of marriage!
Kailo:	Did I write her horoscope? I told you what her parents told me.
Maatu:	I don't know anything. Give us back our money; take her back to her parents.
Kailo:	May I do something else too at your bidding? These issues concern daughters, not goats and sheep! *(Furious)* Send her to her parents, at the behest of this bully!
Maatu:	Then tell me what do I do? Which well shall I jump into?
	(Bhooti comes in.)
Bhooti:	Bebe is not in the enclosure. I don't know where she is.
Kailo:	*(To Bhooti)* Spit on his face if he ever touches you!
	(She leaves. Darshan comes in a little later.)
Darshan:	*(To Maatu)* Here you are! One gets to see you only once in a blue moon. Where have you been all these days? I've gone mad looking for you. I've already been here thrice since morning. I don't know into which abyss you had descended into. Idiot! I wanted to offer you liquor, not poison! *(Taking*

	out a liquor bottle and giving it to him) Take it and get the glasses. *(Looking at Bhooti)* Who's this little girl? Your wife? She's the one you got married to! *(To Bhooti)* Child, bring water from there, a glass or a bowl too! *(Maatu looks at Bhooti, who stands, full of fear)* Don't fear anything child, you're a very wise girl. Go, bring some water and glasses. *(Bhooti goes into the kitchen)* Tell me, why didn't you come to my *Bai's* wedding?
Maatu:	Well, Darshan, we'd drunk a lot the night before yesterday. And then we slept at Ghumanda's tube well. I just couldn't get up in the morning. I regained my senses only in the afternoon.
Darshan:	I don't think you drank Aristocrat Whisky! You must have gulped a fistful of tablets! I'll offer you excellent whisky today, Solan No 1. *(Bhooti brings water. To Bhooti)* May you live long girl! *(Takes out a one-rupee coin from his pocket and gives it to her)* Take it and buy some pakoras from Kaura's shop. Now be off! Quick! *(Bhooti leaves. Darshan pours out the liquor)*
Maatu:	So Darshan, how was the Bai's wedding?
Darshan:	Wedding? It was grand. If you'd come, you would've seen it for yourself. There were more than two hundred people in the wedding procession. My father had given an open invitation to the village that those who wanted to come could join the wedding procession. Plenty of liquor to satisfy everyone. Two buses and ten cars. It was like the whole army of King Akbar!
Maatu:	How could the girl's parents serve so many people?
Darshan:	Do you think that they are paupers who couldn't serve so many people? Their kothi is spread over two bighas! When we were two miles short of their village, Campa Colas ...

Maatu:	Campa Cola! What?
Darshan:	Cold, aerated soft drink. Then omelettes with tea, fish pakora, vegetable pakora, fried liver ...
Maatu:	Laddoo and jalebis too...
Darshan:	What're you saying, you beggar? Who bothers about laddoo and jalebi these days? Now we have barfi, rasgulla, gulab jamun, meat, chicken legs...
Maatu:	Then you too must've spent a lot of money on liquor. It isn't easy to feed two hundred people.
Darshan:	Why would we spend on liquor?
Maatu:	Why? Then who did?
Darshan:	Bai's in-laws. The entire expenditure on buses, cars, liquor and everything, they had already committed. Take it, have this peg.
Maatu:	*(Drinking)* I've heard they gave a lot of dowry also.
Darshan:	What're you asking? How do I tell you, I can't even count! Car, TV, fridge, washing machine ... do you know what that is? ... a machine that washes clothes ... press the electricity button ... ghurrr ... ghurrr ... ghurrr ... and the clothes are washed!
Maatu:	Bhabhi ji, they say is very beautiful.
Darshan:	I tell you; she glows like the flame of *sulfa*. A perfect mustard flower. The first flush of the rising sun. Resplendent like the full moon. If she ever walks through your street, you'll see even the parapets will be illumined! The redolence of the illumination will fill your courtyard.
Jagga:	*(To Darshan)* Kaka ji, please come home! Elder Kaka ji is calling you, just for a minute. He said, 'You may come here immediately after that.'
Darshan:	You go Jaggeya, I'm coming. *(Jagga leaves)* Now, you stay here; I'll be back. Moreover, I'll bring meat for you. A lot of it is still left. And yes, give me that

other stuff of yours. One may drink as much liquor as one can, but this stuff gives a different kick! *(Maatu gives him four intoxicant tablets)* Now I'll experience real ecstasy! *(He puts all the four into his mouth and washes them down with water)* Wait here, I'll be back in a minute.
[Darshan goes out. Maatu sits there, confused. Then he ingests two tablets with water and drinks a large peg of whiskey. He feels dizzy and remembers fragments of what Darshan and Kailo had said to him, in their voices]
Darshan's voice: Cool ... soft drink bottles ... fish pakora ... fried liver...

— Wedding ... it was grand ... more than two hundred people in the wedding procession ...
— Do you think they are paupers...?
— Car ... TV ... Washing machine ... press the button ... ghurrr ... ghurrr
— Like the flame of the sulfa ... mustard flower ... first flush of the rising sun ... redolence will fill your courtyard ...
— Is she your wife ... you got married to her, bastard ... take this coin, girl ... buy pakoras from Kaura's shop ...

Kailo's voice:	Are you a rich Sardar to deserve eighteen-year-old ... you don't have even three acres of land ...
Darshan's voice:	Their kothi is spread over two bighas ...
Kailo's voice:	Don't own even three acres of land, and you're talking about an eighteen-year-old ...
Maatu's voice:	Then what do I do with this kitten ... She wasn't even eight at the time of marriage ... tell me what I should do ...
Darshan's voice:	I tell you; she glows like the flame of the sulfa ... a mustard flower ... first flush of the rising sun ...

	resplendent like the full moon … redolence will fill your courtyard …
	(Kailo comes in. She looks prettier than before).
Kailo:	Hasn't your mother returned as yet? Today I've to give you both a piece of my mind!
	(Maatu behaves as if he has not understood what Kailo has said. In a state of sexual arousal, he gives her a hungry look. Because of the altered sensorium produced by the intoxicants he has consumed, Kailo does not appear to be Kailo to him, but a different, new woman. It appears to him as if she's Darshan's Bhabhi).
Darshan's voice:	Redolence of the illumination will fill your courtyard …
Kailo:	What did I ask you? Why don't you answer? Just see how he is staring lecherously at me!
Maatu:	Darshan has left; the mustard flower! He said, 'your parapets will be illumined. The courtyard will be redolent with the perfumes of the illumination.'
Kailo:	What perfumes, which courtyard! Damn you!
Maatu:	The kothi is spread over two bighas … press the button and ghurrr … ghurrr …
	(Starts laughing)
Kailo:	Are you alright! You bastard, I wish you wouldn't consume so much dope!
Maatu:	How fortunate I am! The full moon! … perfumes … mustard flower, the bottle of wine … I feel like sipping …?
	(He advances towards Kailo)
Kailo:	*(Perceiving his intentions)* Wooh! Low born satyr! Rabid, ravenous!
	(She runs out)
Maatu:	She ran away. *(Bhooti comes in holding a doll in her hands)* No, she's come back again.

[*Bhooti also appears to be a grown-up woman to him. Maatu looks hungrily at her too. Bhooti is scared. She wants to run away but he jumps and stands in front of her and bolts the outer door from inside. Bhooti goes into the kitchen. Maatu follows her and drags her out, imagining her to be Darshan's Bhabhi who glows like sulfa. Darshan's voice 'Maatu, Maatu, open the door, why've you bolted it from inside' and his knocks on the door are heard at short intervals. But Maatu is oblivious to all this. He is devil incarnate and just wants to molest and maul Bhooti, Darshan's Bhabhi to him. Blinded by lust, he is running after Bhooti. Ultimately Bhooti starts panting and picking her up in his arms, he throws her on the cot lying in the courtyard. When he lowers himself on her, a scream escapes Bhooti's mouth. The outer door suddenly opens with a thud. Darshan comes in. On seeing Maatu molesting Bhooti, Darshan slaps him repeatedly on the face.*]

Darshan: You beast! You're molesting a child! Shame on you! Shame on you!!

Maatu: (*Looking with surprise at Bhooti*) Does she look like a child to you?

Darshan: Is she your mother then?

Maatu: Why mother ... she's my ... she's that one who ... with whose arrival, our courtyard is filled with the redolence of lights ...

Darshan: (*Slapping him angrily and abusing him*) You son of a bitch ... you dog, she, who you've made your wife, is like your daughter ...

Maatu: (*looking intently at Bhooti*) My daughter ... then where has she gone?

Darshan: Who?

Maatu: The one with whose arrival ... my courtyard is redolent with lights ...

(He starts crying loudly, striking his head repeatedly with the frame of the cot. Darshan stands there gnashing his teeth in anger)

—Curtain—

ATAMJIT

Atamjit (b. 1950) was born in Amritsar. He taught Punjabi in several colleges of Punjab before retiring as Deputy Director, Department of Higher Education, Punjab. Atamjit popularised the genre of the short play in Punjabi. While staying within the conventions of the dramatic art, he creates multi-layered texts. His subject matter may come from literature, or history, but he addresses burning issues of the day and raises timeless questions confronting humankind. In dealing with eternal human concerns, his texts seem to transcend temporal boundaries. He was given the Sahitya Akademi award in 2009 for his play *Tatti Tavi da Sach* that he returned in 2015. He was also conferred the Sangeet Natak Akademi award in 2010. Excerpts of his play *Murh Aa Lama Ton* (*Come Back from War*) have been included in this anthology.

Come Back from the War
(Excerpts)

Characters

Jiwan Singh:	An Indian soldier fighting for the British in Belgium during the World War I
Soldiers:	Abdullah, Baljit, Dogra, Irfan and others
Sassoon:	Their Officer, the famous English war poet
Bluma:	Wife of a Belgian soldier who has gone out to fight for the British
Phil:	Bluma's father-in-law

Scene 11

(The old Belgian has brought Jiwan Singh to his home. All three are standing, but not looking directly at the others. Indeed, they are avoiding eye contact with each other.)

Phil:	*(Introducing her)* Mr. Singh, Bluma—my daughter-in-law. The Germans killed my grandson, looted our home, took away the horse, and ate all the chicken.
Bluma:	Trampled over all the flowers.
Phil:	My son Alicio is fighting in the war. I feel he too is no more, but she thinks he's alive.
Bluma:	A woman's instinct is never wrong. He'll definitely come back.
Phil:	*(In a choked voice)* But, she doesn't say how we'll survive until he comes back. *(A long silence)* That's why I bring people like you to my home. *(He swiftly walks away)*
Bluma:	Sit down. I'll get you a beer.
Jiwan Singh:	I'm good. Thank you.
Bluma:	I could've worked in a brothel. They need many girls these days. But what would I have said to Alicio when he returns? Are you married?
Jiwan Singh:	Yes. I was married a month before leaving for the war. Mindo is also like you—tall and beautiful.
Bluma:	Do you miss her?
Jiwan Singh:	Miss her? Her memory wrings my heart; she torments me. I go mad without her. Like you, she too is waiting for her man. But what're the chances of my survival? I'm like the grain which may accidently escape the two halves of the grindstone.
Bluma:	Don't talk like this. You'll definitely go to her. May God bless you with beautiful children! *(Sighs)* I've lost my son. Believe me I'm living not only for Alicio but also for the children.
Jiwan Singh:	I don't understand.
Bluma:	When they murdered my son, I ran away. First, they raped our country, then the women. I hid behind the abandoned chicken coops. I saw a child from where I was hiding. He picked up a piece of bread from the heap of garbage and attacked it like crazy. His mother

	came running. I thought she'd snatch the bread and throw it away. She did take it from the child, but then ate it herself. And then both of them began searching for more bread in the pile of trash. There was great difference in the suffering of the two. The tears of the mother had dried up, but the ones from the child's eyes were still flowing.
Jiwan Singh:	Terrible!
Bluma:	I felt I was lucky *(Almost crying)*. My child was saved from this hunger. *(Composing herself)* I meet three customers a week. My earnings from two allow me to buy bread for my father-in-law and myself. With my earnings from the third, I buy bread for the children of the village. Today, I'll use my earnings from you for the children. *(She removes her coat, and moves toward Jiwan Singh. He puts the coat back on her shoulders.)* I've distressed your heart. Perhaps I shouldn't have talked about my sorrows. I'm not familiar with the ways of sex workers. Please forgive me.
Jiwan Singh:	No. Your heart is as beautiful as your face. You're remembering the child who has gone away, I'm dreaming about mine who is yet to come. Actually, children are beyond reach for both of us. You're doing good by connecting with those in the village. They need you very much. *(He takes out a wad of money and tries to give it to Bluma)*
Bluma:	But you ...
Jiwan Singh:	*(Closing her hand over the money)* Keep it. Feed all the children through a *langar*. Let this be my tithe.
Bluma:	But you had come for something else ...
Jiwan Singh:	No ifs and buts. We're talking about innocent children. Don't defile it by bringing in our bodies. Such times require spotless souls. *(Moves toward the door)* If I survive, I'll definitely meet you again.

Bluma: May God grant you a long life.
(He goes out. She looks at his retreating figure for a long time.)

Scene 14

(Abdullah is singing a song)

The cool breeze blows
The swings on the tree flow
Love my life in Kangra ho..
Love my life in Kangra ...

(Abdullah comes out of the trench and starts dancing)

Dogra: Come down. The Germans are close by.
Sassoon: What're you singing?
Abdullah: Song of Kangra, my beautiful town, I was singing of it.
Sassoon: Abdullah, you're always dreaming.
Abdullah: Sahib ji, one can't even cook well without dreams. I first dream the taste, and then fill the food with flavour.
Sassoon: Is Millie also a dream?
Abdullah: She's a dream even when she's right in front of my eyes; she's such a beauty! I shudder in anticipation even as I hear her name.
Sassoon: What'll you show her in your country?
Abdullah: The fort of Kangra. Built on a mountain-top between two rivers, the fort is the pride of the earth. Our region is also called Nagarkot. One side is the *Kot* which means the fort, and the other side is the *Nagar* where a deity presides. The basmati rice of Kangra has the sweet smell of incense, Sahib ji.
Sassoon: Is Kangra a big place in India?
Abdullah: I don't know about India, but my Kangra is huge. At one time it was the capital of Jallandhar.
Baljit: Even I didn't know that.

Dogra: Sahib ji, Kangra is among the strongest forts in Hindustan. It's not easy to rule it. Jahangir won it with a great deal of difficulty from the Rajputs. At times, it was with Hindu kings and at times with Muslim rulers.
Abdullah: Nepali Gurkhas also ruled it at one point of time
Baljit: Sher-e-Punjab's Sikh rule also prevailed in Kangra.
Abdullah: Of course. The Nepali Thapa was vanquished by Maharaja Ranjit Singh.
Dogra: And then Kangra went to the British.
Abdullah: (*Happily*) Kangra belongs to everyone.
Sassoon: What'll you teach Millie first of all?
Dogra: He'll make her sit in front of the oven to blow the smoke and tend to the fire. He'll rest only after the white beauty turns black all over.
Abdullah: What do you know, you Jammu guy—the dreams I have dreamt for my white beauty! I'll take leave, marry her, together we'll pay obeisance at the temple, and then I'll teach her a song
(*Sings*)

The soldier Dogriya Ho
My good soldier, O Dogra.
The pleasant flowing stream
The fragrant breeze of dreams
The majestic mountains surround
The chirping songs around
I miss my Dogriya Ho
My good soldier, O Dogra.

(*Steps out of the trench and starts dancing*) Millie will sing this in my memory:

Come on leave for few days
The blossoms are in bloom
Ask your Sahib to be kind
A bride is waiting for the groom

> *I miss my Dogriya/Dogra Ho*
> *The good soldier – the Dogra Ho*
> *The soldier – the Dogra*
> *My good soldier, O Dogra*
> She'll sing in Kangra, I'll dance in Europe.

Sassoon: Come back to the trench now. The Germans are mad dogs.

Dogra: They'll deep fry you.

Abdullah: *(Does not come down, but sits near the trench.)* I'll take a bullet happily in her name. I just want that she reaches Kangra once. When her scent mingles with the fragrance of Kangra, it'll be a different aroma altogether. This is why I spice the chicken with cinnamon and cardamom as well. *(He sees a man running from afar)* S'soon Sahib, who's that man running? See... he has thrown his rifle in the marsh. How strange!

Irfan: *(Comes running, through the trench)* Sahib ji, there's a message that he's a rebel against the government. He has no sense of nationalism.

Abdullah: O my goodness! He has taken off his uniform as well.

Irfan: The government told him many times to get enrolled. But he kept speaking against war.

Abdullah: He has removed his vest as well...

Irfan: Now the authorities have drafted him as a recruit and have forcibly sent him to the field.

Abdullah: He is stark naked!

Baljit: *(Looks through the scope)* He's really completely naked; not worried about any one.

Abdullah: Wow! He's started dancing. He keeps his Kangra close to his heart, like me.

Baljit: Sir, who can he be? He looks so small.

Sassoon: It seems he's 'big' inside.

Dogra: But he's facing the Germans, who are inhuman.

Sassoon:	Don't know what's happened to the land of Goethe. The people of Beethoven no longer appreciate music or song. The intelligentsia has also given up all this. Great authors, artists, professors, and scientists are in support of war. The bloody nationalists are victims of false pride. Our people are also no less. Except for Russell, everyone else has advocated war in retaliation.
Baljit:	Jiwan Singh says we have also been implored to join the war by Gandhi, Tagore and Lala Lajpat Rai.
Sassoon:	I know. They believe that perhaps on this pretext, the whites will grant freedom to your country. All praise for Einstein. Born in Germany, he has openly declared that war is futile, and nationalism, the measles of mankind.
Baljit:	Really! Is he a leader?
Sassoon:	No, a scientist. These days he lives in Switzerland. Leaders are fighting like the blind. The fools on both sides believe that they're peace-loving. Yet they wish to demolish the respect of the other and build themselves up in the process. Nobody is willing to look within. All're naked in this *hamam*.
Abdullah:	But the really naked guy is outside, Sahib ji. See, he's dancing freely.
Sasoon:	He's unmasking the foolishness of all the wise men. In stripping naked, he has single-handedly ripped the civilised veneer of all nations. He's our Einstein; he has his soul intact. He shouldn't die.
Abdullah:	I'll save him. *(Runs toward him. Everyone implores him to come back, but he doesn't stop. Sounds of gunfire are heard. The bullets hit Abdullah; his moans can be heard. Everybody is shocked into silence. The guns are also silent. Abdullah returns with blood all over his body, and utters his last few words before he dies.)* S'soon Sahib, please forgive me. I could not reach him. I wanted to save him and become the Einstein

of Kangra. I would have declared from the highest point of the fort that human life is the most precious on this earth. Religion, community, and nation—all have their place, but they are nothing in comparison to a human being. Please tell my Millie that she must go to Kangra. Kangra will welcome her with open arms. S'soon Sahib, she'll listen to you. She didn't see my religion, or caste, or my nation. She didn't even consider that I'm a mere cook. She only saw my heart, she loved me, only me. Long live my Millie, long live my Kangra! I love my Kangra, I love my Millie!
(He dies)

Scene 15

(Jiwan Singh is in Bluma's home)

Jiwan Singh: Yesterday, Baljit from my village also left us. A scion of *Jats*, he very enthusiastically enrolled in the army, thinking he'd do something new. What'll I tell his mother? *(Long silence)* But Bluma, will I ever reach Mindo?

Bluma: Definitely. You'll reach her.

Jiwan Singh: Will I find Sucha?

Bluma: For sure, you'll.

Jiwan Singh: How can you have such faith?

Bluma: Because I've nothing left except faith. *(Laughs)* That day I narrated one part of my story. Today I'll tell you the rest. My brother was killed in Louvain—he worked in a library. If Germany was against France and England, why destroy Belgium? If the anger was that Belgium didn't provide passage, why kill civilians? And even if the people had to be taught a lesson, what was the fault of the books? ... Or of the architectural marvels? To destroy even a single book of a nation is sheer meanness. They burnt all the books in Louvain—and my brother. They murdered our art

	as well. But I'm hopeful that art and knowledge will live again. I will look for my child and my brother in them. You may think I am crazy to imagine all this, but without this hope I'll be completely destroyed. I want to live, my friend.
Jiwan Singh:	Doesn't tragedy break us down, Bluma?
Bluma:	Yes, it does, but misfortune also makes us stronger. Yesterday, when I went to get bread for the children, a farmer was ploughing the field. The postman came on a cycle and handed him a telegram. He looked at the telegram for a few minutes, … wiped his tears, and started ploughing again. I asked the postman what was in the telegram. Actually, the farmer's son had died in the war.
Jiwan Singh:	Oh!
Bluma:	Our country is full of poppy flowers. But now I plant roses for those who are dead; and for those who're alive. *(She shows him through the window)* Look, the shrubs are growing. *(Jiwan Singh looks closely)*
Jiwan Singh:	I salute the farmer who continued working in the field. I also salute Bluma who grows the flowers.
Bluma:	Do you know what the meaning of Bluma is? *(She gently pushes down his saluting hand).* It means a flower. A flower may be weak, but nothing can compete with its strength to bloom. It always spreads its fragrance.
Jiwan Singh:	You're right.
Bluma:	Women have the same power; your Mindo too has it.
Jiwan Singh:	You're teaching me how to live!
Bluma:	We're learning from each other. *(Changes the topic)* I like your turban very much. When my Alicio returns, I'll ask him to wear it sometimes. This'll be a way to remember you. *(Jiwan Singh removes his turban and then Mindo's dupatta)* You have lovely hair.

Jiwan Singh: I wanted to show you this—Mindo's *dupatta*. She had worn it for our marriage. *(Covers his head with it, like a veil)* ... Like this.

Bluma: Give it to me. *(Takes it from him and puts it on her head)* How do I look?

Jiwan Singh: Exactly like Mindo.

Bluma: *(Grabs his hand excitedly)* Look, your Mindo is with you. *(He is happy, but she drops his hand)* But my Alicio is not here ... Wait. *(Goes and comes back with a hat)* This hat belongs to Alicio. *(Puts it on his head)* It suits you. Alicio means noble and pure ... You never told me your name.

Jiwan Singh: Jiwan, meaning life!

Bluma: May I say something? You're Alicio at heart.

Jiwan Singh: *(Not knowing what to do)* You're trying to make me happy.

Bluma: No, I'm making myself happy. I give my body to others to feed myself; today I'll give myself to you to satisfy my soul. Come close to me, my heart has blossomed after ages. I find my Alicio in you. *(Hugs him close)* The soft rhythm of love is much better than the drums of war.

(Jiwan Singh also gradually becomes intimate with her.)

Translated by Snehlata Jaswal with inputs from Vivek Sachdev

Swaraj Bir

Swaraj Bir (b. 1958) was born in Verka, Amritsar. He is a medical doctor and an IPS officer and was Director General of Police in Meghalaya. Presently he is the editor of the *Punjabi Tribune*, a well respected daily newspaper. Swaraj Bir is a poet, but is probably better known as a playwright. The themes in his plays are drawn from historical and mythical sources, yet the plays always engage contemporary problems. He makes very powerful use of poetry in the overall organization of his plays. He has written very meaningful texts that deal with contemporary issues such as religion, women, common people and politics. He was awarded the Sahitya Akademi award in 2016 for his play *Massya di Raat*.

Fragrance

(Ujaggar Singh, age 54–56 years, well-built, shaggy grey beard, wearing prison clothes, is pacing around in the jail. Whether he is alive or is a living dead body, who can say? But he has a very dominant presence. His gait is that of a proud man though there is a tinge of sadness to it.)

Ujaggar Singh:

> Flowers wither
> Fragrant paths come to an end
> Courtyards bereft of perfume
> Wizened trees
> Coughing loudly
> Seeking support to stay alive.
> This fragrance, what is it?
> This soul of man, what is it?
> Who am I?
> Standing on the earth,
> Trembling in the wind
> Blubbering inwardly
> Who am I?

Name: Ujaggar Singh. Caste: *Jat*. Profession: Farming. Village: Serai Nathu Mal.

(He speaks about himself as if speaking of someone else) **About thirty or thirty-one years ago, I got married ... my wife is Jaswinder Kaur ... her nickname is Gogi ... A woman like other women** *(Speaking in a little different manner, a little emphatically but patiently, in the manner of a man who wants to convey that what he is saying is very important and is a great truth of life)* **... You understand, what I'm**

saying? ... She's a woman like other ordinary women. ... Yes, *Jenab*, the way women generally are ... By an ordinary woman I mean the one who'll marry where her parents want her to marry ... who'll give birth to children ... will sometimes quarrel with her husband and sometimes with her mother-in-law ... who'll sometimes speak very nicely to him and sometimes pounce upon him like a bitch who has newly given birth to a litter of puppies ... the one who'll go on praising her parents ... Yes, such are the ordinary women we have here ... and *Jenab*, a woman should be like that ... one who is more or less than that doesn't suit us ... and my three children were born to this ordinary woman Gogi ... first a daughter, then a son and then a daughter again. *(a little loudly and pronouncing each word very distinctly)* Yes, I had two daughters and one son.

(In the last sentence, he lays a lot of stress on the words 'yes' and 'had'. The word 'had' strikes like a hammer. A short pause; heavy, brooding silence for a minute. He starts speaking again, laying stress on certain words.)

... And now ... not three, there're only two now ... one daughter and one son ... *(with rising excitement)* ... my Chhoti daughter, yes, my younger daughter, we called her Chhoti ... she died. Yes, Chhoti died ... There are so many people in this world who die young ... and she died ... *(Emphatically, almost yelling)* No, no ... she was murdered ... and that murder ... I committed that murder ... me and my son, we both together ... and I took the entire responsibility ... now I'm in prison ... I have been awarded life imprisonment *(He gets more excited)* ... and I'm not angry about it, no regret and no sorrow. What my son and I did was right ... that Chhoti, she wasn't an ordinary girl ... she was much more than ordinary ... she was hell-bent on bringing disgrace on us. She wanted to marry a low-born ... wanted to publicly disgrace us ... and we ... how could we allow such a thing to happen? Our daughter, a *Jat*, marrying the son of a labourer? If such a thing had happened, what would've been left of us. We would've been nowhere! We tried our best to convince her, to stop her, but she didn't stop seeing that boy ...

(A short pause)

... And one day when she went to the College, I followed her ... I myself saw her standing with that boy ... sitting with him and talking to him ... my blood boiled ... I felt like strangulating both of them there and then ... then I controlled myself with great effort ... came back home and told my wife ... I said 'I won't spare this bastard.' ... My wife Gogi started crying ... she pleaded, 'Don't do such a thing, I'll talk to her.' ... and she did talk to her ... talked to her in private ... beat her up, thrashed her ... but she was so obstinate ... What could one do? ... I don't know what had entered her mind that she insisted on one thing only ... that she'd marry that boy only ... and look at her obstinacy ... she said that if we didn't marry them, she'd herself marry him against our wishes ... I said, I'm also the son of a *Jat*, I won't allow such a thing to happen ...

(A short pause)

One day Gogi was away to her parents ... that evening I discussed it with my son ... and in the night, we talked to Chhoti and told her clearly that if she didn't agree we would hack her to pieces ... but being a true daughter of her father, she wasn't the one to relent ... and my son lost his cool ... he banged her head with a stick ... she screamed loudly ... and then ... I hit her on the head with an axe ... her skull was smashed to pieces ... the entire village turned up ... they took us to the police station ... I confessed to the crime ... I said that I alone had done it, I alone ... my elder brother, the Sarpanch of the village, patted me on my back and said, 'You've acted like a brave lion ... you didn't let our heads be bowed down with shame ... we won't allow you to be hanged.' ... A lawsuit was filed against me and I was given life imprisonment ... now I'm in jail ... Punjab Central Jail ... the biggest jail in Punjab.

(Melodious music. A short pause)

People are unnecessarily scared of jail ... I enjoy great respect here ... everyone says, 'How self-respecting he is ... a man should be like him.' The jail officials respect me ... I can get anything from outside ... There's no bar on anything ... all the prisoners salute me ... they know that I'm different from them ... What I did, I did to save our honour ... not to take revenge against an enemy ... not for money or land either ... what I did, I did to uphold my own prestige and that of my family *(laying great stress on his words)* ... Yes, to uphold the prestige of my family ... I ... killed my own daughter. Yes ... I killed my own daughter.

(A short pause. He starts speaking again, but with a different kind of frenzy and in a manner, as if justifying what he had done.)

... And that daughter of mine ... that Chhoti of mine ... she wasn't an ordinary girl ... she was much more than ordinary ... I wish she had been like my elder daughter. My elder daughter is very nice ... a very ordinary girl ... if Chhoti were like my elder daughter, she too would've been married like her ... would've gone to her in-laws ... lived happily ... but this Chhoti was very obstinate ... one day I slapped her three times and asked her 'Why do you want to marry that bastard' ... Just look at the answer she gave me ... she said ... 'I love him' ...

(A short pause)

... Love ... !

(Music. With a frown on his face, Ujaggar Singh looks into space as if he trying to understand what love is and then gnashing his teeth, he speaks with great anger)

... Love ...!

(Still more angrily and very loudly, laying stress on his words)

... and I hate this word ... this word has destroyed my family ... my daughter was infatuated with that bastard ... forgot her caste, her family status and everything ... was bent upon humiliating me ... Love ... yes ... what did she think of love? ...

(Stops immediately and frowns)

Love ...?

(In a lower voice)

My mother loved me ... I remember ... she used to feed me *choorie* ... after coming back from the school I used to go straight to her lap ...

hugged her ... it gave me great comfort ... As I became an adult, I grew out of my mother's love ... Chhindo *Jheeri* was the first girl I befriended ... and then once Bhola, the son of the gardeners brought a girl from the city ... and we had fun in their garden ... but love ... such a thing never happened.

(Music. Pauses and says very angrily, once again)

... Yes, yes ... such a thing never happened ...!

(Anger subsiding a little he seems to be lost in deep thought)

... Did such a thing never happen? ... No, I'm lying ... *(thoughtfully)* ... Yes, I'm lying ... After all man is man, *Jenab* ... even cattle fall in love ... and I'm, after all, a man ... *(softening)* ... I've a bit of love for my wife Gogi ... and a bit for my elder daughter as well ... yes for both of them, who are ordinary women ... and I love my son the most ... I can lay down my life for him ... yes, it's for this reason only that I took the entire blame on myself ... he's the star of my eyes ... may he always be happy! Next year, he'll be married off ... once he is married may God bless him with a son ... May our family tree flourish ... what else do we have, except him? ... I love him a lot ... Yes, I love my son a lot ...

(Low music. In trying to understand the sentiment of love, Ujaggar Singh's eyes have become moist. In order to control the surging emotion, he presses the corners of his eyes near the nose with his thumb and first finger.)

... You're unnecessarily demoralised Ujaggar Singh ... but what can Ujaggar Singh do? ... What can he do? Ujaggar Singh loved his Chhoti too ... and as I've told you Chhoti wasn't an ordinary girl ... she was extraordinary ... and since her childhood, she loved me a lot ... I wasn't very happy when she was born ... I wanted another son ... but Chhoti was born ... sometimes I feel that what I did with her when she was an adult, if I had done the same thing when she was born ... strangled her to death ... nobody would've come to know ... we wouldn't have earned disrepute ... I wouldn't have seen this jail ... but a person is likely to miss out on an opportunity ... he cannot accomplish everything at the most opportune moment ... Yes, if I'd killed her after her birth ... Oh my God ! What must Ujaggar Singh do? That stupid girl haunts me all the time.

(Music. Ujaggar Singh paces around. A pause)

Yes, she haunts me a lot ... They say when a leaf snaps off from a branch, sap drips from there ... and after all she was my daughter ... she'll be remembered ... and I was saying that when she was born, I hadn't felt happy ...the entire first year passed like that ... I didn't like her even a wee bit ... *(lost in memories)* ... then she started walking ... and then she started lisping. When I would return home in the evening, I would sit on a cot in the courtyard ... and she would come to me sucking her thumb and speaking in her lisping way ... gradually, my heart melted. On those days when I found her asleep after coming back, my home appeared different ... empty, as it were. I waited for her to wake up ... and talk to me in her lisping way ... I would pick her up and take her out ... brought her toffees from Gajji's shop *(very meekly)* ... yes Jenab, I loved Chhoti a lot ...

(A pause)

And our courtyard was quite big ... and I was very fond of growing vegetables ...There's no vegetable I didn't grow in the courtyard ... fenugreek, spinach, tomato, coriander, onion, gourd, okra and many others ... the seeds of radish and turnip were thrown among the fodder plants ... the other vegetables I grew in the courtyard ... Jenab, the vegetables grown at home taste very different ... and my Chhoti, when she was in fourth or fifth standard went to a friend's house and brought from there some seeds and seedlings ... in one bed, she planted the seedlings and in another she scattered the seeds ... I wanted to grow onions and tomatoes in those beds ... the seedlings were ready ... I uprooted the plants grown by her and planted onions and tomatoes in their place ... and what did I see when I came back the next evening? ... that Chhoti had pulled out onions and tomatoes and thrown them out of our door ... I was very angry and scolded her ... and she replied, 'If you can pull out the plants I planted, then why can't I pull out onions and tomatoes planted by you?'... I laughed at that little girl's very simple logic... that day she appeared very affectionate to me... I took her in my lap and hugged her... then we, father and daughter, came to a compromise... and that day, that silly little darling, standing with her arms akimbo was arguing with me as if she were my age!... And she said, 'You grow onions and tomatoes in this bed, and in this one I'll grow flowers... that ends our quarrel.' And she grew flowers... when the right weather arrived, the flowers blossomed... and they exuded fragrance... and one day when I came back late, it was already dark... what wonderful fragrance had spread everywhere in our house!... She had planted the jasmine... it appeared as if the entire house was filled with perfume... that day, yes that day, I liked my home a lot... it appeared as if it were some heaven... she had grown flowering plants of several kinds... marigold... sunflower... there were two rose bushes too... and then I used to bring seeds of flowering plants which she planted and nurtured... And her mother said... 'You've pampered her.'... Chhoti's mother didn't want to send her to college... only I stood by her... she brought many types of seeds from the city and planted them in the courtyard... and she wore only those clothes which had flowers painted on them... and sometimes she embroidered too... on the collar of her shirts, on the hem and on the sleeves... she embroidered flowers everywhere... sometimes I felt that the girl was utterly mad... mad about flowers... she embroidered flowers, planted flowers... embroidered flowers on the pillow covers... embroidered them on *matte* cloth and got them framed in glass *(getting agitated)*... But what kind of a flower it was that she wanted to plant in the courtyard of her life?... *(getting more agitated and angry)*... and I didn't approve of it! *(A little less loudly)*... On the evening of this incident, my son and I decided that first we would try to persuade her... and if she didn't agree, then we would have to do it... after deciding it, my son and I went to the Gurudwara... we offered prayers to the Waheguru... I said... 'Waheguru, give us the strength to carry it out... It's a matter of our prestige, our honour'... And then I smashed the head of the one who planted flowers... *(very loudly, speaking each word distinctly and with great emphasis*) ... Yes ... I smashed her head ... I killed ... my daughter.

(*Violent music. Very disturbed, Ujaggar Singh paces around and tries to control himself. He succeeds and starts speaking in his natural way*)

Many times, I think ... I shouldn't have allowed her to grow flowers when she was a child ... daughters shouldn't be pampered ... and then I think, what if she had planted the flower of her choosing? ... What would've happened then? ... A storm starts raging in my head when I think like this ... *(very loudly)* ... I couldn't have tolerated that flower ... I had to crush it ... and I crushed the one who was thinking of planting that flower ... *Jenab*, the most important thing is honour ... honour has to be kept intact ... and because of what we did, we could save our honour ... so what if there's no fragrance of flowers in it? ... honour, after all, is honour ... the question is of a person's honour ... his prestige ... How does fragrance matter? One can live even when there's no fragrance ... but honour is that garment which if it is torn, leaves a man naked ... yes *Jenab*, man can't live without honour ... only honour is man's life ... how does fragrance matter? ... it's a useless thing ... today I enjoy respect in the entire area ... so what if there's no fragrance in it ...

(*A short pause. Thinking deeply.*)

Fragrance ...?

(*Music. Pause. Ujaggar is gazing into the distant horizon as if fragrance were a sculpture or a picture, which would materialise on the horizon. Feeling embarrassed, he grumbles*).

Fragrance ...?

(*A little more loudly*)

What is fragrance? ... A kind of perfume? ... and why is it liked so much by man? ... Why do such different kinds of scents, perfumes and fragrances come into being? ... What sort of a thing this fragrance is ... does it exist or not? ... And the fragrance of flowers grown by Chhoti still lives in memories. What can Ujaggar Singh do? ... Chhoti haunts me often ...!

(A short pause)

Memories …? Oh my God, what're these memories that you have made? … memories?

(Music. A short pause)

I often wonder why Chhoti's memories haunt me …? Memories …? Not only memories, that accursed darling just cannot be forgotten … I feel as if she's always with me, crying sometimes, and sometimes laughing! … Sometimes sulking, sometimes smiling and sometimes talking to me … and very often I've nightmares … in a dream she's like a witch hacking me to pieces … and she's hacking her brother to pieces … and throwing the pieces into a canal … and in another dream she ties a rakhi on my wrist … and in another one, her wedding is taking place … the *laavaan* ceremony is taking place … the fourth *laanv* is being recited … Chhoti is walking behind her husband … all relatives shower flowers on the couple … they shower rose petals … and then wrapped in *phulkari* Chhoti is sitting by the side of the groom … how beautiful she looks! … and then the groom lifts his *sehra* … and when he lifts his *sehra*, what do I see? … He's the same boy she loved … I snatch the groom's sword and attack him … I slay the groom … and tear the *phulkari* to shreds … and then blood starts oozing from Chhoti's hands adorned with henna … the torn *phulkari* becomes dark red with the groom and Chhoti's blood … I burst into loud laughter … and the people standing there also laugh loudly … and the torn, blood-spattered *phulkari* dries up … and the flowers embroidered on the *phulkari* step out and start flying in the air … the air is filled with the fragrance of those flowers … yes, the air is filled with the fragrance of those flowers … the scent of blood, flowers and henna …

(Music. Pause)

… Yes, fragrance … this fragrance … what kind of a fragrance it is?

(Music. Pause)

Where does this fragrance come from?

(*Music. He looks all around, as if trying to find out the direction from where this fragrance appears to be coming. But he can't find anything and then he starts narrating his story again*).

... and I was talking about dreams ... a very weird kind of a dream I repeatedly see ... it's night ... dark dreadful night ... and our daughters all get up in the middle of the night ... and start planting flowers they love ... and then their parents wake up ... their uncles and brothers wake up ... and hit them on their heads with sticks, slap them, kick them, drag them ... shots are fired ... blood flows in a torrent ... the way it had flowed from Chhoti's head ... girls scream ... and I, drenched in sweat, wake up. There's deep silence everywhere in the jail ... There's no flower here ... but I can smell the fragrance of flowers grown by Chhoti ... I don't know why that fragrance has invaded my nostrils ... why it dwells in my mind ...? And I pray to Waheguru ... 'Waheguru, deliver me from this fragrance ... I did all this after seeking your permission ... to save my own and my family's honour ... Waheguru, you've been very kind ... you gave me the strength and the family honour was saved ... be merciful once more ... deliver me from this fragrance ... In nearby villages people narrate my story to each other ... if this story doesn't have fragrance in it, then what it is? ... Deliver me from this fragrance. I don't want anything else from you. These nightmares are because of that fragrance ... Waheguru, I'm a respectable person ... and how does fragrance matter at all? ... it's a useless thing ... you saved my honour ... this is enough for me ... fragrance is a useless thing ... and then the question is ... should a man protect his honour or not? ... I think a lot ... and this is the answer that I get ... if a man doesn't protect his honour, then he is not a man ... if a man is self-respecting, only then he's a man ... Waheguru, I'm your slave ...I had sought your permission by presenting myself in person before you to do all this in order to save my honour ... and you permitted me ... and saved my honour ... now there're no flowers in our courtyard ... no flowers in this jail ... then, from where does this fragrance emanate? ... Waheguru, save me from this fragrance ... fragrance is a useless thing ... deliver me from it ... fragrance is a useless thing ...

Waheguru, deliver me from this fragrance ... deliver me from this fragrance ... Waheguru, deliver me from this fragrance.'
(He stands with his hands folded, as if in front of Waheguru. The curtain falls.)

Pali Bhupinder Singh

Pali Bhupinder Singh (b. 1965) was born in Jaito, district Faridkot and is an accomplished dramatist of the new generation. His dialogue is crisp and he creates dramatic situations that deeply involve the audience. He examines contemporary society by focussing on the man–woman relationship, and in doing so exposes the fault lines therein. He has also written political satires. He currently teaches at Punjab University, Chandigarh. Given here are some excerpts from his play *Pyasa Kaan*.

The Thirsty Crow
(An excerpt)

A Voice: Professor Atma Ram, the charge against you is that you embezzled five thousand rupees by submitting a false bill for fans received in charity. Is this true?
(In response, Atma Ram's eyes turn red with anger. He pulls the classroom benches around him and very hurriedly improvises a dock in a courtroom, and stands in it.)

Atma Ram: And now, gentle folks, begins that climax of the story which you've never heard before, because the policymakers that be conspired to change that climax for all time to come, I'll show you that climax of the thirsty crow's story which was written neither with stones nor with the water of the pitcher, but with the crow's blood.
(Standing in the middle of the dock)

When reaching the lonely phase of his life the thirsty crow realised that there was very little water in the pitcher; he didn't get worried, as your story goes, rather ...
(Suddenly, martial music begins. He shrieks, his bloodshot eyes reflecting anger.)
Why's there so little water in the pitcher?
(The music becomes loud)
Who drank my share of water?

The voice: Don't ask questions, Professor Sahib! This isn't your court, but of the Management. You tell us if you've something to say in your defence.

Atma Ram: Yes, I will. When after protecting the entire city under the shade of my wings, after fanning people with cool breeze, and after scorching my body in the heat of the sun, I reached this lonely phase in my life, then I found there was very little water in the pitcher. What could I do then?

Second voice: You could've died like your father Mohan Lal. But you shouldn't have demeaned yourself.

Atma Ram: I had risen so high that my home and my family were left far below. Bit by bit, in front of my own eyes, my straw nest became desolate. What remained was one last dream. What could I do? For how long could I go on wrecking my own dreams? In order to teach theories to your children, I made my own children objects of my experiments. When I told you something good, you asked me if my children were doing that. Only for setting examples in front of your children, I shackled my children in a prison of principles, ideals and discipline. See, suffocated in that prison, they died one by one.

Third voice: Keeping these problems of yours in mind we gave you many chances, Atma Ram ji, but it's a pity that you didn't do anything to reform yourself. Your medical reports also clearly show that your mental balance is disturbed. Because of what you've been saying and doing in class, no parents in the city are prepared to send their children to your class. We pity you, otherwise we would have suspended you very long ago.

(Stunned by these allegations, Atma Ram staggers a little)

Atma Ram: Don't do that. Don't take pity on my old age and my loneliness. If you can, then please take pity on this sick education system.

Fourth voice: Keep these sermons of yours to yourself. Tell us clearly if you've something to say in your defence.

Atma Ram: I've already said a lot... it makes no difference. Things remain the same. How sad it is that those who should be answerable at this moment are asking questions. Don't you think that you should've been standing here in my place?

Another voice: *(Very bitterly)* Stop this nonsense! We've already put up with a lot from you! You speak to the students and children against us and the education system. You instigate them against us!

Atma Ram: I only speak the truth.

Another voice: What do you think of yourself? Jesus Christ? Or Socrates? Why don't you talk like a human being?

Atma Ram: Because I don't have the time to talk now. Tomorrow, I give my last lecture in this college, and I need to prepare for that after I get home.

Voice: You'll deliver your last lecture only if we allow you to do that! *(To others)* Friends, the way this man is behaving rudely, my verdict is 'suspension'.

Second voice: Suspension!

(Many voices repeat this verdict)

First voice: It's unanimously decided that Atma Ram is being suspended with immediate effect for being rude, mad, for misguiding children and for embezzling five thousand rupees.

	(Atma Ram is stunned. The word 'suspend' strikes him like a hammer blow)
Atma Ram:	But my last class?
One voice:	You'll meet the class after you're dead!
Atma Ram:	*(Losing his temper)* Okay... I'll meet it after I'm dead, but I'll certainly meet it. I won't leave you. I'll cling to you like a ghost after my death. You won't be able to evade my questions. My questions will reverberate in the streets.
One voice:	Your questions will reverberate in the streets? Just step out of the class. Having turned against you, people are moving around armed with sticks.
	(A roar in the streets. Atma Ram is scared)
ASlogans:	Down with Atma Ram! Down with Atma Ram! Death to Atma Ram! Suspend Atma Ram! There's a clamour in every street, that Atma Ram is a thief!
	(After hearing the last sentence, Atma Ram gets extremely agitated).
Atma Ram:	*(Pained)* Shut up! I say shut up! What did I steal, rascals! Rather I gave, I gave a lot to this system!
	(Recounting his past)
	Full forty years of my life... my youth... my home... all my relations ... my wife, two young sons, one daughter...
	(Whimpering)
	Life always kept calling me ... inviting me to have my feet firmly planted on solid earth ... to have a close look at it, to enjoy all its myriad hues.
	(Moving music is heard. Lights perform a lively dance on the cyclorama. Voices of children laughing can be heard and the shadows of two small children appear, brother and sister, frolicking in a house. A small child with his hands spread out, calls to Atma Ram)
Child:	Papa you come too.
	(Atma Ram closes his eyes tight. His agony is increasing)

Atma Ram:	In order to raise the level of my country and society, I sacrificed all the colourful pleasures of life. I taught two or three times more than the prescribed syllabus in my classes. But whenever I marked the papers, I found that the students had written their answers from help books. What was the end result of my forty years of dedication then? Nobody understood either my theories or experiments; neither at home, nor at the college. Then what's the meaning of my entire life? What did I get out of it? *(Suddenly, his mind is in the grip of intense pain and he throws down all the stools along with blackboard, and screams and then drops down on his knees)* Neither my children nor my students listened to me. Neither an ideal father, nor an ideal teacher ... then who am I? *(Squirming)* I'm a crow ... a crow ... the thirsty crow ... *(Stepping forward he runs all over the stage, as if flying, cawing like a crow)*
A voice:	Stop him! Someone should do something about this madman.
Atma Ram:	Yes, yes *(angrily)*. Do something about this mad crow, otherwise he'll sit on your parapets and cry caw, caw, caw ... plugging your ears with your fingers won't help you, *Jenab*! Into how many openings in your body will you shove your fingers? ... Plug your ears with anything, my voice will make its way into you ... caw ... caw ... caw. *(He yells very loudly)*
One voice:	This professor has gone mad. He has lost his mind.
Another voice:	He should be in an asylum rather than in a college.

Third voice:	He should be stoned and driven out of the city.
Chorus of Voices:	Yes, yes, yes! Hit him! Drive this madman out of the city. Hit him!
Atma Ram:	Mad! Yes, I'm mad! I'm mad! I'm a madman!! *(Behaving like a mad man)* I'll kill ... I'll kill everyone. I have the license to kill everyone. Be warned ... be warned if you send your children to schools and colleges for studies, all of them will die. Some will burn while sitting on the benches, and some will enter toilets after raising their little finger. There'll be the smell of burning flesh. Upset by that, some people will run to Ambedkar Street. There'll be a police picket. They'll try to escape and the police will shoot them in the back. Bullets will be fired ... boom ... boom! On hearing the sound of the gunshots, Gandhi will leave the examination hall and rush into Bhagat Singh's house. The papers will be left behind in the examination hall. The boys will make balls and play with them and the girls will stuff the paper in their hips. Then the chicks will hatch from them. And then the chicks will grow. They'll study in medical college and perform experiments with alcohol. Their mothers will call them for food and they'll look for water to wash their hands with. But there'll be very little water in the pitcher. They'll pick up stones and throw them into the pitcher and it will break. A voice will come from the broken pitcher *(singing) Dum maro dum, mitt jaye gham ... bolo subah sham ... hare Krishna hare Ram ...*
Voice:	He's mad! Hit him! He's mad! Hit-him! *(Imagining some people following him, he runs frightened to a lonely place. He kneels down and puts his head on the ground for some time and then turning towards the audience, addresses them)*

Atma Ram: Now begins the anti-climax. ... It's a lie that on that day the thirsty crow had come to this lonely place in search of water, as you're taught in schools. Rather like a mad man he had been driven away from the city by stones pelted at him. Stones from this side, and from that; stones were being hurled at him from all sides ... so many stones that the entire system had turned into a monolith. His entire body was injured by the stones that hit him; his throat was parched with thirst, but he wasn't afraid.
(His eyes sparkle)
He mustered all his strength and stood up in full glory with his chest puffed out to face the shower of stones.
(He puts a bench on another bench and stands on it. Asking questions to the mad crowd ... loudly, to the mad crowd) Why is sixty-five percent of this pitcher empty? Why is the water in it stagnant? Where has the water of the city gone? Who's trading in thirst? Who? Who? Who?
(Stones continuously strike him ... his questions are creating confusion in the world of shadows. As a result, the hail of stones increases continuously)
In the air, in the space ... in the sky, his questions were thundering like clouds and in response, there was a shower of stories ... and then suddenly ...
(Suddenly a stone strikes his forehead and everything stops)
A stone hit him in the forehead ... a stream of blood gushed out ... another stream flowed downwards and entering his eyes, turned hot because of the fire in his eyes and reached his mouth ... the thirsty crow tasted his blood with his tongue and suddenly ... *(proudly)* his thirst was quenched.

(Lilting music. Atma Ram is licking the blood oozing from his forehead with his fingers.)

Yes, on that day the crow quenched his thirst by sitting on this pitcher; quenched it not with the water from the pitcher, but with his blood. Stones kept hitting him, blood kept flowing and his thirst was quenched, and then he flew away, high into the skies. Forever...

(The music becomes rhythmical. Atma Ram starts flying in the air. The spotlight follows him.)

(Fade out)

Kewal Dhaliwal

Kewal Dhaliwal (b. 1964) was born in village Dhaliwal, district Amritsar. He studied at the National School of Drama. He has given Punjabi theatre new energy and respectability. Like Gursharan Singh, he too became a playwright via theatre. He has a wonderful talent for creating interesting plays based on a story, poem, a painting or life. He has edited many anthologies of plays. In drama, his major contribution is in the field of children's drama, by organising numerous theatre workshops for children apart from writing plays for children which are interesting, moving and carry a message. The Ford Foundation gave him a research grant in 2010–12. He won the National School of Drama's Manohar Singh Smriti Award in 2006 and the Sangeet Natak Akademi award for Direction in 2013.

Bonhomie in the Jungle
(A play for children)

(When the lights come on, a dense forest is seen. Many animals are seen running helter-skelter. Some of them are trembling in fear. Some of them appear petrified with fear and anger. A huge bear pulls the ears of an

elephant. He talks loudly. All the animals stop where they are and watch the bear. All are quiet, as the bear speaks loudly)

The Bear: What has happened? Why're you running here and there? *(Nobody answers)* Has the sky fallen down or is the jungle on fire? *(Nobody speaks. The bear, looking at the dog, says)* You're a watchman, why don't you speak?

The Dog: Our jungle is in danger; very soon we'll neither have a place to live, nor anything to eat.

The Monkey: And we won't have any trees to climb and swing from.

The Deer: We won't have even grass to eat.

The Elephant: But why?

The Fox: They're felling all the trees.

The Bear: Why?

The Squirrel: *(In tears)* They've destroyed my home.

The Rabbit: They've … my …

The Dog: Some dangerous men are moving around. They'll certainly bully us.

The Elephant: Let them come; I'll trample them underfoot.

The Fox: Good, but how many of them will you trample?

The Deer: Yes, how many will you kill?

The Fox: Men are men!

The Cat: They have sticks.

The Sheep: They have axes and daggers.

The Rabbit: They have …

The Deer: They've swords and guns.

The Bear: Keep quiet. *(To the dog)* Are you sure that they're coming to snatch our jungle from us?

The Monkey: Don't they have homes? Why do they want to snatch our jungle?

The Dog: It's quite possible that they have less land. Once at a festival I saw numberless people. It was with great difficulty that I could escape from being trampled under their feet. I'll never go there again. They were so many of them!

The Bear:	This is very serious. We must do something to save our jungle.
The Deer:	The jungle is our life.
The Elephant:	The jungle is our mother.
The Rabbit:	The jungle is our God.
The Bear:	*(Thinking of the gravity of the situation)* This is a very difficult time for us. We must join hands. We must plan something to save our world.
The Dog:	And this scheme would be named SOS, which means 'Save our Souls.'
The Bear:	Very good. SOS will be our code word. Friends, we can save ourselves only if we help each other.
The Squirrel:	*(Laughing)* How can I help this big, fat elephant?
The Cat:	How can I help this dog, who's always pouncing upon me?
The Rabbit:	How can I go near a cat, who's always glowering at me?
The Bear:	You'll never learn anything. Why're you all speaking at the same time? Only one person should speak at a time. *(To the monkey)* You Crooked Tail, give me a banana. *(The monkey gives him a banana)* Good, now imagine that this banana is your mike. Only the person who has this mike shall speak, others'll listen. Let's have a meeting.
The Fish:	Oh! I can't come. But don't worry, there's no need for me to come out of water. We'll have a video conference and use mobile phones.
All of them:	Very good, very good!
	(The parrot gives a mobile phone to each one and they all laugh.
The Bear:	Now you suggest what we should do to save our jungle.
All:	Yes, Sir.
	(They laugh)
The Bear:	Who'll speak first?

All:	I Sir, I Sir.
The Bear:	Keep quiet, only one at a time. Okay, I'll decide. *(Looking at the elephant)* You're the biggest, you speak first.
The Elephant:	*(Holding the banana)* Ha ... ha ... ha ... ha ... but I want to eat it. *(They all laugh)*
The Bear:	*(Rebuking him)* Be warned! It isn't for eating; it's for speaking.
The Elephant:	But what can I say? Yes, I'm big therefore I can trumpet loudly, I can push things, I can fight, I can crush anyone under my feet *(everyone claps)*. I can't climb trees. *(He returns the banana).*
The Bear:	Yes, Crooked Tail, it's your turn now.
The Monkey:	*(Baring his teeth)* This is my banana. I can hop from one branch of a tree to another. I can dance. But I cannot run like the deer.
The Bear:	*(To the rabbit).* Well, Beautiful Eyes, it's your turn now.
The Rabbit:	I'm very small. I can dig long burrows in the earth to live in them. I can enter a burrow from one side of the jungle and come out from the other side. But when I'm above the ground, even a dog can easily catch me. His legs are strong. My legs are small.
The Bear:	*(To the fox)* Well, it's your turn now, Miss Long Nose.
The Fox:	Everybody knows how cunning I am. I can sniff a thing from miles away and tell what it is.
The Bear:	My dear Deer, now you say something.
The Deer:	I'm a good runner but I need open space to run. My beautiful antlers get caught in the branches of the trees.
The Bear:	Would someone else like to add anything?
The Fox:	What do you want to do now?

The Bear:	We'll start a new school. We'll make a nice new syllabus and then start our studies. Everyone will have to study so that we're able to develop good qualities in us and we can face all challenges.
All:	What do you mean by this new syllabus?
The Bear:	We'll understand each other's capabilities.
The Rabbit:	Will I have to learn to climbs a tree?
The Cat:	Will I have to learn how to dig a tunnel?
The Monkey:	Will I compete with the deer in a race?
The Squirrel:	Will I walk like the big-eared elephant?
The Deer:	Will I bark like a dog?
The Elephant:	I wish to fly like a bird.
The Rabbit:	I also wish to swim like fish.
The Cat:	But we don't have these talents in us.
All:	We're all different.
The Bear:	What you all say is right. How can the elephant climb a tree? He'll fall. But he can strengthen the roots of the tree. In the same way the squirrel can't sprint like the deer, because he's very small, but he can bore holes even in mountains. We'll pool all our strengths and provide a really Broad Based Learner Education, which will impart not only bookish knowledge, but will be based on an understanding of the innate qualities of all the organisms. With our special knowledge and abilities, we'll be able to understand the challenges of life and also our inner self. Rather than working singly, we'll work together and all this will give us the strength to face difficult situations.
All:	Very good! Excellent! Let's do it then!
The Rabbit:	*(Jumping up)* It'll be a real school. I'd been going to school daily to learn new things. They taught many new and different things to boys and girls such as dancing, running, painting, speaking and eating.
The Bear:	You're right, this is our real school. Let's join it.

The Elephant:	We'll become competent enough to protect our jungle. We'll be able to protect our land too.
A Big Man:	*(Coming out of the bushes)* Very good, this is a very good school. I too want to join your school.
A Small Man:	Me too.
	(The animals look at him with surprise and fear)
The Dog:	No, you can't be admitted. You are human beings. This school is for animals only, a school for the animals, by the animals. You may leave.
The Monkey:	You've lost your humanity.
The Fox:	You've laid waste our world.
The Cat:	You've laid waste your world too.
The Sheep:	Go away, go away!
Both Men:	But we want to learn new things.
The Rabbit:	You're very clever.
The Small Man:	You're also very smart.
The Bear:	But you have guns.
The Big Man:	We're peace-loving citizens. A school is a temple of learning. We want to join your school as pupils. We consider the entire world as our family. We're also animals, but we've some special abilities in us.
The Bear:	We accept their request on compassionate grounds. Mr. Elephant, do you want to say something?
The Elephant:	I agree with you. We'll teach humanity to these humans.
	(All of them nod in agreement).
The Squirrel:	They'll be able to understand us only when they study in our company.
The Monkey:	I'll learn their language from them.
All:	Well, admit them.
The Bear:	My dear humans, we welcome you on your admission to our school.
The Big Man:	Thank you for your help. We'll live up to your expectations.
	(All of them sing)

Song: We'll study together
           Work together
           For a better world
           A world full of love
           A world with equal opportunities for all
           A world full of mirth and joy
           A world full of love.

7
Prose

Teja Singh

Teja Singh (1894–1958) was born in village Adiala, district Rawalpindi (Pakistan). Along with Gurmukhi he also learnt Urdu and Persian scripts. He did his Masters in English and wrote a few books in the language. He taught History and English at Khalsa College, Amritsar. In Punjabi, he made a significant contribution in the areas of lexicography, autobiography, criticism and essay writing. He also wrote on many subjects related to Sikh religion. He is considered to be the benchmark for Punjabi prose writing. Thus a large number of his sentences became famous as idioms or phrases.

The Love of Home

A house made of bricks and stone does not make a home. 'Home' is the place where one's love and aspirations grow; where one's childhood features a doting mother and siblings; where, after conquering the world, a spirited youth wishes to return with his hard-earned money; where, free from life's trials, one can leisurely live out one's old age with the sweetness akin to the warmth of a mother's lap. A home is the centre of emotions, aspirations and personality of any human being. While the social and national milieu impacts the formation of one's character, the four walls of a home and the environment therein influence it no less. In fact, a person's character is formed within the home itself. It is the mould that shapes one's interests and dispositions. Sometimes when I come across a gentleman with an uncouth, ill-tempered or irritable nature, I pity him in my heart, and wonder how the poor soul must have been deprived of love at home.

I know an old lady who is the very image of kindness and benefaction. Every day, morning and evening, she unfailingly carries out her religious practices and circumambulates at the gurudwara. She cannot bear to see others in pain. Her sensibilities are gentle and pure and she is capable of immense empathy. When she looks at children, she turns into a child herself. However, her temperament is very harsh. She gets irritated at the slightest provocation and is completely beside herself with rage at such times. In such a state, she appears to be totally pitiless and bereft of love, but in reality, even at that point in time, she is as soft and tender as before. Just that this softness and tenderness is hidden behind the veneer of anger. The cause of her anger and agitation can be found by excavating her past, where one finds that she never received any love at home. She had been deserted by her husband in her youth, and her lap never cradled a son or daughter. No child had ever put its tiny arms around her neck and exclaimed, 'Ma! Look, how pretty I am!'

I have known many renowned storytellers who, while narrating stories or lecturing people gathered under canopies, mesmerise them by the miracles of their wisdom and knowledge. But if some miserable or needy person knocks at their door, he might be made to wait for many hours before an audience is granted and, if at all they meet, their heart is not stirred by compassion; their eyes always remain dry like Namrood's grave, never moistened by pity or love. What is the reason for such hard-heartedness? The reason is but this—the gentlemen invest their entire time in flipping through scriptures and writing, or like one gentleman's wife says, 'Your brother spends his life in cars and trains forever carrying his handbag. The love of a home is absent there. As a result, his life becomes devoid of spirit and warmth, remains dry.'

Such preachers and writers project the lives of the masters and prophets as modelled on their own lives, rendering them similarly dry and devoid of homely love. They present Guru Nanak's life in such a manner as if he never passed through a babbling childhood. That right since his childhood he had been delivering nothing but words of wisdom and spirituality, as he did in his mature years. They are ignorant of the fact that the innocence of children, their carefree nature, the love of siblings, being pampered and throwing tantrums are as vital for sculpting great persons as they are for common people. Their thoughts, aspirations and actions evolve naturally through such experiences. For those who would tend to lead an ordinary life, such childhood experiences prepare them for the simple activities of worldly existence; while those who aspire for a higher level of being, for them domestic love, angst and alienation from parents, sisters protecting their brothers at every step—all these create an atmosphere that propels them towards the Lord and teaches them to endure torments and make sacrifices. Having failed to comprehend the essentiality of childhood experiences, those writers have penned down the life of Jesus without even mentioning his childhood, and even portrayed the character of the parents of Buddha and Guru Nanak in very poor light. Had the writers realised that great men too could imbibe positive influences from the environment within their abode, they would have attempted to decipher signs of their emerging greatness in their childhood. Then they would have written reverentially about their parents. The scene from the *janamsakhi* of Guru Nanak which I find most poignant and enthralling is when Guru ji returns home after journeying foreign lands. With a heavy heart, Nanak sends Mardana to the village to find about the well-being of his family members, while he himself stays back at a well outside the village. He exhorts Mardana, 'Please don't tell them that I too have come here.' Mardana goes to mother Tripta ji to enquire about everyone. When he is about to depart, she follows him out of the village and reaches the place where Guru ji was sitting. If one wanted to witness divine reflection in the greatness of a mother, the description of this scene merits reading. The mother is overwhelmed at the sight of her son and her words are so drenched with motherly affection that they far surpass the pathos expressed in the poetry of the highest order and outshine the most intense emotions. She kisses the forehead of her son and says, 'I sacrifice my life for you, my son. I sacrifice my life for the countries you visited. I sacrifice my life for the paths you trod on your way here.' Had it been a philosopher, he would have derisively told his mother, 'Go away. I am not some simple fool. You have come in the guise of *maya* to lead me astray.' No. Instead, Guru ji melted at her words and fell at her feet, crying profusely. Abundant knowledge and meditation were distilled in those tears which were strong enough to nourish the roots of thousands of duties and benefaction.

Was the influence of the love of Bibi Nanaki insignificant on Guru Nanak Sahib? She was the one who had brought him up singing lullabies and protected him from his father's slaps by holding him in her arms. She motivated and encouraged him in his practice of fair trade. If he was 'Nanak', was she not 'Nanaki'?

Was the impact of his wife Khadija less important on the life of Mohammad Sahib? She came to his rescue in difficult times and was the first one to understand him and believe in his ideal of life, constantly encouraging him. Mohammad Sahib used to be terribly exhausted when he experienced revelations from God; it was only Khadija who used to calm him and bring him back to his normal state by lovingly placing his head in her lap and drive away his fatigue.

Had Carlyle loved his wife, he would never have been so furious and ill-tempered. He would remain confined to his room reading and writing while his wife, sitting alone in the corridor, would look at visitors anxiously. If she ever mustered the courage to open his door and peep inside, he would get very irritated and would harshly send her out of the room. Of what benefit to the world is his endless discourse on the subject of 'silence' while his own pen never kept quiet and went on snipping unceasingly, like the scissors of a stupid barber at work? Of what use are his long-winded write-ups through which he flogged and admonished people, while he completely failed in giving any comfort to his wife at home?

A major part of the degeneration of the present day can be traced to shrinking spaces for domestic affairs and an increasingly commercial approach to life. The number of houses is dwindling while hotels are proliferating. Not realising the benign impact of living at home with children and spouse, people prefer the club and hotel life. As a result, people are losing the noble qualities of familial responsibility, fraternal civility, the sweetness and humility which grow only from conduct at home. The interest in one's wife and children is limited to the extent that it enables the man to present his public face. It is rarely observed that the head of the family endeavors to acquire the resources that spur mental, civil or spiritual growth of the family members or tries to enhance for them opportunities for sports, books, healthy entertainment or religious instruction.

It is often deplored that young men and students are socially disengaged, irresponsible, and often transgress the limits of proper conduct. The reason behind it is the adoption of lifestyles prevalent in boarding rather than in their homes. The boy who has stayed in a boarding school since his childhood, has spent most part of his life away from his mother, sister, brother and neighbours, and is devoid of familial qualities (of humility, compassion, respect for fraternity, etc.). In the event of the demise of an aunt, the young man has no clue on how to offer commiserations. His mother has to accompany him and cover it up by saying, 'The boy has come to offer condolence for the aunt.' Without relationships and familial bonds, starved of familial love, when such a young man visits his village after a year and sees girls, he is unable to exercise restraint on his eyes or heart and indulges in rowdiness of various hues.

The foundation of a truly religious life can be laid on the ethos of domestic affairs. But due to dwindling interest of people in domestic affairs, religious life too has now become a mere pretension. Religion has moved out of the homes and entered the marketplace. People have come to hold this erroneous belief that religious outcomes can be obtained by visiting a religious place on a special occasion or listening to a lecture or religious prayer in the hall of a temple. Collective chanting or recitation of prayers with one's wife and children at home is rarely observed. In fact, religious devotion can arise only in a person who collectively engages in religious activity or remembers his God in the company of his family members.

Those people who aspire to reach higher realms of religiosity by renouncing domestic life have as much chance of achieving it as a farmer reaping a harvest by sowing seeds in the air. The so-called great men who avoid domesticity have often deviated from the righteous path. (Why name anyone!) You might have read in the biographies of many men how after remaining celibate for their entire lives, they lost control of their senses at the mere sight of women bathing by the river bank. To escape getting trapped in the vicious cycle of *maya*, many of them went on to live in the jungle clutching a begging bowl in the formative years of their lives. If such people ever found the right track, it was only by following the example of a householder like king Janaka. This is precisely the reason why the Gurus emphasised domestic life because good conduct is cultivated by experiencing a life within home. Relationships such as those with daughter, son, wife, mother, and father are not bonds of *maya* but rather are the sacred moulds created by the Lord for shaping our conduct:

> Mother, father, son all exist because of God
> He alone invests them with relationships.

He who hasn't faced deceit in his day-to-day life would not be able to learn the virtue of uprightness. Similarly, anyone who as a father, mother, brother, son, daughter hasn't fought such obstacles, how would he/she be able to imbibe the characteristics of a father, son, etc. that are born out of these relationships? Qualities like love, compassion, sacrifice or service can never be learnt until one cultivates the ability to love family members and takes initiatives towards their care and protection.

Love for society and country are born only out of the love that is nurtured at home. Only those people resist an attack on their country or the atrocities inflicted on its people who fear that their homes, families, spouse and children are within the range of harm. India is as dear to me as my love for my mud cottage in my village Adiala and its people. I remember the days when, while studying at Rawalpindi, I would go back to my village on Sundays. After crossing Cheer Parhaan I would reach near Trapiaan, from where I could see my village that lay hidden behind a mound. Before catching the enthralling sight of my village, I used to always stand near the mound and prepare my heart before I could actually bring myself to glance at my village. On my return journey too, I used to keep looking back till it disappeared. In fact, many a time I used to retrace my steps after losing sight of the village. How lovely was the village! And my relatives residing in that village were even more beautiful. (But where is all that now? Everyone has disappeared. Now an English or French man might like to visit my village but, alas, not me.)

Gurbax Singh Preetlarhi

Gurbax Singh (1895–1977) was born in Sialkot, Pakistan. He studied engineering at Thompson Engineering College (now IIT) Roorkee and later at the University of Michigan. He was a dreamer and worked hard to make his dreams come true. He founded a town called Preet Nagar situated between Amritsar and Lahore, and persuaded personalities like Balraj Sahni, Nanak Singh and artist Sobha Singh to settle down there. Other greats such as Faiz Ahmad Faiz, Sahir Ludhianavi, Upender Nath Ashk, Kartar Singh Duggal, Balwant Gargi, Mohan Singh and Amrita Pritam were also associated with Preetnagar. The magazine that he started, *Preetlari*, is still being published. He appreciated balance in all things, particularly in personality. He wrote about almost every aspect of life and visualises a common link of love or affection which is vital for a good life. He considers love omnipresent and defines it as an identity rather than a feeling. Like Teja Singh, Gurbax Singh too is a great litterateur of Punjabi. What distinguishes the prose style of Gurbax Singh from Teja Singh is his idealism. This article was written before the formation of the UNO (1945).

A War-free World

Two communities clash due to some religious misunderstanding, innocents get killed, living beings are burnt to death, and houses set on fire. Two countries wage a war for reasons of loss or greed. The blind passion of millions rages, tanks roar, airplanes rain bombs, poisonous gases put innocent masses to eternal sleep, buildings constructed over long periods of time are razed to rubble; the poor public living peacefully are frightened; children cling tightly to their mothers and the mothers look towards their husbands; men try to save themselves from the bullets raining from the sky; animals and birds hide in the trenches. Killed by the bullets of unseen enemies, millions of mothers lose their sons in the battlefield. Pierced by guns, callous shrapnel pricking the eyes, faces torn asunder and hearts slaughtered, loud cries rent the skies and sighs echo all around; the longings, desires and aspirations of life waste away in the form of a river of blood. Why? For what? The innocent, massacred victims are not aware of anything.

Triumphant emperors, chiefs, dictators celebrate their victories; their place of religion decorated with bright lights and offerings made as a mark of gratitude to the Gods, flags are waved, national songs sung and high-powered oratory skills are used to manipulate young men to prepare themselves to kill their enemies and sacrifice their own lives.

No one spares any thought for the sinking heart of the vanquished king, his wailing soul, his desperate entreaties to God, the obliteration of his hope, his sleep-deprived eyes, tormented chest and shattered spirit—no one spares a thought for all this.

Even then the church and the pope pontificate about the world being a singular unified chain and accept offerings from both the vanquished as well as the victor, and offer prayers on behalf of both. Their scriptures exhort us that the world is a river, converging in a single ocean. Then why does such excruciating warfare exist? Is there no other way to arrive at a mutually acceptable solution other than through such a catastrophic war? After all the war is a man-made phenomenon and not a supernatural happening, or a natural calamity like an earthquake.

History bears testimony that in earlier times there used to be no consensus even within a family. The mighty subordinated the weak or killed them. Whenever an opportunity arose, the son would kill his father and begin lording over all his women. By and by, agreements started to take place within the families. It was followed by an internecine war between different families. Thereafter different families united and formed clans; but they clashed, often with the objective of stealing the other's women and cattle and integrating them with their own. By and by, clans united to form a race. Each race fixed the territorial boundaries of its jurisdiction.

Each race appointed its own chief to overcome the difficulties in resolving mutual conflicts. In this manner, as time progressed, small independent settlements were formed at many places and those habitations combined to form provinces, which, in turn, unified to make a big country.

Eventually, courts at lower and higher levels and High Courts were established within a country. Except for a miniscule number, who are communal minded, the rest of the populace abides by the law. They don't seek relief by avenging their rivals. The police maintain peace, judges pronounce judgments and the entire machinery works.

This is evidence of the progress made by humankind. Those who call the past as the Age of Truth (*satyug*) and the present time as the Age of Darkness (*kalyug*) spread negativity and are sadly mistaken. The Age of Truth has not elapsed, rather it always remains the ideal to be achieved by the human race. It is precisely for the attainment of that ideal that the earth has been revolving and the sun shining since eons. Religions had glimpsed a blurred, distant semblance of that ideal; and the focus of all philosophy and the entire quest of science is devoted to the same ideal. Revolutions, wars and religious crusades too are but the steps that explore and stumble and face setbacks while attempting to achieve the very same ideal.

Those people too are sadly mistaken who, based on their assumptions of conflicting interests, surmise that it is impossible to have a long-lasting agreement between different nations. Earlier India too was divided amongst princely states and each princely state had its own laws and vested interests. Each state used to surreptitiously covet the boundaries of the other and big or small battles used to be fought continually. However, despite of the differences in languages and other issues, the population of 40 crores is united now. Different states have the autonomy, their own sources of revenue and expenditure, but all are partners and there is no possibility of inter-state war now.

Thus, a political state that can appear in the realm of imagination can be made to materialise as well. Human thoughts are not totally isolated from the artistry of nature. Today Red Cross and Liberation Army are globally unified secular movements with vast resources.

A common platform of all the nations can also be thought of; the prevalent League of Nations is an incomplete experiment. It might not have proved successful but success is an aggregation of a large number of unsuccessful endeavours. If not in this century or even the next, this common league would definitely become a reality in the century thereafter. Despite the Mussolinis, Kaisers and Hitlers of the world, anti-war human thoughts are hammering the final nails in the coffin of war. This ancient enemy of humankind is making last-ditch efforts. In 1914–15, it caused many fatalities and opened the coffin boxes for them. Then the lids of the coffin boxes were shut but now their nails have been pulled out and the coffins are open again and the horrendous swords are also glistening. It is clear that despite simmering in palpable rage, nations are still uneasy and shy about war. I am hopeful that if ever a world war breaks outs, it would be the last one.

I agree there still exist innumerable reasons for a war in the world. Big empires, big countries located close to countries with less population and vice-versa, iniquitous distribution of necessary goods, war literature, false history, religious bigotry, colour-based discrimination, luxurious palaces, penurious huts—all these are the potential germs that inhere war. However, two indefatigable doctors, science and philosophy, are curbing the evil of these poisonous resources by spreading wisdom and sanity.

These wise doctors have posited new norms and values. Carnegie, Ford, Birla and others are acclaimed for investing in libraries, hospitals and other community works. This unique way of sharing a part of their wealth with others and thereby enhancing one's stature is spreading. Would that day be far off when this idea shall gain sufficient acceptance that instead of ruling over neighbouring countries and plundering them, the greatness of a country would be judged by its efforts to enhance prosperity, education, and freedom of neighbouring nations? I think soon men will realise that no race or nation can hope to retain its own identity by snatching away others' freedom. The British have indeed gained status and respect in the world and one of the reasons for this is their colonisation of India. But they are mistaken if they think that the richness and freedom of India would reduce the prestige and prosperity of England itself. It requires little moral courage and vision to realise that if England sincerely helps India to become free and prosperous like itself, not only India but the entire world can become a virtual heaven. India would heartily and willingly bestow on England the honour of being the most gracious angel of heaven. The Indian heart has a huge element of gratefulness. An independent India walking alongside the English can transform the entire vicious sentiment prevailing in the world by virtue of its own moral strength.

The human race is one. Science has proved that religious boundaries are artificial and that no race is exclusively God's chosen one. Also, the geographical boundaries should not be seen as permanent. The density of the population of Japan, Italy and Germany is 300 per square mile. In Russia, Australia and some other parts of the world, it is not more than 300 humans per mile. By expanding the boundaries of habitable areas, improving the organisation of natural resources and manmade markets by mutual consensus, the causes of war shall be eliminated. This thought would proliferate, gain strength and would become a reality one day.

But my hopes are even higher than this and my dreams are mountain-like. In my mind's eyes, there is a scenario of a shared world of humans, animals and birds. Bernard Shaw had made a very profound statement that the seeds of war cannot be decimated until the time people continue to kill animals for food. It is indeed true that killing hardens the human consciousness. The gushing blood doesn't nauseate the killer Those who kill animals can be easily motivated to kill humans. Perpetration of atrocities on sparrows, parrots, sheep, goats, and cows, lays the foundation for atrocities on humans.

We can trust a day would come when better products would be available for food than meat, better means of entertainment than hunting and better arenas to showcase valour than war. There would be an alternative standard for measuring bravery. Gandhi and Bernard Shaw shall be counted as valiant amongst all those who remained steadfast in the face of all threats, who are not overawed by anyone and who do not hesitate to express the truth; even the sight of death cannot ruffle them.

Many wise men in the world consider war essential for a life of bravery and sing valorous songs about war, felicitate weapons and pay tribute to the killing power. Mussolini, in his philosophy of fascism, lays great stress on war. Many religions too eulogise such an approach towards war.

But doesn't the soul yearn for a scenario of a world where birds sing and fly fearlessly? Where no trap is laid for them, no rope dangles to catch them, no bullet pierces through their chest. The animals should remain happy; leap and jump. The ones who can participate and contribute to the world of humans should be fully compensated. The rights of those who cannot speak should never be trampled. Every human should have the right to work and subsistence; the surplus available at one place should compensate for the deficiency at another place; I envision a world where skills are enhanced, education spreads, light illumines more, superstitions abate, bigotry is wiped out, fallacies vanish, courts dispense justice, markets are shared as per needs, nations coexist sans jealousy and conflicts are resolved by an All-World Parliament. Weapons of war are altogether eliminated and instead of wasting their lives being trained to kill, soldiers learn something productive. The international boycott should cause moral shame as a means to bring straying nations back on the track. In place of cantonments, universities should be visible all around.

Many would find such a scenario improbable but it was not very long ago when everyone had to stay vigilant for their own safety. People used to go armed even for parties, marriages and get-togethers. One member of the family used to guard the house. The condition of frontier *pathans* is still the same and every *pathan* keeps a pistol or gun close to his chest. No one trusts the other; neither does a brother trust his brother nor a father his son; needless to say that the neighbours too do not trust each other.

But in civilised societies, this is no longer required. People sleep in the open, trade freely, joint courts adjudicate, severance of relation with opponents is considered to be sufficient without any need for revenge; many social evils are prevented by the force of moral rectitude.

If a civilised society has been able to reach such a stage then civilised nations too would be able to be bound by a single moral code. I wish to present this moral code as an ideal before conscientious thoughtful people, especially the youth of India because I believe that there is abhorrence for war in the Indian heart and it shuns violence and oppression. Unlike other nations, the ancient history of India is not full of war. The last nail in the coffin of war cannot be hammered until such a nation takes charge of the reins of the International League.

That is why I wish to present before our youth the idea of a war-free world so that communal conflicts and religious bigotry are erased from their minds. I earnestly believe that Indian youth is capable of contributing towards a global destiny and that the despairing sections of humanity await them.

Victor Hugo has beautifully and passionately expressed such sentiments. I conclude this essay by referring to his appeal to the law-makers and guardians of the city. He asked them to join hands and bury their enmity because winning over hatred will win the war. We should fill human hearts with a sense of fraternity. Hugo concluded that education and positive literature will be the substitute for war. In place of destroyers, we will have workers and producers. This will also eliminate boundaries and the culture of hegemony.

Bhagat Singh

Bhagat Singh (1907–31) was born in village Banga, Tehsil Jarhanwala, District Layallpur, now renamed as Faislabad (Pakistan) and was hanged in 1931 at the age of 23 years. Bhagat Singh is respected as a great martyr of India's freedom struggle globally. He was also a thinker and writer. Many of his writings are in Hindi and English. There are approximately a hundred articles and papers written by him in both languages. He also wrote more than a dozen articles in Urdu. Two papers and more than a dozen articles were written by him in

Punjabi which were published in *Kirti* in 1927–28. The range of concerns in his writings is large. He writes on the question of untouchability, student politics, religion, the freedom struggle, *satyagraha* and strikes. He also expounds on Anarchism and Nihilism. His writings are brief but powerful.

Communal Riots and Their Remedy

(*The British Government unleashed a blitzkrieg of vicious propaganda after the communal riots that followed the saga of Jallianwala Bagh in 1919. As a result of this, Kohat witnessed the most barbaric Hindu–Muslim riots in 1924. Following this, a long debate on the communal riots began in the national political consciousness. The need to put an end to such riots was felt by all, but all that was done was to have the Hindu and Muslim leaders come to a formal agreement.* —Kirti [Punjabi monthly])

Presently, the condition of India is extremely pitiable. The followers of one religion are the arch enemies of the other religion. Now, the follower of a particular religion becomes a bitter enemy of other religion *ipso facto*. If anyone doubts it, he simply needs to look at the recent Lahore riots. How brutally were the innocent Hindus and Sikhs killed by the Muslims! The Sikhs, too, retaliated with an unsparing vengeance. These massacres haven't been committed merely to punish the guilty, but for the simple reason that someone was a Hindu, a Sikh or a Muslim. Thus, for Muslims, someone being either a Hindu or a Sikh would be sufficient reason to kill them and likewise to be a Muslim was reason enough to get massacred. God alone can save India under such dire circumstances.

The future of India appears terribly bleak under the prevailing conditions. These 'religions' have doomed the country and no one knows when such religious riots would stop. These riots have shamed India in the eyes of the world. We have seen how everyone gets swept by the deluge of superstitions. Rarely does a Hindu, Muslim or Sikh keep his senses intact while the rest of these so-called religious creatures resort to sticks, swords and pitchforks, and eventually kill each other in a bid to assert the supremacy of their particular religion. Of those remaining, some go to the gallows while others are put behind bars. These 'defenders of religion' regain their senses only after this bloodshed: when the authorities beat their brains out and thus cure them of their mental illness automatically.

It is widely perceived that communal leaders and newspapers instigate these riots. Nowadays, it is better not to say a word about the kind of confusion created by the leaders of India. The very same leaders who claimed to be the vanguard of national liberation and who had been vociferously shouting about 'composite nationality' and 'Swaraj', either keep mum hanging their heads in shame or are swept along the wave of religious bigotry. Those with their heads down are a minority while those who have joined the ranks of the communalists are large in number. When you try to spot a single one you will find them in hundreds. There are very few leaders who sincerely aspire for the public good, and even these sincere leaders are unable to stem the strong tide of communalism. It appears that leadership has become completely bankrupt in India.

Other gentlemen who play a special role in adding fuel to the fire are the scribes.

Earlier, journalism was regarded as a very noble profession, but today it has become dirty. These people pit one community against the other and fuel people's emotions by writing sensational headlines that often result in violent clashes. It is not a stray occurrence happening at one or two places. Rather, a large number of communal riots have been triggered by provocative articles in local newspapers. There were very few scribes who kept their head and were balanced and fair in such turbulent times.

The real duty of the newspapers was to educate, to purge narrow-mindedness from the minds of people, eradicate bigotry, foster amity and communal harmony, and build a composite nationalism, but they have been acting contrary to these principles. They have, rather, spread ignorance, disseminated narrow-mindedness and bigotry, fomented disturbances and annihilated composite nationalism as their chief objectives. This is precisely the reason why I cry tears of blood when I think about this wretched situation and a question arises in my heart, 'What will be the future of India?'

Those who had seen the nationalist fervour during the days of the Non-Cooperation movement find this situation utterly tragic. Those were the days when freedom seemed to be just around the corner but now Swaraj seems like a distant dream. This is the third advantage that these riots have given to the dictatorship of the party. The very survival of bureaucracy had seemed to be under threat and its days appeared numbered, but now it has entrenched itself so powerfully that it is not easy to dislodge it.

If we try to locate the root cause of communal violence, economic factors appear to be the only reason. During the days of the Non-Cooperation movement, leaders and scribes made huge sacrifices. They were ruined economically. After the Non-Cooperation movement lost steam, people became sceptical of its leaders. That is why many of the communal leaders are out of work these days. It is always the issue of livelihood that is at the core of all events in the world. This is the foremost of the three key principles of Karl Marx. The rise of organisations engaged in 'Tabligh', 'Tanzeem' and 'Shudhi' have been based on this principle and this is the prime reason for our present day's indescribable doom.

So, if there could ever be any possible solution to riots, it can only be through improvements in the economic condition of India. Actually, the economic condition of a common man in India is so pathetic that by offering just a quarter of a rupee to someone, a third person can be offended through him. When they suffer from hunger and strife, people readily abandon all principles. Survival makes one do the strangest of things!

But in the present circumstances, it is extremely difficult to bring about any change in the economic conditions because we have a foreign government which does not allow any betterment in the lives of the people. Therefore, we should desperately go for changing it and should not rest until it is thrown out.

To prevent people from fighting with each other, the need of the hour is to create class consciousness. The poor labourers and farmers must be told that capitalists are their real enemies. Therefore, they should remain vigilant about their sophistry and beware of falling prey to their manipulations. The poor, regardless of race, colour, religion or nation have identical rights all over the world. Your wellbeing lies in obliterating distinctions based on colour, creed, race, religion and nation, and uniting together in an attempt to take the power of government into your own hands. You won't lose anything by such endeavours; rather, someday you would attain economic liberation by breaking free of your shackles.

Those acquainted with the history of Russia know that during the reign of the Tsar, diverse communities were always at loggerheads with each other. But the day the workers' regime came into power, the entire scenario changed. No longer do any riots take place there and every human is recognised as an individual rather than by his religious identity. During the Tsar's regime, the economic condition of the people was miserable and this gave rise to riots and communal violence, but today the economic condition of the Russians has improved considerably and awareness about class consciousness has taken firm root. That is why no instance of riots have been heard from Russia lately.

Normally, riots bring terribly depressing news in its wake, but during the Calcutta riots, we heard very heartwarming news. Trade union workers neither participated in those riots nor did they get involved in mutual combat. Rather the Hindus and the Muslims continued to live together amicably and also tried to diffuse the riots. This was a result of the class consciousness in the workers and their understanding of their own class interest. This example of class consciousness shows us a beautiful way to stop communal violence.

We have heard the happy news that the Indian youth are now sick of these incidents of violence and are washing their hands off such religions which foment mutual strife and hatred. They have inculcated such a generosity of spirit that they no longer look at people as Hindus, Muslims or Sikh but first and foremost as human beings and then as Indians. The subscription to such thoughts by the Indian youth augurs well for a bright future of India and indicates that Indians should not get upset at the sight of the riots; rather they should be fully equipped to fight them out and create such an environment that any occurrence of riots is obviated.

The martyrs of 1914–15 had separated religion from politics. They understood that religion is an entirely personal matter of an individual and brooked no interference from others. Nor should it be forced on politics because it does not allow the masses to work together collectively for the public good. This was the reason why during a movement such as Ghadar, people remained cohesively united and while the Sikhs embraced the gallows in large numbers, no less supreme sacrifices were made by the Hindus and the Muslims.

Currently, some politicians seem to have come forward with the intention to keep religion separate from politics. This is a wonderful way to cure the malaise of communal violence and we should encourage it.

If religion is separated from politics, despite of the differences in religious beliefs, we can all stand together in politics.

We hope that the true sympathisers of India will definitely think about the solutions put forward by us and will save India from following the path of self-destruction.

Harinder Singh Roop

Harinder Singh Roop (1907–54) was born in Amritsar. His name cannot be separated from the initial phases of Punjabi prose. He stands parallel to Prof. Puran Singh, Lal Singh Kamla Akali, Principal Teja Singh, Gurbax Singh Preetlarhi, Prof. Sahib Singh and S.S. Amole. His unique narrative style and perspective make him stand out. He had a keen interest in Sikh religion, culture, history and art. He adroitly expressed his views using irony and satire. His prose is fascinating because of its simplicity, purity, and idiomatic and satirical tenor.

Of Sycophants

If you have come in contact with a sycophant, rest assured that you are in for such an enriching experience that you may light the lamps of happiness, distribute sweets all around, invite all and sundry to a meal. Whatever you may do, he is going to valorise you to the skies and sing paeans to every single act of yours. He will eulogise, and the exaggerations would touch such new heights that the Old Iranian poets skilled in the genre of *qaseeda* would pale into insignificance. He would term your clumsily tied turban as a stylish crown; sing high praises about your wrinkled forehead and present it as a sparkling mirror; your beady eyes would be compared to the enormous eyes of a gazelle; your squat nose would be made out to be like the regal nose of Hussain; your hoarse voice would be termed as surpassing the melodious voices of Tansen and Baiju Bawara. Your thick lips would be equated with the delicate pink petals of a flower. Your stained teeth will be touted as brilliantly shining pearls, and your straggly beard the apogee of male handsomeness. He does not hesitate to turn your dark countenance into the brightness of a full moon of the month of Kartik. God forbid if your body resembles a rhino, he would unhesitatingly declare it a soft one. The dust under your feet would be pronounced to be more precious than gold or radium; he will not feel shy of declaring the specks of that dust as the planets Mercury or Venus, and even the Pole Star. People try diverse strategies to hear their own praise; toot their own horn and position themselves at the top. If you have been acquainted with a sycophant, then have no misgivings for he will make up for all your inadequacies. People would be besotted with you by the manner in which he would present you before them. This intoxication is far more potent than that described in their writings on alcohol by Hafiz and Khayyam. You should be grateful that such a man sings your plaudits.

Beware of being swept off your feet by such accolades; even though you are wise like a crow yet this fox would pay you high compliments and, in the process, snatch away the piece of cheese from your mouth and slink away. A swindler is harmless in comparison with such a man; any gambler would concede defeat to him. Since every warrior willingly surrenders before him, you have no means at your disposal to overpower him. You can do nothing and all your intelligence is of no avail. Your education would appear redundant and you would simply be hypnotised the moment you look into his eyes. The sycophant will not let you climb up towards your goal and would infect your virtues like a pest. He is an ominous star for your fair name and if you become a plaything in his hands, you are bound to suffer great losses and self-sabotage your own interests. He has no shame and has completely shunned all integrity. He is not bothered about his own reputation. Why would he be bothered about your reputation? He will deafen you with his applause. You will become totally immune to any other point of view and place your entire trust in him and thus, you would happily and willingly meet your doom. If you are hell-bent on inviting your own ruin who can save you? No angel will alight from the heavens to show you the way; you have to be your own saviour. You and you alone can avert this calamity; get rid of this problem and save yourself from this catastrophe. You should be steadfast and determined not to be swayed by all the acclaim coming your way and to not surrender your rationality before sycophancy. Keep firm control over your mind, as you did while drawing up your will, by retaining your sanity instead of wavering or faltering. One should counter a sycophant with a strategy or a smile; at times just don't pay any attention to what he says; stay nonchalant. If you were to pay even a little bit of attention to him, he would gain latitude and will incline you towards his own stance. If you chose to pay any heed or be maneuvered by him, he would manipulate you into doing illegitimate things. He would escape unscathed and you alone would be held responsible for any wrongdoing.

There was an English emperor named Canute. He was a wise man and used to be always conscious about keeping his wits about him. He kept sycophants at arm's length, never giving them an opportunity to beguile him. But the sycophants too were looking out for an opportunity to entrap him. One day the issue about the territorial boundaries of the state arose. Pouncing on this opportunity, a sycophant bowed reverentially and said, 'The emperor's kingdom extends to the skies and the sun and moon follow your command.' Displaying great courtesy another courtier also got up and looking at the feet of the emperor, said, 'Your majesty, you are the master of heaven and earth. The ocean is afraid of you, and the winds are so much in awe of you that they dare not blow in your presence.'

The king was sure that they were attempting to fool him with their artifice and that he should expose them. The court was dispersed and the next day, he went to the seashore along with such sycophans. A wave rolled onto the sand. The king commanded the wave to go back. But why would it listen to him? Instead, it rolled on and left after wetting his feet. Another one rolled in and came up to his ankles, and yet another, stronger than the ones before, wetted his knees despite his stern orders to the wave to desist. The king was furious and thundered, 'This is my kingdom.' The courtiers stood with heads hanging, utterly humiliated. They were stupefied and rued their stance. The emperor straightened them thoroughly. While such a method is rarely adopted, yet it would save you if you did so.

There is no dearth of those who promote sycophancy; they are found in abundance. Let us name a renowned person who is revered as a poet in Asia. He is one of the wisest men known to the world; he is Sheikh Sa'adi, and the fragrance of his anthology *Gulistan* regales perennially:

> Gar sheh roz ra goyid shab ast ei,
> Babaayad guft ei ke maahe parwin
>
> [If the king calls the day night/then you must concur and exclaim how beautiful the moon in the sky is!]

Why shouldn't a sycophant be fawning away to glory? Why should he desist using this gift? Even a philosopher like Sa'adi is boosting the depressed king's morale and stoking his self-confidence. The moment the sycophant practices his skill, you would get a kick and fall flat on your face! But if you play a trick the way Canute did, then it is the sycophant who would bite the dust.

The sycophant begins his first assault with flattery. The next step is what Sheikh Sa'adi suggests, concurring with all that is said, even if it is blatantly wrong. If it is said that two twos are three, then he will never contradict and correct it to say that it is four; rather he will go on insisting that it is three and not let the other person even think out about the logic behind it. In this manner, the one being flattered foregoes his sanity and becomes a pliant tool in the hands of the sycophant. If the ruler is inclined towards flattery, the sycophant would wholeheartedly concur with him. He never tires of endlessly echoing 'yes' to the ruler. This sort of drama is enacted by numerous actors in the court of a judge or a magistrate from ten to four daily. One doesn't need to ape anyone; as Sir Syed Ahmed Khan had rightly said that it is the height of sycophancy when a sycophant says, 'I am not flattering you.' This assault inflicts a grievous wound which cannot be cured by any medication. Instead, it can only be cured by inflicting more of such wounds. God forbid, if a person gets bitten by a double-tongued snake, his body becomes bloated shortly thereafter. Similarly, whoever succumbs to sycophancy gets addicted to it.

Britishers are the only exception to this rule who have been able to successfully grind their axe through sycophants. After thoroughly examining the Indians, they created a pliant community of them through persuasion, avarice, authority, and above all, by shrewd manipulation, that is, by conferring the titles of Khan Bahadurs, Rai Bahadurs and Sardar Bahadurs.

Balraj Sahni

Balraj Sahni (1913–1973) was born in Rawalpindi (Pakistan). He is famous as an actor but a very few know that he was a Punjabi litterateur. He wrote in several genres: travelogues, plays and essays. Although he talks about various aspects of the world of films and his acting in his essays, his travelogues are exceptionally impressive. Committed to the leftist ideology, he searched out and praised human values. He started writing in his mother tongue on the insistence of Rabindranath Tagore. He has written travelogues of both Russia and Pakistan but the latter has a remarkable emotional quality, as the excerpt below shows.

My Pakistan Travelogue

The train halted. I peered through the window to see the turrets of Lahore station.

I had never missed Lahore much. Mostly, it was Pindi that I desperately longed for. There were many reasons for this. For one, since childhood, I was accustomed to looking at the mountains in the horizon. When I left Pindi and moved to the New Hostel of Government College, Lahore, no mountains were in sight anywhere from its rooftop. I found this to be a major violation of the law of nature. To this day I have not forgotten the restlessness that overwhelmed me then.

Second, the dust storms of Lahore in the summer and the smog during the winters were a kind of hell for me. In our Pindi, dust storms never lasted long and were followed by rain. The dust used to settle down soon and even the loud banging of the doors and windows then used to sound pleasant. The nights turned cool.

On the contrary, in Lahore, once a dust storm started, it would last for many days making it difficult even to breathe. One morning, after rolling up my bed from the roof of the New Hostel, I came to my cubicle and got a scare when I looked at myself in the mirror; my face was coal black. Similarly, in winters, the smog would cause burning sensation not merely in the eyes but in the bones as well.

Moreover, Pindi was a small town. The malevolent policies of the British had not yet taken complete hold over the lives of the people here. Brotherhood and fraternity were alive and kicking; warmth and cordiality permeated friendships. Goodness and humility were still valued. The pernicious plant of communalism was growing but had not still struck a firm root. However, Lahore by virtue of being a big central city had by now been invaded by the culture of the new fashion. The power of money and status had wiped out the old norms of mutual respect. All fair and foul means had been granted legitimacy in the race to overtake others. The whole atmosphere reeked of selfishness and it naturally impacted student life as well. Not merely in sports and education, secret games were being played all around which were very strange and confusing for the boys from small towns. Communal tensions were rising at a ferocious pace and frightening events of the future were casting their shadows clearly before everyone.

Even though I thoroughly enjoyed the vibrant college life in Lahore yet I could never get rid of a feeling of the absurdity of it all. I experienced a vacuity within my being, the reason for which I could not fathom nor was there anyone who could explain it to me. I often thought that there must be some adulteration in the waters of Lahore. I could never call Lahore my very own.

But what came over me today when I saw the ochre-coloured turrets of Lahore station? I felt as if I had been yearning for them for ages. A strong emotion of affection and veneration gushed forth from some hidden source within my being. Before alighting and even setting foot on the ground, I touched the earth with my hands and folded them reverentially in a *pranam*.

Dr. Nazir Ahmed (the present principal of Government College, Lahore) had come to receive me leaving an important university meeting. Due to his presence and his status, the cumbersome stages of customs, immigration, etc. were relaxed for me and I was even respectfully offered tea. Dr. Nazir Ahmed was content that his guest was not bothered to open up his luggage for scrutiny. I, however, was not at all content with such promptness. I longed to unhurriedly explore each and every platform to my heart's content.

It is 4 p.m. I have slept for quite long. My body feels rejuvenated. I want to lunge forward and run on the roads. The same old clock of the Government College tower is ringing; it probably struck eleven. It had the same old nonchalance, about which so many jokes used to be spun. Its tolling arouses strange sensations in me. It is not memories that flash, rather, a profound poise, a kind of calm descends on me like that of a bird suffering from hunger and thirst, savoring the retreat in its nest after a long flight in the scorching sun. From afar the jingling bells of the tongas, sounds of the vendors selling fruit in front of the college ...

The bungalow where I was staying used to be the residence of Mr G. D. Sondhi. The cool dimly lit rooms with meshed doors, a rack for spreading towel in the washroom—all these had been very realistically shown in the film *Bhawani Junction*. Though the film was very low grade, it made me nostalgic for Lahore while I was sitting in a cinema hall in Bombay ten years ago.

In our times, we used to be utterly petrified at the thought of entering these bungalows. The professors carried in themselves a phenomenal fear of the British. That is a thing of the past now. Whenever the bell rings Dr Nazir Ahmed himself attends to the door; there is no peon, no liveried guard. Nazir Sahib has put me up in his own bedroom. He regretted that there was no wardrobe in the room. He said 'Yaar, I have no wardrobe here, you will be inconvenienced. Actually, I do not have many clothes. So why bother! In case you need something, please don't hesitate and let me know, I'll get it sent for you.' This really pleased me. Could I ever have imagined that a principal of the Government College, Lahore would live like this?

Dr Nazir entered the room and said, 'Come on; let's have tea outside in the lawn.' There was no formality in his behaviour as if he understood all my unsaid desires. We walked into the lawn. That velvet grass, well-fed fertile soil, blooming roses in the flower beds, and the dense cool shades of the trees. How could I forget that after coming from Pindi it was in Lahore that my soul had experienced a sense of space for the first time? That I used to run towards Lahore at the slightest pretext...

I recalled that after completing my M.A., I had returned to Pindi and was engaged in a cloth-trading business under my father's patronage. I was newly married. My brother Bhisham was still in Government College, studying for his M.A. He sent a letter—'A new play is being staged at the college next Saturday and Sunday. I am participating as well. Please do come and see.' My father used to keep me under a tight leash, always considering me to be a troublesome bull. I knew very well that his permission if sought, would be denied. Therefore, I left a note on his table on Saturday afternoon and the crux of the note was that 'all government offices observe half Saturday and full Sunday as holidays, and the same rules should also be applicable to the trading offices. How an employee spends his free time should be completely left to his own volition and under this principle, I am leaving for Lahore along with my wife for the weekend and would report back on Monday morning for duty.'

I was aware that there would be uproar at home. A son could be forgiven for leaving home without permission, but never a daughter-in-law. Both of us were immature and prepared to face the consequences upon return. Any punishment that awaited us would be eminently forgettable and was worth taking this chance to go out and have fun.

We reached Lahore, watched the play and had a wonderful time. Next evening, I bought two third-class tickets with the remaining money. We boarded the twelve o'clock train for Pindi. It was very crowded. I seated Dammo in the ladies' compartment. Despite being terribly conscious of my responsibilities as a newly-wed husband, I could not go and look her up the whole night. Early the next morning as soon as I woke up, I hastily got down when the train halted at the next station and walked towards the ladies' compartment. On reaching there I found the compartment empty except for an old woman. I asked her about Dammo, describing her, but she had not seen such a girl. I was aghast. It was a small station and the train started moving. Barely conscious and terribly worried I boarded my coach. May God never push anyone into such a miserable state. Why on earth did I put her in a different coach? Who knows what calamity might have befallen her? Once lost, how would I ever be able to find her? The weak stand no chance of justice even before the law. No one will lend help. How would I face the family on reaching home? The whole town would condemn me, only saying that a fashion crazed man has gone astray and has met his downfall. I realised for the first time in my life that in our country a sense of security and being carefree is so fragile. Was it restricted only to a small minority of high-class elite? And if unfortunately, they too take a wrong step, they also, being dark-skinned, would have to face dire consequences. No help, no support, no one to be approached. The value of a human was not even comparable to an insect...

Half dead, I again raced to the ladies coach at the next stop. I learnt that there was another ladies compartment hitched to the front side of the train. I reached there and saw Dammo, all decked up and without care sitting at the window awaiting Pindi. She was taken aback at my desperate plight and laughed. As the coach was emptying at night, she, along with some other women, had moved to the ladies compartment in the other coach. I had reclaimed the world as quickly as I had lost it. However, I solemnly resolved against such gallivanting in the future. I could never ever forget the extreme fright I experienced then... But I often think if it still is the influential and powerful people alone who are fortunate to get the security meant for the entire public of Pindi and Lahore? What is the situation in my own country, India? Do the common masses still exist only as orphans, even in this era of freedom?

We went out for a drive in the car. From the District Courts Road, we turned towards Ravi Road. There used to be a milestone in front of the college. Whenever I used to cross the road from New Hostel on my way to the college, I used to glance at it spontaneously— 'Rawalpindi – 178 miles, Gujranwala – 39 miles, Jhelum – 118 miles.' Now the size of that milestone has increased fourfold and details of distances of many more destinations have been added: Karachi – 897 miles, Multan – 263...! Lo and behold! There goes the road leading to the Central Training College! On this side of the road, my uncle used to live on Ratting Road and the residence of Prof. Ruchi Ram Sahni was adjacent to it. There used to be a Parsi temple as well and we used to visit Prof. Gulbahar Singh and Prof. Madan Gopal Singh by crossing a lane beside it. The road from Bhaati merges here. We have reached Gurudutt Bhawan! Let me see what the board says ... Why is the driver driving the car so fast?

During my college days, we used to travel down Ravi Road on bicycles or tongas. Today this car is callously changing the geography of my mind. The places that were far-flung in my imagination seem to have shrunk and come very close to each other. I saw the grand minarets of the Jama Masjid and Minto Park appear just in the twinkling of an eye. It is now called Mohammad Iqbal Park. The roundness of Gol Bagh seemed to ostentatiously surround the city. I fixed the surrounding of each place in a brand-new way in my mind, the *samadhi* (mausoleum) of Guru Arjan Dev and Maharaja

Ranjit Singh, and Purana Qila. During my college days, I had never bothered to visit these places. I was a sahib bahadur at that time! I used to saunter on Mall Road or Macleod Road with a sola hat on my head! At best I would go over to Nisbat Road. But this time, I will, like a native, explore all the lanes of Lahore to my heart's content...! I saw an old doorway on the high land in city wall (I've forgotten the name... Kabuli Darwaza?). Watching me look at these things so ravenously, Dr Nazir suggested we spend a night at his ancestral home located in a lane behind the Darwaza. How thrilled I was! This was precisely the hunger that was haunting me and had propelled me towards visiting Pakistan. I desperately longed to hear my very own Punjabi language—Majhi, Lahindi, Pothohari, my own mother-dialects that I had ignored for such a large part of my life. I was guilty of a grievous crime. The languages, however, never neglected me. Seeing me repenting and inclined towards them, they generously opened their arms to embrace me. They began to enrich me by filling my pockets with precious gems and pearls just like my mother used to lavishly fill my pockets with *rewaris, pinnis* (winter sweets) and pine seeds in my childhood. How sweet is the language of Lahoris! Here, it seems immensely fresh, like the golden mustard flowers swaying merrily in the fields, like the bubbling water of the wells. Many of my friends in Bombay do speak this very language but there it sounds somewhat stale to my ears.

A favourite pastime of the dandies of this central region of Punjab is to go for a ride on a cart driven by an elegant horse. Dressed in white muslin kurta or waistcoat and a foppish lungi, with flower garlands in their hands; what handsome, fair and robust faces they have! They rush past so quickly (I would have sworn at them with the choicest expletives were I not in my friend's car!)! What a paragon of handsomeness was this young man! Such a handsome man must be rarely sighted in this world! I am reminded of Waris Shah's

Naazan paalia dudh malaiyan ve
[He has been lovingly nurtured on milk and cream]

Suddenly, my mind flipped 'Forget about it yaar; they are all Muslims... foreigners. They have massacred so many Hindus, torched property extensively and dishonoured such a large number of our women; why have you forgotten all these things?'

'Yes, Okay. Now I will look at them as 'the others' only... but oh my God! What should I really do? They still don't appear to be Muslims, don't look like the 'others'. Let those who had committed such evil deeds pay for it themselves; no one has been appointed as a judge.'

Baghbaanpura is a pretty new habitation. There are beautiful big cement bungalows and a lot of traffic. But I don't see the old Lahori style tongas anywhere! The driver informed me that now the Peshawari tongas are in vogue. In Pindi, only three passengers would sit in a tonga, but here the norm of four passengers still continues. We Pindis used to mock the slow-paced Lahori tongas! So finally, Pindi has won! I felt really pleased with this thought. But, the next day again, the mind underwent the same somersault... 'What do you have to do with Pindi or Lahore? You are unnecessarily wasting your energy over foreign objects.'

'Okay! If I am an outsider, so be it but don't I have the liberty to see Pindi and Lahore and their tongas to my heart's content? May they always be safe and protected from the evil eye! May all their wishes come true! Their children live long...'

That was the building of the Sikh National College. Accordingly, that one must be the road coming from the canal side... Yes, that's correct... the engineering college in Mughalpura which has now been conferred the status of a university. Close by is the *mazar* of Pir Mian Meer who had laid the foundation stone of the Golden Temple at Amritsar. He was the guru of Dara Shikoh; Shikoh had the Upanishads translated into Persian. However, such historical anecdotes seem to have lost their relevance now...

Then we reached Shalimar Bagh where I had had my first smoke triggering an acute cough that made me miserable. My friend and I would recklessly cycle down to the Shalimar very often. We had hidden hopes—today I would definitely see a beautiful girl and she would look at me with eagerness. Then we would strike a friendship and our lives would be rocked by a torrid romance. Alas! By evening all our castles would come crashing down. We would achieve nothing except vagrancy, staring wide-eyed around us, and trying to pass off as 'gentlemen' by smoking but to no avail. However, the twelve-mile ride on the bicycles used to whet our appetites immensely, and we would sometimes go towards 'Stiffles' and at other times towards 'Lorang'. Our crestfallen hopes used to get fresh lease of life by the time we would reach there. Who knows, some beautiful damsel might be waiting for us in the restaurant?

The sun of the future had slunk behind the mountains of the past. Only the fading light of my memories remained in the skies. It was as if I had experienced all romances and played all the games. Now the situation is as in the words of Ghalib:

> Bazeech-e-atfaal hai duniya mere aage
> Hota hai shab-e roz, tamasha mere aage.
>
> [The world is like a child's play/the spectacle is enacted before me day and night.]

Dr Nazir Ahmed has left me to my own devices. Sitting quietly on the verdant grass under the cypress tree we savour our tea. We listen to the evening sounds of silence. Memories of firsthand accounts continue to pop up like fireworks and it felt like a 'festival of lights'! Finally, I did fall in love with one girl and the one to whom I remained devoted my entire life. Both of us, each standing on either side of that arched doorway, had clicked photographs of each other ... How desperately did I try to persuade her whole family for a picnic outing in the Shalimar ... So much of pleading, entreating, politicking and soliciting!

It is through this very arched entrance that hordes of villagers must have come in to see the gaiety of the festival of lights. Oh, the king must have been seated over there. And from behind at the pond, entering from between the *baradari*s on both ends, the performers, the singers and dancers, dressed in their shimmering attire would present themselves before his majesty to showcase their talent ...

Again, the very same repugnant voices rage in my mind. The Shah Jahan of Lahore was, in fact, a Pakistani and the Shah Jahan of Agra was an Indian ... But no, one should not allow such pangs and suffering to rear their head again and again. I have nothing to do with the complexities of politics. I am a guest and Dr Nazir Ahmed is my host. Raising such questions is beyond the realm of propriety. Howsoever I may love it, the Shalimar is not mine. By this logic, Dr Nazir too is unrelated. But why do I want to ask him again and again, 'Nazir Sahib, we have not known each other for long. It was only last year when you visited Bombay that I had met you. Then why do I feel so calm and poised in your company and the same is so rare in Bombay?' Not now, but I will surely ask him. Undoubtedly, Dr Nazir Ahmed is an extraordinary human being.

Just as we were about to get into the car, a middle-aged beggar, holding the finger of an eight-year-old girl dressed in very filthy and tattered clothes, spread her hands before me supplicating, 'Brother, may you have a long life. May Allah fulfill all your desires; shower more prosperity on you; may your children live long...'

Why do tears stream down my unfortunate eyes? What is this woman to me? She is a Pakistani, I an Indian ...

Pritam Singh

Prof. Pritam Singh (1918–2008), one of the renowned philosophers of Punjabi, was born in Patiala. Despite his humble background, he passed MA in English in 1940, MA in Persian in 1941 and MA in Oriental Learning in 1942. He was a scholar of Punjabi, Urdu and Hindi. He was honoured with the Translation Prize by the Sahitya Akademi in 1994. In 2008, Punjab University awarded him an Honorary Degree. Guru Nanak Dev University and Punjabi Sahitya Academy bestowed him with fellowship whereas San Jose State University, California conferred an Honorary Professorship on him. All these honours bestowed upon Prof. Pritam Singh were for his contribution towards study and research works in the field of Punjabi literature and Sikh religion. Besides this, he also contributed to the fields of lexicography and children's literature.

The Importance of History

The community of modern scholars, be it Indian or foreign, has all along been troubled by the despairing lack of purely historical writings in the gamut of the ancient historical literature of our country. Only *Raj Tarangini* may be considered to be the manifestation of our ancestors' interest in historical writing. But its author too has viewed history from the lens of the Puranas. The real history of India is found in the works of the British and other European scholars who came here after the Greeks, Chinese, Arabs, Persians and Moroccans. Our history has been revealed more by our artifacts, coins and sundry rock inscriptions, idols and statues than by written texts. The reason for this is that our forefathers had developed a style of presenting an outstanding individual as an ideal or projecting him as a part of the galaxy of demigods or divine incarnations. This caught the popular eye and was adopted by one and all. Despite epochal changes, this particular style was not abandoned even with the passage of time and the masses were habituated to view history as a puranic tale. When Persian historians like Abul Fazl and Abdul Haq Dehlvi were writing their own historical epics, a writer of Indian background, in the *Janam Sakhi*, writes of Guru Nanak crossing the Sava lakh Parbat (hundred thousand and a quarter mountain) instead of correctly recording the Shivalik Mountains. Instead of Keer Gram (Baij Nath), he makes the Guru travel to the city of insects 'Keerh Nagar'. Similarly, he calls him a modern avatar of Raja Janak in a bid to align the Guru's ideology with some acclaimed source. It is easier to take the mask off the real story, but most of the time there is less of the real story and more of the mask; only a competent explorer can identify the two and distinguish between them. The art of historical exploration in India began with the coming of modern German scholars. After their enterprising efforts, our forefathers' inclination to view history and the puranas through the foreigners' perspective is clearly evident to us. That is why one fails to understand the reasons for our consistent neglect of purely historical writing in current times.

The real significance of history is to lend manifested stability and permanence to the events and the personalities of an era, which otherwise would be lost in the sands of time. Our past gets situated in the womb of the future which results in having an insightful understanding of our culture and its continuity, despite the evolution in our conduct, behaviour and thought. In this manner the greater the preservation of the varied aspects of their past, the people and the country, the more beneficial it would be for them in enriching their cultural prestige. The knowledge of what exactly happened, why, and how gives depth and maturation to our experience. Why did Aurangzeb's empire disintegrate so soon after his death? Why did Maharaja Ranjit Singh's demise sound the death knell for his empire? It is abundantly clear that understanding the real causes would make us wiser. History tends to be misused at times. Undeniably, the present and the future emerge from the womb of the past, and ultimately merge with the past. But this does not mean that we should keep looking backwards. Often times, while attempting to develop a pro-history outlook, people become not just past-oriented but obscurantist as well. They tend to dwell more in the ghosts of the past than in society *per se*. In our country, the historical renaissance had made some Indian scholars past-oriented, and some sought to ideologically subscribe to the past. Thus, normally an intelligent set of people turned their attention away from the present. I consider this as an abuse of history and a misfortune befalling our people. It would have been prudent on our part to be guided by a sense of history to learn valuable lessons from the past, improve our future and deepen our bonds with diverse areas of life. I desire the adoption of history and the shunning of indifference towards it in this context.

In this article, I want to confine myself solely to the history of the Punjab and yearn to see a living, throbbing Punjab through this history.

The efforts made by S. Karam Singh, Baba Prem Singh Hotiwala, and Dr Ganda Singh in this regard are commendable but the goal cannot be achieved through the efforts of a handful. A full army of historians is required for this task. And they must undertake this task in the manner similar to that of the Muslims. The Muslims were very fond of writing travelogues, biographies and history. Al-Biruni's epic *Al Hind* and Ibn Battuta's *Rihla* are ancient books. Babar and Jahangir wrote their autobiographies. Abul Fazl wrote extensive texts about Akbar, and the very concepts of those books bear testimony to the erudition and scholarship of their writer. For example, while writing about Akbar's dietary habits, he has described his daily schedule in detail—what was eaten when and how much. If quails are cooked then how many? From where are they brought? What are the various ways of catching them? Who are the well-known quail hunters of that period? What is the recipe for preparing quails? What are the various spices and in what proportion are they used? How many kinds of dishes are prepared with quails and what are the recipes of each? How many types of quails are there? (There are even drawings of these.) Who are seated with the emperor to share the meal? What is the quantity of the food served, and how many cooks and attendants are on duty to serve? How are the leftovers disposed of? The details of the kitchen are mentioned separately. Each recorded detail has been minutely scrutinised and explained. The same is also true of autobiographies of the Sufis. In *Siyar al-aulia,* the narratives about Baba Farid and Nizamuddin Aulia are largely based on contemporary eyewitness accounts. Additionally there are references of each detail. Poet Hasan Dehlvi was a devout disciple of Hazrat Nizamuddin Aulia and spent one day a week in the august company of the saint. On reaching home, he would scrupulously note down every sentence uttered by the noble saint and recorded each single event occurring at the *dera* (camp). He would then bring back the account and get it endorsed by the Hazrat himself so as to obviate all errors in the final version. There cannot be a more authentic text than Hasan's *Fawaidul-Fawaad.* Even after hundreds of years, Akbar and Hazrat Nizamuddin Aulia continue to occupy the same distinct place in our hearts as they did in their own era, primarily because of these texts. Historians have enormously enriched our lives. Have we ever seen such an authentic and detailed exposition of Punjab's history? With an objective of inculcating an orientation towards history, we had included the history of Punjab in the course prescribed for the Gyani examination conducted by the Punjab University. But in the textbook that was prepared by a first-rate government teacher 'Buddh' was referred to as 'Buddha', 'Ashok' had become 'Ashoka', 'Gupt' had become 'Gupta' and 'Shak Sammat' was written as 'Saaka Sammat'. Such texts provide the strongest arguments in favour of taking immediate cognizance of our history.

While ancient history can be attended to a bit later, more imperative is the need for creating a congenial environment so that the history that is dying before our own eyes could be saved and preserved. Those of us alive today are passing through a momentous period. This is that era about which pastor C.F. Andrews had exclaimed that with his own eyes he had seen five hundred Jesuses being crucified in a single day in the Guru ka baagh. Who were these five hundred Jesus-like persons? Who all were those blessed mothers? Where were they born and where did they grow up? How did they traverse the journey of transformation, unique for each individual, from being a human to the becoming of Jesus? Our historians seem to be a part of the conspiracy of silence. There appears no cogent reason why even a single one could not attain such an exalted status out of these and numerous others who have become Jesus and are visible to us till date the way Hazrat Nizamuddin continues to be with us. During the 1942 Quit India Movement, I used to reside in the neighbourhood of a police station in Jalandhar. In the pitch dark night, the police used to close in on the targeted rural farmer leaders and wreak barbaric atrocities on these valiant men. The piercing sounds from those gut-wrenching incidents would rent the skies through the night. All this happened without any interruptions in all the police stations in those times. After all, who were these amazingly courageous people who had voluntarily renounced comfort to embrace pain and bravely face physical torture at the hands of brutal barbarians? No one knows anything about them. Once I had the opportunity of meeting a senile human ruin in a newspaper office at Patiala who was desperately trying to find someone to recommend his name for a petty pension of fifteen or twenty rupees to enable him to eke out his remaining years. In his request letter addressed to a high officer of PEPSU government, he had written:

> '…Others may or may not be aware, but you do know that my body has become an unbearable burden for me ever since you repeatedly stomped my chest with the heels of your boots in a bid to make me break my resolve of satyagraha in jail…'

There were numerous such living martyrs, who were men of outstanding courage, but today they are an insignificant part of a large crowd of unknown faces and they cannot rightfully claim any special attention from us.

No one knows about the large number of movements that started in Punjab and have faded into oblivion due to our indifference towards history. Who were those pioneering Muslim Sufis or preachers who had come to spread Islam in our towns and villages and the kind of problems they had to face? Is it possible to obtain some details about those who preached Sikhism later on? Do we know anything about the early *Udasi, Nirmale, Sewa Panthi, Suthare Shahi, Namdhari* and the *Nirankari* sages? The achievements and contributions of the brave soldiers of our army, litterateurs, artists, tourists and travelers, outstanding government officers or employees, politicians, scientists, teachers, scholars, sportspersons, industrialists, shopkeepers, workers and farmers—in fact, people from all walks of life—should necessarily have become a part of the narrative of our lives but failed to be so. We can still potentially focus our attention on the biographical aspect. In every kind of movement around us, be it Singh Sabha, Akali, Babbar, Kirti, Ghadar, Congress, Communist, Arya Samaj, Dev Samaj etc., leaders of such sterling qualities, who may be considered to be the pride of entire humanity, have emerged. The opportunity is not lost yet, and we should concentrate on this work now. The act of preserving history should include the biographies of the makers of history which shall consequently become a part of Punjabi literature, thereby making up for the existing deficit.

Besides biographies, there are numerous topics all around that demand our attention. Once the teachers and students of our universities, schools and colleges, our writers, in fact, every educated as well as an uneducated person, cares to realise the essentiality of this, they would find an abundance of virgin topics all around. Some spontaneous thoughts flashed in my mind while I was writing these lines. What do our scholars think of the subjects listed below?

Political, religious, social and other movements; famous *deras* or religious places and other sects; war, martial arts and battles; rulers and states; rivers, post and telegraph, roads, especially ancient trade-routes; managerial services; Punjab under changing modes of governance; wheat, cotton, sugarcane, and potatoes; large industries and handicrafts; primary to university level education and schools; famous villages and towns; ruins and excavations; clans (gotras); castes and tribes; newspapers and journalism; Punjab and Afghanistan; Punjab and Nepal; Punjab and Kashmir; Punjab and Sindh; Punjab and Uttar Pradesh; Punjab and Rajasthan; Punjabis living overseas; the cultural impact of Punjab outside Punjab; dialects, folk literature, superstition, clothes, ornaments, utensils; names of villages, towns and people, rivers and canals, gardens, etc.

When we begin to explore contemporary governance, brotherhood, economy and religion with the intention to conserve the same, from a historical perspective, then it would no longer be possible to overlook those outstanding individuals who are the makers of history. We could then keep them eternally alive through the medium of images, films and writings and revive even those who had earlier passed into oblivion, unnoticed and unsung. How energised would we feel after seeing those sublime souls, not only in their collective but individual form as well, at the very mention of whose names we exclaim in bliss 'Wahe guru, Wahe guru'! During the Indo-China war, the present writer had made a suggestion to the late S. Pratap Singh Kairon, 'Since you are now trying to inculcate a feeling of bravery and patriotism amongst the people, you should take a leaf from an extraordinary incident that occurred in the history Punjab when a *daas* (disciple) of *Param Purukh* had transformed jackals into lions. The valiant sons of Punjab whose deeds of bravery still inspire immense valour amongst Sikhs and Punjabis but remain unknown to others are a source of inspiration too. This opportunity should be seized to catapult them on the national stage immediately because there aren't many valiant heroes in India. Our heroes might otherwise remain victims of narrow-mindedness, but at this juncture, they would be heartily embraced.' As a consequence of this letter, Punjabi University, Patiala had been sanctioned a grant for implementing this project.

The fact of the matter is that there is no dearth of money; publication or preservation too is no big issue. The foremost issue is our own apathy. Else, there is no cogent reason why not even a single manuscript of such a great personality as Guru Nanak Dev could be preserved by us. We have combs, clothes, jutis, beds and cots, and armaments (and this is not a small matter in itself), but the utter negligence in not preserving manuscripts can be ascribed to nothing but our apathy towards history. I wish to cite another example to substantiate this indifference.

There is a village named Hathhoor in district Ludhiana. It was Late S. Attar Singh Bhadauria who first drew attention to some inscriptions dated prior to the era of Guru Nanak Dev. These mentioned the century and era as inscribed in Gurumukhi on the walls of an ancient building in the village (the mausoleum of Rai Firoz). These inscriptions were a testimony to the history of the Gurumukhi script dating further back than even the lifetime of Guru Nanak Dev. Sardar Gurbaksh Singh (G.B. Singh) also copied the writings inscribed on the walls and confirmed the inference of S. Attar Singh. When I visited the site, I discovered that the outer verandah had crumbled while the roof had completely disappeared. The walls still existed there but the rains had washed away the plaster on which the precious writings had been inscribed. However, some portions under the arches remained out of reach from showers and a few faded writings had survived. I traced whatever was traceworthy. It was evident that these walls would not last very long. I wrote to the joint director of the National Archeological Department, Dr Bahadur Chand Chabbra, seeking his help in protecting and preserving these inscriptions. I also went to Delhi to meet with him. He planned a tour and I accompanied him to Hathhoor and some other places. Attempts were made to photograph the inscriptions at Hathhoor, but things didn't progress further. Then, I wrote to S. Pratap Singh Kairon, requesting him to make arrangements for the preservation of this unique building. He forwarded my letter to the director of the Archives department at Patiala; thereafter the matter was ignored. At present, there are no inscriptions there, and the proof of the antiquity of Gurumukhi that could have been saved for posterity has been lost forever to a deaf-mute time.

Can any country of the world with a commitment towards its history, exhibit such ill-disposition?

These are only a few samples which reveal that the vital elements of our past and present which should have flowed into our future have been allowed to be destroyed by crass negligence. We have massacred our history and culture and are guilty of it at local, national and even international levels. We could atone for past crimes and redeem ourselves if we could still develop an orientation towards preserving our history.

Giani Gurdit Singh

Giani Gurdit Singh (1923-2007) was born in village Mitthewal of the former princely state Malerkotla, now a district in Punjab. After his initial studies from Lahore, he began visiting prominent libraries and was soon absorbed in research related to ancient manuscripts. Apart from the libraries of Lahore, Patiala, Amritsar and Kashi (Varanasi) he also studied the manuscripts available with Sikhs of princely states. Giani Gurdit Singh also did editing work for some newspapers. His book *Mera Pind* is a classic work of Punjabi which captures the soul of Punjab. Balraj Sahni said that the book quenched his thirst and made him fall in love with his country. The following piece is a part of this chaptered book that is written in continuity; the book portrays the different facets of the traditional Punjabi life. By using a language that has a distinct flavor and vigour, he presented a vibrant portrayal of rural Punjab.

Be Blessed, O Father!

A twelve-year-old girl was considered mature enough for marriage if we go by the customs of earlier generations. (Now even an 18-year-old is considered too young to marry.) Marrying off young girls was taken to be the highest order of benefaction in villages. If the matchmaker had not already proposed a match for a girl stepping into adolescence, her family initiated efforts to search for one. (Child marriage has been a social problem until the very recent past).

Allowing a girl to remain unmarried by the time she attained maturity was considered to be a sin in our country. The poor girls could hardly be expected to demand to be married off! Daughters and cows seemed to have no voice of their own:

A popular poet expresses the helplessness of girls thus:

> Do daughters and cows have any say, O Sada Ram!

In earlier times when our ancestors were forest-dwellers and did not yet live in urbanised homes, girls must have sought a tree to hide behind and express their shy desires for finding a groom; or maybe they fantasised the tree to be their partner! Their plea might have led their parents to ask them about their preferences between a *gandharva vivah* or a *swayamvar* or they might have chosen to marry on their own.

The tender feelings expressed to an imagined, or even a real, sandalwood tree by the girl are captured in this folk song:

> Why are you standing behind the sandalwood tree, O Daughter!
> I was actually standing beside revered Father
> Praying that he searches for a groom
> O Daughter! What kind of groom should we search for?
> O Father! He should be like the moon amidst the stars!
> Let him be like Kaanha among the moons, find me a groom like Kanhaiya (Lord Krishna)!

> Why are you standing behind the sandalwood tree, O Sister?
> I was standing beside my Brother
> Praying that he searches for a groom!
> O Sister! What kind of groom should we find?
> O Brother! He should be the bravest of the brave!
> Find me a groom like Ram Chander (Lord Rama)!

> Why are you standing behind the sandalwood tree, O Daughter?
> I was standing beside my Maternal Uncle,
> Praying that he searches for a groom,
> O Daughter! What kind of groom should we find?
> O Uncle! The most benevolent in the world,
> Find me a groom like Harish Chander

> My Daughter! I searched, and have found a groom for you!

Another song makes a plea for a rich, prosperous and handsome groom:

> O Father! Please carry out my wish,
> Give me a gem of a groom like Ram.
> O Daughter, I have brought you a groom
> The colour of a (red) *kusumbha* flower
> This Ram-like gem of a man wears a wedding flower-veil
> Like the fragrant *kewda* flower blooming in the gardens.

With the passage of time, the girls lost their freedom to self-select their groom, the control of the parents increased, and the girls' wish for finding a groom turned into entreaties. Emotions expressing requests to the father for finding a prosperous home, a good mother-in-law and father-in-law as the head of the family were depicted in such songs:

> O Father! Send me to a home where a tailor stitches silk clothes,
> May I wear one dress and give another one for dyeing,
> And have clothes aplenty in my coffer;
> May you do this good deed O Father!
> O Father! Send me to a home
> Where a jeweller crafts jewellery
> So, I may wear one and take off another.
> And have jewellery aplenty in my box.
> May I adorn myself every day; may you do this good deed O Father!
> May you earn good fame; may you do this good deed O Father!

Along with a good groom, a good home is also demanded from the righteous father:

> Find a good home for me Father, so I am spared the back-breaking drudgery of repairing mud walls.

A request is made for finding good relatives, especially the mother-in-law and father-in-law. Girls are also concerned that their weddings are not scheduled to be held in an unpropitious season. Like monsoon clouds, apprehensions take various hues, from food being spoilt by showers and to the finery of Shyam (alluding to their groom) being drenched.

> I say to you my Father, O Righteous One
> Don't marry me in the monsoons
> In the monsoons the clouds bring showers
> Shyam ji's dress gets drenched, O Ram ji
> Let someone bring the southern breeze, O Righteous One!
> That Shyam ji's dress dries, O Hare Ram ji

Parents of a comely daughter are not concerned about her wedding alone, but also about refurbishing and decorating their mansion to impress the guest:

> Build high-rise palaces with the help of Kings and Queens,
> Ask for fresh cow dung, bring it, O Kings and Queens,
> Grind the white rice, remind the Kings and Queens,
> O Girl's Father sleeping on the roof, how can you sleep?
> I am not sleeping; I am afflicted with worry
> My virgin daughter, sitting at home, is asking for a groom.

After the spell of four sultry and rainy months, come October and November which are considered auspicious months for marriages due to pleasant weather. The mild cold in the month of October keeps the food from getting spoilt, and the milk does not curdle. A savoury dish of fried dumplings added to yoghurt does not turn sour.

> I ask you, Father, to arrange my marriage in October
> Grains remain unspoilt in the granary; your curd will not turn sour
> O Father, I am your young daughter
> Find me a match and make my feet tinkle with anklets
> O Father, I am your daughter, O Righteous Father.

The sweet wedding songs in beautiful seasons are enriched with the sounds of the flails, and the resonance of the grinding millstones. But October is the time to water the land for rabi crops (gram and cauliflower) sown in the summer months and plough the land for the sowing of the wheat crop, so relatives find it hard to come and get together for the wedding. This may prompt them to cook up a grudge to avoid the trip. Keeping these things in mind, people are compelled to plan the wedding for November.

> I ask you, Father, yes O Father
> Marry me in November,
> The food will not spoil, your relatives will not be annoyed,
> Oh yes, Father, the curd won't go sour.

Traditionally, the girls are meant to be shy; how can they disclose their innermost feelings about their marriage? They bear with whatever the family decides. But friends collectively convey the sentiments of the would-be bride through popular folk songs. This is also an apt time to intensify her feelings when they call upon the father to earn a good deed by marrying off his daughter.

Gurbachan

Gurbachan (b. 1941) was born in Patiala. Even while teaching English in Moti Ram College of Delhi, he remained engaged with Punjabi language, literature and thought. He has written both prose and literary criticism. His prose writings are remarkable for their portrayal of a Punjabi mentality, and especially of how an ordinary Punjabi migrant thinks and lives. Gurbachan works extremely diligently on his language and craft. As a result, his prose is very interesting and creates the illusion of fiction.

This is not Punjab

New York: My name is Harjit Mawi; I used to work as a lecturer in Punjab. Here I am an employee of a security agency; my duty is to guard a residential building.

I have been around for two years. I have acquired many diseases which aren't visible to others. While in Punjab, I had a singular disease—to reach American shores. After reaching here, I have often felt nauseous, though unable to retch.

My other affliction is that the mere thought of spending a penny is anathema to me. Everyone is desperate to accumulate cash here, but I cling to money like a flea. I feel distraught at the mere thought of spending. When natives and poor individuals like me reach America, we begin to act like fleas hanging on to the green dollars. We are stingy even while buying food for the household. It is indeed a disease to be so thrifty without any rhyme or reason. I am well aware of this, but I can't stop myself from being addicted to dollars. Next is the disease that continues to erode me every single day and it is that even before getting married, I considered myself to be impotent. My self-confidence is shattered whenever I think about sex. It appears terribly perilous.

Regularly, one or the other such diseases eats into my entrails and many times the bugs collectively invade me.

It is on setting foot here that one learns that America/New York is a very strange land. After all, we had reached here as economic asylum seekers. We could never experience equality. It can't be predicted how the next generations view this. Our natives who immigrated abroad must have certainly thought along these lines. Here, even after earning on a daily basis, one continues to be impoverished from within. Why is this so?

I have no answers to any of these questions. Earlier I could manage to find answers, was capable of thinking them through, but now even though my thought process is still functional, it has slowed down considerably. Sometimes the thought process comes to a screeching halt and is immobile for many days. If the heart is heavy, one is unable to think clearly. My heart feels heavy all the time. Even my body feels weighed down. I feel tired all the time and this tiredness doesn't ease even with sleep. Sleep deprivation is a regular occurrence. Even as I lie down to sleep, thoughts about going for work hover over me. My eyes have shrunk because of sleep deprivation.

I catch the train for work from the Flushing underground subway. I observe many strange and unfamiliar things on the train. Two sets of people catch my special attention. I clandestinely admire these two types of people. These people are semi-clad women and the hugely built black men. Peeping at the females I feel as if I have managed to see them almost completely nude. I avert my gaze like a gentleman. However, those bodies always seem to be crying out and beckoning me. I have been able to gain this understanding that in a country like the USA, women have obliterated the mystique created around their bodies. The women here wish to convey that the body shouldn't be considered anything more than being simply a body; the moral and cultural trappings built around it are mere snares for the women. These women have blown these snares into smithereens.

Looking at the black guy with a huge frame, I worry that he would punch me square across my jaw in a fit. While in Punjab too I was timid and cowardly, but here, I am a complete goner and feel terribly scared. I remain jittery all the time; probably this nervousness gnaws at the bones of all immigrant Indians. 'Amreeka' has such a weighty ring to it that it keeps the mind oppressed. Similar to intimidation by a demon, we suffer from a sense of intellectual inferiority in front of the whites and a terrible fear of physical assault by the blacks. We bring all these intellectual complexes along with us here. We learn that we are not capable of coping with space/time of this land. That is why we have turned our homes into ghettos. A large number of Asians, especially those connected with the roads, in other words, those who earn by way of simple labour jobs, comprise this category—ghettoised humans.

Since I hold a master's degree and dabble in reading and writing, I keep myself engaged in such philosophical discourses. At times such thoughts crop up in my mind but I can't share them with anyone. Sometimes when I experience acute insomnia and don't feel at ease, some thought germinates within me, but then I find no one to converse with. I have lost all enthusiasm for writing. Sometimes I pen a poem; they have been wandering wantonly in my mind for the last two years. We immigrants write poetry for the simple reason that other genres demand hard work and are time-consuming. By way of poetry, my name too gets included in the list of martyrs of the pen!

During the days when the US Open Lawn Tennis Championship was being held in the stadium in Flushing, I would watch the crowds thronging the stadium, and feel disenchanted. Am I interested in anything at all? I would ruminate. The answer would always be that I am no longer interested in anything. As if I had no control over my days and nights. A routine-bound job and on return to the flat I would simply crash; the next day would be the same at the subway and then at work. This thought often occupies my mind, 'Why do I feel nauseous seeing the crowds go for the tennis matches?'

This issue about nausea is bizarre; I have no idea why it happens abruptly. It could be due to the disenchantment residing deep within me. Maybe I am starved of a conversation with someone I could call my own. Sometimes I am so acutely lonely that I feel like crying. I went to watch a film and the background score was so moving that tears started rolling down my eyes. After the whole day at work, I feel very tense on reaching home. On a day off and all by myself at home, I was about to go off to sleep. The bed was adjacent to Kartara's bed, in the drawing-room. Kartara is from my village and Jagdish has taken him in as a paying guest. No one was home as Sunita and Kartara were both at work and Jagdish leaves at six in the morning and returns at eight at night. I started to think deeply and wondered what actually is bothering me here! Is it because of culture shock? Why am I not in harmony with anything whatsoever?

Jagdish is my elder brother, six years my senior. He is not attached to anyone but there is a bond between us, though it is not obvious. He has no time for household chores. Sunita is his wife and according to her, I am a confused idiot. Like Jagdish, Kartara too works very hard. After back-breaking construction labour, he returns home utterly exhausted. The day he takes off from work, he gets really drunk and rants. Lying on my bed, I was pondering over all this when I suddenly heard a sound from Jagdish's bedroom. Probably Sunita has already returned from work and is at home earlier than me. Maybe she had taken the day off. I don't concern myself with these things. At this house, everyone finds their own way to feed themselves; go to the kitchen and find in the fridge whatever's worth eating or rustle up something to fill one's belly. Sunita doesn't talk much with me or Kartara, implying thereby that it is purely a need-based relationship.

When I was in Punjab, I was distraught and desperately wished to come to America. I was not able to concentrate on anything except being passionately inclined towards writing poetry. My belief was that the young men who have nothing to brag about, start writing poetry. At college functions, I would recite Shiv Kumar's agonised outpourings throatily; it was as if someone had brutally mauled the heart. Girls used to like Shiv Kumar's poetry; I too liked his poetry.

After I arrived in America, once, on an off-day I found it difficult to fall asleep and didn't feel like doing anything. I poured myself a large peg of scotch, found paper and a pen and started to write a poem. I gulped down another peg. How could a poem be composed in an inebriated state? On the blank paper, my mother's visage and at other times my father's screaming face started to flash, 'Yes, my son, you stay confined to home drinking your mother's milk. Why do you need to do anything else?' This had happened at the time my visa had been granted. Ticket purchased, I had to catch the bus for the airport from Jalandhar the next day. I had said, 'I don't feel like leaving.' Father was infuriated.

Destiny had something different in store for me. I got my permanent residency within a year of arriving in America. Others, who had been around for six, seven, even ten years, had not been granted permanent residency; they continued to live illegally and worked on the basis of fake papers.

The lawyer explained that in California, the political asylum cases get settled faster; moreover, they get favourably decided for the educated. They used to think that an MA degree holder won't spread filth in the USA. At the time of the interview, I showed to the interviewing officer a newspaper clipping with a picture of me reciting a poem; I was speaking with a raised hand. I told the American lady officer, 'I am expressing my views at a conference held against the violation of human rights. The state of human rights is so pathetic in India that the representatives of Amnesty International have been barred from entering Punjab. Atrocities are being committed on Sikhs. We Sikhs need freedom. Freedom is every human being's right. Our religion and culture are under immense threat in India. Twenty-five thousand young Sikh boys like me have been butchered in the last five to seven years. I had always faced the imminent danger of being picked up by the police, so I came as a visitor to America.'

All those seeking political asylum use the same idiom.

I had gone there after fully rehearsing to speak in English. They asked me, 'Any proof of you being a college teacher?' It was a fair skinned, beautiful, good natured lady who asked the question. Her facial expressions seemed to indicate that she was sympathetic towards me. I had the bank passbook showing entries of my salary being directly deposited by the college. It also mentioned my designation—lecturer. The lawyers had explained everything beforehand. When I showed the passbook, she said, 'Okay we will let you know soon.' When I apprised the lawyer, he said, 'Your case is clinched. Go and enjoy.'

After I became a permanent resident, Jagdish called at the village. Father was thrilled, but my mother started to cry, saying, 'You murdered Jeeta [me, Harjeet Mawi]. I had a dream that you killed him and dumped his corpse into the river', and she put the phone down wailing. I too could not talk.

Since then everyone has called me lucky. 'Listen, your future generations have been redeemed'. Remaining mum, I too would agree and say that I was lucky indeed. However, at times, I would puzzle over why the hell this matter was considered one of great redemptions? Have the future generations been redeemed or doomed? I felt like screaming openly. This whole quandary is because of the damned Jagdish, who was a waiter and has reduced me to being a mere waiter. His wife? Bloody whore.

I am a meek, timid man, emaciated and faint-hearted. That is why mother had said that I should not go if I didn't feel up to it. She had already told Deesha (Jagdish) that it would be terribly hard on her to pass her days if Jeeta (Harjeet) also left. She held Deesha responsible for my departure. I was extremely perturbed by the situation in Punjab. In America I would at least be rid of such restlessness—and of the police and the gun-toting youth. The professorship that I had managed was against a leave vacancy of six months.

After I had boarded, the plane refused to take off; I remained stuck in India! Allegedly, one of the passengers was a terrorist from Punjab. All the travelers were shunted out. Along with other young boys, I too was profiled for interrogation. The identity card of a college lecturer made things easier for me. The plane took off after two hours. I am not aware if any suspect was caught or not. That was the first instance when I had felt nauseous. It could have been due to my maiden flight, or due to my leaving my native land, or on account of my thoughts about my father, mother and other friends who had come to see me off. Or maybe it was only my own inner weakness. I am intimidated by unfamiliar situations. Earlier I used to feel I would burst into tears. Now I only feel nausea. Neither did I cry then nor do I throw up now. It just feels it could happen at any moment. I feel like my head isn't fastened tightly enough.

One day Didar said to Jagdish, 'Jeeta has some mental issue.'

Sunita often laughs at what I say and would say: 'You have some mental health issue.'

I have no mental health issue. The fact of the matter is that I am easily scared. Terror seems to reside in my bone marrow. When I climb up a ladder, I fear that someone would remove the ladder from underneath. Staying in New York, I had a lurking fear of a black man mugging me. Such incidents happen here on a daily basis and get press coverage. That is why I don't read newspapers.

I wonder if I should seek a doctor's advice; then I feel terribly upset even at the thought. I know I would faint when the doctor would ask for a fee of a hundred dollars. Then the cops would arrive; ambulance and the expenditure to be incurred on all this; I would have to call Jagdish and he would arrive, dropping everything. Sunita would viciously mutter, 'He is a complete idiot.' A few days ago, she said, 'You don't have any guts: you are just like Jagdish.' Didar was listening, he smiled.

One day Didar and I were at home. He had an evening shift that day. He was sitting on the adjacent bed and said, 'Do you know that black guy on the ground floor? That King guy who is a six-footer' I could foretell what he was about to say.

I moved out of the flat before listening to Didar's trash. I started to move towards the park hoping to get rid of my restlessness, I might just throw up. I did not puke.

Every Saturday, while drinking whisky, Jagdish would express his wise thoughts through proclamations: 'After landing in America, in the last seven years, I have never even seen a doctor's face. We have come here to work, not to fall sick.'

I did not talk to Jagdish about my ailment. But it is, in fact, a mental condition arising out of severance from one's own ethos and the inability to integrate with the new atmosphere.

Jagdish would bluntly say, 'It's impossible to earn if one gets into the rut of consulting doctors; we have to send five hundred dollars to father next month.'

As I was coming out of the lift this morning, I saw King. I gasped for breath. Why the hell am I so terrified of this guy? I am scared because he is involved in drugs; also scared because one day after I turned the key and entered the flat, I had barely sat on my bed when I heard King talking to Sunita. Then his voice grew louder and he stormed out in a rage. Sunita slammed her bedroom door and seemed upset at my arrival at home before the scheduled hour. Apparently, she was crying. Maybe she was not crying. Maybe Sunita was not even aware that I was lying in my bed.

King yelled out from the lobby, 'Hey man, where is your fucking brother?'

For a moment I was unable to comprehend if he was saying something to me. 'I am asking you man; where is Jag?' I walked away without answering.

My brother had taken me to his workplace the day after my arrival in New York. I hadn't even recovered from the fatigue of the journey. Jagdish was a head waiter. His bald employer was very pleased with him and was confident that I too would prove to be a hardworking lad. He said, 'I love Indians; very hard-working', and pointing towards the parked bicycles he said, 'Start to supply on the bicycle. It's a simple job; Jagdish will explain it to you.'

Now, the whole day I remain seated in a guard's chair, sometimes doing double duty, sixteen hours. The body gives way. On reaching home, I eat whatever is in the fridge and doze off. All this rush is for making money, a rat race or a dollar race of rats. Just as humans feel repulsed by rats, I feel the same with myself. Trapped in such vicious circles our people appear like rats to me. Back in Punjab, it was a different kind of wantonness; it was the desperation to reach here. Now no desperation of any kind exists. While in Punjab I used to sometimes dabble in poetry. Now, in my mind, there is no space left for poetry. It seems as if all my resources have dried up.

Such is the plight of most of our new immigrants. While I am an educated person, an M.A. in Punjabi hardly counts for anything. Even engineering graduates drive a cab here. The cab drivers don't go back home till they can earn two hundred dollars a day—whether they are able to make them in twelve or in twenty-four hours. Why do these dollars hold such magnetism for our people? Even on the verge of death, their regret is that they won't be able to earn any longer. I too feel that I should keep doing twelve to sixteen hours of duty and there is no point squandering time and energy.

I told my brother that I wished to live separately. 'Don't be stupid. If you live separately, what will you save?' Jagdish argued. He lets out rooms to paying guests. If I leave, he will find someone else. Kartara has been living in the flat ever since he landed here. Everyone's bed is placed in the drawing room. They all sleep there and they have to cook their own food. At times Sunita prepares some vegetable and at other times, nothing.

The Flushing area swarms with immigrants, mainly Chinese, Korean and Punjabis. The entire day is spent at work. It's just passing time, not living.

I don't like this place one bit. I have realized this now. When I landed here, I didn't have a sense of distinction between good and bad; I was obsessed with America. After I came here, a transformation began to take place within me. It was like day mutating into the night. For a while, my mind was dazed by the fact that I have actually reached here. When I get ready and go for work, America is awake and running while the village is asleep; the darkness of the night envelops Punjab then.

Jagdish threw a small party when I got my permanent residency. In a fit, I said, 'Why the hell are you all calling me lucky; what is special about America? What a damned country! I am not happy here and I'm going to go back.'

Kartara was zapped. Just a little while ago he had rued emphatically that he might never get permanent residency. His wife and children were in Punjab. Whenever he was drunk, he call home and talk nonsense to his wife.

Jagdish asked haughtily, 'What do you mean?'

'I mean that a loafer has no life even in America. What does America offer us? Bloody pizza? Our women don't even have time to roll a chapati. They just go on eating and feeding us pizza.'

'I am not your servant, cook your own food and eat.' Sunita knew that I don't relish pizza. Pizza had been ordered today as well.

Silence pervaded. Sunita retired into her bedroom. Kartara kept saying that this guy is acting up since he's got his permanent residency so easily. Jagdish was inebriated by now, 'Look at what Jeeta says! What does America have to offer us? You bastard, what does Punjab have to offer us? Your damn poetry is not worth two cents. You poets are good for nothing; I know everything, bloody dogs! You curse America. You have reached here easily. Look at Didar Singh who had to shell out eight lakh rupees.'

He continued, 'Why do you think at all? If you want to be successful in America, quit thinking.'

'I don't want to be successful, you have already experienced it yourself. You earn so much yet you keep two paying guests at home. You have no clue about your wife's whereabouts or what she does.'

Jagdish said, 'Shut up or I will kill you.' He got up to punch me.

Quickly shoving another peg of whisky down his throat, he came into my room and said, 'If you utter even a single word about Sunita

I will kill you.' He slouched on the bed without eating anything. The microwaved chicken, lying on the table in front of him remained untouched. Sunita was sleeping in her bedroom.

The party to celebrate my permanent residency was a flop. Jagdish and Kartara, both inebriated, had fallen asleep. I switched off the light and went off to sleep. Next day I had a day off work. Jagdish had to catch the subway at six in the morning. I woke up at 10 AM, no one was at home. My head was still spinning because of the whisky.

For many days I remained hounded by the thought that a terrible thing had happened and an unnecessarily unpalatable situation had been created.

One day Jagdish started to say, 'Put your heart into work, earn well, in a few years you will forget all about Punjab; bloody hell! What does it have to offer? What ails you here?'

Sitting close by, Kartara said, 'The problem is that he is unable to digest Black Label; only Bagpiper agrees with him.'

Kartara used to polish off half a bottle on Saturdays and then blabber. He would obliquely glance at Sunita's breasts as she moved around. Jagdish would just turn his face the other way. I used to feel troubled by Kartar's behaviour.

I narrated my woes thoughtfully to Jagdish, 'Other than getting dollars in place of rupees, what else do we get in this damn country? What about the terrible hardship one has to undergo; the humiliation that one has to endure?'

'This poet does not need dollars, he needs the village shit, hmm!'

Suddenly Sunita came in. Looking at me, she said, 'It's better you go back to your Punjab' and walked away to the kitchen.

Didar was relaxing and suddenly burst out, 'People like me also need white boobs, but we are unable to get it; they are very expensive.'

'Just shut up,' said Jagdish.

Sunita laughed. She was listening. While going towards her bedroom she said, 'What rubbish you talk.'

I don't like Sunita at all. Jagdish has got his permanent residency by marrying Sunita. I have not been able to decipher till date why Sunita married Jagdish. Jagdish had been working illegally for seven years. Ever since Kartara has come, he keeps pleading, 'Please organise something for me.' He often says this to Sunita. One day he said, 'Please organise something for me, get some girl ready for me, I am ready to pay up as much as required. Get me married off to some black girl only, I would get the divorce papers from Jeeto.'

Sunita said smilingly, 'There is one easy way; show me one lakh dollars. I will divorce Jagdish and marry you.' Then she started laughing.

I was reading a book. On hearing her, I began sweating. Jagdish was off to work.

Sunita said, 'It is simply a transaction. Every marriage is a transaction; whether the marriage is real or fake, it's business.'

A few days later, I again told Jagdish, 'I am not going to live here. Find me a flat.' He gaped.

Probably he had an intuition about what I was going to say. I said, 'Even though you are elder to me the conduct of your wife is not right.'

He went quiet for some time and then said, 'Where would you go? It would be a wasteful additional expenditure. Even if you share a flat with someone, it will cost you five hundred dollars, and food expenses.'

We were both sitting in the subway.

He suddenly blurted, 'What has Sunita said to you that you are always so curt with her.'

'What will she say to me? I just don't like her.'

'One has to be practical. She was like this before marriage as well. I got a permanent residency because of her. You have reached here because of me. Now we will get father and mother over here.'

'Are you aware that King comes here?'

Jagdish kept mum.

We both took our different paths to work. After about an hour I got a phone call from Jagdish at my workplace, 'This is not Punjab. Stay relaxed. We have to make the best of a bad job.'

Narinder Singh Kapoor

Narinder Singh Kapoor (b. 1944) was born in Rawalpindi. He was a lecturer in English and taught at Nabha, Sangrur and Patiala. Later he also completed MA in Philosophy and Punjabi and became a professor at Punjabi University, Patiala. He continued with his self-growth and did a diploma in French, a degree in journalism, LLB and also PhD in Punjabi journalism. Currently, Kapoor is the most widely read writer of Punjabi prose. His writings stir the imagination of the reader and offer a message of hope.

A Flight in The Sky

One cannot dance merely by tying the ankle bells without the accompanying passion for dance and practice.

A person who obsessively talks only about work can neither make any friends nor love anyone.

One has to put in additional efforts to cultivate any relationship.

There are times when one is able to earn without much effort but saving it would require a great deal of effort.

Success can never be achieved without striving, failure too is impossible without an effort. Those who view life in a sedentary manner akin to seeing photographs in an album can never illumine the paths of others as a lighthouse, nor do they ever venture into deep waters.

Alexander's ambition was far greater than his own self but the world acclaims him because of his enterprise and not his ambition.

The human race is prone to glorifying the past and belittling the present. It doesn't support and encourage a striving man and instead preaches to a loser. People are not invited to explore new frontiers of knowledge, only the known and the familiar are forced to be repeated. However, there exist a few people in every age who make path-breaking efforts and auger a new epoch for mankind.

Some lead their lives in such a manner that causes perennial worry to the Lord.

It has been observed that when one comes to possess more than his needs, he begins to commit excesses; and some bring ruin to the whole nation in the process of their own disaster.

The word 'soul' is used in the context of knowledge and similarly, life can be properly understood only in the context of effort or striving. Wastelands are transformed into vibrant habitations by dint of hard work; in the absence of enterprise, habitations become deserted.

Relationships lose their sheen, break down and, at times, become adversarial if they are not invested with newer interests.

Times past or the nights that have gone by, lost opportunities or friends who passed away, can never be reclaimed. However, it is said that even when everything is snatched from us, what still remains is the future and the endeavour.

It is our mistaken belief that our problems are resolved by mutual discussion. Problems are resolved only if there is an effort towards resolution during the exchange of views. What actually transpires is that the understanding of our own problems deepens through discussions and, with the insights so gained, we are able to transcend the problems. Thus, those problems cease to appear obstructive or insurmountable to us and are resolved on their own.

The more doctrinarian a race or a society becomes, the more it regresses from an entrepreneurial angle.

The dominant tone of the vedas composed in India is of life-affirming action and optimism, whereas the upanishads are more doctrine-based and have a pessimistic tenor.

Human existence is full of agony and is transient. Therefore, any philosophy associated with it is naturally laden with concerns.

Politics exerts pressure on humans from the outside, whereas religion seeks to hold them from within. Politics wields legal control over society while religion pulls the reins through thought processes.

Indian society is more influenced by its cultural traditions than legal codes. Indians are generally listeners and not readers; they are fond of listening rather than reading. They place greater reliance on fate than on enterprise. Science is based on ceaseless effort while religion is founded on mystery.

Science does not oppose religion; it opposes mysticism. In the last century (particularly in the last few decades), the transformation that has taken place in society is the consequence of enterprise. Take a look at your streets and localities to witness the improving lives of those who are making efforts of any kind.

Those who don't have children, travel more, seek more and also go astray more.

Those unmarried either brag or claim to have won wars never fought. In our society, there is a lack of acceptance of a relationship between an older woman and a younger man. Such relationships become subjects of either pity or ridicule because the element of growth is absent from them.

Growth is the fruit of enterprise. Without endeavour there cannot be growth of any kind.

It is said that if you haven't become rich till the age of thirty, then you should abandon the efforts to be wealthy. It is also said that before preaching to others, one must have personally undergone the trials and tribulations of life.

It is amazing that men rule the world but the women are held responsible for all ills. It might be because women are not overly concerned with doctrines; they lay more emphasis on accomplishments and enterprise. Their reactions are more natural, simple and fresh. They are more intuitive and purer of sentiment due to which their decisions are not based on logic, and that is why they do not like debates.

If a man and a woman both bolt a room from the inside after entering it, then as they emerge out of the room, the man would look sad and distraught while the woman would appear to have become wise.

It has been observed that compared to men, women put greater effort into keeping a marriage afloat.

A woman has to be more industrious in every field of life. There is no concept of rights in the world of men It is only a kind of a compromise that women have to make; an attempt at providing an alibi for the enterprise.

A vast majority of people are involved in meaningless endeavours. They strive in areas where they have no ability. And they ignore those areas which portend possibilities for them. Such people try to stop raindrops from falling. This is a race on uncharted roads. A circular race never reaches a marker.

Who has achieved complete success in all his endeavours?

Thinking about someone is a venture towards meeting that person. We remember those who don't come to us themselves and who we are unable to reach. To think of someone is, in fact, an attempt to defer a personal crisis, a way out.

The memories of an unsuccessful love become our experience.

Man is never alone; his reminiscences and experiences provide him with support and sustenance.

Memories too cannot be created without effort; love certainly is an arena of the enterprise.

Education is not possible without efforts.

Without sincere efforts, character building is impossible.

Hard work is basically a respectful form of effort.

The real fruits of hard work are knowledge and character, not wealth and praise.

Kalyug (the age of darkness) necessitates a guru; in Satyug (the age of truth and virtue) or in heaven, even angels are ordinary people.

Industriousness brings forth change and one can never attain insights about time without change. Time is an instrument to measure change. If you want to see the extent of change within you, then look carefully at your friends. The change that is manifest in them resonates with you.

Failure is caused by diverse reasons. One definite reason that leads to failure is putting in less than the requisite amount of labour; inadequate labour ensures failure. The second reason is procrastination; the third is not to finish any work and the fourth is to get deeply involved in the rat race of quickly becoming rich. There are many more ways with which we could play hide and seek with our lives all along.

Great outcomes are never achieved promptly.

A journey is a form of effort.

It is not death, but the cause of death that makes a martyr of a man.

There is beauty even in hell. Those living there cannot identify it; they do not even make an effort to find it. This is, in fact, their punishment.

The unceasing efforts of nature are the cause of the beauty that nature inheres.

No form of art can be learnt by a casual approach. Many aspire to become artists but they lack the courage to put in appropriate efforts.

Getting married is an effort to fight out the long battle of life and strive for it. This is why it is often said that the advice to someone to get married or to go to war should be given after due diligence since both sets of advice have an identical intent.

Despite trying one can never love the person one is afraid of. Unequal relationships are doomed to end in hatred.

The establishment of real democracy would become possible only when attempts would be made to weigh the votes instead of counting them.

You are sure to lose if you seek to fight only for your own rights, but if you also help protect others' rights, then everyone would win.

It is delusional to think that one can survive without engaging with the world. And he suffers from a bigger delusion if he believes that the world would come to a halt in his absence.

Only those enterprises are successful which are affirming for the world, the society and mankind. The effort to 'give away' is far more virtuous than 'to receive'.

God says: Share and I shall give you more. Strive and I shall come to your aid.

We get agitated on hearing the truth as we are accustomed to hearing only falsehood. We get ruffled if anything goes contrary to our habits. Governments are based on falsehood and hence they are afraid of the truth.

Thinking gives birth to rebellion.

With right actions, rebellions fructify into revolutions. Wrong actions make revolutions degenerate into dictatorships. As you sow, so shall you reap.

We are slaves to our ignorance. Knowledge always liberates but no knowledge is possible without striving. Knowledge is not a destination; it is an endless journey. It is a verb and not a noun; not an attainment but an attempt.

That alone happens which is in the realm of possibility. Therefore, efforts must be made to make the possible happen. Someone had prayed: O God, please give me the strength to change whatever can be changed; give me the courage to accept whatever cannot be changed, and give me the wisdom to understand the difference between the two.

The doctor says: I shall make the effort, God will cure.

You won't be able to initiate work, despite making efforts, if you seek the advice of your acquaintances before starting any work.

Those who do not learn from history are condemned to repeat the same mistakes. Those who do learn, commit mistakes too but in new ways and with different efforts.

Only natural efforts particularly bereft of pretense yield success. Just as an instrument without taut strings doesn't produce music, success doesn't embrace pretentious efforts.

Efforts should be so natural that success is their natural consequence.

If one does not become arrogant at the time of victory, then defeat too brings no humiliation.

The larger our island of knowledge, the wider our banks of experience would be.

Knowledge, love and experience lead our efforts towards effacing our hubris.

To feel a sense of security, we attempt to amass wealth. However, wealth itself needs protection and can never give protection to anyone.

Wealth creates many fears.

Wealth and assets multiply desires and hubris is aggravated by power. In this manner, a lust for disproportionate gains swells and our greed severely obstructs the growth of any sustainable relationship. Such situations deplete the possibilities of living and increase the tendencies of murders and suicides.

If individuals are becoming rich and society is regressing, it signifies that there is something fundamentally wrong with our efforts. We will need to change the direction of our endeavours.

It has been observed that as we try to accept the weaknesses of others, we begin to be more in consonance with our own selves. In the same way, the more patient we become, the more emancipated we would be. As our knowledge expands, our dependence on material things lessens, but tremendous efforts are needed to reach such a stage.

Our own path is smoothened as a consequence of our goodwill for others.

I shall try to be worthy of your good wishes and always try to take a flight in the realm of your skies.

Harpal Singh Pannu

Harpal Singh Punnu (b. 1953) was born in village Ghagga in Patiala district. He worked as a teacher in the Religious Studies department at Punjabi University, Patiala and retired as a professor. His prose is full of energy. His main contribution is in presenting in Punjabi the ideas of world-famous philosophers, saints, historians and spiritual devotees. He is full of reverence and devotion towards these personages which provides inspiration to the readers.

Mansur

The name of the Sufi *fakir*, 'Mansur,' reverberates in our hearts at the mere mention of the words 'Ana 'l-Haqq.' These words were the *summum bonum* of his philosophy, the core of his life, and the very same words became the cause of his catastrophic death. The meaning of the words 'Ana 'l-Haqq" is 'I am the truth'. 'Haqq' has two meanings—the truth as well as God. For Mansur, there was no duality between truth and God, and he often proudly proclaimed that he was God. It is not a crime to say so. The Koran has listed ninety-nine names of God and Haqq is one of them. The Sufi fakirs more often used the word 'Haqq' for God in place of the word 'Allah'. In current times, it is no longer considered a sin when we say Allah is omnipresent and since He permeates in every atom, He resides within me as well. But the times of Mansur were different. Mansur's utterance of 'Ana-'l-Haqq' was considered heresy by the faithful. Uttering the word 'Ana 'l-Haqq' was not the only crime he committed. His critics alleged that he believed in the doctrine of incarnations and in rebirth. To him, all men were the prophets of God. He would call someone 'Hazrat Nuh (Noah), and another he would address as Moosa (Moses), and yet another, he would call 'Mohammad.' How could the Muslim brotherhood tolerate such heresy—'I have installed the souls of these prophets within you!' How could such a person be of any significance even if he was a renowned fakir, a scholarly poet and a master of miracles? Blasphemy is blasphemy, and it must stop!

He was arrested under orders of the Khalifa of Baghdad and put behind bars. He was denied food and water for many weeks. He was hung on a cross on the banks of the River Tigris. He would be tortured during the day and in the evening he would be locked up in his prison cell. This went on for nine months. He was executed after being subjected to such barbaric atrocities that to even speak of them is gut-wrenching. Even after a thousand lashes inflicted on him had completely drained him of blood, his hands were chopped off, followed by his feet. His eyeballs were scooped out of their sockets; his tongue hacked off—since it was a tongue that used to utter blasphemies. Thereafter his head was severed from his body. It did not stop even here. His dead body was burnt to ashes and half of the ashes were thrown in the river, while the other half was dispersed in the wind so that this '*kafir*' (heretic) may not be able to finally rise on the Day of

Judgment. Contemporary eyewitness accounts state that every single drop of his blood that was shed echoed 'Ana 'l-Haqq'.

He was martyred. This immortal man was martyred because he revealed the secrets of mysticism to all and sundry. He became a beacon of light for not only his followers but for all saints and sages as well. Al Ghazali, the renowned Islamic scholar, who had reinforced along firm lines the existing foundations of Sharia, also felt compelled to praise Mansur. He wrote, 'All that Mansur expressed was out of his boundless love for Allah.' It is recorded in the Koran 'I am He whom I love, and He whom I love is I. We are two spirits dwelling in one body. If you see Him, you see us both'. Fariduddin Attar wrote, 'He was a consummate martyr who walked the path of Allah. He was like a lion living in a deep forest looking for a few rays of the light of truth, and, in fact, he found the whole sun. He was a diver who discovered treasures of diamonds as he dived in the deep seas and brought them out on the earth and scattered them all over'. Jalaluddin Rumi had registered his protest against the decree of his execution in these words:

> When an unjust judge holds the pen in his hand
> Some Mansur is then martyred on the gallows.

Shabistari in his book *Gulshaan-i-Raz* (Secret Rose Garden) wrote:

'Which tree bore the fruit of 'Ana 'l-Haqq'? 'I am God'—these words are the articulation of an infinite mystery. Other than God Himself, who else can say 'I am God'? Not just Mansur, but each and every mote on this earth is echoing—'I am Haqq, I am the Truth, I am God.' One bush had told Prophet Moosa, 'I am God!' And that bush then became a place of worship. When a man named Mansur uttered these words, the fakir was pilloried and executed. Only the mad wait till Judgment Day to see Allah. In the pilgrimage of the fakirs their journey and the destination become one. They must have merged together this very moment. Those who distinguish between themselves and Allah are the real heretics.'

Jalaluddin Rumi echoes Mansur's voice in the following words—

> I am the word; I am the holy book,
> I am the Bible and the Koran.
> Fire, water, wind and soil, what are they if not me?
> Lies and truth, goodness and evil, tenderness and harshness,
> I am the knowledge, solitude, the light of the faiths
> The deep darkness of hell and its burning fires
> The splendid Heaven and the garden of Eden
> Angels and the demons, body and soul, I am all of these, I am.
> O Shams Tabrez! Tell me what do the words on my lips mean
> You alone can tell, I am the universal soul, I am all of these,
> I am.

Abu Sayed paid his tribute to Mansur in these words:

> You reside in my heart
> All other places, wherever my blood could drop
> It will merge with you
> You are the light of my eyes,
> Wherever my tears would fall
> Those spots will be illumined by your being.

Scholars had attempted to connect Sufi tenets sometimes with Greek philosophy and at other times traced its roots to Zoroastrianism, Buddhism, Christianity and Vedanta. But after Mansur's martyrdom, all Sufis unanimously expressed that Sufism was rooted in the Koran and the Hadith. The Koran proclaims: 'Those, who believe in the invisible, say the *namaz* (prayer), are Momins (believers). I am closer to man than even his own jugular. God is the light of the earth and the sun.'

The beginning of Sufism is ascribed to Faqir Bayazid, who passed away in 909 CE. He was followed by a highly acclaimed saint Junaid of Baghdad. This *fakir* had a large number of pupils who came to him to attain education. Mansur came to his hermitage at the age of twenty-two in 880 CE. Mansur was a handsome young man with dreams resplendent in his eyes. As he bowed for the first time before Junaid, the latter prophesied, 'His blood will sanctify the gallows.' This good-looking young man's name was Hassan bin Mansur bin

Mohammad Al-Baidawi Al-Hallaj and he was born in 858 CE. His grandfather was a Zoroastrian named Sahabi Abu Ayub and his father was Hussain Bin Al Hallaj who was a weaver. A weaver is called Hallaj in Persian. Mansur was born in village Altur in Persia. He studied under Junaid for six years and meditated for another six years at the Kaaba. During these six years he did nothing except meditate. Remaining bare-bodied, he bore the harsh weather of Arabia with equanimity, stoically faceing the scorching sun as well as the brutal cold. Then after the consummation of his long and arduous meditation, he embarked upon a journey on foreign soils. Travelling through Iraq, Persia, Kashmir and Gujarat in India, he reached Aksai Chin via China. In India, he gained knowledge of yoga and tantra from yogis (ascetic monks). Many stories are prevalent about his miraculous powers.

One day, his followers saw that as he raised his hand towards the sky, an apple fell into his hands and he told them that the fruit had come from the Garden of Eden. One of his disciples writes, 'While wandering in the lanes of Baghdad, once he got into a state of spiritual ecstasy and tears began streaming down his eyes. Standing in the centre of the city he said, 'Please save me from the dazzling blaze of God's visage. God has snatched away my 'self' from my own being and refuses to return it. I am deprived of the ability to sing his praises because I have ceased to exist. At times He reveals Himself selectively, so that people should continue to believe in His Being and mankind may not stand in denial of Him. He often keeps Himself concealed so that the people may not be blinded by His effulgence, lose control of their senses and go mad. The distance between Him and me is less than an eyelash. He would soon annihilate me and leave absolutely no trace of mine on earth.'

At the age of fifty, he met Shibli and for the first time ever he uttered 'Ana 'l-Haqq' to him and revealed the secrets of the Divine. Shibli was a scholar and poet of Turkey and was widely known for his scholarship in Baghdad. He is the very same Shibli about whom there are many popular folk songs in Punjabi and in many other languages who allegedly threw a flower at Mansur while others were hurling stones at him. Mansur was arrested for blasphemy and paraded in the streets of Baghdad where the masses had been ordered by the authorities to stone him. Shibli happened to pass that way. He threw a flower at Mansur instead of a stone. Had Shibli not thrown anything at him, then the Khalifa would have punished him for disobeying orders. He did not throw a stone, for he was well aware that Mansur was a mystic. He was apprehensive of being punished for disobedience and did not throw a stone knowing well that Mansur was a complete fakir. As he threw a flower, Mansur wept bitterly and said, 'What have you done? You should have been either a complete stooge of the government or my friend. You should have stoned me if you wanted to obey the ruler. If you were my friend, you should not have been scared of the authorities. By throwing a flower at me you have tried to sail in two boats. I did not expect such behaviour from a scholar like you. I believed that you have realised the secrets of the Divine and are my friend.'

The Khalifa of Baghdad was Al-Muqtadir whose mother Shaghaab was a disciple of Mansur. A minister, Hamid, was also Mansur's follower. That was the reason that a protracted trial lasted against Mansur for blasphemy. Qazi Abu Omar was issuing *fatwa* upon *fatwa* (religious ruling) and Mansur would not say even a word in his own defense. He preferred martyrdom to defense. He said to the people of Baghdad, 'My murder is in accordance with the law, therefore, do justice and execute me!' A passerby asked, 'Why should we kill you?' Mansur replied, 'Because by doing this you will go down in history as ghazis who had performed the holy task of killing a *kafir* (heretic) and I will be known as a martyr. It will do us both good.'

However, the people of Baghdad loved him and could not think ill of him, let alone kill him. Ahmed ibn Hanbal was a zealot leader who had written a significant part of the Hadith, which is a collection of the words and miracles of the Prophet outside of the Koran. Muslims immensely revere the Hadith. Hanbal prepared the case against Mansur; even if it were another Islamic power, the adverse verdict would have been identical, because according to

Islamic sharia saying 'Ana 'l-Haqq' is against the teachings of the Koran, for God is the Absolute Being and none can ever be a part of Him.

Instead of trying to find ways and means to defend himself, Mansur would utter fresh blasphemies. He said, 'Fire is pure because you can see souls dancing in it.' He placed a stone in his hut and called it the Kaaba and started circumambulating it as in a pilgrimage. He said, 'I rule the moon, the stars and the galaxy and turn them around by my own volition.' He exclaimed, 'I shall soon sanctify my beloved's finger with my own blood. That auspicious moment is imminent.' A few stanzas culled from his poem are as follows:

> Meeting you is better than thousands of Heavens
> Hell is nothing but separation from you
> Exonerate the whole world of their sins
> But not mine
> I love you; this sin is unforgivable
> You burnt me a hundred times in the fire of love
> Burn me not a hundred but a thousand times instead
> For our love happens a thousand and not a hundred times.

He wrote:

> Kill me friend, do it quick
> This is the only way to unite with you
> Death would be my life
> And slumber in death will be my waking up
> Being totally obliterated from the world
> Will enhance my stature
> Endless, gigantic status
> Let me be one with water, fire and earth
> Then, on the seeds of love
> Buried in the earth,
> Beauteous maids will
> Shower wine-like water
> You would see this world
> Would be flooded with blooms

When punishments were being meted out to him, he used to be surrounded by people all around. The crowds got restive when the executioner hit his head with an iron rod. People started to pray. Mansur said:

> O people of Baghdad
> You have killed thousands of innocents and unblemished
> Why then do you tremble at punishing this sinner?
> Why did you get scared?

He said:

> O Master, all that You gave me, had You given to these people as well, I wouldn't have met the fate that is being dealt to me.
>
> Or if you had deprived these people, the way You have deprived me even then this would not have happened
>
> But whatever You do is good. Whichever way You keep me is good. Amen!

He was aware that his body would be burnt to ashes. His last poem that was found in his prison cell read:

> My ashes will be my bedspread tomorrow night
> Tomorrow would be a hapless night
> When I will not be able to moisten my bedspread
> with my tears
> I will be with you, You tell me all the time
> Stick around and feast your eyes on variegated love

The case against Mansur was handed over to Ali bin Mussa in the year 911. After investigations, the minister gave his verdict that no case of blasphemy could be proved against Mansur for he had not committed any such breach. However, some of his utterings was found to be objectionable. The minister ordered Mansur's beard to be shaved off; he should be lashed and hung upside down on a tree for four days from morning till evening. In the evening he was to be locked up. Thereafter he would be shackled and thrown in prison. He was held in high esteem within the prison not only by the prisoners but by the staff and officers as well. A separate room was constructed for him and was covered with carpets. He was allowed to keep servants and meet his visitors. The queen would come to hear his sermons and would entreat him not to curse Baghdad. Mansur said, 'Fakirs never curse, but they also do not lie. I do not curse, but truthfully say that I can see Baghdad crumbling. The only difference is that first I shall be obliterated, and the ruin of Baghdad is certain to follow thereafter.'

His fame was spreading far and wide but the power of the zealots was increasing as well, and they had started to threaten the king alleging leniency being shown to the heretic. The king could see the danger from the zealots as they closed in on Baghdad and were raring for a fight. The khalifa was inebriated when he was made to sign the midnight order for Mansur's execution. Early the next morning, on a Tuesday, the order for his execution was read out. The order was for executing Mansur the next day and the day after his body would be burnt and thereafter the ashes were to be dispersed in the wind. Mansur heard the announcement, thanked Allah and immersed himself in meditation. His disciples gathered around him. People asked him many questions. One young man asked, 'Sir, what is love?' Mansur replied, 'Love? You would see it today. Then see it tomorrow and then the day after tomorrow.'

The qazi (magistrate or judge of the Sharia court) asked Mansur, 'You call yourself God but also say the namaz (prayers). God's high praise has been recorded in the Koran; so why do you read the Koran?' Mansur replied, 'The pleasure of hearing self-praise from one's own self far surpasses praise by others.'

When his hands were chopped off, he told the qazi, 'You can see that my hands have been severed. But how will you slash those hands which have reached up to the galaxy?' Then his feet were cut off. Mansur said, 'You have hacked off my feet and you have done well. But how will you cut those feet which go up to the end of the horizon (across the seven heavens)?' He, then, rubbed on his face the blood oozing from his lacerated hands. The qazi asked, 'Why did you do that?' Mansur answered, 'Lovers perform their wuzu with blood and not water.'

Ibrahim, his personal servant, had served him for a very long time. As Mansur was being taken for his execution, he pleaded with folded hands, 'Master, please give something to me also.' Mansur told him, 'I give you back your being. I place you in your own custody. Go and immerse yourself completely in prayer.'

Rushing through the crowds thronging around Mansur, Shibli ran up to him as he was being taken to the gallows. Mansur asked him for a piece of cloth and, wrapping it around his neck, said his last prayers and then, said smilingly, 'The tresses of the beloved have appeared as a noose before me this time around. This is very welcome.'

When the executioner struck Mansur's head with an iron rod, Shibli screamed and tearing off his own clothes, fell down unconscious. Mansur was beheaded and as per the fatwa, other punishments too were meted out. The mute masses of Baghdad wept bitterly. This event took place on 26 March, 922.

Destiny unfolded. Mansur's end marked the beginning of Baghdad's decline. This world-renowned, beautiful city became a place of loot, plunder and murder. The rulers were dethroned and fatal attacks became the order of the day. Mansur himself had written, 'The sun rises and sets every day but the suns that rise in the heart never ever sets.'

We very much become the person the way we submit ourselves before Almighty. An individual worshipping idol is a stone himself; if you worship human beings you will be a human being; and if you completely immerse yourself in the worship of God, then only a Mansur can tell what heights you would achieve!

A couplet penned by Bhai Nand Lal is:

> 'If you have uttered the name of Mansur, keep the rope over your shoulders. because the executioner could pretend that he has forgotten his rope back home. So, be concerned about the noose before you mention Mansur.'

Balbir Madhopuri

Balbir Madhopuri (b. 1955) was born in village Madhopur of Jalandhar district. His childhood was difficult. He had to start working as farm labour at the tender age of nine years but he never abandoned his resolve to achieve something worthwhile in his life and pursued education despite challenges. He retired as a Deputy Director from the Ministry of Information and Broadcasting. He was also a senior editor of the magazine *Yojana* (Punjabi edition) and later of *Samkali Sahit*. He is a poet, editor and translator. He has translated over thirty books into Punjabi. His autobiography *Chhangiya Rukh* where he fearlessly depicts the visible and invisible excesses perpetrated on the Dalits, oppressed and downtrodden is one of his best-known works. His literary strength in prose lies in his spontaneity, simplicity and honesty. This book has been translated into many languages. In Pakistan, it was published in Shahmukhi script. In 2013, the Sahitya Akademi awarded him the national award for translation of the book *Raj Kamal Choudharydian Chonvian Kahanian*.

The Humanist Slap

'He is my dear friend... Our friendship goes back some thirty-five years. He is an outstanding poet, and a writer of ghazals. His ghazals reflect the humanist view, and he is from our area...' Dr Gurucharan Singh Muhay, the editor of the Punjabi edition of *Yojana* introduced me to a person with a well-starched beard and red turban.

'Which department are you in?' I enquired of the poet.

'I am a free bird... roam about and compose poetry ... it is my wife who works.'

'He spends his days on the roads, working on the ghazals that are in the process of being written, and his evenings are spent in the coffee house, and afternoons, he spends in the chandu khana,' Dr Muhay handed out his information about his poet friend.

'Chandu khana?'

'Yes, where musical evenings are held ... you must come with me one of these days. I'll introduce you to other writers and poets ... one should not sit in a room all day!' Dr Muhay continued eagerly, 'He is a large-hearted man. He doesn't let anyone pay in the coffee house—what payment does one receive by reciting poem in kavi darbars (poet assemblies)! He is enjoying himself at the expense of his wife ... she is a very good woman!'

The ghazal writer was smiling all the while. I felt that this man was a parasite, without any work or source of income.

'You haven't told me anything about him,' the poet said.

'He is an assistant editor here. His name is Balbir Chand, but he calls himself Balbir Madhopuri.' Muhay introduced me with some irony. To escape this daily humiliation, I had recently got my name officially changed to the present one.

The meetings were held in the afternoon outside the PTI building on Parliament Street. But no one talked about culture or literature; they were so preoccupied with backbiting, criticism, and jealousy. I avoided these meetings.

Days turned into months. Muhay and his other editorial colleagues would talk for hours about their religious interests and activities. They would debate over the various ways of making life better, higher, for the work one does, because our wealth would not accompany us in the afterlife, etc., and these discussions would stretch out endlessly. They disturbed my world. They called their guru Satguru, the true God, or Purna Satguru, the perfect God. They tried to persuade me to attend their religious meetings and would often comment on the need for a guru. They called me stupid. I was tense and upset at not being able to finish my official assignments on time.

... One evening I was obliged to go with them to attend a satsang of their guru, Ved Prakash, in a posh residential area in New Delhi. Muhay's poet friend had also begun attending these religious assemblies. Discussions at these meetings would focus on spiritual, scientific, and technological development. I liked the atmosphere. I began attending these meetings along with Muhay.

... One day, at one such meeting, D.D. Sharma said, 'Pitaji, in Guru Ravidas's bani ...'

'Guru? He was not even a saint! The Gurbani calls him a bhakt, a devotee,' Satguru Sharma, who was addressed as Pitaji by one and all, explained what was not asked, interrupting the question. The one who had asked the question did not say anything further, perhaps because he felt that it was not appropriate to argue with the guru.

The Satguru carried on, 'I was Yagyavalkya Rishi in my last birth, and Gargi was my wife then. She is now with me in the form of my daughter, Sheela.'

Everyone present looked at one another, wondering how the Guru had complete knowledge of the previous and future births and the whole universe.

'Pitaji, we have heard that this world is sweet. Who knows about the hereafter, for none has seen it', I repeated what I had often heard.

'The Guru is great, no one knows the Guru's power ... whatever he does, is right; he is as pure as the lotus ... Companions of many births come together to keep an account of one another's doings', Ved Prakash Sharma delivered many such discourses on the eternal and the unknown.

'Pitaji, you are a complete guru; help us demolish the differences and discriminations of caste so that everyone is deemed equal', I gave words to my deepest desire.

'Look! All this is the consequence of karma, actions of our previous births. Satguru does not interfere in these things, but teaches you to accept them—that would give you peace. You can yourself see, we wash our faces again and again, look at the mirror time and again, but how much attention do we pay to our feet?'

I acquired the real knowledge of what it meant to be a shudra, by attending these assemblies of the Purna Satguru. Then, I discussed it with Muhay. He said, 'It is the result of births and deeds. You keep on the straight path, you will be blessed—if a soul is full of faith and trust then alone can it know belief, reverence and devotion.'

After the satsang, a well-dressed young man told a few people, 'He is my uncle, but don't be misled or duped by him. He drinks chicken soup and also liquor occasionally.'

No one paid much attention to this boy.

'... Even if for a moment one accepts that there is an earlier birth, how can one accept a wife of the earlier birth as a daughter in this?' I asked Muhay.

'To criticise or to hear anyone else criticise the Guru is a sin', Muhayans wered curtly.

'But what is the harm in trying to find out the truth?'

His son Sukhbir answered my question, 'If you are making allegations, then I am going to get to the bottom of this affair.'

Kicking his scooter to life, he roared off, coming back after some time, with dejection written all over his face, and said, 'I spoke to this daughter of Pitaji. She says She is "neither married nor a virgin, all because of her father".

After this confirmation, I thought of those shlokas of Brahmaji, which he had uttered while persuading his daughter, Padma, to yield to him—that one can have sex with mother, daughter or sister, for the sake of progeny. It seemed to me that perhaps the Satguru may have been inspired by that!

Muhay noticed my dilemma, and he said, 'One has read and heard plenty of nonsense in Indian mythology, but this seems to have come true.'

All the good feelings that I had for the Guru and his satsang were wiped clean from my mind, the way corrupted files disappeared from my office computer. Despite pressing every button, the monitor showed blank. I felt redeemed.

Muhay and some of his like-minded friends now started a full-scale enquiry, like an investigating committee. 'We'll close this shop of his,' Muhay declared. Somehow the know-all guru had come to know of this determined declaration.

Earlier, Muhay and many of his friends would have dismissed the charge of the Guru being a tantrik, but now they themselves levelled this charge against him. The Guru could no longer amass wealth through his satsang.

In an attempt to cover up his misdeeds, the Guru told one of the satsangis who was close to him, 'All the Scheduled Castes have come together against me.'

The man who had declared himself the father of all, now revealed how obscurantist his views still were.

Muhay was bitter and angry, 'We have been duped. We have been humiliated. My family was connected with the Radhasoami sect for more than seventy-eight years ... I have spent nights weeping.'

'And that writer woman?' I tried to shock him.

'After fourteen years of living together, she has left me, saying that you were, and even now are, a chamar.'

Muhay was sad and dejcted, his face had shrunk and he would pass his hand over his grey beard. It seemed as if he was about to tear it out.

Dr Muhay was soon promoted as deputy secretary. He came to see me every five or seven days. As he walked in one day, he said, 'Come, let's go to the chandu khana. We will meet some friends .. .'

'Gurucharan, how much longer before you retire?' His poet friend asked, after greeting Muhay.

'Six months.'

'After that you can sit here with this cobbler and his shoe-polishing kit, and I too will come here regularly, so that we can meet.'

Dr Muhay ignored his bitter comment, and tried to steer the conversation in another direction.

'Gurucharan, what am I saying! You can get a shoe-polishing kit and sit with the cobbler here—and we will continue seeing each other...' the poet repeated what he had said, pointing to the cobbler who was busy repairing some shoes.

'Yaar, I have a degree in homeopathy. I will help people by dispensing medicines. Then, I have plenty of experience, and can work as a journalist in English and Punjabi. I am an M.A. One shouldn't say such things to friends.'

After a few days, Dr Muhay and I visited some old friends. After enquiring about the process of retirement from government service, the poet again said, 'Gurcharan, I had advised you earlier that you should sit here under this neem tree with a shoe-polishing kit. And it would be a way for us to keep on meeting each other ...'

Dr Muhay slapped the poet hard. I tried to ignore it by turning away. Then, as I watched them obliquely, I saw Mohan Singh Berry separating them and trying to talk some sense into them.

I realized that even the mind of the other low castes had been deeply affected by the inhuman treatment meted out to them for centuries. We would like Scheduled Castes and backward castes to unite, but the terrible wounds inflicted on their psyche, and the deep divisions created by these wounds, will not allow them to mingle and be one. The scheduled castes had organised the movement for reservations for the backward classes after the Mandal Commission report, but the backward classes were used by the upper castes in their own interests. There was rioting and arson and lives were lost.

I was still thinking of these issues, when a few days later a colleague MK Rao from Andhra Pradesh came to Delhi. When I had recounted to him what had happened, he said, 'There is no need to worry. When I was elected the president of our association, one of our senior officers, who had always projected himself as a Gandhian said, "How can we allow the scheduled castes to sit with us?" Then, when I was the general secretary of the state unit of SFI, and we invited the communist leaders for a meal during the Telengana assembly elections, the village headman refused to come to our homes. But otherwise, the headman is very progressive.'

It seemed to me that the curse of caste has permeated our society and there is no indication of its dying out soon. Then, it suddenly occurred to me that the Muhay formula may be the most effective method of establishing social equality—to deliver a sharp humanist slap on the face of casteism!

Translated by Tripti Jain

Glossary

Arooz	the poetics of ghazal, originally a Turkish form of poetry. It has been imitated in Persian, Urdu, Hindi and Punjabi.
Baba	grandfather, an elderly person or even a sage or an enlightened soul
Baiju Bawra	a renowned musician, who was Tansen's contemporary and was believed to be more popular than Tansen
Bar	some regions in Pakistani Punjab. Primarily the *bar* denotes to a forest area between the two rivers, for example, Saandal *bar* was the territory between Ravi and Chenab. Other *bar*s were Neeli, Ganji, Kiran and Gondal
Barat	wedding procession
Baradari	community
Bhabhi	brother's wife
Bhai jaan	expression of endearment for brother, or an intimate friend
Bhai	elder brother; an informal way of addressing a friend
Bhua	father's sister
Bikrami	the calendar followed by many Punjabi Hindus; as per this calendar, the year starts on 13 March, with the advent of spring
Boli	a folk song with a rousing rhythm, generally having humorous or satiric content
Braham/Brahm	the Supreme Consciousness or Formless God, not to be confused with Brahma, a Hindu god
Chacha	father's younger brother, with whom nephews and nieces are generally quite close.
Chamar	a dalit community, now classified as a scheduled caste, that generally was engaged in leather-making
Chhindo Jheeran	Chhindo is the name of a girl who belonged to the Jheer caste. Jheers were traditionally water carriers. In rural Punjab, it was quite common to fix identity on the basis of caste.

Chobara	covered part of the roof, which does not have walls and doors like a regular room
Choorie	a traditional Punjabi sweetmeat made with crushed unleavened bread (roti) mixed with butter or ghee and sugar.
Chowdhry/ Chowdhary	honorific used for the headman of a village, trade or community or for political leaders orprominent persons
Chulha	earthen stove, widely used in Punjab
Chunni	also known as dupatta; a long scarf worn by women in India and some South Asian countries to cover their head and shoulders
Deor	husband's younger brother
Doabia	the word 'doab' means land between two rivers. Indus-Sagar Doab (Indus and Jhelum doab), Chaj Doab (Chanab and Jhelum doab), Rachna Doab (Ravi and Chenab doab) are famous doabs in Pakistan. In the East Punjab, the area between Sutlej and Beas is a famous doab, which is knwon as Bist Doab. But a person residing in the Satlej and Beas 'doab' area is referred to as *doabia*.
Doli	the palanquin in which the bride would travel to her husband's house. Nowadays the term is used to signify the departure of the bride even though a palanquin is no longer used.
Dupatta	length of cloth to cover the head and upper body by women in Punjab and other parts of India, and at times used as a veil
Fakir	religious ascetic or holy man who survives primarily on alms
Gaana	ceremonial multicoloured thread tied round the wrist
Gandharva Vivah	love marriage. It is one of the eight Hindu marriages in classical texts.
Ghadar	a political movement of the early twentieth century which was organised by oversees Indians with an objective to overthrow the British rule in India
Ghagra	long skirt
Gulli-danda	a game played with one short, sharp, whittled piece of wood being struck by a stick.
Gurmukh	one who listens to his Guru and follows the path shown by the Guru. Another spiritual meaning of Gurmukh is

Glossary

	one who has realised his Guru within himself and remains in his will. The opposite is Manmukh, one who follows material pursuits or desire as dictated by his mind.
Hafiz	one who knows the Quran by heart
Halva	an Indian confection made of flour, sugar and ghee
Hammam	a communal bathhouse, usually with separate baths for men and women
Indra	the king of gods in Hindu mythology
Janam Sakhi	Chronicle of Birth (of Guru Nanak)
Jand	*Butea frondosa*, considered a sacred tree. Its wood is used as timber, and its resin is used in local cuisine.
Jat	usually a landed Punjabi who is traditionally engaged in agriculture
Jathedar	chosen leader of high esteem to head a group of Sikhs (jatha)
Jethani	wife of husband's elder brother
Kaaba	located in Mecca, Saudi Arabia. It is considered to be the holiest shrine in Islam
Kafi	A form of Sufi poetry, usually written in Punjabi and Sindhi. The word kafi is derived from Arabic *kaaf* meaning *group*. As a form of poetry, it is derived from *qasidah*. *Kafi* is also a raga in Hindustani music. There is a practice of singing kafi poetry in Punjabi Sufiana music.
Kaintha	a necklace, worn by both men and women in Punjab
Kalidas	a Classical Sanskrit writer, who lived in fourth or fifth century CE. He is widely regarded as the greatest Indian poet and dramatist in the Sanskrit language. His plays and poetry are primarily based on the Vedas, the *Mahabharata* and the Puranas.
Kanjak	among Hindus, the ninth and tenth day of Navratra are for the worship of goddess Durga. On these two days, nine young girls, symbolic of the nine forms of Goddess Durga, are worshipped (kanjak puja or kanya puja). Kanjak signifies purity and innocence, and also strength.
Kangra	a hilly region in erstwhile Punjab (now in Himachal Pradesh)
Kattak/Kartik	month of the Hindu calendar corresponding to 15 October to 15 November

Kavishar	a person who sings out the poetry he writes
Khalifa	successor, leader or ruler
Keekar	tree that belongs to the family of Acacia, that is commonly seen in many parts of Punjab
Kulfi	frozen dessert (like ice cream) made by reducing and thickening milk. It is poured into conical moulds, frozen and served with sweet rice noodles called *faluda*.
Kurti	long shirt worn by women
La Ilaha Illallah Muhammad Rasulallah	Muslim prayer which means 'May Allah's Peace, Mercy and Blessings be upon all of you.'
Laagi	a village menial who is paid for performing customs. Generally, barbers were assigned such duties and were paid for it.
Laavaan	According to the Sikh marriage traditions, the marriage ceremony is performed in the presence of the Sikh holy scripture, Sri Guru Granth Sahib. It involves four circumambulations around the Holy Granth by the bridegroom followed by the bride. Each circumambulation is known as *laanv* and a Sikh priest (known as *granthi*) reads out wedding hymns from the Holy Granth coinciding with each circumambulation. The entire ceremony is known as *laanvaan*.
Lambardar (also Numberdar or Nambardar)	a title given to powerful families of landlords of the village or town, a state-privileged status which is hereditary and has wide-ranging powers. The lambardar gets many perks for performing these duties.
Langar	free kitchen that feeds everybody irrespective of caste, creed, status or nationality
Lehnga	women's skirt, mainly worn in Punjab
Maharaj	honorific for addressing someone in a higher position
Malin	gardener (female)
Mazar	tomb, grave or shrine
Mirasi	people belonging to the *mirasi* community in India and Pakistan are traditional singers and dancers.

	They were generally employed by noblemen as entertainers in their courts. Now, the word *mirasi* is used to refer to a person who is flippant and likes to crack jokes or is a clever raconteur.
Muklawa	the ritual return of the bride to her parents' house after marriage. The husband would come to take his wife back. The period of stay may range from a few days to a few months. In the case of a child bride, the duration may be a few years (till she attains puberty). Conversely, in Hindus and Sikhs, muklawa is the first time departure of the bride to her husband's house after her marriage.
Murshid	guru or spiritual master
Nain	barber's wife. In villages in Punjab, a barber is often addressed informally as Raja. He is assigned the job of performing minor rituals, especially those related to marriage. The barber's wife performs a similar role.
Namdhari	Indian religious group that considers themselves a sect of Sikhism. According to Namdharis the line of Sikh Gurus did not end with Guru Gobind Singh but continued with Namdhari leaders.
Neem	an evergreen tree (*Azadirachta indica*) whose leaves, bark and fruit have medicinal value according to Ayurveda.
Nirankari	'the formless one'. A sect of Sikhism based on a reform movement founded by Baba Sayal Das that sought to restore the beliefs and practices of Sikhs which were prevalent in Guru Nanak Dev's time.
Nirmale	'those without blemish'. They comprise a Sikh tradition of ascetics founded by Guru Gobind Singh in the seventeenth century.
Param Purukh	the Supreme Being; it refers to God imagined as man
Parshad	consecrated food
Phulkari	a shawl embroidered with patterns, worn on ceremonial occasions by women and by brides in particular on the occasion of their wedding.
Phuphar	father's sister's (bhua's) husband
Pothi	scripture or book
Pingal	the theory of poetry as given by Acharya Pingala, a poet and mathematician. It is also known as *Chhandshastra*.

Qalandar	a Sufi saint who belongs to the Qalandari Sufi order; a person who has advanced in Sufi mysticism; one who has risen above all systems. Sometimes, the term is used to refer to god.
Qaseeda	odes of high praise
Qazi	magistrate or judge
Rajputs	a set of patrilineal clans originating from Rajasthan and spread over north of India.
Rakhi	an ornamental wristband presented during the festival of *Raksha Bandhan* as an amulet or token of respect and affection, typically by a woman or a girl to her brother or a man that she regards as a brother. The bond enjoins the brother to protect his sister from harm.
Salu	a red wrap, plain or embroidered, worn by a woman during a wedding
Sahibji	suffix or noun often used as an expression of respect for seniors
Samadhi	heightened state of consciousness in deep meditation
Sardar	chief, leader, commander: an appellative for a Sikh
Sawan	the rainy season in north India, roughly in July and August
Sehra	sort of chaplet; strings of beads or flowers with a plume worn by the bridegroom on his head, which covers his face
Seth	rich man, generally a businessman and/or a money-lender
Sewa Panthi	a philanthropist order started by Bhai Kanhaiya, after he became a Sikh of the ninth guru, Guru Tegh Bahadur, who instructed Kanhaiya to go forth and serve humanity
Sher-e-Punjab	reference to Maharaja Ranjit Singh, the only Sikh ruler (1780–1839) of Punjab who ruled it and other areas extending to Afghanistan in the west and Kashmir in the north from 1799 to 1839
Shudhi	purification
Siharfi	siharfi (literally, Golden Alphabet) is a form of Sufi poetry in which every line of a poem or stanza begins with the succeeding letter of the Arabic alphabet. The first two poems in this collection begin with *alif* and last two poems begin with *noon*.

Suhagan	married woman
Sulfa	mixture of tobacco and cannabis, smoked as an intoxicant
Suthare Shahi	a mendicant order which owed its origin to Suthra Shah (1625–82), disciple of Guru Hargobind
Sutthan	loose trousers worn below the kurti by women
Swang	dialogue
Swaraj	self-rule
Swayamvar	choosing a groom out of many suitors, a practice in ancient India.
Tabligh	an Islamic missionary organisation that focuses on following Islam as it was practised during the times of the Prophet.
Tahli	a deciduous tree (*Dalbergia sissoo*) valued for its timber; it is also used for making furniture and joinery; also known as shisham in Hindi; widely distributed across north India
Taiya	father's elder brother
Taka	equivalent to two paisas or pennies in that time. An *anna* would be two takas. These were sufficient for small purchases; a *rupee* had considerable purchase value then.
Takht Hazara	a town in Pakistan, the birthplace of Ranjha, the protagonist of the famous love legend of Heer–Ranjha
Tansen	an accomplished musician in the court of Akbar
Tanzeem	an Islamic organisation with focus on following the Quran and Sunnah
Trinjan	a space in the house exclusively for women where they could rest, chat or spin, weave, embroider, knit, etc.
Udasi	a religious sect of ascetic sadhus who were interpreters of Sikh philosophy and custodians of Sikh shrines till the Akali movement
Vanjara	a travelling tradesman, who sells things of daily use in villages
Vey	an interjection often used by women while informally addressing a man

Wagah	Wagah is a village in Pakistan near India-Pakistan border. It is also known as Wagha-Attari border. Attari is the last Indian village on the border in Amritsar district.
Wah-e-Guru ji ki Fateh	Sikh greeting; part of 'Wah-e-Guru ji ka khalsa, Wah-e-Guru ji ki fateh'
Wuzu	ritualistic cleansing of body parts in Islam